PRAISE FOR
BRAND MANAGEMENT

'In an era where marketing is everything and branding is the core of marketing, the importance of this book cannot be overstated. The two accomplished marketing academics, Jaywant Singh and Paurav Shukla, offer an authoritative and comprehensive discussion of all aspects of branding that makes this book a must-read for business students and practitioners alike.'
Bodo B Schlegelmilch, Professor Emeritus, WU Vienna University of Economics and Business, Bualuang ASEAN Chair Professor, Thammasat University, Bangkok

'This comprehensive, timely and highly accessible gem of a book provides a state-of-the art perspective on branding in today's world. Grounded in research, the book and its concepts are highly relevant to both students and practitioners interested in branding.'
Debbie MacInnis, Emerita Professor of Marketing, Marshall School of Business, University of Southern California

'This is not just another book about branding concepts! This is a book that has been long awaited, a book that holistically addresses the entire branding process, from the meaning of the branding concept to how to build and manage a brand. The book offers a pragmatic guide to why branding is important and how it works, and will become a requisite text for anyone involved in a branding project. It provides an essential discussion of current research on branding and should be a 'must-read' for all students studying branding.'
Nicholas J Ashill, Professor of Marketing and RC Chair, School of Marketing and International Business, Wellington School of Business and Government, Victoria University of Wellington – Te Herenga Waka, New Zealand

'Provides a fresh and useful survey of branding concepts, research and applications. Progressing from the core ideas and historical origins of branding, the text proceeds to thoroughly cover modern scholarly research and contemporary industry applications. The work is an invaluable resource both for students learning about branding and for scholars requiring a comprehensive reference on work in the area.'
Malcolm Wright, Fellow of ANZMAC, MSA Charitable Trust Chair in Marketing, Massey Business School – Te Kura Whai Pakihi, New Zealand

'Offers an in-depth coverage of key concepts, practical case studies and actionable frameworks. An extremely valuable resource for anyone looking to learn about branding, or to elevate their brand strategy and drive impactful results.'
Rodrigo Guesalaga, Professor of Marketing, Faculty of Economics and Business, Alberto Hurtado University, Chile

'Written by two top research academics, this book has provided a comprehensive and thorough account of branding and brand management in the global context. Current, relevant and interesting case studies and illustrations have been presented throughout the book, which have added to its uniqueness. I highly recommend that this book be used as a core text book in any brand management courses taught at the undergraduate and postgraduate levels, as well as a key reference for any DBA and PhD students.'
T C Melewar, Professor of Marketing and Strategy, Department of Marketing, Branding and Tourism, Middlesex University London

'Dr Singh and Dr Shukla's *Brand Management: Principles and Applications for Effective Branding* offers a comprehensive guide to mastering the art of branding. Through its insightful exploration of brand principles and real-world applications, this book is an invaluable resource for marketers and business professionals aiming to enhance their brand strategy.'
Iain Brown, Head of Data Science, SAS Northern Europe

'What a brand stands for and how you keep it relevant is at the heart of many organizations' focus. This work provides real life examples and insights on those very considerations.'
Carmela Crisafulli, Director, Development Marketing EMEAA, IHG Hotels and Resorts

'A comprehensive textbook that demystifies branding, offers actionable frameworks, and shows how to apply them through a myriad of case studies.'
Amitava Chattopadhyay, The GlaxoSmithKline Chaired Professor of Corporate Innovation INSEAD, France

Brand Management

Principles and applications for effective branding

Jaywant Singh
Paurav Shukla

KoganPage

First published in Great Britain and the United States in 2024 by Kogan Page Limited

2nd Floor, 45 Gee Street
London
EC1V 3RS
United Kingdom

8 W 38th Street, Suite 902
New York, NY 10018
USA

www.koganpage.com

Kogan Page books are printed on paper from sustainable forests.

© Jaywant Singh, Paurav Shukla 2024

The rights of Jaywant Singh and Paurav Shukla to be identified as the authors of this work have been asserted by them in accordance with the Copyright, Designs and Patents Act 1988.

ISBNs

Hardback	978 1 3986 1 1603
Paperback	978 1 3986 1 1580
Ebook	978 1 3986 1 1597

British Library Cataloguing-in-Publication Data
A CIP record for this book is available from the British Library.

Library of Congress Control Number
2024934065

Typeset by Integra Software Services, Pondicherry
Print production managed by Jellyfish
Printed and bound by CPI Group (UK) Ltd, Croydon, CR0 4YY

CONTENTS

PART TWO Building brands – principles and applications

PART THREE Managing contemporary brands

LIST OF FIGURES AND TABLES

Figures

Tables

WALKTHROUGH OF TEXTBOOK FEATURES AND ONLINE RESOURCES

Chapter overview

Highlights the main issues and topics that will be covered in each chapter.

In this chapter, we delineate brands through history – how and why branding began and developed through ancient, medieval and modern eras. We bring in new perspectives on the existence of the core concepts of modern branding throughout history.

Learning outcomes

A bulleted list at the beginning of each chapter summarizes what you can expect to learn, to help you to track your progress.

Upon reading this chapter, you should be able to

- Understand how the need for branding took roots
- Develop insights into the historical journey of branding, through ancient, medieval and modern times

Case studies and real-world examples

A range of case studies and real-world examples illustrates how key ideas and theories are operating in practice to help you to place the concepts discussed in real-life context.

CASE STUDY – Time travel through the Nestlé story

1 Please visit the history of Nestlé on the webpage below, and answer the following questions: www.nestle.com/about/history/nestle-company-history

2 Evaluate the critical factors leading to the creation of brand Nestlé.

3 Critically examine the landmark changes in branding of Nestlé through the history.

4 Discuss the changing focus on consumers convenience, wellbeing and shared values in Nestlé's branding in modern times.

5 Critically reflect on Nestlé's current branding strategy and recommend steps the brand should take to help ensure its long-term success.

Scholarly debate boxes

Students are directed to publications that have been key to theoretical debates in the subject and encouraged to critically reflect on them.

'Branding in practice' boxes

In each chapter, the application of branding concepts and theories is illustrated through real-world examples.

Branding in practice – Why logos are going simple

In recent years, some brands have simplified their logos by removing or adapting design elements such as name (e.g., Mastercard, Uber etc.), colours (i.e., Apple, Instagram), shades (e.g., Google), depth (e.g., Dell) and fonts (e.g., Burberry, Chanel) among others.

Exercise questions

These can be used in tutorials or small study groups to stimulate debate and critical thinking.

1 What are the main patterns of buyer behaviour?
2 How can the empirical generalization patterns help brand managers?

Key terms/quotes boxes

These boxes give explanations of key terms and concepts in the book to highlight them for your learning.

Chapter summary

Draws together the main threads of the chapter and summarizes the key learning points.

Key learning points/concepts

Key learning points at the end of each chapter summarize the main themes of the chapter and act as a useful revision tool.

Key concepts

- Patterns of buyer behaviour
- Empirical generalizations in branding
- Modelling brand buying behaviour
- The psychology of branding
- Theories that influence branding research

References

Detailed references provide quick and easy access to the research and underpinning sources behind the chapter.

Online resources:

This book includes online resources for lecturers comprising:

- Chapter slides
- Instructor manual
- Exercises
- Further real-world examples

> These resources can be accessed through the Kogan Page website:
> www.koganpage.com/brand-management

PART ONE
Introduction – the foundations of brand management

Brand – the concept and meanings

01

Overview

In this chapter, we first introduce the basic concepts of a brand and how a product transforms into a brand. In the following section, we elaborate upon the central place of branding in all walks of life, and identify the popular definitions of branding and its varied meanings. We then show the pervasive reach of branding in all aspects of humanity such as for individuals, groups, societies, governments and ideologies. In the last section, we highlight the importance of branding for all stakeholders involved. Overall, this chapter provides the foundations for learning the discipline of branding.

Key learning outcomes

Upon reading this chapter, you should be able to

- Understand the difference between a product and a brand
- Develop deeper understanding of branding definitions and associated meanings
- Develop insights into the pervasiveness of branding
- Appreciate the scholarly debate on the foundations of branding
- Recognize the importance of branding for different stakeholders

How does a product become a brand?

To comprehend the concept of brand, it is necessary to understand the idea of a product. The overall notion of product is easily understood by most people through its physical manifestation. A product can be much more than its physical aspects. For instance, a watch or a pen can be identified as a physical product, whereas a bank or an insurance policy can be identified as service products. They satisfy different needs and wants of their customers. Thus, a product is anything that meets the functional needs of customers.[1] Moreover, a product is almost always a combination of the tangible and intangible.[2] For example, a watch is bought to tell the time, and a pen to write. Similarly, a service product like a bank is used to satisfy financial transactions and other financial needs. An insurance policy is bought for reducing customer safety concerns. Thus, a product can also be identified as the total package of benefits the customer receives upon purchase of the product.

To achieve meaningful engagement with customers, a company should consider both the tangible and intangible benefits that the product delivers. In other words, companies should think beyond the functional aspects of its products. The product engagement matrix[3] provides a useful direction for companies to integrate both tangible and intangible benefits, as shown in Figure 1.1.

As a fundamental principle, a product satisfies customer needs through its core benefits. For instance, a hotel offers 'shelter' away from home or a soft drink quenches 'thirst'. A generic product is a somewhat rudimentary difference that may exist between competing products in a particular industry or sector. For instance, two Italian restaurants on the same street of a city may use the same ingredients to make a margarita pizza. However, their shape and size may differ

Figure 1.1   Product engagement matrix

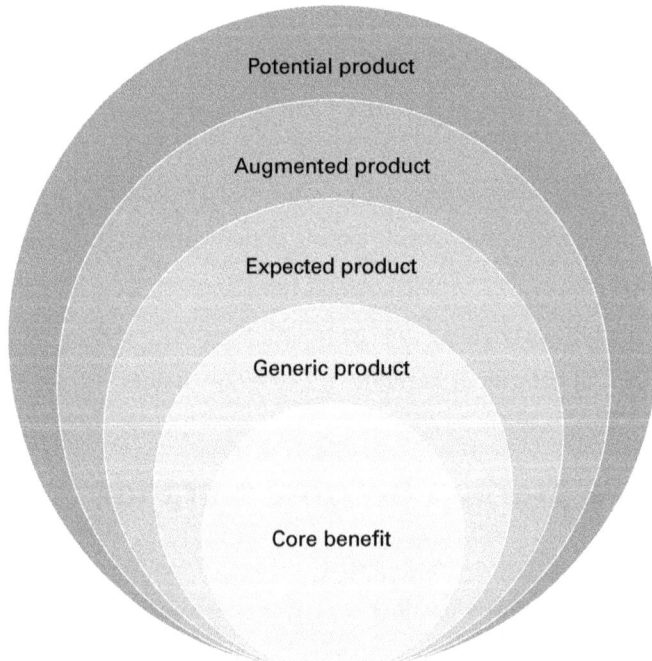

Potential product

Augmented product

Expected product

Generic product

Core benefit

SOURCE Adapted from Levitt (1980)

somewhat. In most cases, the generic product differences are not salient to the customers. The salient differences are observed by the customers at the expected product levels. The expected product reflects customers' minimal purchase conditions. These could include price, delivery terms, customer service provision and novelty. Extending the Italian restaurant example, customers may expect reasonable price, prompt delivery, good customer service and a range of flavours to satisfy their need to eat. Many products use a variety of expected product characteristics to differentiate themselves. For instance, a Bic pen is available for less than £1, while on the other hand, a Montblanc pen can cost a hundred times more. While both pens satisfy the same functional need for writing, customer expectations differ significantly from a social value perspective.

An augmented product is something that the customer has never thought about or expected. The unprompted 'augmentation' beyond the expected product can substantially help companies to differentiate their product from competitors and create 'aha' moments. Such augmentation can also strengthen the customer-brand relationships as the customer feels more valued. For instance, the Italian restaurant can provide a free drink with the order of a pizza. In addition, for health conscious customers, a restaurant can provide information regarding calorie content and sourcing of ingredients from sustainable sources. Such augmentation exceeds the normal expectations of the customer and may create greater satisfaction and garner customer loyalty over a period. Product augmentation comes with its own risks as well. For instance, companies cannot always augment products or services on a continuous basis. Moreover, some customers, due to their own financial constraints or value preference, may prefer the basic product and may not be willing to pay for augmentation. Hence, a company should embark on a systematic programme of customer-benefitting and, therefore, customer-retaining product augmentation.

Everything that is done by a firm to attract and retain customers on a regular basis is called the potential product. This may involve product feature innovations through market research and investments in product or service R&D. For instance, since its launch of the path-defining smartphone, iPhone, Apple has regularly introduced an improved version that builds on its predecessors. The latest iPhone boasts a new operating system, better camera hardware and software, and a variety of other features that differentiate it from earlier versions as well as competitors. These potential product differentiations can help a product create substantial value in customer minds and lead to strong relationships.

Products at the most basic level satisfy customers' functional needs. However, a customer attaches value to a product in proportion to its perceived ability to help solve their problem or meet their needs. In today's highly competitive marketplace, satisfying such needs may not help companies stand out and be noticed. Most companies aim to differentiate or distinguish their products from competitors by highlighting their unique features or elements. They achieve this by creating a brand.

Brand definitions and meanings

According to the American Marketing Association (AMA), a brand can be defined as a specific name, symbol or design – or, more usually, some combination of these – that is used to distinguish a particular seller's product. At a simplistic level, identifying a name or developing a logo, etc. can be the basis of branding. However, brand is seen though a multi-dimensional lens by practitioners. Figure 1.2 shows how practitioners think about a brand in real life.[4]

Figure 1.2   Multi-dimensional view of a brand from academic-practitioner perspective

SOURCE Adapted from de Chernatony and Dall'Olmo Riley (1998)

Brand as a legal instrument demonstrates the mark or ownership and at the same time protects a company's products and image through copyrights and trademarks laws. A logo helps a brand in differentiating through visual identity and name. It also helps a brand highlight quality assurance. At the corporate level, a brand allows a firm to highlight its organizational culture, people and personality over a long-term horizon. Brand can act as shorthand for rapid recognizability and speedy decision making. Moreover, a brand can instil confidence among its customers through its quality associations which in turn reduce risk perceptions and enhances trustworthiness.

Brands can also act as an identity system beyond a name. They can highlight the direction, meaning and strategic positioning within the marketplace. Moreover, brand as an identity system can provide a protective barrier and communicate essence to its stakeholders. Image in consumers' minds can allow a brand to clearly differentiate itself and also establish its customer-centric credentials. Consumers' image perceptions of a brand is their reality and thus can help a firm in developing and enhancing customer-brand relationships. When a brand and customer values match, the product becomes more desirable in customer minds. The values can be psychological such as brand personality and image that add to the functionality aspects of the product. These values are generally conveyed through advertising and packaging. Customers tend to buy brands that fit with the subjective meaning they value. As brands evolve to meet such requirements through their aesthetics, supply chain, customer service and other marketing activities, customers are ready to pay a premium price for the perceived enhanced experience they will gain from engaging with the brand. Brands create a belief in the consistent performance of the product and thus add value in customer minds and enhance customer-brand relationships.

Brands are multifaceted entities. The concept and meaning of brands have evolved over the decades. Scholars have attached symbolic, cultural, attitudinal and behavioural aspects. Brands and an individual's identity are interlinked wherein brands are also suggested to reflect an individual's personal, interpersonal and social selves, and vice versa.[5] While there is no universally accepted definition of a brand, the interpretations and meanings have enriched the field of branding through the inclusion of a variety of branding traits in the definitions. For example, brands are identified as risk reducers at the point of purchase decisions.[6] Brands are also defined as value enhancers[7] through their relational associations.[8] From a semiotics perspective, brands can be a physical entity and/or a mental representation.[9] Brand is also defined from the perspective of its visible traits such as the name, logo, term, sign, symbol or design, or a combination of these. Leading marketing practitioners such as David Ogilvy and Tim Ambler define brand from the perspective of image and personality[10] and as a promise that consumers believe in.[11] Building on these aspects, scholars highlight a brand as a dynamically evolving concept that captures the product's essence, its meaning and its direction.[12][13]

What can be branded?

As described earlier, a brand is not just a name or a logo but an identity representation of a company and its values. Without branding, a company may struggle in differentiating its products and services. In most cases, due to competition, customers will also struggle in identifying the unique facets of a product without clear branding. Thus, it is imperative for companies to build brands. Brands provide customers with the knowledge structure about the product. When exposed to the brand in the marketplace, the brand-driven knowledge structures act as mental shortcuts in helping customers to recognize and visualize the product that leads to a quicker and confident purchase decisions.

Therefore, anything can be branded. This includes products, services, people, destinations, concepts, ideologies, religion and anything else. Branding for each of these aspects has flourished in recent years. In the following paragraphs, we provide examples of successful branding for the aspects listed.

Product brands

Physical products are easiest to imagine from a branding perspective. The tangibility of products makes it easier for companies to create brands. Tangible products can effortlessly be displayed and packaged and thus brand name, logo and other such visual aspects can be attached to them with ease. For instance, a commodity such as water, when packaged in a bottle, becomes a branded product. While people may not normally pay for tap water, the same water can be bottled and branded with a price tag. Moreover, due to branding, people tend to associate bottled water with a different level of purity and quality as compared to tap water. This has resulted in the rise of global bottled water market brands such as Dasani from Coca-Cola, Aquafina from Pepsi, Perrier from Nestlé, among many others. This has also resulted in a large market for mineral water along with a variety of other new sub-categories such as vitamin water, flavoured water and smart water. Such branding activities has led to the global bottled water market being valued at $283 billion in 2021 and is expected to expand at a compound annual growth rate (CAGR) of 6.7 per cent from 2022 to 2030.[14]

Product branding is not only useful for business to consumer (B2C) markets but also for business to business (B2B) markets. B2B markets differ from B2C markets in terms of order size and frequency of order itself. B2B orders tend to be larger and infrequent and are dependent on derived demand from B2C market.[15] Hence, creating a product brand is quite critical in setting out a unique identity and strong relationships that influence a business buyer's trust perceptions. A number of large B2B brands exist within physical goods market, as outlined in Table 1.1.

Table 1.1   Examples of large B2B product brands

Sector	Examples of large B2B product brands
Coal mining	China Shenhua Energy Co, BHP Billiton, Coal India, Shaanxi Coal
Steel	China Baowu Group, ArcelorMittal, Ansteel, Nippon Steel
Glass	Saint Gobain, PPG Industries, Corning International, AGC, Kyocera
Aircraft manufacturing	Boeing, Airbus, Lockheed Martin, Raytheon, Rolls Royce
Textiles	Toray, V.F. Corp, Shenzhou International Group, Reliance Industries
Machine manufacturing	Caterpillar, John Deere, CNH Industrial, ABB, Linde Enterprises, Daikin, Komatsu
Forestry	Oji paper, Stora Enso, West Fraser Timber, Weyerhaeuser, Universal Forest

SOURCE Zippia.com[16]

Product branding has transformed many other sectors within the B2C market as well. For instance, the home technology market has expanded rapidly within the last two decades. Brands such as Apple, Amazon, Google have become globally known with their product brands, from the Apple iPhone and Amazon Echo to Google Nest and Home branded products. More traditional products such as toothpaste and television also have distinct brands.

Service brands

Globally, in most of the developed economies services industry has overtaken the manufacturing sector. For instance, within the USA, service sector contributes 77.31 per cent of the overall GDP.[17] Similarly, in the UK the service industry accounts for 79 per cent of the total UK economic output.[18] In France and Japan, service industry contributed 70.16 per cent[19] and 75 per cent respectively. In countries such as Germany with a strong manufacturing sector, service industry still contributes almost 70 per cent of the overall GDP.[20] Such growth of service industry across large developed markets has resulted in differentiation initiatives by companies. This has in turn propelled the growth of service brands.

Compared to product brands, services are somewhat difficult to brand due to their inherent characteristics. Services differ from products due to their intangibility, perishability, inseparability and variability.[21] Services are intangible because they can often not be seen, tasted, felt, heard or smelled before they are purchased. Similarly, services cannot be stored and are inseparable as their production and consumption occurs simultaneously. Due to human involvement, there is a substantial variability challenge in delivery of services.

For instance, insurance or financial products like a mortgage cannot be felt or seen and can only be experienced after the service has been provided. Moreover, when claiming an insurance, a customer may receive differing levels and quality of service from the same company due to service variability.

The growth of service industry and its challenges have led to substantial research establishing services marketing as a field of study in itself.[22] An alternative perspective emerged claiming that service provision rather than goods is fundamental to economic exchange.[23]

Thus, service brands dominate in every industry sector. In the physical retail sector including grocery, clothing and healthcare, global brands compete with local brands. For instance, within the grocery sector, brands such as Wal-Mart, Tesco and Carrefour have a global footprint. These retailers use branding elements with their own distinct store atmospherics to entice and engage consumers. Similarly, in the internet-based service economy, many dominant brands exist including Amazon, Alphabet, Meta and eBay, among others, which have created their own service eco-systems. Within the technology industry, the e-commerce and smartphone revolution has resulted in global service brands in fields such as:

- travel and hospitality (e.g. Expedia, Tripadvisor, etc.)
- games (e.g. Candy Crush, Fortnite, Angry Birds, etc.)
- music (e.g. Spotify, iTunes, TuneIn, etc.)
- education (e.g. Coursera, EdX, Duolingo, etc.)
- dating (e.g. match.com, Tinder, eHarmony, Bumble, etc.)

These service brands have disrupted their industry sector which was dominated by traditional brick and mortar players.

BRANDING IN PRACTICE
Service brand transformation: the demise
of Blockbuster and the rise of Netflix

Blockbuster opened its first movie-rental store in 1985 in Texas, USA. For the two decades between 1990 and early 2000s, it was the dominant player in the VHS tap rental market. While a small rental store offered a few hundred movie choices to rent, a Blockbuster store could have a selection of 8,000 movies. Within the first five years, the company had more than a thousand stores across the USA. Viacom, a US-based media conglomerate, bought Blockbuster for $8.4 billion in 1994. Blockbuster made a significant chunk of revenue from late fees, almost 16 per cent of it, which frustrated many customers.

According to Reed Hastings, the co-founder of Netflix, one of his key motivations for starting the company was because he did not want to pay the $40 fine he was charged by Blockbuster. Netflix started as a mail-order DVD rental business with no late fees and a monthly flat rate in the year 1997. In 2000, Netflix founders Reed Hastings and Marc Randolph tried to sell Netflix to Blockbuster for $50 million and was turned away by then-CEO John Antioco. At that time, Blockbuster was widely considered a visionary leader in the home entertainment market with more than 9,000 stores globally and $5.9 billion in revenues.

However, competitors such as Redbox and Netflix, with their no late fees and quicker rental options, started gaining rapid market share by mid-2000s. In 2004, Blockbuster decided to end their late fees charge which was estimated to have cost the company $200 million. Moreover, it also entered a new online rental market with a new venture, Blockbuster Online, which was already dominated by Netflix.

Using the facets and complexities of services as a competitive advantage over a products-focused business, Netflix transformed the home entertainment sector. It was able to build a novel service business model utilizing technological advancements, including the vast improvements in internet speed and storage infrastructure.

From 2003 to 2005, Blockbuster lost 75 per cent of its market value and filed for bankruptcy in 2010. While Netflix remains a dominant global brand with $29.7 billion revenue in 2021.

This case highlights the continuous and dynamic nature of the service industry wherein branding plays a key role along with technology transformation.

SOURCES www.businessinsider.com/rise-and-fall-of-blockbuster?r=US&IR=T#today-the-blockbuster-franchise-has-dwindled-to-just-one-store-in-bend-oregon-which-has-been-turned-into-an-airbnb-15; https://finance.yahoo.com/news/netflix-reed-hastings-streaming-wars-blockbuster-120914436.html

Person brands

Similar to products and services, people also possess intrinsic qualities that are reflected and perceived by the external world. Moreover, every person has a name and thus in a generic sense, everyone has a person brand of some kind.[24] Personal brand reflects individual characteristics with a motive of establishing a distinctive image in the minds of the target audience. While person branding has been in existence for a long period of time, academic research pertaining to this phenomenon is gaining popularity in recent years. For instance, impression management theory has been used as a lens to examine the ways in which people create, manage and communicate their person brand.[25] People use a variety of defensive (excuse, justification, disclaimer, self-handicapping and apology) and assertive (ingratiation, intimidation, supplication, entitlement, enhancement, blasting and exemplification) impression management tactics to build their brand.[26]

Historically, rulers across civilizations created their person brands by creating unique monuments. For instance, the Pharaohs built pyramids and temples with their own name inscribed throughout these monuments. Ancient kings in Greece, Persia, India, China, Mayan and Aztec civilizations used facets of person branding by creating impressive monuments and artefacts glorifying their achievements and personality. For instance, in ancient India, king Ashoka's stone engraved edicts communicated the personal ideology of the ruler for his subjects to follow.

Over time, person brands have become popular in different fields. For instance, artists and sculptors such as Leonardo da Vinci, Donatello and Caravaggio, economists such as Adam Smith and John Maynard Keynes, scientists such as Copernicus, Newton and Einstein are examples of person brands. In recent years, person brands have grown substantially. Politicians such as Winston Churchill, Jacinda Ardern and Donald Trump have created their own branded personas built around their personal ideologies. Following such personal ideologies can act as a double-edged sword. For instance, Donald Trump was banned from using various social media such as Twitter for his divisive political rhetoric on a variety of socio-political issues. To sustain his person brand, the ex-president Trump even created his own social media platform, Truth Social. Person branding has allowed many other politicians to use their characteristics to gain senior business leader positions and earn substantial revenues. For example, ex-British deputy prime minister Nick Clegg has become President of Global Affairs of Meta.

Person brands are also highly influential in the world of business. Some famous business CEOs and entrepreneurs have created person brands that are at times more popular and recognized than the companies they are associated with. For example, Richard Branson (Virgin), Bill Gates (Microsoft), Steve Jobs (Apple), Jack Welch (GE), Jack Ma (Alibaba), Jeff Bezos (Amazon), Mark Zuckerberg (Facebook) and Elon Musk (Tesla and Twitter) have created and curated their person brands that are recognized globally. At times their charisma has helped but also hindered their company's growth prospects. For instance, Elon Musk was sued by the Securities and Exchange Commission of the USA in August 2018 and had to agree for some of his tweets to be vetted by a lawyer which had a substantial impact on Tesla's market valuation.[27]

Similar to person brands in political and business domains, person brands also exist in other social domains. For example, in the early 1990s, several fashion models, including Claudia Schiffer, Heidi Klum, Naomi Campbell and Kate Moss, gained worldwide popularity through their work with haute couture brands and commercial modelling. These supermodels charted a new drive for fashion trends globally and became household names. Similarly, with the increasing penetration of television globally, many news anchors and journalists also established their person brands. Celebrities associated with Hollywood and other film and drama industries also have strong person brands. For instance, popular Hollywood actress Angelina Jolie used her person brand to highlight the plight of refugees for over 20 years as a UN refugee agency ambassador.

Person brands and social media

With the rise of internet and social media, a novel type of person brand has emerged as social media influencers. Traditional celebrities bring meaning to the endorsement process from the roles they assume in their careers which they use in turn to build their social media profiles.[28] For instance, footballer Cristiano Ronaldo has the highest number of followers overall (more than 510 million on Instagram) which is based on his footballing prowess. Similarly, the musician Justin Bieber has amassed 455 million followers on Instagram. Many of these influencers are not always celebrities known for their work in social, political and business domains. However, they develop their expertise over time in a particular domain by regularly engaging and posting on various social media platforms and gaining followers. Their continuous endeavours in the field of their choice and views create their person brand. These influencers have become brands in themselves purely capitalizing on the growth and popularity of social media as compared to traditional celebrities.

Destination brands

Travelling has always been part of human need. From the early migration of humans from Africa to all parts of the world to recent global immigration trends, humans have an innate need to explore new horizons. With the advent of robust public transport and cheap air travel, there has been a significant rise in the number of people travelling globally. As destinations compete with each other to attract visitors, branding has become crucial in this domain. Governments across the world are spending a substantial amount of resources on promoting their destinations to global visitors. For instance, island countries such as the Seychelles and Dominican Republic spend nearly 22 per cent of their GDP on tourism marketing, promotion and visitor-related infrastructure.[29] Even large markets such as the USA and the UK spend substantial resources on destination branding. For instance, the USA destination marketing body, Brand USA, received more than $250 million in funding from the federal government in 2022 alone to promote tourism.[30] According to Visit Britain, inbound tourism was worth more than £28 billion to the UK economy in 2019, its third largest service export and a major part of British trade.[31]

Destination branding encompasses branding of nations, cities and places. It allows the promoters of destinations to increase tourist traffic as well as makes the destination more attractive for businesses which in turn plays a critical role in the globalizing of the destination as well as growth of the local economy. For instance, when a government promotes a destination and develops primary travel infrastructure, it attracts secondary infrastructure including airlines, hotels and hospitality sectors. The availability of transport, accommodation and culinary delights in turn bring visitor traffic, leading to economic growth at the regional and in some cases national levels.

As part of their destination branding exercise, some governments have created memorable campaigns with global recognizability and recall. For instance, Malaysian government's campaign slogan 'Malaysia, Truly Asia' or the 'Incredible !ndia' campaign by the Government of India since 2002 have captured the imaginations of millions of tourists. Destination branding can be used to not only promote the place but demonstrate the unique aspects associated with its culture, food, heritage and people. For instance, in 2012, Visit Britain, the official tourism body of Great Britain, launched a four-year £25 million campaign to promote tourism coinciding with the London Olympic Games. The Love Great Britain campaign focused on culture, heritage, sport, music, nature, food and shopping and partnered with the James Bond movie *Skyfall* as well as Paddington Bear. The nation of Iceland used the campaign 'Iceland Hour' after the eruption of the Eyjafjallajökull volcano in 2010 to re-build its reputation as a tourism destination.

Branding of ideologies and religion

Thinking about some of the oldest brands in the world, one would observe religion and ideologies as brands with immense staying power. For instance, from a branding perspective 'Buddha', 'Krishna', 'Jesus Christ' and other similar religious figures have a global presence and recognition for millennia and not just centuries. Similarly, every religion differentiates itself from others through its unique symbols and design aesthetics. Moreover, the strength of branding of ideologies and religion has led to numerous sub-brands within each religion that people strongly attach themselves with. Within Christianity, while Catholic and Protestant ideologies dominate, each is further divided into many other sects and beliefs with their own unique symbolism, mythology and motifs. The same appears to be the case for Hinduism and Islam as well. Images and symbolism remain central to religious branding. Symbols such as ॐ (aum) and swastika in Hinduism, menorah, the seven-branched candelabrum and star of David in Judaism, the Christian cross, the khanda in Sikhism and Torii in Shinto are deeply imbued in people's psyche and are pertinent reminders of the distinctive identity of the religion.

In recent times, religious organizations and their associated groups have assigned significant resources to branding. This rise of resource allocation is associated with several societal changes, including work replacing church as a place for social connection; the cultural upheaval of the 1960s wherein baby boomers widely rejected the faith of their families; and by the 1990s the rise of spiritual alternatives provided via cable TV and the internet globally.[32] This has resulted in a huge increase in spending on branding by religious organizations across online and offline media. Religious organizations have used the same branding principles as their commercial counterparts such as leaders' persona, symbolisms, mythologies, speeches, quotes and language to appeal to their existing followers and acquire new ones.

Commercial brands have also adapted their products and services to cater to the belief systems of religious communities. For instance, McDonald's introduced halal meat in countries where a majority of the population is Muslim. However, in countries such as the UK, they do not offer such a choice.[33] Brands that are deeply rooted in their religious belief system consolidate their image accordingly to attract and engage their target audience. For example, some brands keep their stores closed on Sundays or support certain religious gatherings, groups or events. Chick-fil-A, the third-largest food chain in the USA, remains shut on Sundays, reflecting their founder Truett Cathy's Christian faith.[34] Mecca-Cola, a brand that originated in Paris, France, was founded in protest against the political ideology of the West in the Middle East, particularly towards the Muslim majority countries.[35] Such examples illustrate how some brands build their identity around religious belief systems.

The importance of brands for companies

As described above, anything can be branded and more importantly, branding ensures organizational success. Brands not only help the organization but also other stakeholders as well. For instance, consumers make product quality, price and other relevant consumption decision judgements based on the brands they see. Similarly, people who are not consuming but only observing the brands also make judgements about the person in possession of the brand. Thus, brands serve functional as well as emotional and social purposes.

Brands have become highly valuable for companies. This is reflected in increasing investment in branding activities globally. Brand is an intangible asset, and their value resides in the perceptions of the customers and the market.[36] Thus, many managers assume that brand equity and brand value are the same. While both brand equity and brand value are educated estimates of how much a brand is worth, there is a subtle difference between these terms. Brand equity refers to the importance of a brand in the customer's eyes, while brand value is the financial significance the brand carries.[37]

> Brand value has traditionally been regarded as part of the company's goodwill which is the extra worth of a business over and above the value of physical assets. Hence, finance professionals and accountants tend to take brand value into account when a business is sold. Thus, the intangible value of a brand does not appear on the balance sheet.

However, there is an ever-increasing emphasis on brand value in corporate communications including investor reports and directors' statements in annual reports. Moreover, brand is increasingly considered an acceptable security for asset-backed financing.[38]

This importance of brands has led to a number of metrices that determine the value of a brand. These metrices use a variety of parameters to calculate the total financial value of a brand. Brand valuation was first developed by the British branding agency Interbrand in the 1980s. Several other companies also launched their brand valuation metrics. For example, Millward Brown, now part of Kantar, also developed its own brand valuation methodology termed Brand Z. Similarly, Young and Rubicam's brand valuation model, which is now called VMLY&R and is a subsidiary of WPP, also gained popularity within the market. Brand valuation involves a variety of approaches including the cost, market and the income approach. For instance, Interbrand uses three key components for their brand valuation: an analysis of the financial performance of the branded products or services, the role the brand plays in purchase decisions and the brand's competitive strength.[39] Table 1.2 provides the top 10 global brands and their valuation based on Interbrand's methodology.

Table 1.2   Best global brands 2023

Rank	Brand name	Value (in US$ mn)	% increase YoY
1	Apple	482,215	18%
2	Microsoft	278,288	32%
3	Amazon	274,819	10%
4	Google	251,751	28%
5	Toyota	59,787	10%
6	Coca-Cola	57,535	0%
7	Mercedes-Benz	56,103	10%
9	Disney	50,325	14%
10	Nike	50,289	18%

SOURCE Interbrand annual global ranking, 2022[40]

Scholarly debate

Ehrenberg A S, Uncles, M D and Goodhardt, G J (2004) Understanding brand performance measures: using Dirichlet benchmarks, *Journal of Business Research*, 57 (12), 1307–25

Keller, K L and Lehmann, D R (2003) How do brands create value? *Marketing Management*, 12 (3), 26–31

Chapter summary

This chapter began by defining a product and how companies can use a variety of engagement levels to build relationships with consumers. We then identified the pivotal role that brands play in building strong relationships with the consumers. We also identified several definitions of brand and the multidimensional view of a brand from both academic and practitioners' perspectives. Anything can be branded including products, services, people, organizations, destinations, ideologies and religions. The importance of brands is captured in its financial valuation. As markets evolve, brands evolve too and thus branding has become a key facet for business success.

Key concepts

- Product
- Brand as a multidimensional entity
- Branding applications
- Product, service, person, destination, ideologies and religion
- Brand meaning
- Financial value of a brand

Exercise questions

1 Define a product and discuss how companies can achieve meaningful engagement with consumers using product engagement matrix.

2 Explain the multidimensional view of a brand.

3 Can anything be branded? Discuss using examples.

4 You have been invited as a consultant by a national tourism agency of your home country. Their management board is currently sceptical about branding the nation and its culture. Explain how branding can enhance tourist perceptions of your home country using other successful campaigns as examples.

5 Using the internet, compare and contrast different brand valuation techniques.

6 Explain the importance of a brand from the perspectives of an organization and a consumer.

CASE STUDY

The new model of sharing economy

This case shows how modern information technology is helping brands and individuals become more collaborative.

Adam Smith, the father of modern economics, noted that a person who seeks only his own profit may still end up making choices that benefit others economically, guided by an 'invisible hand'. Imagine an economy where self-interest isn't just good for you, it also benefits society as a whole. This concept, dubbed the 'sharing economy',[41] is emerging alongside traditional economic models. While self-interest still drives most productivity, technology is pushing boundaries and making collaborations easier.

There has been a lot of hype about how IT would change the economy, so it is important to separate the truly transformative changes from those that simply make it easier to do what we were already doing. Three main trends stand out:

1 Wider reach: Technology empowers individuals to offer goods and services to larger audiences. Take accommodation, for instance, websites like Airbnb connect homeowners with global travellers, bypassing limitations faced by traditional hotels. This doesn't alter the pursuit of self-interest, but it optimizes resource utilization by filling previously empty rooms. Similarly, online platforms match individuals with diverse personal service needs, creating a win-win for both parties.

2 True sharing: Barter, once deemed inefficient, is making a comeback thanks to the internet. House swaps and car sharing platforms expand possibilities, allowing more people to experience different lifestyles and optimize resource use. Carpooling websites offer a modern twist on hitchhiking, connecting drivers with passengers for efficient travel. This trend goes beyond economics, reflecting a shift towards experiences and a less materialistic view of success.

3 Sharing in creation: The open-source software movement, Wikipedia and artists exploring alternative copyright models showcase how voluntary, collaborative work can yield valuable products. This 'anti-Taylorism' approach disrupts traditional production methods; but it's not an alternative to capitalism, rather a complement.

These emerging sharing trends all serve to complement, not replace, capitalism. Much like traditional free market economics, collaborative consumption models thrive on trust and supporting structures. Reviews, ratings and clear licensing allow sharing economy companies to regulate themselves without top-down rules.

However, some degree of government oversight helps instil confidence when handling private assets. The aim of the government should not be to forcibly institutionalize sharing where it does not arise organically, nor to restrict it where it proves useful, rather, regulators and businesses alike should focus on empowering those who voluntarily opt into collaborative ecosystems, providing the guardrails they need to participate securely. By embracing both self-interest and collective benefit, the economy may enjoy the best of both the invisible hand and its more visible, collaborative counterpart.

Case questions

1 How is technology transforming consumption trends and driving the sharing economy?

2 Find examples online of the sharing economy from food, travel, transportation and crowdfunding sectors.

3 From your perspective, what challenges are faced by the sharing economy brands?

4 What role should governments play in sharing economy system according to you?

Endnotes

1 Doyle, P and Stern, P (2006) *Marketing Management and Strategy*, Pearson Education

2 Levitt, T (1980) Marketing success through differentiation – of anything, *Harvard Business Review*, Jan–Feb, 83–91

3 Ibid.

4 de Chernatony, L and Dall'Olmo Riley, F (1998) Defining a 'brand': Beyond the literature with experts' interpretations, *Journal of Marketing Management*, 14 (5), 417–43

5 Bagozzi, R P, Romani, S, Grappi, S and Zarantonello, L (2021) Psychological underpinnings of brands, *Annual Review of Psychology*, 72, 585–607

6 Assael, H (1984) *Consumer Behavior and Marketing Action*, Kent Pub. Co.

7 De Chernatony, L (2010) *Creating Powerful Brands*, Routledge

8 Blackston, M (1992) A brand with an attitude: A suitable case for treatment, *Journal of the Market Research Society*, 34 (3), 231–42

9 Stern, B B (2006) What does brand mean? Historical-analysis method and construct definition, *Journal of the Academy of Marketing Science*, 34 (2), 216–23

10 Ogilvy, D (2013) *Ogilvy on Advertising*, Vintage

11 Ambler, T (1992) *Need-to-Know Marketing: An accessible AZ guide*, Century Business

12 Kapferer, J N (1994) *Strategic Brand Management: New approaches to creating and evaluating brand equity*, Simon and Schuster

13 Goodyear, M (1993) Reviewing the concept of brands and branding, *Marketing and Research Today*, 21 (2), 75–79

14 www.grandviewresearch.com/industry-analysis/bottled-water-market (archived at https://perma.cc/2XEK-LXVV)

15 Keller, K L and Kotler, P (2022) Branding in B2B firms, in *Handbook of Business-to-Business Marketing*, Edward Elgar Publishing, pp 205–24

16 Zippia (2022) The 10 largest coal mining companies in the United States, Zippia.com, 26 July, www.zippia.com/advice/largest-coal-mining-companies/ (archived at https://perma.cc/8TZJ-BUFC)

17 www.statista.com/statistics/270001/distribution-of-gross-domestic-product-gdp-across-economic-sectors-in-the-us/ (archived at https://perma.cc/WK7N-HKQS)

18 https://commonslibrary.parliament.uk/research-briefings/sn02786/#:~:text=The%20service%20industries%20accounted%20for,employment%20in%20July%2D September%202022 (archived at https://perma.cc/8AA3-54RA).

19 www.statista.com/statistics/270352/distribution-of-gross-domestic-product-gdp-across-economic-sectors-in-france/ (archived at https://perma.cc/VJD7-UJGG)

20 www.statista.com/statistics/295519/germany-share-of-economic-sectors-in-gross-domestic-product/ (archived at https://perma.cc/YC9A-X7Q5)

21 Kotler, P, Keller, K L and Chernev, A (2021) *Marketing Management – Global Edition*, Pearson

22 Zeithaml, V A, Parasuraman, A and Berry, L L (1985) Problems and strategies in services marketing, *Journal of Marketing*, 49 (2), 33–46. Also see Lovelock, C and Patterson, P (2015) *Services Marketing*, Pearson Australia

23 Vargo Stephen, L and Lusch Robert, F (2004) Evolving to a new dominant logic for marketing, *Journal of Marketing*, 68 (1), 1–17

24 Rangarajan, D, Gelb, B D and Vandaveer, A (2017) Strategic personal branding—And how it pays off, *Business Horizons*, 60 (5), 657–66

25 Bolino, M, Long, D and Turnley, W (2016) Impression management in organizations: Critical questions, answers, and areas for future research, *Annual Review of Organizational Psychology and Organizational Behavior*, 3 (1), 377–406

26 Lee, S J, Quigley, B M, Nesler, M S, Corbett, A B and Tedeschi, J T (1999) Development of a self-presentation tactics scale, *Personality and Individual Differences*, 26 (4), 701–22

27 www.theguardian.com/technology/2022/mar/08/elon-musk-seeks-end-us-restrictions-tweets (archived at https://perma.cc/GC8K-PULY)

28 Breberina, J, Shukla, P and Rosendo-Rios, V (2021) When endorsers behave badly: Consumer self-expression and negative meaning transfer, *International Journal of Advertising*, 1–25

29 www.cnbc.com/2016/09/29/tourism-how-much-do-countries-spend-to-attract-tourists.html (archived at https://perma.cc/WH6U-LHGE)

30 www.hotelmanagement-network.com/comment/us-tourism-funding-boost/ (archived at https://perma.cc/DJA7-RX7Q)

31 www.visitbritain.org/visitbritain-launches-multi-million-pound-global-campaign-drive-inbound-tourism (archived at https://perma.cc/2LAE-U2C5)

32 Einstein, M (2008) *Brands of Faith: Marketing religion in a commercial age*, Routledge

33 www.mcdonalds.com/gb/en-gb/help/faq/do-you-have-any-halal-restaurants.html (archived at https://perma.cc/7QS9-CDL3)

34 www.businessinsider.com/chick-fil-a-closed-on-sunday-business-strategy-2019-6?r=US&IR=T (archived at https://perma.cc/VE3D-E35W)

35 https://meccacolagroup.com/the-founer-and-you/ (archived at https://perma.cc/5AWL-U9BH)

36 https://online.hbs.edu/blog/post/whats-in-a-brand-the-value-of-the-brand-and-how-to-record-it (archived at https://perma.cc/6L36-YDTD)

37 https://prophet.com/2022/01/brand-equity-vs-brand-value/ (archived at https://perma.cc/GQW5-EM8K)

38 https://interbrand.com/london/thinking/financial-applications-for-brand-valuation/ (archived at https://perma.cc/RS36-T2WA)

39 https://interbrand.com/thinking/best-global-brands-2021-methodology/ (archived at https://perma.cc/8796-53R2)

40 https://interbrand.com/best-brands/ (archived at https://perma.cc/AY7Y-WTAX)

41 www.ft.com/content/ddf5de76-0105-11e3-a90a-00144feab7de (archived at https://perma.cc/7WH6-ZXA8)

The evolution of branding   02

Overview

In this chapter, we delineate brands through history – how and why branding began and developed through ancient, medieval and modern eras. We bring in new perspectives on the existence of the core concepts of modern branding throughout history. We identify the original drivers that led to the modern-day branding concepts and then discuss how branding emerged more potent and omnipresent in the modern times. The chapter ends with reflections on the future for brands.

Key learning outcomes

Upon reading this chapter, you should be able to

- Understand how the need for branding took roots
- Develop insights into the historical journey of branding, through ancient, medieval and modern times
- Understand how the basic concepts of branding developed through the ages and morphed into modern branding lexicon
- Appreciate the scholarly debate on the history of branding
- Develop insights into the forces shaping the contemporary and future paths for branding

The evolution of the word 'brand'

Brands were used throughout history as conveyers of information and image or meaning.[1] This occurs because brand as a word serves a dual function of being both a noun and a verb. Brand as a noun refers to various entities such as products, people, places and ideas.[2] As a verb, brand refers to the seller's or producer's approach to make their goods and/or services meaningful through naming and communicating the features or benefits.[3] According to the *Oxford English Dictionary*, the word brand was first found in the Old English (Anglo-Saxon) that emerged from Germanic languages. It appears as a noun in the epic poem *Beowulf* (ca. 1000) and as a verb in Wycliffe's religious tract *An Apology for Lollard Doctrines*.[4] Dual-function words such as brand are highly flexible as they can be combined into multiword noun phrases (e.g. brand identity, brand loyalty, brand equity) and verbal phrases (e.g. corporate brand-ing, brand-ed service) which can extend and enhance the meaning. Thus, brand was used for 15 centuries before it entered marketing lexicon in 1922, when it appeared as the multiword noun phrase brand name in the publication *Hotel World*, to describe a trade or proprietary name.[5]

In its original meaning brand was used in the poem *Beowulf* as a synonym for sword. The usage of the term brand is associated with the old Germanic *brinn-an* or with the Norse word *brandr* that is loosely associated as an act, means or result of burning. Moreover, through its evolution, the word brand had both positive and negative meanings which emerged through the practice of branding throughout history. As described earlier, traders and merchants from Indus valley civilizations used seals that distinguished their goods from others. Thus, the mark was stamped on the goods. The positive idea associated with brand reflects the burning of a mark on goods or animals such as cattle, horses, etc. to clearly establish origin, ownership and distinctive identity. However, the word also conveyed negative meaning when it was used to communicate the idea of disgrace stamped on something or someone. For instance, in British colonial slave regimes, branding of African American slaves was widespread for identification or punishment purposes.[6]

The genesis of branding across ages

As discussed in the previous chapter, branding has become firmly established as a key component of business success. Brand as a concept remains multifaceted and thus multitudes of meanings are attached with it. The notion of brand, however, has been observed throughout the development of the human civilization. At its core, brand is something that distinguishes a seller from competitors. From ancient to modern times, brands have played two key roles for their owners: (a) conveyer of information regarding origin, quality and other relevant aspects attached with a product or service; and (b) conveyer of image or meaning relating to status, power, value and/or personality to both consumers and channel members.[7] Many historical branding practices focused on former rather than the latter.

Branding in ancient civilizations

Branding as a business practice is not a new concept. Historians, archaeologists and scholars from other disciplines such as sociology and anthropology have suggested that some form of brand and branding had existed since the early periods of the human civilization. The need for branding emerged as trade started flourishing within and between expanding ancient civilizations. To clearly identify their goods, sellers started using pictorial symbols sometimes accompanied by additional text. These early versions of brands are termed proto-brands by researchers.[8] The earliest evidence of such proto-branding is observed in Egyptian wine jars and other ceramic goods found throughout Mesopotamia.[9] The first extensive evidence of proto-brands were found when archaeologists excavated two regions of the Indus Valley civilization in Harappa and Mohenjo-Daro (2600–1700 BCE). The stone and bronze craftsmen in these ancient cities created little square seals, with animal and geometric motifs, which were then sold to the merchants, who used these seals for branding purposes to distinguish their goods from others. These seals have also been found in archaeological excavations around Mesopotamia and Failaka in Persian Gulf suggesting extensive use of brand marks in these trading operations. These seals with their imagery and text have been shown to indicate the origin, identity of the owner and aided the sorting, storage and transportation both by resellers and relevant authorities.

Similar to early Bronze Age Indus civilization, in the middle Bronze Age (2000–1500 BCE), in Shang China, carved bone and tortoise-shell-based crests provide evidence of a substantial state-run operation that was organized around 'Zu' or kin groups. These crests appear on pottery, flags, cooking pots, wine vessels, horse plumes, fences and other goods.[10] It is argued that these crests could allow others to identify the product origin and also infer quality on the basis of that.[11] In the late Bronze Age (1500–100 BCE), the trade centres grew in the Eastern Mediterranean with seafaring communities of Canaanites (Phoenicians), Minoans and Mycenaean Greeks taking a central role as the key middlemen in the Near Eastern trading system.[12] Cyprus copper emerged as a high status good, similar to Egyptian gold.

These practices adopted by early civilizations were continued by late Bronze Age and Iron Age producers and merchants. For instance, Tyrian jugs that were stylishly decorated with bands or red, black and maroon paint that reflected the origin and quality.[13] Similarly, modern archaeologists are able to trace different Greek pots back to their respective makers and workshops by comparing the very individualistic decorations. Greek potters started labelling their work as early as 7th century BCE with some vases containing inscriptions of the men who made them, similar to modern-day craftsmen signatures.[14] The labelling conveyed origin and quality perceptions and at the same time invoked power and image value of the good as status symbols of their time.

While the focus of early branding effort was on differentiating goods such as pottery, metal, cotton and other such produce, there is also evidence of service brands in ancient history. For instance, Takshashila, considered to be one of the earliest centres of higher learning in the world, had students representing India, Central Asia, China and other countries. Similar centres for higher learning emerged in various other parts of the world including Alexandria, Athens and ancient India. These were destinations of higher learning and thus excellent examples of destination branding apart from the services they offered.

BRANDING IN PRACTICE
Ancient Egypt and India

To demonstrate their power and status over subjects, Egyptian rulers built vast structures such as the pyramids and the temples. Karnak temple in Luxor was the largest such complex in the world when it was built. Each of the temples and sub-temples had their own distinctive identities associated with the rulers of the time. The power of such structures is seen even today as Karnak is the second most visited site in Egypt after the Giza pyramids.

In India, post-4th century BCE, the rise of Buddhism happened rapidly and that can also be attributed to how the thoughts of the Buddha were communicated across South and Southeast Asia. Various statues of Buddha emerged throughout the ancient world including Bamyan in present-day Afghanistan and Leshan Giant Buddha in China. In India, religious art in the form of murals, statues and paintings in the rock-cut Ajanta caves captured the life stories and message of the Buddha. Such religious iconography served as brand communication adopted later by other religions as well.

Figure 2.1   Temples in ancient Egypt and India were seats of religion and sources of brand communication

SOURCE Authors

Branding through the Middle Ages

Throughout the Middle Ages and up to the early 20th century, the use of brand as the conveyer of information remained consistent. The origin and quality signals were associated with craftsmen, guilds or cities, which led to the rise of industrial clusters. Moreover, the growing commerce and international trade spurred the need for clear distinction for goods coming from different sources. Certain places gained regional, international and even global prominence for their speciality products. For instance, Chinese silk and porcelain, Venetian Murano glass, Indian spices, Japanese gold, West African ivory and salt from Sahara were in high demand throughout the world markets.

The international trade routes such as the Silk Road led to the emergence of important world-renowned trading centres such as Xi'an from the east to Samarkand, Baghdad and Damascus in the Middle East and Central Asia, to Constantinople and Venice in the West.[15] With the growing demand of unique goods, novel forms of people brands emerged including artists, sculptors, poets and scientists. For instance, works of poets such as Rumi, Omar Khayyam and Ferdowsi were disseminated far and wide through the trade routes. Similarly, books on a variety of topics from Indian and Arabic scientists, including Bhaskara, Muhammad ibn Musa al-Khwarizmi, were read widely. Further, as Europe entered the Renaissance period, painters and sculptors such as Leonardo da Vinci, Michaelangelo, Raphael, Donatello, Caravaggio and Filippo Brunelleschi, among many others, became brands in themselves and gained fame for their work internationally.

Similar to the Chinese systems of kin groups in ancient times, early guild-like associations existed in most civilizations.[16] From the 11th century onwards, however, guilds started taking a more structured form across Europe as craftsmen united to protect their common interests.[17] Guilds controlled trade in many cities and shaped the flow of labour and production. By controlling the supply and demand for various specialist goods, guilds were able to establish their own distinctive identities. While guilds helped create unique brands and supported their members through their trade monopoly locally and regionally in most cases, scholars also argue that many guilds turned primarily into profit-seeking entities. This, in turn, inhibited quality, skills and innovation.[18]

The Industrial Revolution

The Industrial Revolution acted as a catalyst for a new wave of branding propagated by some of the pioneering multinational companies of the time such as the East India Company and the Dutch East India Company. Initially starting as trading companies, these organizations flourished as they engaged in the export and import of a variety of commodities including clothing, machinery, spices, tea and opium from a number of different European and Asian countries. With intensified trading and competition, the need for a distinctive brand name, mark and/or logo became even more pronounced, which contributed towards modern branding practices.

Companies such as Twinings, a tea company established in London in 1707, decided to differentiate itself through an elaborate logo in 1787, which is considered the oldest commercial logo in continuous use.[19] However, the oldest commercial logo belonging to a business that still exists today is attributed to the lager brand Stella Artois. The origin of the logo can be traced to 1366 with the establishment of Den Hoorn Brewery in Leuven, Belgium. The two horns in the Stella Artois brand have remained part of the brand logo since 1366, while other features such as the text, font and style have changed over the years. Table 2.1 lists some of the oldest brand logos of companies that still exist today.

Similar to a goods-centred economy, the service economy also flourished throughout history. While the goods travelled across countries and kingdoms, services were predominantly localized. Many such service-oriented brands have survived for centuries and continue to trade today, predominantly in the hospitality and education sectors. For instance, the oldest continuously operating hotel brand in the world, Nishiyama Onsen Keiunkan in Japan, was established in the year 705 and has been

Table 2.1 Examples of old brands and the introduction of their logo

Brand name	Year of company establishment	Logo first used	Industry
Stella Artois	1366	1366	Beverage
Twinings	1707	1787	Beverage
Bass Ale	1777	1876	Beverage
Peugeot	1810	1850	Automotive
Shell	1833	1904	Energy
Levi Strauss	1837	1886	Clothing
Louis Vuitton	1854	1896	Luxury
Sherwin-Williams	1866	1905	Chemicals
Nestlé	1868	1868	Food
Heinz	1869	1869	Food
Prudential	1875	1896	Insurance
Coca-Cola	1886	1886	Beverage
Johnson & Johnson	1886	1887	Healthcare

operated by 52 generations of the same family over the past 1,300 years.[20] Similarly, the oldest continuously run restaurant brand in the world, St Peter Stiftskulinarium in Austria, came into existence in the year 803.[21] Shishi High School in Chengdu, China opened in 143–141 BCE and is claimed to be the oldest existing school in the world.[22] Such examples show the existence of service brands that have stood the test of time. In contrast to the historic period, global service brands have emerged and flourished in the modern times across many traditional and new sectors.

Branding in the modern world

With the arrival of the 20th century, due to technological and logistical advancements, multinational corporation emerged that were producing and selling their goods and services in many different countries. Brands such as Nestlé, Coca-Cola, IBM and Ford Motor Company initially exported their products in various foreign markets and then opened factories in different parts of the world. These brands became household names in many international markets. The two world wars in the 20th century altered the scope and scale of the demand and supply for goods and services.

At the start of the 20th century, most industry sectors were highly fragmented, largely served by local or at best regional players. During World War I, however, the US government in particular enforced the idea of 'simplification' in the US industry, which then resulted in a standardization movement.[23] A survey of 84 product categories in 1929 showed a substantial reduction in variation within a decade.[24] For example, the variation in bed blanket sizes reduced from 78 to 12, and from 33 variations in hospital beds when they were standardized to one size fits all. This had a significant effect on market competition where small manufacturers almost vanished and were replaced by large, integrated operations producing standard-sized products. Emergence of these large corporations allowed mass production and mass marketing as well as a standardized approach to branding.

However, post-World War II, technological and logistical advancements combined with greater market access and consumer affluence meant that managers were able to provide a greater variety of products and services, driving a gradual move from the extreme forms of standardization. This was also supported by the management thinkers of that time, who promoted the initial strategic orientation for 'market segmentation'.[25][26] The movement was predominantly geared toward the aggregation of the submarket or the market class rather than customization at an individual level.[27] As different segments were created by marketers, a variety of corresponding brands, sub-brands and their variants were developed. However, with most products looking functionally similar, marketing and brand managers were faced with the task of creating a unique identity for their products in a cluttered marketplace.

This led to the use of a variety of psychological techniques for distinguishing a product from the competition. The increasing use of segmentation-driven communication included factual information as well as emotional triggers. For instance, marketers started using gender- and age-based stereotypes in advertising, as demonstrated in the examples in Figure 2.1. To develop an emotional connection with consumers, marketers increasingly used movie stars and famous sports personalities as endorsers of their products. Further, the advent of colour TV in 1951 provided a novel medium for brands to communicate their identities beyond billboards, radio and other signage mediums.

The increasing use of psychology led to accusations of manipulation from and mistrust towards marketing. Scholars argued that the increased consumer choice and related marketing activities were not particularly beneficial to the consumer themselves, rather it brought profit to the industry.[28] However, at the same time, critical scholars also acknowledged the improvements in the quality of life afforded by the growth of industry.[29] Thus, the growth of industry and brands led to critical debates regarding the benefits accruing from economic growth versus the ethics related to the growing reliance on often zealous and sometimes manipulative marketing practices.

Growing importance of product quality

As products proliferated and competition grew across markets globally post-World War II, product quality became a paramount factor for consumer choice. Companies highlighted their product quality throughout their communications. Interestingly, an American engineer and mathematical physicist, W. Edwards Deming, who helped develop the sampling techniques for Census and Labour statistics in the USA and Japan, led a completely new movement focusing on quality management that was embraced by the Japanese firms.[30] Through his training of engineers and managers, Deming created the Total Quality Management (TQM) idea. Many Japanese firms including Yamaha, Toyota and Sony applied Deming's quality management ideas in their manufacturing and supply chains resulting in substantial productivity and quality gains. With their relentless pursuit of quality improvement, these companies became trusted household brands in many parts of the world and have continued to flourish globally.

Throughout the 1980s and 1990s, globalization fuelled economic growth which led to a healthy middle class in markets across the Americas, Europe and Asia. Consequently, companies started taking into account cultural and regional differences and adapted their branding practices accordingly. This led to scholarly debate regarding the suitability of standardization versus customization approaches.[31,32] Firms started following different branding philosophies for their international operations. Many brands such as Apple, Microsoft, McDonald's and Sony adopted standardization, while others, including Nestlé, P&G and Unilever, developed or acquired numerous local/regional brands in their portfolios. A further approach emerged that bridged the standardization versus customization debate in the early 1990s wherein to benefit from the economies of scale some firms adopted a *glocal* approach. Through this approach, brands aimed to pursue standardization with a relevant local adaptation in product offerings and communications, as seen in the example below.

BRANDING IN PRACTICE
McDonald's approach to glocalization

McDonald's, an American firm, is one of the largest fast-food chains in the world with more than 38,000 outlets in over 100 countries.[33] Started in 1940 by brothers Maurice (Mac) and Richard McDonald in California, USA, the company pioneered an efficient format of service by creating a limited menu that included hamburgers, potato chips, drinks and pies as well as a self-service counter eliminating the need to be served on a table by staff.[34] In the 1950s, Ray Kroc joined the brothers as a franchise agent and launched the first McDonald's franchise. In 1961, Kroc took over McDonald's Corporation.

Kroc was a firm believer in standardization and set out exacting standards from food preparation to cleaning which were taught at the Hamburger University to franchisees. He also launched the highly recognizable double-arch M design logo. McDonald's offers the same décor and processes throughout the world through standardization. Moreover, it offers several products with the same brand name globally including McChicken, McNuggets, McFlurry and Happy Meal.

However, with its international expansion the firm has increasingly customized its menu and communications in many markets. For instance, in Japan, in spring, McDonald's offers Teri Tama Burger while in autumn it sells the Tsukimi Burger.[35] In India, to avoid the cultural taboo attached to beef consumption, McDonald's launched the Chicken Maharajah Mac.[36] Further, to serve the large vegetarian population of India, a separate vegetarian kitchen and other menu items such as the McAloo Tikki Burger were added. To serve Islamic markets, McDonald's replaced pork with fish in its menu, and offered Halal meat as well as a special menu for Ramadan festivities.[37]

As shown above, McDonald's standardization approach helps in achieving uniform speed and efficiency of supply chain and service, cleanliness and hygiene. At the same time, customization responding to cultural, religious and local palettes assists the brand in satisfying customers globally.

The internet age

The advent of the internet and its commercialization in the mid-1990s created a new avenue for branding. The internet-driven digital economy grew at a rapid pace and many brands were quick to adapt while others were late adopters. The internet was an equalizer for small and large brands alike. Brands could easily reach out to a vast body of consumers globally through their website and other social media as they grew in prominence over the years. The internet also led to online-only brands such as Amazon, eBay, Google and Facebook.

The digital transformation grounded in internet technology assisted brand communication in a variety of ways. Brands were now able to communicate their message to a wider audience. From a demand-side, the internet allowed brands to convey their story through a variety of means beyond the traditional newspaper and television adverts such as blog posts, videos, photos and social media. In the pre-internet world, most brand communication was a one-to-many endeavour wherein the brand promoted itself via traditional means. The internet allowed customers to co-create brand message which led to many-to-many communications. On the supply side, brands were able to coordinate the flow of goods and services globally through the power of continuous connectivity leading to significant growth in international trade. Within the last two decades, brands' spend on digital media has increased manyfold compared to traditional media.

The future for brands

As these sections have shown, branding has evolved throughout human history. From the simple seal that identified goods by a specific merchant, branding has developed into a multidimensional endeavour that encompasses both science and art and benefits from knowledge emanating across disciplines such as anthropology, sociology, psychology, economics, management and mathematics. In recent decades, branding has developed as a discipline of its own and is aided by continuous robust research which is driving the future of branding.

Ample avenues exist for brands to evolve further. Modern technology allows brands to build their voice in a cluttered marketplace. The advances in neuroscience, cognitive psychology and the emergence of techniques associated with Big Data analytics are helping branding researchers to understand the individual and social psychology and behaviours on an unprecedented scale. As a result, many brands are moving towards hyper-personalization. For instance, based on cookies and other predictive analytics-based approaches, brands are able to personalize individual digital experiences taking into account individual socio-demographic, geography, psychographic and behavioural variables. Amazon customizes its webpages and recommendations depending on the aforementioned variables as consumers search through its website. Similarly, all social media platforms track visitor activities and customize content and customer experience accordingly.

Such changes, driven by information asymmetry wherein brands possess substantial amounts of data and information about customers, is leading to a power imbalance in the market. The available data and analytics have allowed brands to gain deep insights about their customers, tipping the balance in their favour. Such market power held by brands can sometimes lead to manipulative practices that can harm their customers' interests and wellbeing. To avert such imbalances, governments and policy makers have created interventions including the European General Data Protection Regulation (GDPR)[38] which enables greater protection to consumers regarding the use of their personal data by brands.

Supplemented by technological advances, branding will continue to evolve. While traditional principles and concepts – such as brand elements, brand architecture, brand loyalty and equity, brand positioning, communication and engagement, brand extension and cobranding – will continue to hold their sway, the approach will become more sophisticated. Customer data is generated in unprecedented volumes in today's marketplace on a continuous basis. Capturing, curating and managing this data in a meaningful way is going to be a major challenge for the brands beyond the segmentation and targeting objectives. Such data will also assist brands in offering increasing transparency and consumer protection which can become future differentiators for the brands to aspire for. Brands that transfer the power of data to their customers may reap significant rewards in reputation and trust.

As we move towards the future, brands will have to play an increasingly important role as societal flagbearers in regards to sustainability and social responsibility. Recent research shows that consumers expect their brands to be doing more 'good' and not 'less bad'.[39] Moreover, consumers increasingly expect brands to take an ethical stance[40] and even at times a social activist stance.[41] In future, brands will have to authentically demonstrate their sustainability and social responsibility credentials to gain consumer appreciation and engagement. While such initiatives may not lead to increasing sales or profitability, with greater consumer consciousness about future of the planet and human welfare issues, it is imperative for the brands to integrate these activities for their long-term survival and success.

Chapter summary

This chapter first discussed the evolution of the term 'brand'. We then identified how branding as a practice evolved in ancient civilizations across the world as merchants needed to differentiate their goods from other competitors to highlight their origin and quality. The practice of branding did not change much throughout the middle ages. However, increasing global trade led to newer concepts such as people branding which evolved through the expertise of master craftspeople of the time. The roots of modern branding practices can be traced back to the Industrial Revolution in Europe with many multinational brands emerging in the 17th century and onwards. We also discussed the parallel evolution of service brands. The chapter also reflected on modern branding practices from the start of the 20th century, pre- and post-World Wars I and II. We also discussed the impact of the digital revolution and the future of branding. Understanding the growth and evolution of branding will allow you to comprehend the deep roots of this discipline throughout human history and appreciate the consistency as well as the evolutionary characteristics of branding.

Key concepts

- Defining brands
- Branding history
  - Branding in ancient civilizations
  - Branding through the Middle Ages
  - Branding in the modern world
- The future of branding

Exercise questions

1 Discuss the evolution of the word brand.

2 What were the key drivers for branding in ancient civilizations? Explain with examples.

3 Did branding practice differ throughout ancient civilizations to the Middle Ages? Why and how?

4 How did branding evolve in 20th century? What were the primary drivers?

5 Explain with examples the key considerations that brands will have to take into account for success in the 21st century.

CASE STUDY   Time travel through the Nestlé story

Please read the history of Nestlé, and do the following:

1   Evaluate the critical factors leading to the creation of brand Nestlé.

2   Critically examine the landmark changes in the branding of Nestlé through history.

3   Discuss the changing focus on consumer convenience, wellbeing and shared values in Nestlé's branding in modern times.

4   Critically reflect on Nestlé's current branding strategy and recommend steps the brand should take to help ensure its long-term success.

SOURCE www.nestle.com/about/history/nestle-company-history

Endnotes

1   Moore, K and Reid, S (2008) The birth of brand: 4000 years of branding, *Business History*, 50 (4), 419–32

2   Stern, B B (2006) What does brand mean? Historical-analysis method and construct definition, *Journal of the Academy of Marketing Science*, 34 (2), 216–23

3   Calder, B J and Reagan, S J (2001) *Brand Design*. In Dawn Iacobucci (ed.), *Kellogg on Marketing*, John Wiley, New York, pp 58–73

4   Brand names on menus? 1922, *Oxford English Dictionary* 2022:II.9

5   Ibid.

6   Bastos, W and Levy, S J (2012) A history of the concept of branding: Practice and theory, *Journal of Historical Research in Marketing*, 4 (3), 347–68

7   Moore, K, and Reid, S (2008) The birth of brand: 4000 years of branding, *Business History*, 50 (4), 419–32

8   Ibid.

9   Wengrow, D (2008) Prehistories of commodity branding, *Current Anthropology*, 49 (1), 7–34

10   Moore, K and Lewis, D C (2009) *The Origins of Globalization*, Routledge

11   Eckhardt, G M and Bengtsson, A (2010) A brief history of branding in China, *Journal of Macromarketing*, 30 (3), 210–21

12   Moore, K and Reid, S (2008) The birth of brand: 4000 years of branding, *Business History*, 50 (4), 419–32

13 Harrison, R J (1988) *Spain at the Dawn of History: Iberians, Phoenicians and Greeks*, Thames and Hudson, London

14 Osborne, R (1998) *Archaic and Classical Greek Art*, Oxford University Press

15 Frankopan, P (2015) *The Silk Roads: A new history of the world*, Bloomsbury Publishing

16 Epstein, Steven A (1995) *Wage Labor and Guilds in Medieval Europe*, University of North Carolina Press, Chapel Hill, NC, pp 10–49

17 www.britannica.com/topic/guild-trade-association (archived at https://perma.cc/QV34-M5GU)

18 Ogilvie, S (2004) Guilds, efficiency, and social capital: Evidence from German proto-industry, *The Economic History Review*, 57 (2), 286–333

19 https://twinings.co.uk/blogs/news/history-of-twinings (archived at https://perma.cc/VC5N-T3BR)

20 https://keiunkan.co.jp/en/ (archived at https://perma.cc/MAS6-TBB6)

21 www.stpeter.at/en/ (archived at https://perma.cc/GR86-BXW4)

22 www.oldest.org/culture/schools/ (archived at https://perma.cc/7X9H-RX37)

23 Lampel, J and Mintzberg, H (1996) Customizing customization, *Sloan Management Review*, 38 (1), 21–30

24 Alford, L P (1929) Industry: Part 2 – technical changes in manufacturing industries, in *Recent Economic Changes in the United States*, vols 1 and 2, NBER, pp 96–166

25 Levitt, T (1960) Marketing myopia, *Harvard Business Review*, 38 (4), 24–47

26 Smith, W R (1956) Product differentiation and market segmentation as alternative marketing strategies, *Journal of Marketing*, 21 (1), 3–8

27 Lampel, J and Mintzberg, H (1996) Customizing customization, *Sloan Management Review*, 38 (1), 21–30

28 Lazarsfeld, P F (1941) Remarks on administrative and critical communications research, *Zeitschrift für Sozialforschung*, 9 (1), 2–16

29 Tadajewski, M (2010) Towards a history of critical marketing studies, *Journal of Marketing Management*, 26 (9–10), 773–824

30 https://asq.org/quality-resources/total-quality-management/tqm-history (archived at https://perma.cc/42JX-WNBU)

31 Levitt, T (1983) The globalization of markets, *Harvard Business Review*, May–June, 92–102

32 Douglas, S P and Wind, Y (1987) The myth of globalization, *Columbia Journal of World Business*, 22 (4), 19–29

33 https://corporate.mcdonalds.com/corpmcd/franchising-overview.html (archived at https://perma.cc/RWJ8-F9C6)

34 www.britannica.com/topic/McDonalds (archived at https://perma.cc/9YUE-X4GW)

35 www.daytranslations.com/blog/mcdonalds-international-strategy-adapting-around-the-world/ (archived at https://perma.cc/CC2M-2XK2)

36 www.bbc.co.uk/news/business-30115555 (archived at https://perma.cc/576F-FSA9)

37 www.daytranslations.com/blog/mcdonalds-international-strategy-adapting-around-the-world/ (archived at https://perma.cc/CC2M-2XK2)

38 https://gdpr.eu/ (archived at https://perma.cc/8H35-9EBY)

39 Davies, I A, Lee, Z and Ahonkhai, I (2012), Do consumers care about ethical-luxury?, *Journal of Business Ethics*, 106 (1), 37–51

40 Singh, J (2016) The influence of CSR and ethical self-identity in consumer evaluation of cobrands, *Journal of Business Ethics*, 138 (2), 311–26

41 Moorman, C (2020) Commentary: Brand activism in a political world, *Journal of Public Policy & Marketing*, 39 (4), 388–92

Research streams in branding 03

Overview

The focus of this chapter is to provide an overview of research traditions in branding. In the first section we explain the key developments and empirical research on brand buying behaviour. This part focuses on 'how' consumers buy their brands. In the second section we bring in the research on 'why' consumers buy and relate to their brands, that is, the research underpinned by the psychology of branding. In the third section, we highlight key research on branding through the lenses of sociology and anthropology.

Key learning outcomes

Upon reading this chapter, you should be able to

- Develop understanding on different research streams in branding
- Gain knowledge on the three main aspects of branding research
- Understand how the theories and insights from different disciplines inform branding research
- Appreciate the scholarly debate on branding research
- Develop insights into of the latest branding research

How do consumers buy brands?

A major challenge in branding research has centred around consumer buying behaviour. While brand buying remains a highly complex phenomenon, brand managers have consistently aimed to maximize their sales and profits through understanding how their brands are being bought by the buyers. Consequently, models that identify brand buying patterns emanating from mathematics and statistics disciplines enable brand managers to manage the inventory as well as understand their brand's levels of loyalty in the competitive markets, i.e. how much customers stick with the brand. In addition, forecasting models provide estimates of future brand sales and assist with product planning. Such models have become well-established and widely adopted by the branding practitioners. In the following section, we provide an overview of the research on how people buy their brands.

Understanding brand buying through consumer panel data

People engage in buying various goods and services using a variety of means. With the proliferation of products and services with seemingly similar features across markets, understanding consumer choice processes has been a critical issue for marketing researchers. How do consumers choose one brand over the others? This question has garnered significant interest among research scholars and practitioners. Scholars initially suggested that when faced with products similar in features, general qualities and external appearance, consumers preferred a brand based on their previous buying experience, advertising or recommendation.[1] The question remained at the forefront for researchers, however, due to lack of robust data collection methods – the measurement of actual brand preference and purchase remained scarce. In 1942, H L Churchill advocated the use of panels of consumers who agreed to record their purchases on a regular basis in a diary. The diary was then used to analyse how different brands were bought by the consumers.

One of the first consumer panels that recorded consumer preferences and behaviour was run by Chicago Tribune. The data was analysed by George Brown in 1953 to understand customer preference.[2] Brown showed that the consumers could be divided into four segments based on their buying record for a brand: sole buyers, divided buyers, unstable buyers and no buyers. Such analyses of historical buying record became popular. Later researchers used panel data to further establish how consumers were buying their brands.[3][4] In the UK, the Attwood Panel similarly collected continuous purchase data across several product categories. Taylor Neslon (UK), Sofres (France), Frank Small (Australia), Intersearch (USA) and Research International (UK) were other popular consumer panels operating in the 1960s and onwards. Through mergers and acquisitions the panels grew in size and became established as providers of robust purchase data on how consumers were buying brands across categories over time. Currently, the Kantar Group, IRIWorldwide, GfK, Nielsen and Dentsu are some of the major providers of consumer panel data.

Empirical generalizations in marketing

A substantial amount of research evidence employing panel data has emerged over the past six decades. This body of research focuses solely on examining how consumers buy their brands, and empirically establishing patterns in brand buying behaviour. One of the pioneer scholars is Andrew Ehrenberg, who, with his colleagues, observed empirically generalizable patterns of buyer behaviour in purchase data. These patterns were then juxtaposed with mathematical modelling to establish lawlike relationships of buying.

The underlying precepts of this body of research lie in the scientific tradition of generalizing empirical results that are generated in different conditions. The phenomenon is now well-established as 'empirical generalizations' which has laid the foundations for studying how consumers buy their brands. One of the leading scholars espousing the tradition was Frank Bass who defined empirical generalizations as a pattern or regularity that repeats in different circumstances and which can be described simply by mathematical, graphic or symbolic methods.[5] Ehrenberg suggested that the lawlike relationships of science are descriptive generalizations, and they are also the building blocks of higher-level theory and explanation.[6]

In marketing literature, studies based on empirical generalizations have been developing steadily over time. Patrick Barwise added another perspective to the discussion with his listing of five characteristics of a good empirical generalization: scope, precision, parsimony, usefulness and link with theory.[7] A good empirical generalization, for example, will have a wide scope in terms of results showing consistent patterns under different conditions, contexts, countries, product categories and period. Similarly, the generalized results will demonstrate higher precision in terms of replicability of the results. Parsimony in research refers to the use of fewer variables to predict a generalizable outcome. Often there may be a trade-off between scope and parsimony, however, with repeated generalizations, a parsimonious model can emerge. Good empirical generalizations should also provide useful benchmarks to the marketing practitioners, who should be able to apply the patterns for realistic marketing decisions. Further, linking empirical generalizations with theory is critical to establish that the predictions are reliable, explainable and the reason some generalizations may not hold under certain conditions.

Other scholars further advocated the use of replication studies across multiple sets of data covering a wide range of conditions to establish the scope of empirical generalizations.[8] [9] Empirical generalizations can thus be transformed into the building blocks of scientific knowledge. The idea of using multiple sets of data is central to producing generalizable results that lead to empirically grounded theory.[10] Such results are, in turn, highly useful and applicable for branding practice, as demonstrated in the following 'Branding in practice' box.

BRANDING IN PRACTICE
Empirical generalizations in brand management

The systematic study of brand performance metrics has led to generalizable patterns, as summarized here:

- Brand penetrations vary within a product category and are much lower for smaller brands.

- Average buying frequencies do not vary much amongst brands in a category. Underlying these averages, some individuals are heavy buyers and others light buyers.

- Smaller brands not only have fewer buyers than larger brands, but buyers of smaller brands also buy the brand slightly less often than do buyers of bigger brands – the so-called double jeopardy effect.[11]

- 100% loyal buyers are relatively rare – in one year, almost all buyers of a typical brand are multi-brand buyers and divided in their loyalty.

- Levels of loyalty are higher in shorter-length periods, mainly because there are fewer opportunities to purchase different brands in shorter periods compared to longer periods.

- Most buyers of a brand also buy other brands leading to the duplication of purchase, which correlates with brand penetration.

SOURCE Singh and Crisafulli (2022)

Challenges of generalizability

In general, in management and marketing research there is a distinct lack of studies that are replicated across various contexts to establish generalizability. The reliance on a single data source has also taken roots in managerial practice, where brand managers often rely on cross-sectional studies for branding decisions. Studies with a single set of data may be considered anecdotal in nature as the business manager might want to know, for instance, whether or not a planned communications campaign will have a productive impact across the sector. Such practices that rely on a single data source pose a question about the scientific rigour and practical applicability of the results. Given that the results are not tested or re-validated across varying contexts, their generalizability remains unclear. In this regard, in academic inquiry, meta-analytic studies are increasingly gaining popularity.

A meta-analysis that combines the results of dozens or hundreds of comparable studies may reveal a replicable pattern in the data, which forms the basis of an empirical generalization that is highly informative to the decision makers.[12] In the past, studies have illustrated how meta-analysis has produced empirical generalizations concerning parameters in models of advertising, price, diffusion and consumer behaviour.[13] In pricing research, the results of 1,851 published price response estimates were used to conclude that average brand-level price elasticities are –2.62.[14] In practical applications, price elasticities may indicate levels of brand loyalty. This suggests that a price increase might not lead to a reduction in sales, and the brand should aim for a lower price elasticity figure. Thus, the meta-analytical result of –2.62 could serve as a benchmark for pricing decisions. Similarly, in a meta-analysis of 290 studies on brand relationship elasticity that denotes the relationship between brand relationship strength and customer brand loyalty, the overall elasticity was found to be 0.44. The figure can help managers to estimate the percentage increase in customer loyalty resulting from investments in brand relationship activities.[15] In branding research, such studies can help managers in using empirically generalizable research findings for robust decision-making.

Use of modelling in branding research

Over the years, marketing scholars have developed models using mathematical and statistical principles. These models have been widely used by branding practitioners to understand brand buying behaviour and predict future buyer behaviour. Broadly, the models are classified as being either decision or descriptive models. John D Little, in 1994, contrasted the two approaches: decision models are for solving problems whereas descriptive models seek to uncover marketing phenomena and to represent them.[16] Decision models include marketing activities that are controllable by the organization, such as price, sales promotion and advertising, and leave out others. Decision models often utilize popular statistical technique such as logit modelling. Descriptive models such as the Hendry, first-order Markov, NBD, NBD–Dirichlet, on the other hand, aim to descriptively provide information on the phenomena, for instance, patterns of buying or repeat purchase behaviour.

Managers and researchers use decision models to identify potential solutions to their current marketing problems by attempting to determine causality; for example, the impact of price discount on sales, the influence of advertising on market shares or whether personal selling or advertising would have a stronger impact on sales.[17] Critiques have, however, pointed out several deficiencies in decision modelling approaches.[18] For instance, decision models are said to be simplistic, and are unable to account for all possible variables that could influence a causal outcome. In the afore mentioned example of the influence of advertising on market shares, several other variables could impact causality, such as brand equity, promotional activities of competitors, the weather, seasonality, availability, amongst others. Similarly, the predictive capability of such models is doubtful, given the contextual and temporal issues involved. For instance, a brand manager predicting ice cream sales would need access to accurate weather data that also accounts for weather fluctuations. Such data is hard to come by and could lead to sub-optimal marketing decisions. Causal inferences derived from decision models have also been questioned, due to the dynamic consumption experiences and practices in the digital environment.

Descriptive models typically examine large-scale purchase data and derive information and patterns that can be used to describe present and predict future buying behaviour. Descriptive models have been hailed as being more useful for realistic marketing decisions. The models identify patterns of purchase behaviour, and provide insights and predictable benchmarks for evaluating change. As in many other areas of engineering and other sciences, models which successfully describe generalizable marketing phenomena first show us what, where, how and how much. However, they can then also help in deciding what to do and why.[19] For instance, models such as the NBD-Dirichlet provide benchmarks for evaluating the market performance of brands, as well as predicting the future buyer behaviour. The model fits over a wide range of contexts, and time periods, and has spawned a substantial body of academic papers, and found applications in marketing practice.[20] Descriptive models have been critiqued for lacking the function of explaining the psychology of purchase behaviour; in other words, why consumers buy brand A over brand B.

Why do consumers buy brands?

The research on the reasons for purchase of brand products/services has developed in parallel to the research traditions discussed in the preceding sections. Since the publication of one of the first books in the domain, *The Science of Advertising*, by Edwin Balmer 1910, the academic discipline of marketing started taking shape. Academic journals such as the *Harvard Business Review* (est. 1922), *Journal of Retailing* (est. 1925) and the *Journal of Marketing* (est. 1936) provided a platform for disseminating research findings and spurred further academic research in marketing and branding. The issue of why consumers buy has been the research focus for marketing researchers since the start of the formal academic research tradition. For instance, the first issue of the *Journal of Marketing* published an article titled 'Why people buy at department stores' (1936).[21]

Several established academic disciplines such as sociology, social psychology, anthropology, psychology, economics, statistics and mathematics shaped the branding and marketing thought. Drawing from these, researchers developed new branding ideas and terminology. For instance, in the 1950s and the 1960s, terms such as brand loyalty, brand segmentation, lifestyle branding and marketing mix were coined. Similarly, in the 1970s and 1980s, terms such as brand positioning, brand equity, social and relationship marketing emerged. Further developments were in the areas of brand identity, relationship branding, brand communities, not-for-profit branding and brand origin throughout the 1990s and early 20th century.[22] In the following sections, we bring together some of the theories in respective disciplines that have been influential in shaping the discourse and research in branding.

Psychology and sociology

Psychology is the scientific study of the human mind and its functions, especially those affecting behaviour in a given context. Sociology, on the other hand, is the scientific study of social life, group behaviour, social change, and social causes and consequences of human behaviour. These disciplines have impacted branding research in a substantial way, especially in understanding why consumers buy one brand over others, why they connect or disengage with their brands, and why they continue patronizing their brand.

The discipline of psychology has profoundly influenced branding thought and literature in modern times. Psychological theories, such as attribution theory, balance theory, cognitive dissonance, elaboration likelihood model and self-identity theory, have impacted research on enhancing our understanding of consumers and their relationship with brands.

Similarly, theories from the discipline of sociology have guided some pathbreaking research on branding. Theories such as symbolic interactionism, impression management, social exchange and social capital, amongst others, have played an important role in shaping research in branding. A brief overview of some of the prominent theories is provided in Table 3.1.

In terms of brand consumption behaviour, a distinct branch that has developed in recent years is that of consumer culture theory.[23] Scholarly work in the field emanates from social anthropology and ethnographic and netnographic studies rooted in other disciplines.[24] The consumer culture theory denotes that consumption choices are grounded in cultural and social norms. The study of subcultures has spawned research in understanding the impact and dynamics of brand communities as well as how consumer identities evolve and impact global brand consumption behaviour.[25][26]

Economics and behavioural sciences

While psychological and sociological theories examine individual and group behaviour, theories in economics, in particular behavioural economics, focus on the

Table 3.1 Prominent theories and their applications in branding

Theory	Key source	Meaning	Application
Attribution theory	Heider, F (1958) *The Psychology of Interpersonal Relations*, Wiley, New York	Accounts for how individuals perceive the causes of everyday experience, as being either external or internal.	A toothpaste brand communicates that it is the most preferred brand for the dentists. The quality of the brand is attributed to the dentists' preference.
Cognitive dissonance theory	Festinger, L (1957) *A Theory of Cognitive Dissonance*, Stanford University Press, California	People strive for consistency. A person who experiences internal inconsistency tends to become psychologically uncomfortable and is motivated to reduce the cognitive dissonance.	When a consumer realizes that their preferred brand is from a country that they have a negative opinion of, then their preference for the brand may change.
Elaboration likelihood model	Petty, R E and Cacioppo, J T (1986) *Communication and Persuasion: Central and peripheral routes to attitude change*, Springer-Verlag, Berlin, Germany	Focusing on attitude change, the ELM proposes two major routes to persuasion: the central route (careful evaluation and processing) and the peripheral route (simple inferences and low involvement).	A car brand advertises catering to both central and peripheral routes through communicating various features of the car, such as speed, design, colour, safety and fuel efficiency.
Social-identity theory	Tajfel, H and Turner, J C (1979) An integrative theory of intergroup conflict, in W G Austin and S Worchel (eds.) *The Social Psychology of Intergroup Relations*, Brooks/ Cole, Monterey, CA, pp 33–47	People identify themselves based on their affiliation with social groups (ingroup), or being excluded from such groups (outgroup).	A brand highlights the nature of the people who use their products or services (e.g. celebrities – luxury).

(*continued*)

Table 3.1 (Continued)

Theory	Key source	Meaning	Application
Impression management	Goffman, E (1959) *The Presentation of Self in Everyday Life*, Penguin, Garden City, NY	It is a conscious or subconscious process in which people attempt to influence the perceptions of other people about a person, object or event by regulating and controlling information in social interaction.	A brand highlights its sustainability credentials for people who would want to be seen as pro-environment.
Social exchange theory	Thibaut, N and Kelley, H (1959) *The Social Psychology of Groups*, Wiley, New York	Social exchange theory proposes that social behaviour is the result of an exchange process. The purpose of this exchange is to maximize benefits and minimize costs.	A brand communicates its unique benefits in comparison to the competitors.
Persuasion knowledge theory	Friestad, M and Wright, P (1994) The persuasion knowledge model: How people cope with persuasion attempts, *Journal of Consumer Research*, 21 (1), 131	People are aware when there is a persuasion attempt made to change their beliefs. Such persuasion knowledge suppresses their attitude change.	A brand in its communications attempts to avert persuasion knowledge by using subtle signals.
Social capital theory	Bourdieu, P (1987) *Distinction: A social critique of the judgement of taste*, Harvard University Press	Individuals and groups function together to create a shared identity, norms and values that foster relationships.	In the digital space, a brand enables customer reviews to influence purchase amongst consumers.

economic value and agency perspectives. For instance, the well-known game theory, which examines how people base their decisions on the expected behaviour of others, has been applied in branding research to investigate the competitive behaviour of brands' advertising and pricing strategies.[27] Signalling theory, another landmark development in economics that derives from the principles of information asymmetry, has had profound influence on branding research.[28] Scholars have employed signalling theory to examine a variety of branding contexts, such as corporate branding, digital branding, luxury branding, brand communications transparency and advertising.[29]

A group of theories that examines value as a construct grounded in exchange of goods and services has also informed branding research.[30] The theory of value has been used to examine areas such as retail branding, brand communications, luxury branding, digital branding, employer branding, place branding and the branding of sustainable goods.[31] In behavioural economics, Daniel Kahneman and Amos Tversky provide evidence that people behaved irrationally in uncertain conditions, contradicting the economic theory of expected utility maximization.[32] Known as the prospect theory, the research has had a tremendous influence in understanding perceived fairness, loss aversion, emotions and attitudes in branding.[33]

With the advent of the digital age, branding researchers have employed the network effects theory to understand how consumers relate to their brands in the digital space.[34] The theory states that the value of a product or service increases with a greater number of users engaging in consumption. The theory finds applications in studying the effectiveness of social media messaging of brands, brand crisis communications, mobile platforms, brand extensions, brand popularity and brand communities.[35]

Chapter summary

After providing an overview, the chapter delved into the specific research traditions or streams in branding. In the first part, the chapter encapsulated the key question of how consumers buy their brands. In this part, the chapter summarized key research emerging from mathematical sciences. Here the empirical generalizations tradition is discussed, with examples of key research and how the stream developed over the decades. That section also included the use of quantitative modelling in branding research. In the following section, the chapter brings together views on why consumers buy brands, delving into a number of theories from psychology, social psychology, sociology, economics and other disciplines, with examples of applications in branding research.

Key concepts

- Patterns of buyer behaviour
- Empirical generalizations in branding

- Modelling brand buying behaviour
- The psychology of branding
- Theories that influence branding research

Exercise questions

1 What are the main patterns of buyer behaviour?

2 How can the empirical generalization patterns help brand managers?

3 What the main traditions of branding research?

4 Name three theories that you think are important to understand branding research and explain their contributions to the domain.

5 How has economics influenced branding thought?

Endnotes

1 Copeland, M T (1923) Relation of consumers' buying habits to marketing methods, *Harvard Business Review*, 1 (2), 282–89

2 Brown, G H (1953) Brand loyalty—fact or fiction? *Advertising Age*, 24 (26 January), cited in A S Ehrenberg and G J Goodhardt (1968) A comparison of American and British repeat-buying habits, *Journal of Marketing Research*, 5 (1), 29–33

3 Cunningham, R M (1956) Brand loyalty – what, where, how much, *Harvard Business Review*, 34 (1), 116–28

4 Oakes, R H (1957) Resale price maintenance in Chicago, 1953–55 (A Study of Three Products), *The Journal of Business*, 30 (2), 109–30

5 Bass, F (1995) Empirical generalisations and marketing science: A personal view, *Marketing Science*, 14 (3), G6–G19

6 Ehrenberg, A S C (1972/88) *Repeat-Buying: Facts, theory and applications*, 1st and 2nd edns, Griffin, London; Oxford University Press, New York

7 Barwise, P (1995) Good empirical generalisations, *Marketing Science*, 14 (3), Part 2 of 2

8 Singh, J and Crisafulli, B (2022 *Brands and Consumers: A research overview*, Routledge, London

9 Easley, R W and Madden, C S (2013) Replication revisited: Introduction to the special section on replication in business research, *Journal of Business Research*, 66 (9), 1375–76

10 Ehrenberg, A S (1994) Theory or well-based results: Which comes first? in G Laurent, G L Lilien and B Pras (eds.) *Research Traditions in Marketing*, vol. 5, Springer Science and Business Media, Dordrecht, Netherlands

11 Ehrenberg, A S C, Uncles, M D and Goodhardt, G J (2004) Understanding brand performance measures: Using Dirichlet benchmarks, *Journal of Business Research*, 57 (12), 1307–25

12 Hanssens, D M (2018) The value of empirical generalizations in marketing, *Journal of the Academy of Marketing Science*, 46 (1), 6–8

13 Farley, J, Lehmann D, and Sawyer, A (1995) Empirical marketing generalisation using meta-analysis, *Marketing Science*, 14 (3), Part 2 of 2

14 Bijmolt, T H A, van Heerde, H J and Pieters, R G M (2005) New empirical generalizations on the determinants of price elasticity, *Journal of Marketing Research*, 42 (2), 141–56

15 Khamitov, M, Wang, X and Thomson, M (2019) How well do consumer-brand relationships drive customer brand loyalty? Generalizations from a meta-analysis of brand relationship elasticities, *Journal of Consumer Research*, 46 (3), 435–59

16 Little, J D C (1994) Modeling market response in large customer panels, in R C Blattberg, R Glazer and J D C Little (eds.), *The Marketing Information Revolution*, Harvard Business School Press, Boston, MA, pp 150–72

17 Leeflang, P S and Wittink, D R (2000) Building models for marketing decisions: Past, present and future, *International Journal of Research in Marketing*, 17 (2–3), 105–26

18 Ehrenberg, A S, Barnard, N R and Sharp, B (2000) Decision models or descriptive models?, *International Journal of Research in Marketing*, 17 (2–3), 147–58

19 Ibid.

20 Ehrenberg, A S C, Uncles, M D and Goodhardt, G J (2004) Understanding brand performance measures: Using Dirichlet benchmarks, *Journal of Business Research*, 57 (12), 1307–25

21 McDermott, L M (1936) Why people buy at department stores, *Journal of Marketing*, 1 (1), 53–55

22 Hampf, A and Lindberg-Repo, K (2011) *Branding: The past, present, and future: A study of the evolution and future of branding*, Hanken School of Economics

23 Arnould, E J and Thompson, C J (2005) Consumer culture theory (CCT): Twenty years of research, *Journal of Consumer Research*, 31 (4), 868–82

24 Kozinets, R V (2002) The field behind the screen: Using netnography for marketing research in online communities, *Journal of Marketing Research*, 39 (1), 61–72

25 Muniz Jr, A M and O'Guinn, T C (2001) Brand community, *Journal of Consumer Research*, 27 (4), 412–32

26 Fournier, S and Lee, L (2009) Getting brand communities right, *Harvard Business Review*, 87 (4), 105–11

27 Milberg, S J, Cuneo, A and Langlois, C (2019) Should leading brand manufacturers supply private label brands to retailers: Calibrating the trade-offs, *Industrial Marketing Management*, 76, 192–202

28 Connelly, B L, Certo, S T, Ireland, R D and Reutzel, C R (2011) Signaling theory: A review and assessment, *Journal of Management*, 37 (1), 39–67

29 Mandler, T, Bartsch, F and Han, C M (2021) Brand credibility and marketplace globalization: The role of perceived brand globalness and localness, *Journal of International Business Studies*, 52, 1559–90

30 Sheth, J N, Newman, B I and Gross, B L (1991) Why we buy what we buy: A theory of consumption values, *Journal of Business Research*, 22 (2), 159–70

31 Shukla, P (2020) *Luxury Value Perceptions: A cross-cultural perspective*, Aalto University Press

32 Kahneman, D (2011) *Thinking, Fast and Slow*, Penguin, London

33 Rossiter, J R (2019) A critique of prospect theory and framing with particular reference to consumer decisions, *Journal of Consumer Behaviour*, 18 (5), 399–405

34 Katz, M L and Shapiro, C (1985) Network externalities, competition, and compatibility, *The American Economic Review*, 75 (3), 424–40

35 Kumar, V, Nim, N and Agarwal, A (2021) Platform-based mobile payments adoption in emerging and developed countries: Role of country-level heterogeneity and network effects, *Journal of International Business Studies*, 52, 1529–58

PART TWO
Building brands – principles and applications

Brand features 04

Overview

In this chapter, we first describe the fundamental values that make brand features effective through our novel ALARM framework. We discuss brand features through the lens of the ALARM framework, with illustrations. In the first two sections, we provide theoretical understanding of the use and purposes of brand feature strategy. In the last section, we explain the need for a consistent brand feature strategy (CBFS) along with the reasons for pursuing the strategy. The last section also includes examples of brands that pursue the CBFS in practice effectively.

Key learning outcomes

Upon reading this chapter, you should be able to

- Understand the essential values that make brand features effective
- Know the different features of a brand
- Learn about the ALARM framework
- Understand how the ALARM framework can guide the development of brand features
- Appreciate the importance of CBFS for effective branding

What are the essential values for brand features?

For effective branding, there are essential values that shape the brand features. These values are grounding principles through which brands can communicate and differentiate effectively in the marketplace. Over time, these values aid brands in strengthening their associations through brand features. These essential values are encapsulated in the ALARM acronym of brand features: *Appealing, Legitimate, Applicable, Recognizable, Meaningful.*

Appealing

Brands by nature are created to connect and communicate with target customers. Thus, a fundamental condition for any successful brand is that it is appealing to the audience that it is aiming to connect with.[1] To achieve this appeal, a brand has to evoke a feeling of interest and likeability. Appealing brands can communicate both utilitarian as well as hedonic aspects of the product or the service associated. One of the core features of appealing brands is that it generates customer curiosity and in turn may create a desire for the brand.

Legitimate

As stated in Chapter 2, brands were created to distinguish and protect the identity of the owner. Initially used as a protection mechanism, in today's world brands have become highly valuable for their owners. Consequently, relevant legal frameworks have emerged to support and protect the brand owners. Thus, legal aspects of legitimacy are deeply connected with the brand. Moreover, legitimacy is reflected in customers' perspective where customers feel trust in the brand. Legitimacy can be achieved through a consistent approach in brand communication across a variety of platforms and media. Such consistency over a period of time can help brands in signalling their legitimacy and be identified as genuine and reliable.

Applicable

In communicating a brand's message, the brand owner is offering to fulfil the promise that the brand has made to its customers. A brand has to highlight why and how it is suitable and fitting for task accomplishment. Thus, applicability is key to a brand's success. For many day-to-day brands, applicability gets highlighted in the usefulness and utilitarian benefits. This creates heuristics, or shortcuts, in customers' minds for decision making. For many high involvement brands, the applicability aspect can help customers signal their identity.

Recognizable

A brand's core purpose is to distinguish the brand from its competitors. Hence, recognizability plays a highly important role in brand's success. Without recognizability among its target population and beyond, a brand may not exist for long. To achieve recognizability, a brand has to establish its distinction clearly. Moreover, the distinction that the brand wishes to convey has to be observable and understandable by its target market. Without obvious and clearly perceivable brand benefits, a brand will not achieve recognizability.

Meaningful

In increasingly competitive markets, a prime role of a brand is to communicate its meaningfulness in a succinct and swift manner. Thus, brands communicate inherent meanings that are not explicitly or directly expressed. Meaningfulness is a major challenge for brands due to a variety of cross-cultural and language-related aspects that influence the inference of meanings. Thus, when conveying meaning, brands need to be compatible with the rules of the language, culture and symbols. Meaningfulness allows customers to create a strong emotional and/or cognitive attachment with the brand. It also conveys the brand's relevance and usefulness to its target market.

A summary of the features is shown in Table 4.1.

Brand features/assets

A brand is recognized by its components, or features, such as its logo, name, characters, slogans and packaging. Each of these features help a brand to distinguish itself from its competitors. These features enable the brand to create memory traces that are useful during brand recall and recognition. For example, a Stanford University study found that children as young as three–five years old were able to distinguish between non-branded and McDonald's chicken nuggets.[2] Features act as shortcuts to ascertain the brand's intangible and tangible elements, such as quality and value.

Brand name

Brand name is a fundamental and critical feature that leads to effective branding. Brand name helps generate brand recognition and recall. When the need arises for a product in a particular category, brand recognition is vital as it forms the consumers' awareness set. For example, think of a famous cola brand. The chances are that you either thought of Coca-Cola or Pepsi. Similarly, when thinking about a social media platform, people may immediately recall brands such as Instagram, Snapchat, Facebook and Twitter, among others. These names are appealing to customers and tend to arouse interest and likeability within the target market.

Companies spend a substantial amount of resources in finding a brand name that is easy to pronounce and distinguishable to global audiences. For instance, one of the world's largest manufacturers of white goods with a revenue of more than $27 billion, Haier Corporation, was founded as Qingdao Refrigerator Company. However, as it entered global markets, to resonate with global consumers, the brand name was changed to Haier Corporation.[3] Brand names increasing carry a financial value that is used by many firms in their financial statements. For example, the most valued

Table 4.1 ALARM features of a brand

Brand features	Brand name	Logo	Slogan	Persona	Digital presence	Sounds and jingles	Packaging
Appealing	Allows brand recall	Aids brand recognition	Evokes memory traces and brand associations	Anthropomorphizes a brand	Enhances engagement	Refreshes memory and brand associations	Allows brand recall and recognition at the point of purchase
Legitimate	Allows protectability	Allows protectability	Reinforces brand legitimacy	Deters copycat branding	Extends protectability through increased visibility	Additional avenue for brand protectability	Strengthens brand trust
Applicable	Somewhat limited	Allows malleability	Allows malleability	Limited	Allows co-creation and enhances engagement	Limited	Allows malleability
Recognizable	Increases brand recognition and recall	Increases brand recognition and recall	Allows extra identification	Enhances brand knowledge	Adds further layers of brand connection and knowledge	Allows extra identification	Provides relevant information
Meaningful	Allows recall of product features	Can explain product characteristics	Evokes brand usage situations	Allows increased self-brand connection	Stretches brand meaning in a variety of contexts	Evokes brand usage situations	Helps brands explain product features

brand name in the world according to Interbrand is Apple, which was valued at more than $400 billion in 2022.[4]

With this type of valuation attached to brand names, many brands spend a significant amount of financial and legal expense on protecting their brand name.

BRANDING IN PRACTICE
Apple's brand name protection troubles in China

In the year 2002, Apple filed for a trademark bid for its iPhone brand in China. However, this was not approved until the year 2013. In the meantime, in 2007, a Chinese technology company, Xintong Tiandi, filed its application to trademark 'IPHONE' for its leather products, which was later approved in 2010. Xintong Tiandi sells mostly handbags, mobile phone cases and other leather goods.

In the year 2012, Apple initiated legal proceedings against Xintong Tiandi with the Chinese Trademark Authority. However, the authority ruled in favour of the Chinese manufacturer. Apple then sued the Chinese firm in the lower Beijing court and later on to the higher court after losing its appeal. The higher court also ruled in favour of Xintong Tiandi.

As iPhones went on sale in China in the year 2009, the high court ruling stated that Apple could not establish that its brand iPhone was familiar among Chinese consumers in 2007 when Xintong Tiandi filed its trademark application.

SOURCES www.bbc.co.uk/news/business-36200481; www.reuters.com/article/us-apple-china-idUSKCN0XV0YH; image courtesy: www.billboard.com/pro/apple-loses-iphone-trademark-case-china/

A brand name can convey meaningfulness. It allows customers to recall what the brand stands for and its functions. These meanings can be associated with utilitarian, hedonic and innovative aspects of a brand. For instance, customers may not know what Minnesota Mining and Manufacturing Company does, however, when they encounter 3M branded products while shopping (Post-it notes and many other household and industrial products), it reminds them of the innovative nature of the company.

Another example is that of yoghurts, which may be regular purchases for many people. When thinking of yogurt brands such as Activia and Benecol, people are reminded of the gut health benefits associated with this yogurt product category and the brand simultaneously. Research shows that brand name can also allow people to make quality inferences.[5] Many retail brand names including Walmart, Target, Tesco, Carrefour and Marks and Spencer carry particular quality- and price-associated meanings.

Logo

A logo is a fundamental aspect of a brand's visual identity. A logo consists of text and/or symbols that communicate a business's core values and are a vital tool for brand recognition. A good logo should be distinctive, appropriate, practical, graphic and simple in form. A logo is a dynamic rather than static element for many brands. It evolves and reforms depending on how the organization transforms itself on its journey. Nike is a good example of this. The Nike logo wasn't always the swoosh as we know in current times. The company was founded in 1964 as 'Blue Ribbon Sports' and the logo was a set of interlacing letters (BRS) with the name of the brand underneath. However, as Nike became more popular among customers worldwide, in 1971 a graphic design student named Carolyn Davidson helped the brand create the swoosh logo with Nike written over it in lower-case font. Over the years, the Nike logo has also changed with the brand name in upper-case font, from black and white to red and white and recently the dropping of the brand name altogether with just the swoosh on most Nike products. It shows the prominence that the swoosh logo has acquired over time as it is now recognizable even without the brand name.

Sometimes brands have to change their logos for cultural, language or historical reasons. For instance, Starbucks sued a San Francisco-based cartoonist for creating a parody of its logo in 1998. Similarly, in the year 2000, it went to court seeking an injunction against a Japanese coffee chain company that had a similar logo. However, the company itself decided to change its logo when entering the Kingdom of Saudi Arabia by removing the mermaid from the logo and only keeping the crown.[6] The decision was taken to accommodate the cultural sensitivities, local religious beliefs, social norms and laws.

Sometimes, due to historical associations, brands continue to use a different name or logo for the same product in different countries. However, effective brands aim to create consistency in logo design through colours, style and formats. For instance, Walkers, a well-known brand of potato crisps in the UK, is known as Lay's in most of Europe and the US as well as in India. However, in Australia it is labelled Smith's. A consistent feature across these different brand names is the font style and the yellow/red background. Thus, the brand keeps certain aspects of the logo static while remaining dynamic in other areas.

While brands can evolve and adapt over time and to align with various cultures, logos can also allow brands to traverse the boundaries of culture and language altogether. Logos are a major vehicle for brands to express their meaningfulness. With the incorporation of image and other symbolic elements, logos can allow brands to traverse the boundaries of culture and language. For instance, the arrow at the bottom of Amazon logo seems like a smiley face, but it is more than that. The arrow is pointed from the letter A to the letter Z with an aim to represent the fact that Amazon offers a huge variety of products. Moreover, the smiley face depicts Amazon's relentless focus on customer satisfaction. Similarly, Fanta's logo uses the orange fruit in the background. Orange as a fruit is associated with freshness around the world. Moreover, it also conveys the taste of Fanta. In addition, the colour orange is considered energetic and is represents excitement and enthusiasm, which again allows emphasis of Fanta's association with youthfulness.

BRANDING IN PRACTICE
Why logos are going simple

In recent years, some brands have simplified their logos by removing or adapting design elements such as name (e.g. Mastercard, Uber, etc.), colours (i.e. Apple, Instagram), shades (e.g. Google), depth (e.g. Dell) and fonts (e.g. Burberry, Chanel).

The minimalistic trend in brand logo design is driven by three important aspects. Firstly, simple logos are more memorable and fewer elements in a logo have implications for easier recognition and recall.

Secondly, digital transformation is playing a big role in logo design. Most people now spend a substantial amount of time on their digital devices and in particular on smartphones. In the digital landscape, with multiple brands vying for customer attention rendering complex logos in high quality can take up more bandwidth and thus affect the speed at which the logo is delivered on the webpage. Moreover, smaller and complex elements may not be seen and recognized easily in the crowded landscape of mobile apps on the smartphone screen. Moving to a simple design allows companies to work across both offline and online mediums more effectively.

Thirdly, in the marketplace, there is a move towards developing minimalistic design which is associated with modernity. Thus, there is normative pressure that is driving the change towards simple logos. However, redesigning logos may not always work in the favour as brands will need to make new memory associations with the logo. This may require significant investment of time and resources from both the brand as well as the customers and thus could be a risky endeavour.

Slogan

'Have a break, have a _____!' Most people who are familiar with the famous Nestlé brand around the world would fill up the blank with the word KitKat. This shows the power of slogans in creating memory traces. Slogans help brands establish their dominance through easy memorability and brand associations. Moreover, by highlighting brand features, slogans allow companies to convey aspects of the product and in turn the desire for a brand. For instance, Kentucky Fried Chicken's (KFC) long-standing slogan 'It's finger lickin' good', reminds consumers about the taste of the brand's chicken and creates desire.

Slogans help brands make legitimacy claims. BMW proclaims to be the 'ultimate driving machine'. Similarly, Carlsberg declares itself as 'probably the best lager in the world' and Redbull 'gives you wings'. Slogans become memorable over time and can create such strong associations that even when a brand retires a slogan from its campaigning, it can still exist within the vernacular. For instance, Nike sparingly uses its slogan 'Just do it!' in its packaging and other campaigning compared to past decades. However, the slogan is strongly attached to the brand.

Sometimes slogans designed at the start of a brand's inception to connect with a target market can limit the brand's expression. For example, in 2006, Dunkin' Donuts, which is currently re-branded as Dunkin', launched a new slogan 'America Runs on Dunkin" changing its historical slogan 'Time to make the donuts'. The slogan is specific to a market and thus may not translate well in many other markets in which Dunkin' is present.

Slogans help customers relate to brand usage situations. As discussed earlier, KitKat is associated with taking a break from the routine, Nike is associated with taking healthy actions and McDonald's slogan 'I'm lovin it!' evokes action towards having tasty fast food. Thus, slogans also allow meaning making through communicating usage-related messages.

Slogans can also create a strong emotional attachment for a product or a brand. One highly successful slogan, 'Diamonds are forever' from De Beers Diamond Company, has helped the firm create emotional connections with customers globally. However, as demonstrated in the Branding in practice box that follows, brands should be careful when developing their slogans, as they may not be appropriate when translated through a different linguistic and cultural lens. Thus, creating meaningful yet culturally neutral slogans is important for brands.

BRANDING IN PRACTICE
When brand names and slogans don't travel well culturally!

If misunderstood or mistranslated, brand names and slogans can cause substantial harm to the brand. For instance, confectionery giant Cadbury's committed a major blunder in its slogan by comparing a brand of chocolate to the disputed territory of Kashmir between India and Pakistan and describing both as 'too good to share'. Moreover, the blunder occurred in an advertisement to promote Cadbury's Temptations brand on India's Independence Day. The newspaper campaign featured a map of India showing the war-torn area of Jammu and Kashmir shaded over. Written in bold across the shaded area was the message 'I'm good. I'm tempting. I'm too good to share. What am I? Cadbury's Temptations or Kashmir?' Cadbury's India

Limited was forced by the Indian public and media to apologize for the advert.

When Mitsubishi released the Pajero model in the 1980s it hadn't considered that the word Pajero is associated with negative connotations in Spanish. Therefore, Mitsubishi had to change the name to Mitsubishi Montero in all Spanish-speaking countries. Similarly, Ford had to change the name of its car brand Pinto for the Brazilian market as Pinto in Brazilian Portuguese refers to small male genitalia. The brand was re-named as Corcel which means a horse or steed.

SOURCES www.theguardian.com/media/2002/aug/20/advertising.india#:~:text=Confectionery%20 giant%20Cadbury%27s%20has%20committed,brand%20on%20India%27s%20independence%20day; www.goodbadmarketing.com/davidfrank/famous-marketing-language-translation-blunders/

Persona

Many organizations humanize their brands by using a variety of animate and inanimate characters to further delineate themselves in the marketplace and build stronger connections with their customers. For example, Ronald McDonald is a cartoonish character developed by the McDonald's corporation. The colourful-clothes-wearing clown allows the brand to create an appeal to younger consumers. On the other hand, brands such as Geico uses an animated lizard, M&M use coloured chocolate mascots, Churchill insurance has a dog, Old Speckled Hen ale uses Henry the fox and comparison website comparethemarket.com uses meerkats that speak in a human voice. Moreover, some brands use photos of their founders such as Uncle Ben's. Using a persona allows companies to anthropomorphize their brand which appeals to many customers.

Animals and inanimate objects that use human voices or have human-like expressions have always fascinated mankind. This has been captured in a variety of mythical tales across civilizations including the sphinx in Egypt, Narasimha in India, Minotaur in Greek, Gonggong in China and Saqra in South America. Moreover, modern tales such as *Alice in Wonderland, Peter Rabbit, Paddington* and *Jungle Book* have also used anthropomorphism to weave their stories. In modern times a number of animation studios have emerged and successfully engaged audiences globally through anthropomorphized characters including Mickey Mouse and Angry Birds, among many others. As customers across the world have built strong emotional identifications with such characters, brands have often integrated them in their persona. Such efforts allow brands to build quick reference points, emotional engagement and transfer of meanings that are associated with these characters on the brand.

Another popular trend in utilizing brand persona can be seen in co-branding. For instance, Mickey Mouse, a Disney character, has been used by Sugerfina, Kate Spade, Uniqlo, Adidas and Gucci, among many others. The following Branding in practice box shows how Angry Birds have been used by brands across the globe.

BRANDING IN PRACTICE

Angry Birds work for Rovio and its alliance partners!

Rovio Entertainment, a Finnish video game developer, released the Angry Birds game in December 2009. The game was based on stylized wingless birds that were cannoned from a slingshot over a variety of structures that held 'bad piggies'. The game became an instant success on mobile phones and other platforms. In order to ride on the success of the game and its characters globally, many brands entered into an alliance with Rovio.

The brand persona attached with Angry Birds led to a number of successful alliances including both for-profit and not-for-profit organizations. For instance, Burger King created toys and augmented reality experiences using Angry Birds. Similarly, the multinational sports entertainment company Topgolf offered an interactive golf experience involving Angry Birds. Global sports brands such as the Chicago Bulls and English premier league club Everton have also become Angry Birds alliance partners. Moreover, education-oriented brands such as Duo lingo and Kahoot have also engaged with Angry Birds. UNICEF and Rovio have built an alliance to further support adolescent education in a number of emerging markets.

Such alliances help both brands to enhance their image among customers. Research has shown that the positive image of the brands become substantially enhanced through the spillover of perceptions of the partnering brands on to the alliance benefiting both partners.

SOURCES www.rovio.com/articles/category/brand-partnerships/; Singh, J (2016) The influence of CSR and ethical self-identity in consumer evaluation of cobrands, *Journal of Business Ethics*, 138 (2), 311–26

Persona creates unique associations which strengthen the brand's recognizability among customers and at the same time deter copycat brands from taking advantage of all the initial investment that a brand has made towards its success. Anthropomorphizing helps create a strong and multidimensional meaning that provides a substantial protective layer for the brand. Success of such anthropomorphizing may attract other brands to copy the original brand persona. However, the multidimensional meaning that is created due to brand persona allows customers to distinguish between the original and the copycat brand. Thus, brand persona offers protection against such practices.

Digital presence

Historically, marketing and branding were communicated mostly through printed press, TV and other outdoor media outlets. However, the commercialization of the internet transformed this landscape. Today, it is unusual for a brand to not have digital presence in some form. The need for digital presence became particularly acute post-March 2020 when the Covid-19 pandemic hit globally. With physical stores being shut down, digital presence became vital for brand survival. Digital presence can take many forms including websites, blogs, social media interactions, image- and video-based engagement as well as livestreaming and metaverse.

The advent of digital marketplaces has led to novel forms of businesses including digital-only and sharing economy brands. For instance, global fashion brands such as Asos, banks such as Starling and Monzo, B2B brands such as Alibaba and eBay, and multi-brand stores such as jd.com and Wayfair have successfully emerged as purely digital players. The digital marketplace has also spawned another novel business model known as the 'sharing economy' wherein assets and services are shared between private parties online, either free or for a fee. Global giants such as Uber, Airbnb, Ola, Facebook Marketplace and Fiverr became globally successful and recognized brands through the sharing economy.

Digital presence is key for today's brands and more importantly it plays a pivotal role in creating appeal to wider audiences and enhancement of engagement. For example, Gymshark, a UK-based fitness apparel and accessories brand, started in 2012 and was valued at more than £1 billion in 2020. The brand started selling bodybuilding supplements and its own fitness apparel through its website in 2013 with about £500 per day worth of sales. However, by 2016, the brand was using all forms of digital presence including social media campaigns, its website and other means of digital customer engagement. In 2016, Gymshark was named the fastest growing company in the UK by the *Sunday Times*.[7]

BRANDING IN PRACTICE

Retail reversal: digital-only brands going physical

The popularity and success of many of these digital-only brands has allowed them to build their presence in brick-and-mortar markets as well, reversing the trend of physical stores moving into digital space. For instance, Amazon has created its Amazon Go stores where it utilizes advanced digital technologies to offer an immersive and engaging retail experience for its customers.

Away is an American luggage and travel accessories retailer based in New York that started its operations in 2015 as an online-only retailer. The company improved upon traditional suitcase designs by adding features such as built-in batteries in their luggage for charging mobile devices. It found a sweet spot between super-premium and inexpensive luggage. Away benefited a lot from its digital presence wherein customers and social media influencers used the brand to co-create their travel experiences using the brand's colourful suitcases. Its products have become highly popular among international travellers and while continuing to strengthen its online presence, Away decided to launch their first physical store in 2016. Since then, the brand has launched several other stores in large cities across the world including London, Boston, Toronto, Chicago, Dallas and San Francisco. The brand has also partnered with large retail organizations such as Nordstorm to create pop-up stores that aids brand visibility and recognition.

Many other brands such as Casper (mattresses), Allbirds (sustainable shoes and clothing), Knix (undergarments) and Billie (Razor and other grooming products for women) have also moved into building physical retail presence.

This retail reversal from digital to physical also shows the need for brands to embrace an omnichannel presence. At the same time, it also allows digital-only brands to compete head-on against other physical retail brands.

SOURCES www.shopify.com/uk/retail/dtc-to-brick-and-mortar; https://econsultancy.com/how-away-luggage-built-travel-brand-through-storytelling/;www.awaytravel.com/stores

Digital presence is a boon, particularly for small brands. Apart from connecting with customers globally, digital presence can help brands increase their visibility and recognition to a wider society. This can increase market penetration and at the same time help the brand compete and protect itself from copycats. Digital presence is comparatively less resource-intensive and thus allows brands to represent themselves in a meaningful manner and gain a foothold in the market. It also helps such brands establish a revenue stream that in turn can aid further expansion.

Similarly, for large and established brands, digital presence acts as a mechanism for brand recall and self-brand connection. Moreover, it allows multiway communication between the brand and the customer, customer and customer and customer and brand. Today, many large retail brands across different categories, including grocery, fashion, homeware, and food and beverages, have built a strong digital presence to create customer engagement. Some of these brands also sell their products directly to their customers as well as via other online retailers. For instance, Argos, a multi-brand catalogue retailer of home furnishings and electronics in the UK, continues to offer an omnichannel experience to its customers. It has also partnered with its parent company Sainsbury's, a grocery retailer, to deliver products bought at Argos online in Sainsbury's stores. On the other hand, brands such as Coke and Pepsi have built digital presence predominantly to create excitement, connection and engagement to encourage repeat buying.

Sounds and jingles

Sound is one of the key senses through which human beings perceive stimuli. Sounds can startle, shock, soothe and please us and in turn attract our attention through auditory reflexes. Sounds can thus create both affective and cognitive triggers. Brands have used sounds to attract attention and create strong association beyond the visual stimuli such as logo, brand name and persona. Marketers historically have relied on visual elements more than appealing to other senses.[8]

Sonic branding, the idea of using sound-based communication, has become popular over time as part of sensory marketing.

Visual cues may remain one of the key elements of connecting with customers. Sonic branding can also prove a potent tool to refresh customer memories, create brand salience, foster unaided recall, and generate distinctive cognitive and affective responses. For instance, brands such as the BBC and Intel have used sonic branding to create appropriate associations that appeal and remind people globally about these brands when they hear the tunes without seeing the brand. Many other brands such as Netflix, Colgate and Tic Tac have used just pure sounds to build a unique brand identity.

Some brands have extended sonic branding further by developing a jingle beyond just the sound profile. For instance, McDonald's worked with pop star Justin Timberlake to create the jingle for 'I'm Lovin' It' which was launched globally in 2003, and continues to be the sonic profile for the brand globally. Similarly, the Green Giant jingle, 'Ho, ho, ho, Green Giant' has been used by the firm since the 1960s, giving the brand a strong unaided recall score.

As seen in Table 4.2, sonic branding can create a number of affective and cognitive responses.

Table 4.2 Top 10 sonic brands in the USA

Brand	Unaided recall (48 hours)	Emotions identified by customers
Liberty Mutual	96%	Familiar, happy, unique, authentic
State Farm	96%	Familiar, likeable, trustworthy, authentic
Farmer's Insurance	95%	Familiar, unique, likeable, authentic
Nationwide	92%	Familiar, likeable, unique, trustworthy
Little Caesars	93%	Familiar, unique, authentic, likeable
Intel	93%	Familiar, likeable, unique, authentic
Arby's	90%	Familiar, unique, authentic, likeable
T-Mobile	91%	Familiar, happy, unique, likeable
Safelite	90%	Familiar, likeable unique, authentic
O'Reilly Auto Parts	90%	Familiar, happy, unique, authentic

SOURCE Veritonic audio logo index 2020[9]

Sonic branding not only creates familiarity but also provides enduring brand power that induces positive emotions such as happiness, likeability, uniqueness and authenticity from people. Moreover, it also adds a further layer of protection for a brand that is hard to copy. Many visual elements including the logos and the design aspects are copied world over. For instance, a Chinese retail chain, Chrisdien Deny, with more than 500 stores across China, has its name, logo and fonts and other visual elements very similar to Christian Dior.[10] Many other brands also copy other visual elements, such as the casual wear brand Clio Coddle which has a green crocodile logo reminiscent of Lacoste.[11] Across many emerging markets, sneakers are emblazoned with Adidos, Hike, Cnoverse and Fuma – featuring a smoking puma – and there are SQNY and PenesamiG batteries and Johnnie Worker Red and Black Labial whisky.[12] While these visual elements can easily be copied, sonic branding elements are hard to copy because of their inherent audio signals and thus can be copyrighted.[13]

Sonic branding can also allow consumers to take action as sounds and jingles can involve action orientation. For instance, the British price comparison portal Go Compare uses its jingle to ask people to go to the website to view a variety of price comparisons. Similarly, KitKat's famous jingle 'Gimme a Break' encourages consumers towards an action, that is, having a break and eating a KitKat. Jingles and sounds can thus evoke brand usage situations in consumer minds and increase engagement.

Packaging

Packaging is one of the oldest forms of communicating a brand. From a simple brown bag to highly elaborate design, packaging is a powerful visual element that appeals to consumer senses. For example, the packaging of a Chivas Regal whisky bottle clearly communicates the sense of conspicuous consumption and luxury. Similarly, perfume brands heavily rely on packaging to attract consumer attention.

Packaging is a strategic decision for brands as it is the first point of real contact between a consumer and the brand's product. Consumers may have seen the logo or slogan of a brand before and may have heard the jingle. Thus, packaging has a critical role to play in appealing and communicating the brand elements to the consumer. For example, the packaging of Cadbury's chocolate contains the unique purple colour and the font style that reminds consumers of the brand elements at the point of purchase. Similarly, Kellogg's frequently uses the colour yellow across its cereal brand packaging which not only attracts consumers' attention but also helps them build a stronger connection with the morning breakfast and sunshine which is consistent with the brightness of the yellow colour. Surf, a Unilever brand, expresses its product characteristics such as fragrance through pictorial representations of flowers including lavender, lily, and jasmine via its packaging.

An important function of packaging beyond communication is protecting the product from spillage and pilferage. Moreover, appropriate packaging can also help a brand become more sustainable. For instance, Amazon has invested a substantial amount of resources in developing frustration-free packaging that aims to reduce waste, offers protective design, increases recyclable material usage and is easy to open. By the end of 2021, Amazon claims to have more than 2 million products that qualify for frustration-free packaging across its platform. The company also claimed to have avoided over 30,000 tons of plastic across North America in 2021 through its packaging innovations.[14] Most supermarket brands, such as Walmart, Tesco, Waitrose and Sainsbury's, have moved away from single-use plastic bags to 'bags for life' and are now currently promoting plastic-free wrappings and packaging. Good packaging allows consumers to handle the product content in an appropriate manner and avoid damage. Thus, packaging, in turn, increases consumer trust in the brand, reduces carbon footprint and helps promote its sustainability credentials.

Creative packaging can arouse curiosity in consumers which can lead to a variety of cognitive actions. Packaging can convey both originality and relevance of the brand. Research shows that these elements of packaging can arouse curiosity and motivation to process the information and design of the packaging, which positively affects brand attitude and purchase intentions.[15] Packaging also conveys the design aesthetics of the brand. For instance, Apple uses a minimalist and sleek packaging design which is consistent with its product and branding. On the other hand, many health supplements and complementary medicines are regularly accused of excessive product information on their packaging.[16]

Packaging acts as a powerful medium to convey a brand's features. Packaging used creatively can clearly show the product inside and communicate its functions. For instance, frozen vegetables are packaged in plastic bags with pictures of the product inside. Packaging can also act as a simple instruction manual in several product categories including toys, cookware and electronics.

Scholarly debate

Escalas, J E (2004) Narrative processing: Building consumer connections to brands, *Journal of Consumer Psychology*, 14 (1–2), 168–80

Keller, K L (2000) The brand report card, *Harvard Business Review*, 78 (1), 147–58

Creating brand appeals through a consistent brand feature strategy (CBFS)

As discussed above, the ALARM framework allows brands to differentiate and communicate their core message in a unique way using a variety of brand features. However, these features do not work in isolation and a brand needs a cohesive and consistent brand feature strategy to be successful in the marketplace. With such integration, consistency as well as branding effectiveness is enhanced. Consistent brand feature strategy (CBFS) requires all levels of an organization to be in sync with the branding strategy. As described in the ALARM framework, CBFS, if used appropriately, will help a brand create a consistent appeal among its customers using a combination of brand features. Moreover, due to the consistency of approach, legitimacy of the brand communication will increase through enhanced consumer trust. CBFS will also help a brand improve its recognizability because consumers will be able to comprehend similarities in the brand features. In summary, CBFS can help a brand increase its meaningfulness among its target consumers.

Many large brands have successfully developed CBFS. For instance, Louis Vuitton, the world's largest luxury brand, started in 1854 in Paris as an innovative producer of flat-topped trunks. In 1896, the iconic LV monogram was introduced by the company.[17] Since then, the brand has consistently used the monogram and other brand features consistently. The brand logo and name have appeared across the range of their products. The brand has also used a variety of slogans. However, each of them has consistently aimed to create distinctiveness through communicating the class, quality and heritage of the brand. Slogans such as 'Show me your luggage and I'll tell you who you are' in the 1920s, to recent ones such as 'the spirit of travel' highlight the brand's ethos consistently. Moreover, the brand has employed Hollywood celebrities such as Sean Connery, Julia Roberts, Angelina Jolie, Emma Stone, prominent sportspersons such as Muhammad Ali, Pele, Maradona, Andre Agassi, politicians such as Mikhail Gorbachev and musicians such as Keith Richards as ambassadors to personify the brand's luxury message. The distinctive packaging of the brand is recognized globally. In addition, the brand has hired top creative directors and collaborated with globally renowned artist such as Takashi Murakami to consistently demonstrate the brand's artistic pedigree. Further, the brand has collaborated with top art museums across the world to showcase its creativity and innovativeness and its bold experiments with brand aesthetics. Louis Vuitton has also spent substantial resources on developing its digital presence through its website and other digital avenues. Its website demonstrates the brand features consistently. A consequence of such concerted efforts has made Louis Vuitton one of the world's leading luxury brands. For example, in the Interbrand top 100 global brands list, Louis Vuitton has consistently remained the top luxury brand with a brand valuation of nearly $45 billion.[18] In addition, such efforts have led to substantial social media presence for the brand. On Facebook the brand has more than 25 million followers, and on visual social media such as Instagram the brand has more than 50 million followers.

Chapter summary

This chapter began by identifying essential values that shape brand features through our novel ALARM framework. The ALARM framework encapsulates five key values: *Appealing, Legitimate, Applicable, Recognizable, Meaningful*. Each value guides brand feature development for effective branding. A brand can utilize several features in combination: brand name, brand logo, slogan, persona, digital presence, sounds and jingles, and packaging. Each of these features help a brand communicate its core message and values. However, this has to be done consistently, as explained in the discussion of CBFS. A consistent approach will ensure an effective brand management process for the organization.

Key concepts

- Brand values
- ALARM framework
  - ○ Appealing, Legitimate, Applicable, Recognizable, Meaningful
- Brand features
  - ○ brand name, brand logo, slogan, persona, digital presence, sounds and jingles, and packaging
- Consistent brand feature strategy (CBFS)

Exercise questions

1 What are the essential values of a brand? Explain the ALARM framework in detail with examples.
2 What are brand features? Explain various brand features using examples.
3 How can brand features be integrated through ALARM framework?
4 Why should brands employ a consistent brand feature strategy (CBFS)?
5 Identify a brand and apply the ALARM framework and CBFS.

CASE STUDY   Marc Jacobs' Heaven line and pop culture

Introduction

Fashion branding is a complex and dynamic process that involves creating and communicating a distinctive identity and value proposition for a fashion product or service. Fashion brands need to constantly adapt to the changing preferences and expectations of their target customers, as well as the competitive and environmental forces that shape the fashion industry. One of the challenges that fashion brands face is how to appeal to younger generations, who have different tastes, values and behaviours to older ones.

This case study examines Heaven by Marc Jacobs, a sub-label of the renowned fashion brand Marc Jacobs, which was launched in the fall of 2020 as a collaboration between Marc Jacobs and Ava Nirui, a multi-talented artist who rose to fame on Instagram for her creative bootlegs of luxury brands. Ava played with the names of Marc Jacobs, Dior, Chanel and Louis Vuitton to create a tongue-in-cheek take. For example, she created a white hoodie embroidered with 'Mark Jacobes est 1985' which became very popular among youths. She also created goods such as asthma inhalers, basketballs and toothpaste tubes with tongue-in-cheek names and logos based on luxury fashion brands.

This case study explores how Heaven by Marc Jacobs uses nostalgia and pop culture as key elements of its branding strategy, and how it resonates with Millennials and Gen Zs, who are the main target customers of the sub-label. The case study also analyses the strengths and weaknesses of Heaven by Marc Jacobs, and the opportunities and threats that it faces in the fast-changing fashion industry.

Background

Marc Jacobs is one of the most influential and successful fashion designers in the world, who has been at the forefront of fashion trends and innovations for over three decades. He started his own label, Marc Jacobs, in the mid-1980s, and became the creative director of Louis Vuitton in 1997, where he transformed the luxury brand into a global fashion powerhouse. He also launched a lower-priced line, Marc by Marc Jacobs, in 2001, which was popular among young and fashion-conscious consumers. Marc Jacobs is known for his eclectic and rebellious style, which mixes high and low culture, vintage and contemporary influences, and grunge and glamour aesthetics.

However, in recent years, Marc Jacobs has faced some difficulties and challenges in maintaining its relevance and profitability in the fashion industry. The brand's aesthetics had become out of sync with the minimal and utilitarian trends that dominated the 2010s, and the brand had suffered from declining sales, store closures and lay-offs. The brand also discontinued its Marc by Marc Jacobs line in 2015, which was a major source of revenue and customer loyalty. The brand's parent company, LVMH, had expressed concerns about the brand's performance and future prospects. While LVMH did not disclose the brand's financial performance, analysts in 2018 estimated that the LVMH-owned brand had been losing $61 million annually for some years, registering flat revenues – a sharp drop from the estimated $1 billion in revenue it was making in 2015.

In order to revitalize the brand and restore its profitability, Marc Jacobs appointed Eric Marechalle as the chief executive in 2017, who joined from Kenzo, another LVMH-owned fashion brand. Marechalle implemented a series of strategic changes, such as streamlining the brand's operations, reducing costs, improving quality, expanding distribution channels, and enhancing its digital and social media presence. He also supported Marc Jacobs' creative vision and encouraged him to pursue new projects and collaborations that would reinvigorate the brand's identity and appeal. One of these projects was Heaven by Marc Jacobs, a sub-label that Marc Jacobs and Ava Nirui launched together in the autumn of 2020.

Heaven by Marc Jacobs

Heaven by Marc Jacobs is a playful and eclectic sub-label that draws inspiration from Marc Jacobs' past collections, shows and campaigns, often recreating some of his most iconic designs. The sub-label also incorporates Nirui's artistic sensibility and style, which is characterized by her creative bootlegs of luxury brands, her nostalgic references to the 1990s and 2000s pop culture, and her diverse network of friends and idols. The sub-label offers baby tees, grungy cardigans, printed mini dresses, nylon shoulder bags and eccentric accessories that fit the aesthetic and taste of Millennials and Gen Zs, who are the main target customers of the sub-label. The sub-label also features collaborations with various artists and celebrities, such as Kate Moss, Nicki Minaj, Brian Molko and Gen Z singer Beabadoobee, al of whom appear in the sub-label's campaigns and events.

This sub-label has a nostalgic vibe that appeals to Millennials who grew up with Marc Jacobs in its 1990s and 2000s glory days, when the brand was known for its grunge influence and quilted "It" Stam bags. For that generation, Heaven reminds them of Marc by Marc Jacobs, the lower-priced line that was discontinued in 2015, and which was often their first introduction to the Marc Jacobs world. But Heaven also attracts Gen Zs, who seem to enjoy nostalgia as much as Millennials and have a diverse and flexible fashion sense that combines vintage references with current trends. Heaven also benefits from the popularity and influence of the celebrities and artists who wear and endorse the sub-label, such as Bella Hadid, Olivia Rodrigo, Dua Lipa and Doja Cat.

The sub-label has a distinctive identity that differentiates it from Marc Jacobs' main line and other competitors in the market. In doing so, Heaven is a brand that celebrates the past, embraces the present and looks forward to the future.

Analysis

Heaven by Marc Jacobs is a successful case of nostalgia and pop culture in fashion branding, as it leverages the history and heritage of the Marc Jacobs brand, as well as the cultural and personal references of Nirui and her collaborators, to create a unique and appealing value proposition for younger customers. The sub-label also demonstrates the creative synergy and mutual respect between Marc Jacobs and Nirui, who share a similar vision and style, and who complement each other's strengths and weaknesses. The sub-label also benefits from the strategic support and guidance of Marechalle, who provides the necessary resources and expertise to ensure the sub-label's operational and financial viability.

However, Heaven by Marc Jacobs also faces some challenges and threats that could affect its sustainability and growth in the long term. One of the challenges is how to maintain the sub-label's relevance and freshness in the fast-changing and competitive fashion industry, where trends and customer preferences can shift quickly and unpredictably. The sub-label also needs to balance its creative freedom and experimentation with its commercial objectives and expectations, as it needs to generate enough sales and profits to justify its existence and investment. It also needs to manage its relationship and alignment with the Marc Jacobs brand, as it needs to avoid cannibalizing or diluting the brand's main line and image, while also benefiting from the brand's reputation and resources.

Case questions

1   Market segments such as Gen Z have different expectations from luxury brands. Applying the ALARM framework, identify the ways in which a brand like Heaven can engage with Gen Z.

2   Gen Z are digital natives. How would you use digital presence brand features to connect with this cohort of customers?

3   Beyond digital presence, how can a brand like Heaven create a consistent brand feature strategy (CBFS) to engage with its customers?

Endnotes

1   Schmitt, B H and Simonson, A (1997) *Marketing Aesthetics: The strategic management of brands, identity, and image*, Free Press, New York

2   Science Daily (2007) Old McDonald's has a hold on kids' taste buds, study finds, 8 August, www.sciencedaily.com/releases/2007/08/070806161214.htm (archived at https://perma.cc/R4AY-AM6U)

3 Cakici, N M and Shukla, P (2017) Country-of-origin misclassification awareness and consumers' behavioral intentions: Moderating roles of consumer affinity, animosity, and product knowledge, *International Marketing Review*

4 https://interbrand.com/best-brands/ (archived at https://perma.cc/8LU8-47S9)

5 Rao, A R and Monroe, K B (1989) The effect of price, brand name, and store name on buyers' perceptions of product quality: An integrative review, *Journal of Marketing Research*, 26 (3), 351–57

6 www.washingtonpost.com/archive/opinions/2002/01/26/the-saudi-sellout/71c3ca17-277b-43e8-9a8c-9d9c9cc1e3d3/ (archived at https://perma.cc/SGZ4-JS7V)

7 www.thetimes.co.uk/article/gymshark-launched-by-ben-francis-bulks-up-69838cls9 (archived at https://perma.cc/94E3-GBE2)

8 www.marketingweek.com/ritson-brand-assets-senses/ (archived at https://perma.cc/JZ7Y-2363)

9 www.veritonic.com/audio-logo-index (archived at https://perma.cc/N6TN-RPP2)

10 www.nytimes.com/2014/12/27/business/international/adidas-and-hotwind-in-china-brands-evoke-foreign-names-even-if-theyre-gibberish.html (archived at https://perma.cc/XZK5-N82P)

11 www.thedrum.com/news/2015/02/20/art-fakery-chinas-most-notable-sham-brands (archived at https://perma.cc/XVP9-GNLA)

12 https://photogallery.indiatimes.com/celebs/celeb-themes/funny-fake-brands/johnnie-worker-black-labial-scotch-whiskey/morphshow/47896366.cms (archived at https://perma.cc/EG7S-CRCT)

13 Gustafsson, C (2015) Sonic branding: A consumer-oriented literature review, *Journal of Brand Management*, 22 (1), 20–37

14 https://sustainability.aboutamazon.com/environment/packaging (archived at https://perma.cc/R2LJ-4XY7)

15 Shukla, P, Singh, J and Wang, W (2022) The influence of creative packaging design on customer motivation to process and purchase decisions, *Journal of Business Research*, 147, 338–47

16 www.creativebydefinition.com/supplement-packaging.html (archived at https://perma.cc/43P3-FRUZ)

17 www.lvmh.com/group/milestones-lvmh/1593-to-the-present/ (archived at https://perma.cc/FR8N-84PQ)

18 https://interbrand.com/best-global-brands/louis-vuitton/ (archived at https://perma.cc/5S56-YH38)

Brand loyalty and brand equity

05

Overview

In this chapter, we first introduce the concept of brand loyalty and discuss why it remains important from a managerial perspective. We then consider the debates on the varied approaches to brand loyalty, including behavioural and attitudinal measurement and management. We also provide an overall view on the current state of the debate. Further, we explain the concept of brand equity and provide details on different ways of measurement. Bringing in the current business approaches to measuring brand equity and brand valuation, we give illustrations of some well-known brand valuation tools.

Key learning outcomes

Upon reading this chapter, you should be able to

- Know about the relevance and importance of brand loyalty for businesses
- Understand the ways in which brand loyalty is measured and managed
- Learn about the current debate on brand loyalty
- Understand the different meanings and measurements of brand equity
- Learn about popular brand valuation tools

Relevance and definitions of brand loyalty

Loyalty is something that consumers exhibit in their interactions with the brands. Managers want their customers to be loyal to their brands. Loyalty is extremely important for brands as in having loyal customers, managers can be certain that a group of customers will continue to buy their products and services in the foreseeable future. Thus, brand loyalty allows managers a degree of certainty about their business in competitive markets and ensures financial stability.

The concept of loyalty is multifaceted. Brand loyalty could mean an emotional and/or attitudinal connection with the brand. It could also manifest in a customer buying the brand repeatedly over a period by showing behavioural loyalty.

BRANDING IN PRACTICE

Brand Keys Loyalty Engagement Index shows relevance of brand loyalty

Brand Keys, a brand research consultancy headquartered in the USA, has been conducting an annual survey of North American consumers asking them about their attitudinal preference towards thousands of brands in more than 110 categories since 1996.

It claims to identify the category drivers that establish customer loyalty to brands and in turn drive profits. According to the agency, the brands that come closest to meeting or exceeding the category ideal position tend to achieve the highest level of customer engagement and loyalty over a future 12- to 18-month period.

In its latest report, new brand leaders, returning brand leaders and brands that owned the loyalty of customers for a long period of time were identified (see Table 5.1).

SOURCES https://brandkeys.com/customer-loyalty-engagement-index/; https://thecustomer.net/brand-keys-customer-loyalty-engagement-index-finds-seismic-changes-in-loyalty-rankings/

Table 5.1 Brand loyalty leaders

New brand loyalty leaders	Returning brand loyalty leaders	Brands that own loyalty for more than a decade
Corona Extra	McDonald's	Discover Card (26 years running)
Disney+	Uber	Google (23 years)
Enterprise Rent-A-Car	The NFL	Domino's (19 years)
Aquafina	Chase	Dunkin' (17 years)
Traders Joe's	L'Oréal	Konica Minolta (16 years)
Booking.com	Apple (headphones)	Hyundai (14 years)
Oscar Meyer	Chipotle	AT&T Wireless (14 years)
Epsom	Dick's Sporting Goods	Amazon.com (12 years)
Levi Strauss	CVS	Home Depot (11 years)
H&R Block	Samsung (smartphones)	
LEGO	Colgate	
Dannon		
Don Julio Tequila		
Drury Hotels		

The concept of loyalty is grounded in the notion of 'faithful adherence', as per the meaning given by *Oxford English Dictionary*. Such adherence is multifaceted by its concept, as it could reflect adherence towards a person, a product, a service or an ideology, amongst others. As discussed in Chapter 2, however, all the above can be branded: David Beckham is a person as well as a brand, Tesla is an automobile company and a brand, and Google is search service provider and a brand.

Scholars have debated and often skirted around the expressions 'customer loyalty' versus 'brand loyalty'. Loyalty is seen as inherent to people who express their loyalty to a brand. On the other hand, loyalty is also driven by brands. Loyalty-related terms such as commitment, recommendation, share and retention are applicable to both customers and brands. Therefore, customer loyalty and brand loyalty are inextricably linked terms and can be used interchangeably.

Scholarly beginnings

As discussed in earlier chapters, scholars began to conceptualize and define a variety of branding constructs, including brand loyalty, in the 1970s. Scholars and practitioners including Jacob Jacoby, Jagdish Sheth, C Whan Park and David Kyner led the debate on conceptualizing brand loyalty. For example, Jacoby defined loyalty as a non-random behavioural response, expressed over time, by some decision-making unit, with respect to one or more alternative brands, which is a function of psychological processes (decision-making, evaluation).[1] This definition puts forth the faithful adherence to a particular brand among competing brands by an individual or a household (decision-making unit) over a period of time. Further to that, scholars also defined brand loyalty as a positively biased response that captures a emotive, evaluative and behavioural response.[2] The debate on brand loyalty further developed as scholars started identifying its varying components. For instance, Richard Oliver argued that loyalty involves four facets including cognitive (loyalty to objective information), affective (loyalty based on liking or preference), conative (loyalty through intentions and behaviours) and action (effortful search and purchase of the brand and avoiding all alternatives).[3]

These conceptualizations and definitions show the complex and multifaceted nature of brand loyalty. This has led to researchers questioning the constructs and its relevance. For instance, if a consumer buys a product repeatedly without any attitudinal or emotional connection, is it loyalty? Alternatively, if an individual shows a strong preference and liking toward a brand but is not going to be able to buy it for the foreseeable future, is it loyalty as well? Scholars argue that not all loyal brand relationships are alike in strength or in character[4] and thus there exists a confusion regarding the nature and relevance of brand loyalty. In the following section, we discuss the different approaches that capture the various facets of brand loyalty.

Different approaches to brand loyalty

Brand loyalty can manifest itself in three distinct forms, namely share, retention and recommendation. For example, consumers demonstrate loyalty by consistently buying one brand above all other competitors and thus give a high market share to their desired brand. Consumers could also buy that brand for a considerable period showing brand retention. Moreover, consumers may become advocates of the brand by recommending it to other potential customers. While the first two forms of loyalty show a behavioural inclination, the latter shows an attitudinal preference. In addition to the above, brand loyalty is also category-dependent. For instance, fast-moving consumer goods (FMCG) such as soap, shampoo, etc. are bought regularly and so it is comparatively easy to observe both behavioural and attitudinal loyalty. However, loyalty is difficult to capture for shopping or speciality products such as TVs, computers, cars, luxury goods. Thus, scholars and practitioners use different facets of brand loyalty to understand and capture its multifaceted nature. In the following section, we capture the behavioural and attitudinal approaches of brand loyalty.

Behavioural approach

The behavioural approach of loyalty is predominantly focused on measuring loyalty through well-established measures such as repeat-buying, market share, market penetration, average purchase frequency and share of category requirements. These measures are recorded by third-party companies such as IRI, Kantar Group, GfK and Nielsen using large scanner panels. These consumer panels record the purchases of many hundreds or thousands of individual or households on a continuous basis over several years. Such large-scale panels provide brand, category and socio-demographic-based insights to companies about the actual purchases of their brands by the consumers in the dataset. Brands benefit from such insights by evaluating their market competitiveness across many different brands within a category across various types of markets. In doing so, brands can identify the levels of loyalty using the well-established loyalty measures stated above. Brands can also get relevant consumer purchase data from large-scale retailers. For instance, retailers such as Tesco, Wal-Mart and Sainsbury's share a variety of data about their customers' purchase patterns through proprietary platforms. However, such retailer data, while being vast, contains the purchase patterns from their own loyalty programmes. Consumers who belong to such loyalty programmes tend to purchase from specific stores more often to attain greater loyalty rewards. Thus, single-retailer-based panel data creates a skewed picture of customer loyalty and market competitiveness.

The behavioural approach to loyalty has provided substantial insights into understanding how people buy different brands across categories. One of the major insights of the behavioural approach is that many markets are near-stationary, wherein the market share of brands does not change much. Sometimes, over a longer period there may be some changes in consumption behaviour which could lead to a change in the market. For instance, lager drinking increased in the UK throughout the 1980s with a corresponding decline in the consumption of bitter beer. Such changes in consumption behaviour are rather rare as consumers tend to buy from a repertoire of brands within a category driven largely by habit.

A similar change occurred in the early 2000s when Australian wine makers marketed their brands in the UK market based on the types of grapes and usage occasion. Wine was previously marketed based on the concept of *terroir*, which refers to the unique combination of natural factors associated with any particular vineyard, such as quality, product complexity or vineyard prestige, highlighted by French wineries. Thus, wine was largely associated with regions such as Champagne, Bordeaux, Brittany and Savoy. The Australian strategy of marketing their brands based on the types of grapes and usage occasion simplified the consumers' choice as it did not require the complexities associated with guessing wine qualities based on *terroir*. Such simplification in choice allowed young consumers in particular to easily understand and adopt wines from Australia, replacing lager beer as their first choice of alcoholic drink in many situations. As noted earlier, though, such category level consumption shifts do not happen often. Markets are largely stationary at brand and category level, as observed in most large-scale empirical studies.[5] [6]

BRANDING IN PRACTICE
Brand performance measures used for understanding behavioural loyalty

Companies use a variety of brand performance measures to understand and capture behavioural loyalty. Some of the regularly used measures and their definitions are provided here.

Market share: denotes the percentage of total category sales the brand accounts for.

$$\text{Market share} = \frac{\text{Total purchases of the brand}}{\text{Total purchases of the category}}$$

Market penetration: the proportion of the population who buy the item at least once in a given time-period.

$$\text{Penetration} = \frac{\text{The number buying the brand at least once}}{\text{The total number of potential customers}}$$

Average purchase frequency: the average number of purchases made by households who buy at all in a given period.

100% loyal buyers: buy only one single brand of that product category throughout the time period of analysis.

Share of category requirements: measures each brand's market share among the group of householders that bought the brand at least once during the time period under consideration.

Duplication of purchase: the number of purchasers of a brand who also purchase another brand in the same period (i.e. buyers of brand X also buying brand Y).

Based on the above measures there are several brand-level buying patterns established in scholarly research. See the Branding in practice box in Chapter 3 on page 40.

Attitude-based approach

While the behavioural approach to brand loyalty emerged from large-scale panel data, the attitude-based approach is grounded in capturing consumer preference and attitudes through a variety of techniques including focus groups, surveys and experiments. Another fundamental difference between behavioural and attitudinal approaches to brand loyalty is their measurement itself. Behavioural loyalty is captured through actual behavioural data, while attitudinal loyalty is measured through self-reported measures that may or may not result in actual behaviour. For brand managers, behavioural measures give a more accurate portrayal of the competitive structure of the market as compared to attitudinal measures. However, behavioural purchase data is more expensive and scarcer in certain markets or categories. This creates accessibility constraints for smaller and medium-sized brands. Hence, many such small and medium-sized brands rely on attitudinal measures of brand loyalty to understand their customers.

The attitude-based approach to brand loyalty has developed substantially over the past six decades within the field of marketing. Early proponents of the approach argued that for true brand loyalty to exist, strong attitudinal commitment from the customer was a fundamental condition.[7] Attitudinal loyalty is seen as a consistently favourable set of beliefs toward the purchased brand.[8] Researchers have measured attitudinal loyalty through a variety of questions based on preference, purchase likelihood, recommendation likelihood, affective commitment, repeat purchase likelihood, positive beliefs and feelings – relative to competing brands.[9] The attitude-based approach has led to the development of unique branding constructs, including self-brand connection,[10] brand commitment,[11] brand trust[12] and brand love.[13] By comparing the strength of these attitudes toward the brand against the competitors, researchers and managers can predict purchase and repeat patronage toward the brand.

Synthesizing the brand loyalty debate

While scholars continue to debate about the relevance and applications of behavioural and/or attitudinal approaches to brand loyalty, both have significant merits and weaknesses. For instance, the behavioural approach provides insights on customers' actual purchasing behaviour and loyalty towards brands. It does not, however, offer information about the psychology behind the brand choice. For instance, why a brand was preferred over its competitors. On the other hand, the attitudinal approach highlights the psychology of brand choice and brand loyalty. This approach, however, mostly captures customer intentions and attitudes that may not result in actual behaviour, for example purchase.

While theorizing the construct of brand loyalty, many scholars have reflected on the intertwined nature of attitudinal and behavioural approaches.[14] In fact, brand loyalty in real life reflects both attitudinal and behavioural components. If there is no liking or commitment towards the brand, and the customer still keeps on buying it regularly, it may be because of habit or unavailability of competing brands. Similarly, a customer may have strong feelings towards the brand and follow all relevant media information, but may not have the means to purchase the brand. Either of the above cases can reflect brand loyalty. The former is an example of habitual loyalty while the latter depicts positive attitudes which may not result in purchase. Thus, by comprehending both attitudinal and behavioural aspects of brand loyalty, managers can make better decisions about their brands.

BRANDING IN PRACTICE
Usefulness of loyalty programmes: fact versus fiction

It is believed that an average North American household is part of more than 30 loyalty programmes.[15] The loyalty management market was valued more than $21 billion and is expected to be greater than $71 billion by 2026.[16] The usefulness of loyalty programmes, however, is debatable.

The importance of brand loyalty and the surrounding debate has led many companies to introduce a variety of loyalty programmes. For instance, one of the largest retailers in the UK, Tesco, launched its loyalty programme 'Clubcard' in 1995. Similarly, most airlines and their alliance partners run their own loyalty programmes relating to air miles accrued. Many managers assume that loyalty programmes lead to substantial rewards for the organization as loyal customers are less costly to serve and spend more than other customers and they also act as brand advocates spreading positive word-of-mouth for the company.[17] However, substantial academic research relating to loyalty programmes has established that in most cases loyalty programmes do not enhance either attitudinal or behavioural loyalty.[18]

A loyalty programme is built with a notion that upfront expenditure in creating loyal customers will result in much greater future returns. Contrarily, research shows that many of the loyalty programmes produce substantial liabilities for the firm.[19] Evidence clearly shows that heavy buyers continue to buy more, irrespective of being part of a loyalty programme or not. Moreover, as loyalty programme members, they claim extra rewards, but do not change their purchase behaviour.[20] The overwhelming evidence thus suggests that loyalty programmes largely benefit customers but not the brand in most cases.[21] Thus, loyalty programmes remain largely organization-driven initiatives with little impact on brand loyalty among their customers.

The debate on the usefulness of loyalty programme is summed up nicely in this quote from a manager representing the Millennium Hotel Group, 'Honestly, I don't know what, if anything, it actually does for me.'[22]

What is brand equity?

Brand equity is a frequently used term in the field of branding. Businesses and scholars have offered varying interpretations of the concept. The concept became popular in the 1990s with scholars such as David Aaker and Kevin Lane Keller leading the debate. Brand is by nature intangible and thus identifying the equity of a brand has always been challenging. This is further compounded by definitional challenges arising due to a lack of agreement on the nature, constituents and outcomes relating to brand equity. Some scholars and marketers have attempted to examine brand equity through the lenses of economics and finance. Their aim remains to attach a financial value to a brand which can demonstrate the profit potential of the brand in the market. This finance-driven approach has led companies to identify and promote the value of their brand, reflected in the balance sheet as 'goodwill', when acquiring a firm.

The other approach to brand equity is based on customers' perceptions and attitudes towards the brand. Grounded mainly in psychology and sociology, this approach aims to capture how customers prefer one brand over the other through their image perceptions, symbolism and behavioural intentions. Kevin Lane Keller conceptualized brand equity through this approach and developed a framework named 'customer-based brand equity'.[23] Customer-based brand equity (CBBE) is defined as the differential effect of brand knowledge on consumer response to the marketing of the brand. This framework examines customers' brand knowledge through the subcomponents of brand awareness and brand image. Brand awareness is measured by asking customers about their brand recall and recognition. Brand image is measured through favourability, strength and uniqueness of brand associations, and types of brand associations that are captured in brand-related attributes, benefits and attitudes. Brand attributes take into account a variety of marketing mix aspects such as price, packaging and user imagery. Brand benefits reflect the functional, experiential and symbolic aspects associated with the brand.

Brand strength vs brand size debate

Managers can use the CBBE framework to ascertain their brand's health in a competitive marketplace and also to identify their customers' views about competing brands. Focusing on this attitudinal-approach-driven CBBE framework, companies can discover the strength of their brand's association in customer minds compared to their competitors. In this regard, companies can also identify the strengths and weaknesses of their brand on a variety of CBBE components as well as overall market position of their brand. For instance, a brand could have higher awareness (i.e. recall and recognition) but may not have a strong brand image. Such a brand can then focus on building better brand image by communicating the uniqueness of its associations and attributes.

Strength of CBBE does not mean that a strong brand will be a market leader. There is no clear evidence that the strength of CBBE and the size of the brand are correlated.[24] A brand with a strong CBBE may have a small market share. For instance, Ferrari is a highly recognized automobile brand, but its market share within the overall automobile sector is small. Compared to Ferrari, Ford may not have the same strength of CBBE but has a much larger market share. Moreover, the strength of CBBE does not relate to future success in terms of market share either.[25] Brands such as Kodak, Polaroid and Nokia which were some of the largest players in their sectors for a number of years and still evoke a significant degree of CBBE, are however brands that have failed in consumer markets.

Measuring brand equity

With the variations in conceptualizing brand equity, researchers and practitioners have attempted to measure brand equity in a variety of ways. Several important considerations have been taken into account by researchers in regard to measuring brand equity including perceptual measures such as perceived quality, brand loyalty and brand awareness/associations.[26] [27] Researchers have also identified several behavioural measures such as buying frequency, market penetration, share of category requirements, level of loyalty among buyers and market share to estimate behavioural loyalty as a proxy for brand equity.[28]

While academic research on measuring brand equity has included attitudinal and behavioural aspects, a number of practitioner frameworks have also gained prominence. Noteworthy among them are Interbrand's Brand Valuation (see Table 5.2), Brand Asset Valuator by VMLY&R and BrandZ from Kantar. Each of these brand equity frameworks utilize a different methodology.

Interbrand's Brand Valuation includes three variables, namely financial forecast, role of brand and brand strength.[29] Financial forecast measures the overall financial return or after-tax operating profit. Role of brand measures the purchase decision attribution specifically assigned to the brand devoid of other factors such as price, convenience or product features. Brand strength measures 10 factors based on internal and external dimensions that determine the brand's ability to generate loyalty and resultant demand and profit in the future compared to other industry players.

Developed in conjunction with academic partners from a number of universities, Brand Asset Valuator by VMLY&R captures brand equity through brand strength and brand stature.[30] Brand strength is measured based on the future growth potential of a brand through two sub-dimensions, differentiation and relevance. Similarly, brand stature, or the current operating value of a brand, is measured through esteem and knowledge sub-dimensions. Differentiation reflects a brand's ability to capture attention in the cultural landscape and is identified as a powerful driver of curiosity, advocacy and pricing power. Relevance, on the other hand, relates to the appropriateness and meaningfulness of the brand to consumers, which, in turn, drives brand consideration and trial. Esteem depicts how highly regarded a brand is and how well it delivers on its promises, leading to trial and commitment. Finally, knowledge sub-dimension captures the depth of understanding people have of a brand – both its positive and negative information.

Similarly, the BrandZ framework by Kantar utilizes a methodology combining a financial matrix with perceptual attributes of the brands.[31] The framework aims to identify brand-related attribution by capturing financial information from annual reports and other sources such as Kantar Worldpanel and Kantar Retail IQ data. This data is coupled with perceptual matrices on brand power that is captured through the meaningfulness, differentiation and salience of a brand in consumer

Table 5.2   Interbrand's top 10 best global brands 2022

Ranking	Brand name	Brand value (in mn $)	Change since last year
1	Apple	482,215	+18%
2	Microsoft	278,288	+32%
3	Amazon	274,819	+10%
4	Google	251,751	+28%
5	Samsung	87,689	+17%
6	Toyota	59,757	+10%
7	Coca-Cola	57,535	0%
8	Mercedes-Benz	56,103	+10%
9	Disney	50,325	+14%
10	Nike	50,289	+18%

SOURCE https://interbrand.com/best-global-brands/

minds. Using predictive algorithms based on the combination of financial and per-ceptual data, future value is assigned to the brand.

As is evident from the industry-based brand equity frameworks, a combination of financial, attitudinal and behavioural measures is utilized to measure brand equity. These frameworks, which are proprietary to their respective firms, lead to annual brand reports or rankings such as the BrandZ top 100 Most Valuable Global Brands or Interbrand's Best Global Brands.

Chapter summary

This chapter focuses on two key constructs in the branding domain: brand loyalty and brand equity. The chapter began by describing the relevance of brand loyalty and its varying definitions leading to a critical debate on the nature of brand loyalty. Brand loyalty has been approached from a behavioural or attitudinal perspective: both approaches provide unique insights into the relationship between a consumer and a brand. We highlight the need to synthesize the two approaches. The chapter questions the over-reliance on and the problems with the usefulness of customer loy-alty programmes and considers how brand equity and its measurement approaches remain contentious. Brand equity is useful for organizations in identifying the value of the potential acquisition. The chapter also provides insights into the academic framework of consumer-based brand equity (CBBE) as well as the behavioural approach for measuring brand equity. Further, a detailed discussion on industry frameworks that measure brand equity is provided.

Key concepts

- Brand loyalty
  - ○ Behavioural brand loyalty
  - ○ Attitudinal brand loyalty
- Brand loyalty programmes
- Brand equity
  - ○ Brand strength and size
- Consumer-based brand equity (CBBE)
- Brand equity measurements

Exercise questions

1 Critically discuss the concept of brand loyalty.

2 What are the approaches to brand loyalty? How do they differ?

3 Describe brand performance measures. How can these measures help managers understand and estimate brand loyalty?

4 What is brand equity? Why and when does it matter for an organization?

5 Explain the different ways in which brand equity has been examined in academic research.

6 Review and critically analyse the three industry-based brand equity measurement frameworks.

CASE STUDY   'Data for a discount: are customer loyalty programs ever a good deal?'

Read the article from *The Guardian*, which explores the use of loyalty programmes in Australia. It looks specifically into how loyalty schemes make use of customer data, providing information on buying habits, needs and preferences, as well as movements (e.g. where a customer shops). The benefits of the actual loyalty scheme may not always be obvious to the individual, and neither is what information is being collected or how. More importantly, what is the data used for?

SOURCE www.theguardian.com/australia-news/2022/sep/20/data-for-a-discount-are-customer-loyalty-programs-ever-a-good-deal

Case questions

1 Based on the case study and academic research evidence, reflect critically on the usefulness of customer loyalty programmes.

2 Given the increasing restriction on data usage and privacy regulations, how should companies manage loyalty databases?

3 Reflect critically on the future of customer loyalty programmes in the digital age.

4 Discuss how AI may impact the operationalization and management of customer loyalty programmes.

Endnotes

1 Jacoby, J (1971) Brand loyalty: A conceptual definition, *Proceedings of the Annual Convention of the American Psychological Association*, 6 (2), 655–56

2 Sheth, J N and Whan Park, C (1974) A theory of multidimensional brand loyalty, in *NA – Advances in Consumer Research,* vol. 1, eds. S Ward and P Wright, Association for Consumer Research, Ann Arbor, MI, pp 449–59

3 Oliver, R L (1999) Whence consumer loyalty?, *Journal of Marketing*, 63 (4_suppl), 33–44

4 Fournier, S and Yao, J L (1997) Reviving brand loyalty: A reconceptualization within the framework of consumer-brand relationships, *International Journal of Research in Marketing*, 14 (5), 451–72

5 Ehrenberg, A S, Uncles, M D and Goodhardt, G J (2004) Understanding brand performance measures: Using Dirichlet benchmarks, *Journal of Business Research*, 57 (12), 1307–25

6 Sharp, B and Romaniuk, J (2016) *How Brands Grow*, Oxford University Press

7 Jacoby, J and Chestnut, R W (1978) *Brand Loyalty: Measurement and management*, John Wiley and Sons

8 Uncles, M D, Dowling, G R and Hammond, K (2003) Customer loyalty and customer loyalty programs, *Journal of Consumer Marketing*, 20 (4), 294–316

9 Dick, A S and Basu, K (1994) Customer loyalty: Toward an integrated conceptual framework, *Journal of the Academy of Marketing Science*, 22, 99–113

10 Escalas, J E and Bettman, J R (2003) You are what they eat: The influence of reference groups on consumers' connections to brands, *Journal of Consumer Psychology*, 13 (3), 339–48

11 Singh, J, Shukla, P and Schlegelmilch, B B (2022) Desire, need, and obligation: Examining commitment to luxury brands in emerging markets, *International Business Review*, 31 (3), 101947

12 Chaudhuri, A and Holbrook, M B (2001) The chain of effects from brand trust and brand affect to brand performance: The role of brand loyalty, *Journal of Marketing*, 65 (2), 81–93

13 Batra, R, Ahuvia, A and Bagozzi, R P (2012) Brand love, *Journal of Marketing*, 76 (2), 1–16

14 Dick, A S and Basu, K (1994) Customer loyalty: Toward an integrated conceptual framework, *Journal of the Academy of Marketing Science*, 22, 99–113

15 Kim, J J, Steinhoff, L and Palmatier, R W (2021) An emerging theory of loyalty program dynamics, *Journal of the Academy of Marketing Science*, 49, 71–95

16 Fortune Business Insights (2019) Loyalty Management Market Size, Growth: Industry Report 2026, www.fortunebusinessinsights.com/industry-reports/loyalty-management-market-101166 (archived at https://perma.cc/XTP4-EKDJ)

17 Reinartz, W and Kumar, V (2002) The mismanagement of customer loyalty, *Harvard Business Review*, 80 (7), 86–94

18 Uncles, M D, Dowling, G R and Hammond, K (2003) Customer loyalty and customer loyalty programs, *Journal of Consumer Marketing*, 20 (4), 294–316

19 Shugan, S M (2005) Brand loyalty programs: Are they shams?, *Marketing Science*, 24 (2), 185–93

20 Liu, Y (2007) The long-term impact of loyalty programs on consumer purchase behavior and loyalty, *Journal of Marketing*, 71 (4), 19–35

21 Kim, J J, Steinhoff, L and Palmatier, R W (2021) An emerging theory of loyalty program dynamics, *Journal of the Academy of Marketing Science*, 49, 71–95

22 McCall, M and Voorhees, C (2010) The drivers of loyalty program success: An organizing framework and research agenda, *Cornell Hospitality Quarterly*, 51 (1), 35–52

23 Keller, K L (1993) Conceptualizing, measuring, and managing customer-based brand equity, *Journal of Marketing*, 57 (1), 1–22

24 Goodhardt, G J (1999) Letters to the Editor: Strong and weak brands, *International Journal of Advertising*, 18, 190

25 Ehrenberg, A S, Uncles, M D and Goodhardt, G J (2004) Understanding brand performance measures: Using Dirichlet benchmarks, *Journal of Business Research*, 57 (12), 1307–25

26 Yoo, B and Donthu, N (2001) Developing and validating a multidimensional consumer-based brand equity scale, *Journal of Business Research*, 52 (1), 1–14

27 Christodoulides, G and De Chernatony, L (2010) Consumer-based brand equity conceptualisation and measurement: A literature review, *International Journal of Market Research*, 52 (1), 43–66

28 Romaniuk, J and Nenycz-Thiel, M (2013) Behavioral brand loyalty and consumer brand associations, *Journal of Business Research*, 66 (1), 67–72

29 https://interbrand.com/thinking/best-global-brands-2021-methodology/ (archived at https://perma.cc/QXU4-GQ7F)

30 www.bavgroup.com/about-bav (archived at https://perma.cc/FSF5-K59S)

31 www.ft.com/content/051725be-bc78-11e2-9519-00144feab7de (archived at https://perma.cc/ST54-VRQR) and www.youtube.com/watch?v=WcPakbqewp4 (archived at https://perma.cc/F2TE-EJB5)

Brand positioning   06

Overview

In this chapter, we first introduce the concept of brand positioning and how it influences marketing practice. We then include the well-known concepts of brand association, image and symbolism. We also provide an overview of points of parity and points of difference as effective tools for assessing brand positioning. In the sections following, we consider practical tools of brand positioning in the form of associative network theory and perceptual maps. The chapter ends with a discussion on how customer segmentation bases can be employed to position the brand and target relevant segments.

Key learning outcomes

Upon reading this chapter, you should be able to

- Understand what brand positioning is and its central role in marketing
- Comprehend the concepts of brand association, image and symbolism
- Understand how to use points of parity and points of difference in brand positioning
- Gain insights into associative network theory and perceptual maps as important tools for determining brand positioning
- Know how customer segmentation bases are used for positioning

What is the positioning of a brand?

Think about colour red. Now, think about a cola brand. Which brand came to mind? When asked, most consumers tend to answer Coca-Cola. Think about the 'best search engine'. It is highly likely that you thought 'Google'. The colour red for cola or the word for best search engine is associated with a particular brand in consumer minds. This, in its simplest form, is brand positioning.

Brand positioning is defined as the place a brand occupies in the minds of consumers based on one or more distinctive characteristics in comparison to competitors. The idea of positioning emerged from product management literature. Management consultants Al Ries and Jack Trout coined the term product positioning in the early 1970s. They identified product form, package size and price when compared to competitors as a way in which a firm can differentiate its products.[1] Product differentiation is about the features of a product that distinguishes it from its competitors. Brand positioning relates to the communication of differentiating elements of the product to consumers.

Brand positioning, over the years, has become an important element in marketing strategy. Most successful brands have a clear positioning in consumer minds, as highlighted in the earlier examples of Coca-Cola and Google. Similarly, Red Bull has a clear positioning advantage as an energy drink by associating itself with extreme sports. Brands such as Xerox and Google have achieved such strong positioning that they have become synonymous with their respective product categories, photocopying and information search on the internet.

Brand positioning is analogous to a schema that exists in consumer minds. A schema is a cognitive structure that represents consumers' expectations about a product category which is developed over time.[2] A brand-positioning-related schema takes shape based on the value ascribed to various brand attributes, and the variability present across brands. For example, when considering cars, consumers assign different value to attributes such as price, quality, design, safety, status, style and performance, among many others. Volvo is associated with the safety attribute. A consumer who assigns the highest value to safety in purchasing a car is more likely to prefer Volvo above others. Thus, Volvo's brand positioning on safety features allows alignment with consumer expectations. To affirm consumer views and expectations about the brand, Volvo's brand communication often prominently features the safety attribute, creating a virtuous cycle and strong brand positioning in consumer minds.

BRANDING IN PRACTICE
Positioning in the dentifrice market

When thinking about toothpaste how do you differentiate between various brands? Table 6.1 shows the positioning put forward by many global toothpaste brands.

Table 6.1　Toothpaste brand positioning

Brand	Positioning
Colgate Total	Fights full range of oral health problems
Close-up	Whitener, great breath for kissing
Crest	Powerful fluoride cavity fighter
Aim	Milder taste than other brands, kid-friendly
Arm & Hammer	Popular baking soda mixed with toothpaste
Aquafresh	Kills germs, for young adults
Biotene	Reduces bacteria and germs in mouth
Oral-B	High quality, dentist approved
Rembrandt	Higher-quality whitening
Sensodyne	Especially for sensitive teeth
Mentadent	Baking soda and peroxide for fresh breath

While brands aim to position their products using a variety of positioning statements, it is well-known that most consumers hardly differentiate between brands in most categories. This is particularly true for low-involvement products. One of the reasons for such reduced differentiation is the development of sub-brands and market proliferation where many of these positions overlap.[3] For instance, Colgate not only has its 'original Total toothpaste', but currently has 54 variants,[4] some of which are listed here:

- Colgate cool stripe
- Colgate white charcoal whitening toothpaste
- Colgate max white extra care sensitive protect whitening toothpaste
- Colgate total advanced deep clean toothpaste
- Colgate sensitive instant relief repair and prevent
- Colgate white sparkle diamonds whitening toothpaste
- Colgate sensitive with sensiform toothpaste
- Colgate max white purple reveal toothpaste
- Colgate deep clean with baking soda toothpaste

These variants substantially overlap with the positioning of other toothpaste brands in the market, thus, reducing the clear differentiation that brands wish to derive.

Brand association, image and brand symbolism

In the previous chapter, we briefly discussed the importance of brand image, associations and symbolism for brand equity and loyalty. These aspects also play a critical role in brand positioning.

Brand association

Brand associations are fundamental memory cues that help consumers remember and recall a brand based on a variety of triggers including a brand name, logo, a narrative or any other stimuli. Research has shown that brand associations are critical in our understanding of inference making,[5] categorization,[6] product evaluation,[7,8] persuasion[9] and brand equity.[10,11] Two distinct theoretical mechanisms have been proposed in explaining how brand associations affect consumer decision making. The first path, grounded in the Human Associative Memory (HAM) theory,[12] proposes that declarative knowledge is represented as a network of concept nodes connected by links that are strengthened each time two events co-occur. The more a brand name co-occurs with a benefit association, either through indirect or direct experience, the stronger the link between the brand name and the benefit association.

An alternative theory explaining the power of brand associations is adaptive network theory,[13] which is grounded in the classical conditioning literature.[14] According to this theory, association strengths update and evolve as cues interact, and often compete, to predict outcomes.[15] Thus, while HAM theory explains that cues are learned independently, adaptive network theory holds that cues interact, wherein the strength of the association between a brand name and a benefit depends on how uniquely a brand name can be associated to a benefit and vice versa. Hence, in the case of brand associations, the famous neuroscience expression 'neurons that fire together, wire together' is relevant. The more a particular benefit association is attached to a brand, the stronger the association becomes and in turn will lead to stronger brand related memory and recall. For example, when buying electronic products, quality is an important consideration. In this regard, Sony has built a strong association with the word quality worldwide. Such associations can act as a buffer against consumer backlash when the occasional quality transgression or brand crisis occurs. For instance, Sony has been involved in many product recalls due to product quality issues.[16,17] However, it has still maintained its brand position due to the strength of its quality association.

A popular theory in brand communication is the associative network memory model. It describes how brands are perceived by consumers based on their memory cues. Building on the HAM theory, it argues that the network of nodes and connecting links within consumer minds regarding a brand influences brand equity. Various nodes such as a brand name, logo and other visual or sensory signals connect with features such as quality, price, image, etc. and these associative linkages, in turn, determine brand equity. The linkages can be either positive or negative. For example, a fast-food brand such as McDonald's could easily be recognized because of a strong associative network memory including the brand name, the yellow colour of the logo, its mascot and design elements, which is connected with positive features such as fast service and negative features such as unhealthy food.

Brand image

Brand image is another fundamental aspect of brand positioning. Brand image refers to the perception, reputation and overall impression that a company or product evokes in the minds of consumers and the public.[18] It is a critical aspect of brand equity,[19] as it influences consumer behaviour and purchasing decisions. Brand image, using the theory of mental representations, can be seen as consisting of two subconstructs, namely, brand attitude – which examines the valence reflected in the pleasantness or unpleasantness of an emotional stimulus – and brand strength – cognitive elements associated with a brand.[20]

Brand attitude

The brand attitude component of brand image captures the positive or negative feelings about a brand and its attributes. In the previous section, we highlighted the quality attribute of brand Sony. In addition, consumers' attitudes towards brand Sony can be shaped by many other attributes, such as visual aesthetics, brand communications, customer experiences and interactions with the brand across different platforms such as social media, physical retail stores and other channels. All these attributes, either individually or in combination, lead to the accumulation of positive or negative feelings over a period, and can contribute towards the development of brand attitude for Sony. Brand attitude, thus, is a dynamic construct that continuously evolves as a consumer gets exposed to brand-related stimuli and develops an emotional response. A consumer may possess a strong positive attitude towards a brand, however, if the brand behaves in a morally inappropriate way or its products harm consumers in some way, the brand attitude can turn negative. For instance, consumers in general held positive brand attitudes towards Volkswagen, one of the largest manufacturers of automobiles in the world, which built a reputation around high-quality engineering. When it was found to be faking emission test results using either hardware or software, consumer attitudes towards the brand changed into negative.[21] Alternatively, if a brand continues to fulfil its promise consistently and focuses on enhancing customer experience through some of the above identified attributes, negative attitudes can change to positive as well. Many brands emerging from Japan, Taiwan and South Korea which have become global names today, such as Toyota, Mitsubishi, Asus, Acer, Samsung and Hyundai, have overcome initial scepticism from consumers in Western countries and have successfully created positive brand attitudes.

Brand strength

The other component of brand image, brand strength, refers to the ease of retrieving the brand name from memory, through the range of associations that a brand has created in the consumer minds over a period.[22] Brand strength, thus, builds over time, through the number of associations, uniqueness of these associations and also the strength of associations. Researchers in philosophy and cognitive psychology highlighted that humans tend to create a mental image of things that are not actually present to the senses, based on the existing associations they have through their imagination.[23] This has substantial implications for brand strength: researchers in branding have shown that brands with a bigger market share have a greater number of associations in consumer minds.[24] For instance, when thinking about the brand Apple, the likely associations are user-friendly, iPhone, expensive, iTunes, iPad, innovation, beautiful, design, elegance, Steve Jobs, cool, stylish, among others. On the other hand, if asked about another brand operating in electronics market, such as ZTE or HTC, people tend not to identify as many associations as Apple and more importantly the strength of the association is not as strong. Hence, the brand image of these brands compared to Apple is weak. However, there are brands that have a uniqueness in their associations in consumer minds that are difficult for others to replicate. Google as a brand has a unique association with online information search. This unique association and its strength make it harder for other search engines to complete with Google in online information search.

A well-crafted brand image, which utilizes the brand attitude and brand strength, creates a distinct and favourable identity for a brand, conveying its values, personality and unique selling propositions. Maintaining a positive and consistent brand image is essential for building trust, fostering brand loyalty and ultimately gaining a competitive edge in the market. As consumers often associate emotions and feelings with brands, a strong brand image can lead to deep connections, turning customers into brand advocates and ambassadors.

Brand symbolism

Brand symbolism refers to the use of symbols, icons and visual cues by a company to represent its brand identity and values.[25] These symbols often transcend language barriers and become a powerful means of communication with consumers through sound as well,[26] which we discussed in Chapter 4. Brand symbolism research is rooted in semiotics, the study of signs and symbols and their use or interpretations. One of the most iconic examples is the bitten apple logo used by Apple, which evolved from its original design of Newton sitting under an apple tree. The apple symbolizes knowledge, discovery and the quest for enlightenment, aligning perfectly with the company's focus on innovative technology and user-friendly products. This symbolism fosters an emotional connection with consumers, inspiring a sense of aspiration and sophistication.[27] Another notable example of brand symbolism is the Nike 'swoosh' logo. The simple yet dynamic swoosh represents motion, speed and victory. It embodies the brand's commitment to excellence, athleticism and determination, making it a universally recognized symbol. The swoosh has become synonymous with Nike's brand personality, creating a strong association between the logo and the company's core values, which, in turn, drives brand equity and consumer trust. Brand symbolism, when executed effectively, can create a lasting impression and shape brand perceptions and distinctiveness.

Branding researchers have particularly focused on the socio-cultural meanings of signs, symbols and icons present in the society. Beyond the visual aspects that brand symbolism offers, the social-cultural interpretations allow individuals to use brands to represent their self-identity, group-identity, social-identity and even cultural-identity.[28] A substantive body of research in this domain is contained in the consumer culture theory (CCT) literature.[29] Consumer culture theory researchers argue that brand symbolism acts as a social representation that enable communities to communicate, behave and orient themselves.[30] Due to such social interpretations, brands are interwoven in consumer narratives and experiences, and are in turn mythologized and anthropomorphized.[31]

Ascribing humanlike attributes to brands (i.e. brand anthropomorphism) has been found to enhance consumers' ability to recognize the inherent values of a brand.[32] Many brands have utilized the power of social narratives and used anthropomorphic elements to create strong self-brand connections. By humanizing their narrative, many brands have become icons in their own rights. For example, the Duracell bunny, Tony the Tiger for Kellogg's Frosties, Ronald McDonald for McDonald's, cheetah of Cheetos, meerkats of Comparethemarket.com are all well-known examples of brand anthropomorphism. Research shows that anthropomorphizing primes the mental representation of fun, which in turn increases consumers' focus on approaching self-rewards. The self-rewards focus makes consumers more likely to consume in a more indulgent fashion.[33] However, brand anthropomorphism is not always beneficial. Research highlights that anthropomorphizing a brand becomes a detrimental marketing strategy when consumers are driven by distinctiveness motives.[34] Brands can overcome this challenge through supporting consumers' identity expression.

Scholarly debate

Parris, D L and Guzmán, F (2023) Evolving brand boundaries and expectations: looking back on brand equity, brand loyalty, and brand image research to move forward, *Journal of Product & Brand Management*, 32 (2), 191–234

Sharma, M and Rahman, Z (2022) Anthropomorphic brand management: an integrated review and research agenda, *Journal of Business Research*, 149, 463–75

Points of convergence and divergence

The discussed constructs of brand association, image and symbolism are key drivers that allow a brand to distinguish itself in the marketplace. Some of the associations that consumers have in their minds about a brand could be similar to competing brands, while certain attributes, visuals and motifs could be unique to the brand. The similarity of associations between competing brands is referred to as points of convergence (PoC), while the unique features of a brand as compared to competitors, offer points of divergence (PoD). Consumers use a variety of attributes to derive PoC and PoD, including quality, price, image, status and location, among others. For example, while very different in how they provide rating for a movie (point of divergence), both IMDB.com and Rottontomatoes.com in general are associated with movie ratings and reviews (point of convergence). Similarly, handbags from H&M and Gucci both have lots of similarities in their functionality (PoC), however, they differ substantially in regard to quality, price, brand image and status (PoD). Moreover, two closely competing brands may also have PoC and PoD. For example, Coca-Cola and Pepsi heavily use the colours red and blue respectively to create PoD in their communications.

PoCs could be observed at product category level and between direct competitors. At product category level, PoC is mostly associated with common tangible features observed across competitors within a given sector or industry. For example, most automobiles have certain common features in terms of wheels, doors, governor, dashboard, seats and engine, etc. These features help establish the product as an automobile in consumer minds. Product category level convergence evolves as the industry advances. For instance, automobile transmission systems have continued to evolve wherein automobiles now have fossil fuel (either petrol or diesel), hybrid and electric versions. Directly competing brands within most industries have many similar features. While leading brands may aim to avoid such convergence, follower brands can take advantage of such convergence to increase choice confidence among consumers.[35] A famous case of direct competitor convergence was observed when

Apple sued Samsung in various parts of the world for copying its design features, wherein both parties settled after seven years long legal battle in courts.[36]

PoDs, many times, are features unique to a brand, or strong positive/negative mental associations a consumer may have that allow clear distinction between competing brands. PoDs can emerge from features associated with objective or subjective performance as well as other abstract or imagery aspects. For instance, a brand promoting 4k television will objectively be able to show how its product is better than competing HD television brands. Additionally, consumers also use subjective performance elements in their decision-making process. For example, a German automobile is assumed to be better engineered than a South Korean counterpart. Similarly, an Italian fashion brand is subjectively assessed as superior in terms of design and aesthetics as compared to brands from other countries. Such subjective assessments of country-of-origin effect are driven by consumer mental associations as highlighted.

Perceptual map

A perceptual map, also known as a positioning map, is a graphical representation that helps managers understand how consumers perceive competing brands within a specific product category. It reflects consumer perceptions rather than market share, sales- or revenue-based figures. It provides a visual tool for analysing the competitive landscape and the relationships between various attributes or qualities that consumers associate with products. Perceptual maps typically depict two or more relevant product- or brand-related dimensions along axes, with each axis representing a distinct attribute, feature or characteristic that influences consumer perceptions about the brand. For example, a perceptual map may have economical versus expensive on the X axis and high versus low quality on the Y axis for several brands in the same product category (see Figure 6.1). By plotting different brands or products on these axes, brands can identify assess their own positioning against the competitors, potential gaps in the market and make informed decisions about areas for differentiation or improvement.

Perceptual maps are regularly used in marketing, branding and strategy development. Creating an effective perceptual map requires careful data collection and analysis. Market research tools, including surveys and focus groups, are commonly used to gather consumer perceptions and preferences related to various product attributes. Once the data is collected, it is plotted onto the map wherein the features are identified on the X and the Y axis. Each brand is then represented as a point on this axis, as shown in the example figure. The relative distances between these points on the map indicate how consumers perceive the differences between them. Brands that are close to each other on the map are perceived as similar in terms of the attributes or features being measured, while those farther apart are seen as more distinct. By interpreting the map, businesses can identify opportunities to differentiate their offerings, adjust their marketing strategies and address any gaps in consumer perceptions. Overall, perceptual maps serve as powerful tools for serving two objectives: (a) understanding a brand's competitive landscape, and (b) developing effective positioning strategy in relation to competitors.

BRANDING IN PRACTICE
Brand positioning for fashion industry

The fashion industry is a hypercompetitive, multi-billion dollar sector consisting of very small to large global brands. It also consists of brands that serve all income groups of the market. You could buy a pair of jeans trousers for $12 from George and for $3,000 from Dolce & Gabbana. With such high levels of competitive diversity, a perceptual map can offer a quick reference about how consumers perceive fashion brands.

The following perceptual map, based on a student survey conducted by the authors, uses the two dimensions of price (high versus low) and style (traditional versus trendy) that demonstrates how consumers perceived different fashion brands on these dimensions.

Figure 6.1   Perceptual map based on student survey conducted by authors

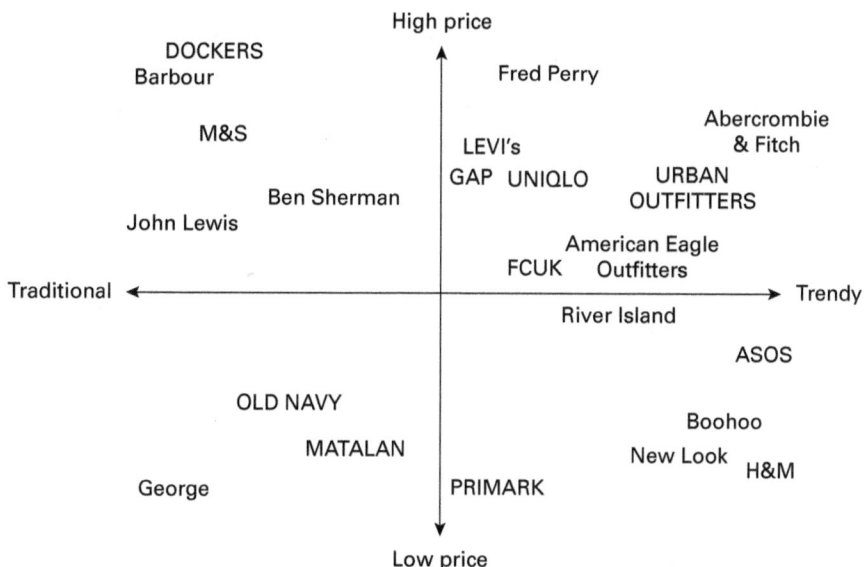

The perceptual map shown offers several insights. First, it offers different brands' position on those dimensions. Second, it also shows specific clusters of brands which consumers perceive to be similar to each other. For example, Boohoo, New Look and H&M are a cluster of brands that are competing in the trendy and low-price quadrant. Similarly, Levi's, Gap and Uniqlo are seen as quite similar to each other. However, these brands are distinct from some of the traditional brands such as M&S, Ben Sherman or Barbour. Third, this perceptual map also demonstrates certain gaps that exist within the market currently based on consumer perceptions. For instance, a brand that is mid-priced and follows new trends set by brands like Asos and Zara could enjoy a unique position. Similarly, a traditional brand that is mid-priced could also find itself in a distinct position in the market.

Most brands do not start with a clear positioning vis-à-vis competitors. The positioning is formed as the brand evolves, because it is based on consumer perceptions. Once a position is formed, changing consumer perceptions is highly resource intensive. However, a perceptual map can provide a brand with a direction in which they may aspire to move. The following Branding in practice box provides an illustration of perceptual map for fashion industry.

Segmentation bases and brand positioning

Segmentation is a core aspect of marketing that is associated with the paradigm of Segmentation, Targeting and Positioning (STP).[37] By dividing customers into separate groupings based on their socio-demographics (e.g. age, gender, income, etc.) and socio-psychographics (e.g. price consciousness, status orientation, etc.), managers can target appropriate segments that fit with their brand positioning in the market. Segmentation allows brands to better understand their customers, improve product development, acquire new customers and retain regular customers, and optimize their performance and spend on marketing campaigns by choosing appropriate media.[38]

There are four major bases for customer segmentation in business to consumer (B2C) markets: demographic, geographic, psychographic and behavioural. Demographic segmentation pertains to various socio-demographic variables such as age, gender, income, marital status and education. Geographic segmentation focuses on a variety of variables including area, postcode, city, region, county, province and country. Psychographic segmentation takes into account lifestyle, personality, values and such other psychological motivations that drive consumer decision making. Finally, behavioural segmentation is driven by occasion and other market-specific behaviours that consumers display in their consumption practices. An important aspect while understanding customer segmentation bases is to remember that these segmentation bases are not exclusive and, in most cases, overlap. For example, in the fashion industry perceptual map, a brand like Asos targets young consumers (demographic segmentation), who wish to be seen as trendy (psychographic segmentation), and most of these consumers tend to live in the Western developed markets (geographic segmentation). Similarly, Ferrero, which owns the brand Kinder, sees a spike in sales of Kinder Egg around Easter times and for its other brand Ferrero Rocher around Christmas (behavioural segmentation).

These segmentation bases which evolved in physical markets are also extremely useful for online marketplaces. In the digital domain, brands have a plethora of customer data that can be utilized to develop even more meaningful segmentation that can take into account all segmentation bases and multiple variables within it. For instance, using Facebook's advertisement platform, a brand can decide to use various segmentation bases depending on its campaign objectives such as sales, lead generation, engagement, sales promotion, increasing web traffic or awareness. The brand can then choose to target customers who live in a certain neighbourhood, area, region, city or country (geographic segmentation), age, gender, education level and field of study, income, life events including birthdays and anniversaries, social groups or networks, relationship status, employment status and work industry (demographic segmentation), hobbies and interests that include business, entertainment, sports, activities, family and relationships (psychographic segmentation) and variety of behaviours including digital activities, device usage, travel, web-browsing patterns, purchase behaviours (behavioural segmentation) in a single campaign. The rise of Big Data-based segmentation analysis has further crystallized the usefulness of segmentation bases which allows better targeting and positioning.

BRANDING IN PRACTICE
Major segmentation systems offered by specialist companies

As just illustrated, segmentation can become a complex exercise as one starts adding more variables in the mix. To help brands achieve their aims, a number of leading market research and data analytics firms have developed segmentation systems. Herein, three of the leading such segmentation systems are discussed – PRIZM, Mosaic and Acorn. These systems can be useful in improving brands' overall efficiency and effectiveness in reaching their target audiences. By leveraging these systems, brands can customize their segmentation, targeting and positioning strategy effectively. Thus, they can strengthen their marketing efforts and services to provide enhanced value to their specific consumer groups.

Potential Rating Index by ZIP Market (PRIZM), developed by Claritas, is a segmentation tool that utilizes all the segmentation bases, to classify USA-based households into 68 segments.[39] It utilizes a combination of data sources, including socio-economic rank (income, education, occupation and home value) as well as 11 life-stage groups and 14 social groups. Life-stage groups are based on age, affluence and the presence of children. Social groups are based on affluence and whether they live in a city, second-tier city, the suburbs or small towns and rural areas. The tool also incorporates various offline and online data sources that capture purchase behaviours and media behaviours including TV, cable, internet browsing, social media, podcast listening, mobile, audio and print behaviours.

Mosaic is a consumer classification system developed by the information services and analytics firm Experian to classify and identify the structure of UK society.[40] It aims to categorize individuals and households into 15 groups and 66 types based on a wide range of factors, including demographic, lifestyle, buying behaviour and attitudes. Mosaic provides insights into consumer preferences, spending patterns, media consumption habits and other relevant characteristics. Using Big Data analytics including the latest satellite remote sensing technology, global data and machine learning algorithms, Experian have also created a segmentation tool called Worldview that offers geo-level demographic attributes for 250 by 250 metre grids globally.

Acorn is a geo-demographic segmentation of residential neighbourhoods in the UK. It classifies more than 1.6 million postcodes in the country into one of 65 types. The 65 types aggregate into 22 Acorn groups which lie within 7 Acorn categories at the top level.[41] These types are based on 800 variables that describe the consumers.

Chapter summary

This chapter focused on a vital component of brand management – brand position-ing. We first defined what brand positioning is and how this schema can help brands in distinguishing themselves in a competitive marketplace. Brand positioning is per-ceptual. Managers can easily conceptualize the intended positioning for their brand. However, in practice, it is much more complex and takes considerable time and re-sources to achieve a desired position in consumer minds in comparison with the competitors. Brand association, brand image and brand symbolism play a vital role in developing and achieving brand positioning. Brands should clearly understand their points of convergence (PoC) and points of divergence (PoD) in order to devise effective brand communications. Perceptual maps are an important tool for managers in understanding their brand's PoC and PoD against competitors. Utilizing a variety of segmentation bases brands can connect better with their target market through appropriate positioning.

Key concepts

- Brand positioning
- Segmentation, targeting and positioning
- Brand association
- Brand image
- Brand symbolism
- Points of convergence (PoC) and points of divergence (PoD)
- Perceptual map
- Segmentation bases
  - Demographic
  - Geographic
  - Psychographic
  - Behavioural

Exercise questions

1 Visit the Colgate toothpaste website (www.colgate.com/en-gb/products/toothpaste) and examine the variants of the original toothpaste brand. If given a choice, how would you consolidate or differentiate Colgate's positioning in the market?

2 Following your Colgate exercise, now visit the Arm & Hammer (www.armandhammer.com/oral-care/toothpastes) and Aquafresh (www.aquafresh.com/products.html) websites and examine the brand positioning of their sub-products. What would you suggest both of these brands do with regards to their brand positioning?

3 Given that Colgate, Arm & Hammer and Aquafresh offer similar variants of toothpaste catering to similar oral health issues, how do you think they are differentiated in consumer minds?

4 Identify points of convergence (PoC) and points of divergence (PoD) for a minimum of 10 brands in the following categories: (a) fashion; (b) automobiles; and (c) smartphones.

5 Draw a perceptual map for a product category of your choice.

6 Identify segmentation bases utilized by prominent brands in: (a) shampoo; (b) sports clothing; (c) sneakers; (d) washing machines; and (e) airlines.

CASE STUDY Gymshark

Read the article in *Forbes* about the development and growth of the sports apparel brand GymShark. In it, GymShark's approach is summarized as:

- Staying humble
- Focusing on customer needs
- Being visionaries
- Building an influencer community
- Assembling a dream team
- Documenting everything
- Building the founder's profile

SOURCE www.forbes.com/sites/jodiecook/2020/08/17/how-gymshark-became-a-13bn-brand-and-what-we-can-learn/?sh=22d3fe9176ed

Case questions

1 Based on the case study, discuss how Gymshark was able to create its unique positioning in the athleisure market.

2 Draw a perceptual map of the athleisure market using any two criteria of your choice.

3 Thinking about segmentation bases, which particular segmentation bases and variables were used by Gymshark in targeting its customers?

4 What types of brand associations, image and symbolic facets of brand positioning were used by Gymshark?

Endnotes

1 Ries, A, and Trout, J (1972) The positioning era cometh, *Advertising Age*, 24 (4), 35–38

2 Sujan, M and Bettman, J R (1989) The effects of brand positioning strategies on consumers' brand and category perceptions: Some insights from schema research, *Journal of Marketing Research*, 26 (4), 454–67

3 Singh, J, Ehrenberg, A and Goodhardt, G (2008) Measuring customer loyalty to product variants, *International Journal of Market Research*, 50 (4), 513–32

4 www.colgate.com/en-gb/products/toothpaste (archived at https://perma.cc/KV29-MDQ5)

5 Alba, J W, Hutchinson, J W and Lynch Jr, J G (1991) Memory and decision making, in *Handbook of Consumer Behavior*, ed. T S Robertson and H H Kassarjian, Prentice-Hall, Englewood Cliffs, NJ, pp 1–49

6 Sujan, M (1985) Consumer knowledge: Effects on evaluation strategies mediating consumer judgments, *Journal of Consumer Research*, 12 (June), 31–46

7 Broniarczyk, S M and Alba, J W (1994) The importance of the brand in brand extension, *Journal of Marketing Research*, 31 (May), 214–28

8 Schnittka, O, Sattler, H and Zenker, S (2012) Advanced brand concept maps: A new approach for evaluating the favorability of brand association networks, *International Journal of Research in Marketing*, 29 (3), 265–74

9 Greenwald, A G and Leavitt, C (1984) Audience involvement in advertising: Four levels, *Journal of Consumer Research*, 11 (June), 581–92

10 Keller, K L (1993) Conceptualizing, measuring, and managing customer-based brand equity, *Journal of Marketing*, 57 (January), 1–22

11 Sasmita, J and Mohd Suki, N (2015) Young consumers' insights on brand equity: Effects of brand association, brand loyalty, brand awareness, and brand image, *International Journal of Retail & Distribution Management*, 43 (3), 276–92

12 Anderson, J R and Bower, G H (1973) *Human Associative Memory*, Halstead, New York

13 van Osselaer, S M J and Alba, J W (2000) Consumer learning and brand equity, *Journal of Consumer Research*, 27 (June), 1–16

14 Gluck, M A and Bower, G H (1988) From conditioning to category learning: An adaptive network model, *Journal of Experimental Psychology: General*, 117 (September), 227–47

15 Van Osselaer, S M J and Janiszewski, C (2001) Two ways of learning brand associations, *Journal of Consumer Research*, 28 (2), 202–23

16 www.laptopmag.com/articles/sony-vaio-batteries-recalled#:~:text=Sony%20is%20recalling%20the%20lithium,overheat%2C%20risking%20burns%20and%20fire (archived at https://perma.cc/JT7X-L6ZD)

17 www.cpsc.gov/Recalls/2016/Sony-Recalls-VAIO-Laptop-Computer-Battery-Packs (archived at https://perma.cc/BL6X-NEEJ)

18 Patterson, M (1999) Re-appraising the concept of brand image, *Journal of Brand Management*, 6, 409–26

19 Faircloth, J B, Capella, L M and Alford, B L (2001) The effect of brand attitude and brand image on brand equity, *Journal of Marketing Theory and Practice*, 9 (3), 61–75

20 East, R, Singh, J, Wright, M and Vanhuele, M (2021) *Consumer Behaviour: Applications in marketing*, 4th edn, Sage, London

21 https://knowledge.wharton.upenn.edu/podcast/knowledge-at-wharton-podcast/volkswagen-diesel-scandal/ (archived at https://perma.cc/GGW6-C7UP)

22 East, R, Singh, J, Wright, M and Vanhuele, M (2021) *Consumer Behaviour: Applications in marketing*, 4th edn, Sage, London

23 Mckellar, P (1957) *Imagination and Thinking: A psychological analysis*, Basic Books, Oxford,

24 Romaniuk, J (2013) Modeling mental market share, *Journal of Business Research*, 66 (2), 188–95

25 Holt, D B (2005) How societies desire brands: Using cultural theory to explain brand symbolism, in *Inside Consumption*, Routledge, pp 273–91

26 Klink, R R (2000) Creating brand names with meaning: The use of sound symbolism, *Marketing Letters*, 11, 5–20

27 https://edition.cnn.com/2011/10/06/opinion/apple-logo/index.html (archived at https://perma.cc/G2EB-EZ7N)

28 Schmitt, B (2012) The consumer psychology of brands, *Journal of Consumer Psychology*, 22 (1), 7–17

29 Arnould, E J and Thompson, C J (2005) Consumer culture theory (CCT): Twenty years of research, *Journal of Consumer Research*, 31 (4), 868–82

30 Woodside, A G, Sood, S and Miller, K E (2008) When consumers and brands talk: Storytelling theory and research in psychology and marketing, *Psychology & Marketing*, 25 (2), 97–145

31 Holt, D B (2004) *How Brands Become Icons: The principles of cultural branding*, Harvard Business Press, Boston

32 Morhart, F, Malär, L, Guèvremont, A, Girardin, F and Grohmann, B (2015) Brand authenticity: An integrative framework and measurement scale, *Journal of Consumer Psychology*, 25 (2), 200–18

33 Nenkov, G Y and Scott, M L (2014) 'So cute I could eat it up': Priming effects of cute products on indulgent consumption, *Journal of Consumer Research*, 41 (2), 326–41

34 Puzakova, M and Aggarwal, P (2018) Brands as rivals: Consumer pursuit of distinctiveness and the role of brand anthropomorphism, *Journal of Consumer Research*, 45 (4), 869–88

35 Wang, Q and Shukla, P (2013) Linking sources of consumer confusion to decision satisfaction: The role of choice goals, *Psychology & Marketing*, 30 (4), 295–304

36 www.theverge.com/2018/6/27/17510908/apple-samsung-settle-patent-battle-over-copying-iphone (archived at https://perma.cc/S8DM-JH9V)

37 Kotler, P (2017) Philip Kotler: Some of my adventures in marketing, *Journal of Historical Research in Marketing*, 9 (2), 203–08

38 Dibb, S (1999) Criteria guiding segmentation implementation: Reviewing the evidence, *Journal of Strategic Marketing*, 7 (2), 107–29

39 https://claritas.com/prizm-premier/ (archived at https://perma.cc/QX4W-9S2V)

40 www.experian.co.uk/business/platforms/mosaic (archived at https://perma.cc/2FUW-P74U)

41 https://acorn.caci.co.uk/ (archived at https://perma.cc/JW8M-VMKP)

Brand communication

07

Overview

In this chapter, we first discuss how a brand's primary function pertains to communication. We then introduce the prevalent theories in advertising including AIDA, ATR and ELM. We also provide an overall view on the current state of the debate. Further, we bring in the signalling role of brands, from economics and evolutionary psychology perspectives. In the section, we take a novel perspective on how brand communication influences individual identities, both social and personal, and in turn how individual identities are shaped to be congruent with the brand. In the following two sections, we introduce two powerful theories that provide deeper understanding of individuals' relationships with brands, where brand communication aggravates compensatory consumption and often functions as a tool for individuals' impression management. This chapter contains some well-known cases in brand communication.

Key learning outcomes

Upon reading this chapter, you should be able to

- Understand how brands function as a communication tool
- Learn about the well-known theories in brand communication
- Understand the debate on how brands shape identities
- Develop insights on psychological theories that influence brand communication
- Be informed about the role of brand communication in the digital age

Brand as the key communication tool

As mentioned in earlier chapters, brands are a vital tool for any organization in communicating their distinctiveness from competitors. In Chapter 4, we discussed how brand features such as Appealing, Legitimate, Applicable, Recognizable, and Meaningful (ALARM), coupled with brand elements such as the name, logo, slogan, persona, digital presence, sounds and jingles, and packaging, help brands to distinguish themselves.

Companies use their brand elements in a variety of ways to communicate their brand identity to the wider public. Moreover, depending on the aim of the communication, such as information, persuasion, image creation, reassurance and reminder, brand elements are used differently by companies. For example, in many parts of the world, orange juice was not considered a breakfast drink, even 30 years ago. While oranges were consumed, orange juice was not a staple part of breakfast.[1] This changed considerably when Del Monte Foods, one of the largest producers and distributors of processed fruits and juices, ran a worldwide campaign featuring British actor Brian Jackson in the mid-1980s. The campaign's slogan, 'The man from Del Monte, he say yes!'[2] became an instant catchphrase leading to the acceptance of orange juice as a breakfast drink. Within a decade of the campaign execution, a report from the US Department of Agriculture (USDA) in 2003 concluded that on any given day only 5 per cent of US citizens consumed fresh oranges while 21 per cent consumed orange juice.[3]

While Del Monte aimed to change usage behaviour relating to the consumption of its product, Stella Artois, the lager brand, used brand communication to change consumer perceptions towards paying a higher price. Due to its higher alcohol content, the brand had to pay higher duty in the United Kingdom, which made the cost higher compared to the competitors. Stella launched the 'reassuringly expensive' campaign with the help of advertising agency Lowe to create a positive assurance that by being more expensive, its premium lager was better than the cheaper brands.[4] Using highly creative advertisements that used themes such as war movies, silent comedy and surrealism to portray an image of sophistication associated with the beverage, the brand was able to capture the public imagination.

De Beers, a leading diamond consortium that specializes in diamond mining, extraction, retail and trading, created a completely new behaviour globally through brand communication, also known as the 'diamond invention'.[5] When the company discovered massive diamond mines in South Africa in the late 19th century, they realized that only by maintaining the fiction that diamonds are scarce and invaluable could diamond prices be kept high. By controlling all the facets of the diamond business from mining to retail, the company was able to control the supply and by using the brand communication, it increased the demand. In the mid-1930s, the brand used communication to persuade young American men that diamonds were synonymous with romance and the measure of a men's personal and professional success directly correlated with the size and the quality of diamond that they purchased for their partner. Moreover, they also campaigned to convince young women that love was measured through a gift received, a diamond.[6] The brand communicated this through idols of romance including Hollywood personalities, political leaders, their spouses and daughters. The company also created a weekly service which provided 125 leading newspapers with descriptions of the diamonds worn by movie stars. Such communication tactics honed over the years have resulted in global success. For instance, in Japan, the percentage of first-time brides who receive a diamond engagement ring increased from 5 per cent in 1965 to 77 per cent in 1995. Similarly, in China, one of the fastest-growing retail markets for diamonds, less than 1 per cent of first-time brides received a diamond engagement ring in 1994, but this increased to 31 per cent in 2010 and over 50 per cent in 2019.[7][8]

While brand communication can help a brand create distinctiveness and propel its market share and revenues, if the claims made in the brand communication are not supported in product functionality, customers will not stay connected with the brand. Exaggerations about product performance through brand communication can backfire when the product does not meet customer expectations.[9] The issue of robust and valid claims in brand communication had led to research on communication ethics,[10] product harm[11] and brand transgression.[12] This has also culminated in related regulations and appropriate legislative bodies that examine miscommunications and false claims. For instance, in the UK, the advertising watchdog ASA (Advertising Standards Authority) banned a campaign by Toyota and Hyundai for making exaggerated claims about the speed at which their electric cars can be charged and misleading consumers about the availability of rapid-charging points across the UK and Ireland.[13] Similarly, the watchdog also banned a series of advertisements from HSBC for being misleading about its green credentials. The bank did not mention its financing of fossil fuel projects or links to deforestation.[14]

Theories in brand communication

Along with the development of brand communication, research interest has grown in this domain. A number of prominent theories have emerged over the past few decades aiming to explain the underlying processes involved in brand communication, mainly in advertising. These theories are grouped as 'strong' and 'weak' theories of communications. These two contrasting perspectives provide insights into the impact and role of communication in shaping consumer attitudes and behaviours.

The strong theory of communication is also termed as the persuasive view, which characterizes the role of communication as having a strong influence on shaping the receivers' actions, attitudes and behaviours. Communication from this theoretical viewpoint is seen as a potent tool that can influence consumer desires, emotions and could also drive cultural norms. In contrast, the weak theory assumes the role of communication as a means to convey information to potential consumers as well as to remind existing consumers about the brand. This viewpoint espouses communication

Figure 7.1   Hierarchy of Effects models

AIDA	DAGMAR
Awareness	Awareness
Interest	Comprehension
Desire	Conviction
Action	Action

as a source of information that can help consumers make informed decisions by themselves. It proposes that the brand communication should be focused on details about features, benefits, prices and availability of the brand, and such information will, in turn, help consumers in their decision making. While these theories offer different perspectives, brand communication can serve both persuasive and informative functions depending on the context and the specific goals set by the managers.

Several important theories in the field of brand communication have emerged including Hierarchy of Effects models such as AIDA and DAGMAR (see Figure 7.1), as well as other process theories such as Elaboration Likelihood Model (ELM) and Advertising, Trial and Reinforcement (ATR). Hierarchy of effects models build on the notion that consumers move through a series of stages in their decision-making process. The AIDA model, as the name suggests, includes four hierarchical components, namely Awareness, Interest, Desire and Action. The DAGMAR model, which stands for Defining Advertising Goals for Measured Advertising Results, identifies the sequence of hierarchy as Awareness, Comprehension, Conviction and Action.[15] Figure 7.1 provides a comparison of the hierarchy.

The process-based account of brand communication is reflected in theories such as Elaboration Likelihood Model (ELM) and Advertising, Trial and Reinforcement (ATR). ELM describes the change of attitude through two major routes of persuasion: the central route and the peripheral route (see Figure 7.2).[16] When the message recipient has the motivation and the ability to think about the message and its topic, they use the central route. However, consumers use peripheral route when they have little or no interest in the subject and have lesser ability to process the message. In the peripheral route, consumers rely on heuristics and rules of thumb in message processing.

The ATR model highlights that brand communication works for the existing buyers of a brand (see Figure 7.3).[17] The central assumption of this theory is that the main

Figure 7.2 Elaboration Likelihood Model (ELM)

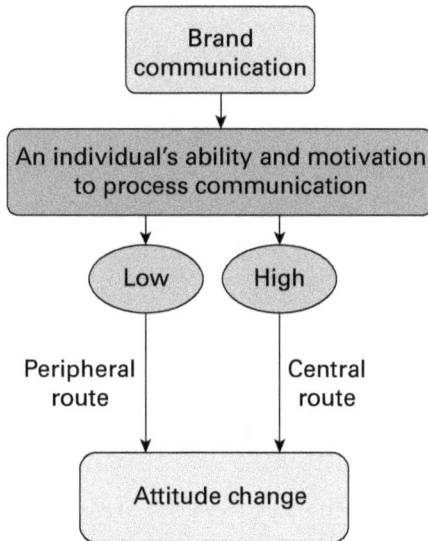

SOURCE Adapted from Petty and Cacioppo (1986)

Figure 7.3 Advertising, Trial and Reinforcement (ATR) model

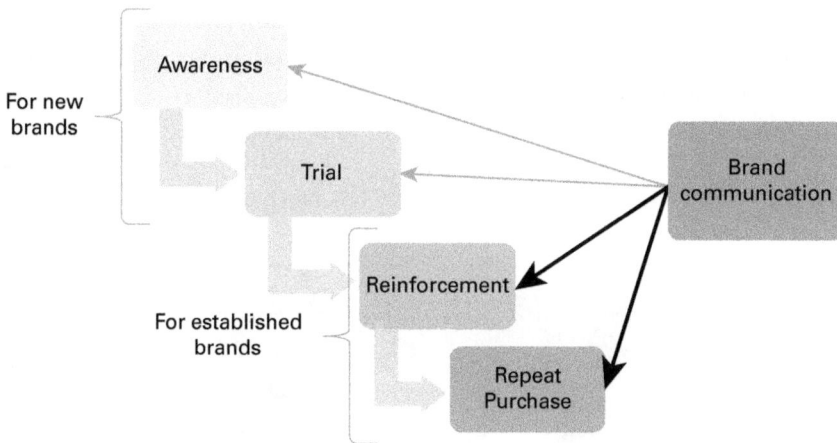

role of brand communication 'is to reinforce feelings of satisfaction with brands already bought'.[18] In this theory, consumers first gain awareness or interest, which leads to trial purchase, which in turn leads to a repeat-buying habit. However, for frequently bought products, repeat buying is the central determinant of sales volume and thus the role of brand communication in this situation is to reinforce rather than be persuasive. It means that when buyers are already aware of the brand, the role of communication is to reinforce their existing knowledge and beliefs about the brand, which can lead to repeat purchase. To maintain the market share through repeat purchase, communication mainly works through reminding and reinforcing the brand message, as denoted in the bold black arrows in Figure 7.3.

Each of the above theories offer an interesting account for brand communication, however, they have also been criticized for their specific limitations. For instance, ELM has been criticized for its descriptive nature,[19] unable to account for the changing levels of consumer involvement, the possibility that consumers may use both central and peripheral routes simultaneously,[20] and the role of situations, person and product categories that may lead to variance in chosen routes.[21] Similarly, Hierarchy of Effects models have been criticized for their lack of applicability to established brands when awareness is already present.[22]

Brands as communication signals

Most brands use visual and/or auditory elements to signal who they are to the wider population (Figure 7.4). These elements allow brands to convey their message about the brand's identity, image, functionality, distinctiveness, usage, status and other such aspects. Consumers, in turn, often utilize these brand elements to signal their own identity as well. Thus, brands fulfil two important roles: (a) communicate the product and its benefits; and (b) aid consumers in communicating their identity. These two roles are explained through signalling theory. The communication from the brand about the product and its benefits can be illustrated through the economics perspective of signalling theory. On the other hand, the consumer signalling through brand is grounded within the evolution biology and social psychology fields.

Figure 7.4   Electric cars are employing their green credentials as brand communication signals

SOURCE Unsplash (Michael Marais)

The economics perspective of signalling theory is based on the core idea of 'information asymmetry'. Information asymmetry pertains to the inequalities of knowledge between market actors, such as sellers and buyers.[23] The concept of signalling in economics was originally highlighted by Nobel laureate Michael Spence in his seminal work.[24] Spence argued that there is a knowledge gap between the sender and the receiver of a message. The sender aims to fill that gap by providing more information. In the branding context, this is highly relevant as in a competitive marketplace buyers may not possess the relevant information about every product or brand. Thus, it is paramount for brands to communicate their ability to fulfil customer expectations. Brands can do that by highlighting their functionality, novelty, social approval and many such other attributes.

This is relevant for every brand but even more important for new products. For instance, in the fast-growing electric car market, new brands are emerging at a rapid rate. Each automobile brand is highlighting their specific features pertaining to electric cars in terms of mileage on a single charge, speed of charging and electricity consumption, as well as their collaborative networks such as network of charging points and beneficial electricity supplier tariffs. Such information can alleviate knowledge gaps among potential electric car buyers.

While this information is available in the market, receivers may still remain sceptical, due to the reliability of information, one of the key conditions of signalling theory. For instance, while many electric car makers claim substantial mileage on a single charge, a study by the consumer body Which? found that since 2017 only one electric car met the official Worldwide Harmonized Light Vehicle Test Procedure (WLTP) that pertains to the mileage of the car in ideal road conditions.[25] Thus, a reliability signal challenge exists for electric cars in terms of their official mileage on a single charge. Electric car brands can provide transparent information about the ideal and real mileage and enhance their reliability signals.

On one hand, brands communicate their features, while on the other, consumers also use brands to signal their identity. In this regard, a substantial body of consumer research exists that is derived from evolutionary biology and social psychology.[26] [27] Research in evolutionary biology highlights that men use brands conspicuously, driven predominantly by their short-term mating motives,[28] while women use conspicuous brands to deter other female rivals,[29] and signal their mating standards to men and thereby deter undesirable pursuers.[30]

Many luxury brands highlight their logos prominently on their products which enables consumers to communicate their status.[31] Brands also use a variety of other signals to communicate their position in the market to assure consumers of their reliable signals. For example, in the UK retail market brands use a variety of positions, such as number 1 (Tesco), low price (Lidl and Asda), high quality (M&S and Waitrose) and frozen food (Iceland). Such signals can shape consumers' own preferences and identities. Price-conscious or quality-conscious consumers may prefer retailer brands that match with their identities.

BRANDING IN PRACTICE
Signalling misadventures at Starbucks

Starbucks, a global coffee brand, courted controversy regarding its stance on the Black Lives Matter (BLM) movement. As BLM gathered pace around the USA and in many other markets where Starbucks products are sold, the company announced its support via social media and press releases. It also pledged to donate $1 million to organizations promoting racial equity, diversity and inclusivity.

While signalling support towards the BLM movement publicly, Starbucks, initially, told its employees that they could not wear clothing and accessories that supported the movement, stating violation of the company's dress code policy. The company stated that employees were 'not permitted to wear buttons or pins that advocate a political, religious or personal issue'. However, such double-standards were shared by the employees on social media and the company received substantial public backlash.

Following the public uproar, Starbucks reversed its decision and handed out buttons supporting the cause. Moreover, the company also announced that it would design and distribute 250,000 T-shirts that feature a series of protest picket signs, including one that says 'Black Lives Matter'.

This example highlights the pivotal role of reliable and consistent signals in brand communication. When brands demonstrate consistent signals about their actions and intent, it can dampen hypocrisy perceptions and strengthen positive brand image.

The interactive relationship between brand communication and individual identities

Brands are part of consumers' daily lives and are woven into their life narratives. Thus, consumers attach meanings to their brands, knowingly or unknowingly, intentionally or unintentionally.[32] Consumers have beliefs about themselves, called self-concepts, which are reflected in their consumption of the brands. Consumers hold several types of self-concept. For instance, actual self reflects the attributes that the consumer actually possesses, such as level of intelligence, academic achievements and attractiveness.[33] The ideal self represents what the consumer would like to portray themselves to be which, in turn, motivates them to change, improve and achieve higher standards.[34] The social self refers to how the individual thinks other people perceive them. The ought self represents the sense of duty, obligation and responsibilities,[35] and the extended self is created by external objects such as brands that one possesses or surrounds oneself with.[36] [37]

Brand communication aids consumers to establish and manage their self-concepts and thus the relationship between the individual and social identity is intertwined. Social identity reflects a consumer's perceived membership of a relevant social group. Social groups are identified as in-group and out-groups. Research shows that consumers buy and consume brands that match with their in-groups and avoid brands preferred by their out-groups.[38] When consumers discover that the brand preferred by them and their in-group is rejected by others, they demonstrate defensive behaviours such as advocating the brand, and even trading up to a premium version of the brand.[39] Research also shows that consumers use different types of brands to negotiate their identity in a variety of settings.[40]

Many successful brands understand and utilize this interactive nature of identity through their communications. For instance, Dove, a personal care brand from Unilever, realized from its market research that the traditional fashion-model-driven aspirational marketing that focused on an ideal self was causing anxiety among its consumers. Its research showed that only 2 per cent of women considered themselves beautiful. In response to this, Dove created its 'real beauty' campaign, which employed women with different body shapes and colours as models. The campaign was an instant success globally and the brand sales increased from $2 billion a year to $4 billion within three years of the campaign.[41]

BRANDING IN PRACTICE

'Don't Buy This Jacket'! Patagonia invokes consumers' ought and ideal selves

Patagonia, founded in 1973 by climbing enthusiast Yvon Chouinard, has continuously focused on environmental sustainability in its brand communication. In 2011, on Black Friday, Patagonia launched a full-page advertisement in the *New York Times*, with the slogan 'Don't Buy This Jacket'.[42] Black Friday is celebrated in the United States as the day after Thanksgiving in the month of November, and traditionally marks the start of the Christmas shopping season, with high discounts offered on the day to attract shoppers. Patagonia, instead of encouraging the shopping spree like other brands, decided to address the issue of consumerism head on through this advertisement. The campaign aimed at establishing Patagonia as a leading brand selling sustainable products.

The advert also highlighted the environmental costs of producing the jacket and by promoting anti-consumption, the brand took a stance against fast fashion. Moreover, the common threats initiative pledge launched by the brand at the same time focused on reducing consumption, repairing, reusing and recycling goods. The campaign's communication appealed to consumers' responsibilities and aspirations towards securing the planet's future, connecting with their 'ought and ideal selves'. The campaign was highly successful for the brand in terms of sales gain, and at the same time, in raising awareness regarding the issues of consumerism, fast fashion and its environmental impact.[43]

Brand communication and compensatory consumption in the digital age

As discussed in the earlier section, brands are an important aspect of expressing consumer identities. Consumers regularly define themselves through their craft, hobbies, work and education which are recognized by others as indicators of attainments. When such indicators of attainment are lacking or weak, consumers use alternative symbols of self-definition to compensate their own shortcomings.[44] In this regard, brands have become prominent avenues of alternative symbols of self-completion. For example, a low-income consumer may invest in buying high-end products such as luxury brands as a compensation mechanism of their lack of wealth (i.e. indicator of attainment). This phenomenon is called compensatory consumption, defined as a reactionary consumption behaviour to quell or eliminate the experienced self-identity threat.[45] Compensatory consumption can take many forms depending on the lack of attainments and the standard of comparison. For instance, if your neighbour (i.e. standard of comparison) bought a new automobile, you may decide to buy a new car or another conspicuous product to attain symbolic self-completion. Research points out that consumers typically offset comparisons to higher status and wealthier individuals by identifying an alternative domain in which they believe they fare more favourably than the higher-status person and by displaying success and achievement in these domains.[46] For example, consumers of inexpensive cars display car bumper stickers relating to golf club membership and marathon completion, which highlight their membership or accomplishments in another domain.

Brands have long understood consumers' need for symbolic self-completion and resultant compensatory consumption. In this regard, brands use a variety of tactics to induce compensatory consumption. In sectors such as make-up, cosmetics, fashion and other personal care brands have used highly attractive models and celebrities, perpetuating the ideal of body shape in their communications. For example, in the oral hygiene market, a toothpaste brand communicating 'whiter than white' teeth can make the receivers feel inadequate about the whiteness of their own teeth, leading to the purchase of the brand. Such brand communication can create a discrepancy between the target consumers' actual and ideal selves, which, in turn, would drive the need for compensatory consumption.

Compensatory consumption is further pronounced in digital environments due to constant and continuously evolving comparative standards of attainment. While research is still nascent in this area, the concept is highly applicable in the context of digital consumption. Social media influencers induce the desire for further consumption of products that they endorse through creating a sense of discrepancy amongst the followers. Similarly, other consumers posting their lifestyle and brand choices on social media platforms such as Instagram, Facebook, Snapchat and TikTok may also create a lack of self-attainment perceptions. The digital environment can, thus, induce compensatory consumption. While many brands regularly engage with social media and the influencers in promoting their products to increase sales, they should remain aware of the precepts of ethical marketing and responsible behaviour.

Brand as tools for individual impression management

Another important theory from social psychology that enriches the domain of brand signalling is impression management. Emerging from the seminal work by Erving Goffman, this theory describes efforts by a consumer to create and maintain their identity to match with the image held by their target audience.[47] While impression management has been studied extensively in organizational psychology and organization management literature,[48] marketing and brand management domains have yet to explore the applications. By engaging in impression management, consumers project their desired image and avoid portraying an undesired image.[49] Researchers suggest that consumers use two types of impression management tactics, namely defensive and assertive.[50]

Defensive tactics are employed to defend or restore an identity, and include excuses, justifications, disclaimers, self-handicapping and apologies. On the other hand, assertive tactics are used for developing or maintaining identities and include tactics such as ingratiation, intimidation, supplication, entitlement, enhancement, and exemplification.[51] For example, consumers use brands that promote their sustainability credentials as part of their exemplification tactic so they can present themselves as having social consciousness. Similarly, consumers also employ ingratiation regularly by flattering others' brand choices and giving expensive gifts. Power dressing is associated with intimidation tactics. Given that consumers use impression management regularly, further research can reveal insights into applications in brand communication.

In the digital age, signalling through brand communication has evolved further. In recent years, a number of social media platforms such as Instagram and Snapchat have emerged that focus on the visual representation. Consequently, many consumers use brands to curate their own identity in a desirable fashion. Examples of such behaviour can be found in people conspicuously highlighting clothing and hairstyles and image projection using specific brands that are related to high status on social media. The tendency to manage one's online impression using brands has fuelled the growth of multibillion dollar industries including luxury goods, personal grooming, diet, cosmetics and exotic tourism. Accordingly, brands have strengthened their presence on social media platforms.

Scholarly debate

Bolino, M, Long, D and Turnley, W (2016) Impression management in organizations: Critical questions, answers, and areas for future research, *Annual Review of Organizational Psychology and Organizational Behavior*, 3, 377–406

Lee, S J, Quigley, B M, Nesler, M S, Corbett, A B and Tedeschi, J T (1999) Development of a self-presentation tactics scale, *Personality and Individual Differences*, 26 (4), 701–22

In conclusion, the theories from the different disciplines discussed above enrich our understanding of how brand communication functions. It is, however, important to consider that while offering deeper insights into the underlying processes that drive consumer-brand relationships, many of these theories may seem overlapping in their scope and meaning. For example, self-concept- and identity-related theories reflect on consumer's sense of self as it is, as well as within a group and society, and impression management theory offer how consumers signal and manage their identity. Similarly, the different hierarchy of effects models discussed are flexible and allow brands to adapt their campaigns, depending on the communication aims (i.e. awareness, persuasion, image creation) and market position (e.g. new or established). Overall, the advancements in knowledge provide insights about multiple ways that brands can achieve the goal of building strong customer relationships.

Chapter summary

In this chapter, we first understood how brands play a vital role in communicating the value and ethos of a firm. Moreover, through the examples of brands such as Del Monte, De Beers and others, we also learned how brand communication is critical to the success of an organization. Thereafter, we explored the various theories of brand communication that emerge from the field of advertising including the different Hierarchy of Effects models, ELM and ATR. Brand communication as signalling has been studied from a variety of lenses including economics, evolutionary biology and psychology. While the economics-driven perspective offers a way to understand how brands can signal their position in the market, the psychology-driven research shows how consumers use brands to signal their own identity. Thus, brand communication and individual identity at both personal and social levels are intertwined. In today's digital age, brands also allow consumers an avenue to fulfil their identity-driven goals through compensatory consumption. Moreover, consumers regularly use brands to manage their impression in both offline and online domains. In summary, brand communication has assumed even greater importance as a strategic tool for organizational success.

Key concepts

- Brand communication
- Hierarchy of effects model
  - AIDA
  - DAGMAR
  - ELM
  - ATR
- Brand signalling
- Self-identity
- Social identity
- Compensatory consumption
- Impression management

Exercise questions

1 Using your own examples, explain how brand communication can help companies achieve success.

2 Critically reflect on why brand communication is vital in today's market.

3 Explain the hierarchy of effects models and critically reflect on their advantages and shortcomings.

4 Brands are intertwined with consumer identities. Explain, providing examples.

5 Using examples, discuss how and why consumers use brands as compensatory consumption tools.

6 Discuss the impression management tactics through the usage of brands that you have observed amongst your peers.

CASE STUDY   How to develop a jewellery icon

Introduction

Luxury jewellery brands often rely on 'iconic' designs to build brand recognition and drive sales growth. These signature pieces encapsulate a brand's history and aesthetic, provide an aspirational entry point for customers and can account for a significant portion of revenue. An icon transcends mere adornment; it embodies a brand's narrative, resonates with diverse audiences and fuels financial success. This case study analyses how iconic designs have supported the business strategies and performance of leading jewellery houses like Cartier, Bulgari and Chaumet.

Chaumet's Bee My Love collection

The 243-year-old French jewellery brand Chaumet is known for its exclusive tiaras but has also successfully developed iconic ranges like 'Bee My Love' at more accessible price points. The bee motif alludes to Chaumet's history as the official jeweller of Napoleon Bonaparte, who adopted the bee symbol. The Bee My Love collection includes plain gold rings from €1,090 up to diamond-encrusted designs at €98,600. As Chaumet CEO Jean-Marc Mansvelt notes, building icons requires long-term discipline and investment. But ultimately only the customer can make an icon successful with continuous engagement and purchase of the brand. Bee My Love represents Chaumet's origins and has become central to its brand narrative and revenue mix.

Cartier's Trinity and Love collections

Cartier's Trinity design originated in 1924 from a custom ring commission but has evolved into a globally recognized icon available in jewellery, watches and accessories. The silk Trinity cord bracelet retails for £720, providing an affordable entry point into the brand. Cartier's Love collection originated in 1969 as couple's bracelets but truly took off commercially with its symbolic design and aspirational sentiment. HSBC estimates that Love now generates nearly 20 per cent of Cartier's €10 billion annual revenues. Although initially organic creations, Cartier has since strategically invested in marketing and innovation around Trinity and Love to fully capitalize on their iconic status.

Bulgari's city-inspired icons

Bulgari has taken the more deliberate approach of linking its iconic designs with brand heritage. Its snake-shaped Serpenti range references ancient Roman mythology, while the round Diva and B.Zero1 collection alludes to Rome's famous Colosseum amphitheatre. Bulgari CEO Jean-Christophe Babin notes these vertical and horizontal adaptations have made Serpenti in particular commercially successful across diverse product categories. The strategy provides focus to Bulgari's icon efforts and consistency across its marketing communications.

Conclusion

Iconic designs have proven essential for luxury jewellery brands in establishing identity, connecting with customers and sustaining long-term sales growth. The quest for an iconic collection is a strategic endeavour demanding a delicate balance between tradition and innovation. Yet, icons cannot be artificially manufactured, and rely on authentic brand narratives combined with targeted brand communications, which can lead to strong consumer demand. Thus, building an icon requires more than just price tags. The most successful jewellery houses have strategically invested around organic icon innovations to fully capture their commercial potential.

Case questions

1 'Building an icon requires discipline... time and money.' Explain the statement in terms of brand communication.

2 The case discusses brands at various stages of iconicity. Using the ATR model, discuss how established and new brands should use brand communication.

3 The case states 'But ultimately only the customer can make an icon successful with continuous engagement and purchase of the brand'. Reflect critically on the intertwined nature of brand communication and consumer identity.

4 Imagine that you are the head of brand communication for the Serpenti range and are tasked with building a digital identity for this icon. What kind of digital brand communication and impression management tactics will you use to motivate your target consumers to engage with your brand through sharing, liking and commenting?

Endnotes

1 www.bbc.com/future/article/20220627-how-orange-juice-took-over-the-breakfast-table (archived at https://perma.cc/F8GQ-RZKD)

2 https://en.wikipedia.org/wiki/Man_from_Del_Monte (archived at https://perma.cc/BL6H-37XN)

3 www.ers.usda.gov/publications/pub-details/?pubid=37013 (archived at https://perma.cc/TPH5-AHKA)

4 O'Shaugnessy, J and O'Shaughnessy, N (2003) *Persuasion in Advertising*, Routledge

5 Epstein, E J (1982) Have you ever tried to sell a diamond?, *Atlantic Monthly*, 23, 363, www.theatlantic.com/magazine/archive/1982/02/have-you-ever-tried-to-sell-a-diamond/304575/ (archived at https://perma.cc/66T5-FDMX)

6 Friedman, U (2015) How an ad campaign invented the diamond engagement ring, *Atlantic Monthly*, www.theatlantic.com/international/archive/2015/02/how-an-ad-campaign-invented-the-diamond-engagement-ring/385376/ (archived at https://perma.cc/NU24-SHVH)

7 www.buzzfeednews.com/article/sapna/about-31-of-chinese-couples-using-diamond-engagement-rings-u#.rd2weWN6J (archived at https://perma.cc/YLK4-4GB9)

8 https://daxueconsulting.com/china-diamond-market/ (archived at https://perma.cc/G5C4-4Q2X)

9 Shiv, B, Carmon, Z and Ariely, D (2005) Ruminating about placebo effects of marketing actions, *Journal of Marketing Research*, 42 (4), 410–14

10 Cheney, G, May, S and Munshi, D (eds.) (2011) *The Handbook of Communication Ethics*, Routledge

11 Cleeren, K, Dekimpe, M G and Van Heerde, H J (2017) Marketing research on product-harm crises: A review, managerial implications, and an agenda for future research, *Journal of the Academy of Marketing Science*, 45, 593–615

12 Khamitov, M, Grégoire, Y and Suri, A (2020) A systematic review of brand transgression, service failure recovery and product-harm crisis: Integration and guiding insights, *Journal of the Academy of Marketing Science*, 48, 519–42

13 www.theguardian.com/media/2023/jun/28/advertising-watchdog-bans-hyundai-and-toyota-electric-car-ads (archived at https://perma.cc/LV6Y-QK2R)

14 www.ft.com/content/197dbd75-e0a6-4c1a-aef8-3b6dc60b4baf (archived at https://perma.cc/4EES-Q28Q)

15 Vakratsas, D and Ambler, T (1999) How advertising works: What do we really know?, *Journal of Marketing*, 63 (1), 26–43

16 Petty, R E and Cacioppo, J T (1986) *The Elaboration Likelihood Model of Persuasion*, Springer, New York, pp 1–24

17 Ehrenberg, A S (2000) Repetitive advertising and the consumer, *Journal of Advertising Research*, 40 (6), 39–48

18 Ehrenberg, A S (1974) Repetitive advertising and the consumer, *Journal of Advertising Research*, 14 (2), 25–34

19 Kitchen, P J, Kerr, G, Schultz, D E, McColl, R and Pals, H (2014) The elaboration likelihood model: Review, critique and research agenda, *European Journal of Marketing*, 48 (11/12), 2033–50

20 MacKenzie, S B, Lutz, R J and Belch, G E (1986) The role of attitude toward the ad as a mediator of advertising effectiveness: A test of competing explanations, *Journal of Marketing Research*, 23 (2), 130–43

21 Bitner, M J and Obermiller, C (1985) The elaboration likelihood model: Limitations and extensions in marketing, *ACR North American Advances*, 12, 420–25

22 Ehrenberg, A S (1974) Repetitive advertising and the consumer, *Journal of Advertising Research*, 14 (2), 25–34

23 Akerlof, G A (1970) The market for 'lemons': Quality uncertainty and the market mechanism, *The Quarterly Journal of Economics*, 84 (3), 488–500

24 Michael, S (1973) Job market signaling, *The Quarterly Journal of Economics*, 87, 354–74

25 www.which.co.uk/news/article/revealed-the-truth-about-electric-car-mileage-aC1bt9t5jU50 (archived at https://perma.cc/MHT5-UC6C)

26 Park, J K and John, D R (2010) Got to get you into my life: Do brand personalities rub off on consumers?, *Journal of Consumer Research*, 37 (4), 655–69

27 Dubois, D, Rucker, D D and Galinsky, A D (2012) Super size me: Product size as a signal of status, *Journal of Consumer Research*, 38 (6), 1047–62

28 Sundie, J M, Kenrick, D T, Griskevicius, V, Tybur, J M, Vohs, K D and Beal, D J (2011) Peacocks, Porsches, and Thorstein Veblen: Conspicuous consumption as a sexual signaling system, *Journal of Personality and Social Psychology*, 100 (4), 664–80

29 Wang, Y and Griskevicius, V (2014) Conspicuous consumption, relationships, and rivals: Women's luxury products as signals to other women, *Journal of Consumer Research*, 40 (5), 834–54

30 Chen, Q, Wang, Y and Ordabayeva, N (2023) The mate screening motive: How women use luxury consumption to signal to men, *Journal of Consumer Research*, 50 (2), 303–21

31 Han, Y J, Nunes, J C and Drèze, X (2010) Signaling status with luxury goods: The role of brand prominence, *Journal of Marketing*, 74 (4), 15–30

32 Belk, R W (1988) Possessions and the extended self, *Journal of Consumer Research*, 15 (2), 139–68

33 Sirgy, M J (1982) Self-concept in consumer behavior: A critical review, *Journal of Consumer Research*, 9 (3), 287–300

34 Landon Jr, E L (1974) Self concept, ideal self concept, and consumer purchase intentions, *Journal of Consumer Research*, 1 (2), 44–51

35 Higgins, E T (1987) Self-discrepancy: A theory relating self and affect, *Psychological Review*, 94 (3), 319–40

36 Reed, A (2002) Social identity as a useful perspective for self-concept-based consumer research, *Psychology & Marketing*, 19 (3), 235–66

37 Belk, R W (1988) Possessions and the extended self, *Journal of Consumer Research*, 15 (2), 139–68

38 Escalas, J E and Bettman, J R (2003) You are what they eat: The influence of reference groups on consumers' connections to brands, *Journal of Consumer Psychology*, 13 (3), 339–48

39 Khalifa, D and Shukla, P (2017) Me, my brand and I: Consumer responses to luxury brand rejection, *Journal of Business Research*, 81, 156–62

40 Banerjee, M, Shukla, P and Ashill, N J (2022) Situational ethnicity and identity negotiation: 'indifference' as an identity negotiation mechanism, *International Marketing Review*, 39 (1), 55–79

41 https://priceweber.com/2022/06/13/advertising-to-the-real-self-vs-the-ideal-self-when-do-we-become-friends/ (archived at https://perma.cc/CSA8-W3HN)

42 https://eu.patagonia.com/gb/en/stories/dont-buy-this-jacket-black-friday-and-the-new-york-times/story-18615.html (archived at https://perma.cc/M6VA-XLAR)

43 www.marketingweek.com/case-study-patagonias-dont-buy-this-jacket-campaign/ (archived at https://perma.cc/Y488-6SEX)

44 Wicklund, R A and Gollwitzer, P M (1981) Symbolic self-completion, attempted influence, and self-deprecation, *Basic and Applied Social Psychology*, 2 (2), 89–114

45 Kim, S and Rucker, D D (2012) Bracing for the psychological storm: Proactive versus reactive compensatory consumption, *Journal of Consumer Research*, 39 (4), 815–30

46 Goor, D, Keinan, A and Ordabayeva, N (2021) Status pivoting, *Journal of Consumer Research*, 47 (6), 978–1002

47 Goffmann, E (1959), *The Presentation of Self in Everyday Life*, Double Day, New York

48 Bolino, M, Long, D and Turnley, W (2016) Impression management in organizations: Critical questions, answers, and areas for future research, *Annual Review of Organizational Psychology and Organizational Behavior*, 3, 377–406

49 Berger, J and Heath, C (2007) Where consumers diverge from others: Identity signaling and product domains, *Journal of Consumer Research*, 34, 121–34

50 Tedeschi, J T and Melburg, V (1984), Impression management and influence in the organization, *Research in the Sociology of Organizations*, 3, 31–58

51 Lee, S-J, Quigley, B M, Nesler, M S, Corbett, A B and Tedeschi, J T (1999), Development of a self-presentation tactics scale, *Personality and Individual Differences*, 26 (4), 701–22

Consumer-brand relationships 08

Overview

In this chapter, we provide the origins of consumer-brand relationship, tracing the beginnings from relationship to marketing research. In the section following, we present an overview of some of the key concepts used in consumer-brand relationships, including self-brand connection, brand trust and commitment, brand attachment, brand engagement and brand love. We then explore the role played by consumer-brand relationships in influencing customer experience. The final section includes the latest developments in brand experience via digital and social media.

Key learning outcomes

Upon reading this chapter, you should be able to

- Understand how the notion of consumer-brand relationships research developed
- Gain insights on some of the key current concepts in consumer-brand relationships
- Critically understand the role of consumer-brand relationships in influencing customer experience
- Explore how consumer-brand relationships function in the digital and social media era

Origins and concepts of consumer-brand relationships

Brands are a bridge between the company and the consumer. For a company to be successful, they have to build a strong relationship between the consumer and a brand (Figure 8.1). The debate on the importance of this relationship between the consumer and the brand emerged with the development of relationship marketing theory in the mid-1990s.[1] Historically, as discussed in Chapters 1 and 2, brands were observed as merely identifiers of products or services for centuries, if not millennia. However, with the development of relationship marketing theory, scholars have grappled with questions such as whether, why and in what forms consumers seek and value relationships with brands.[2] Initial conceptualizations within this theory highlighted that consumers engage in relational market behaviour due to personal, social and institutional influences.[3] These influences coupled with consumers' motivation to simplify their decision making, information processing, reduce perceived risks and maintain cognitive consistency and a state of psychological comfort, were identified as major drivers of consumption choice. Researchers also suggested that family and social norms, peer group pressures, government mandates, religious tenets, employer influences and marketer policies also motivated consumers to build strong relationships with brands and organizations.[4]

In a seminal article, Susan Fournier criticized the traditional transactional nature of consumer-brand relationships in the business-to-consumer markets. The

Figure 8.1   Consumers search for a brand with which they feel connected

SOURCE Khuc Le Thanh Danh on Unsplash

author opined that the B2C markets can learn from how B2B sector partnerships evolve between suppliers and manufacturers.[5] Fournier proposed a renewed perspective that builds on relationship marketing theory, and argues that brands should be animated, humanized and personalized to form a relational bond with consumers. This perspective emphasizes that consumers form relationships with brands in the same way as people-to-people relations. Hence, brands have transitioned from mere transactional products or services to entities that play relational roles in people's lives. Fournier's work also emphasizes the dynamic nature of customer-brand relationships and the interplay between attachment and detachment. The work also reaffirms the earlier research on empirical generalizations (see Chapter 3), that customers do not exhibit unwavering loyalty to a single brand; instead, it recognizes that customers might engage with multiple brands, forming connections that vary in intensity and duration. Fournier's insights into the origins of customer-brand relationships underscore the complex interplay between individual identity, cultural context and brand symbolism. This perspective underscores the importance of understanding consumer behaviour beyond transactional exchanges, acknowledging the role of emotions, memories and aspirations in shaping enduring brand relationships.

The development of relational perspective allowed other researchers to examine consumer-brand relationships from varied angles. This led to a number of relationships-related constructs that are observed in people-to-people relationship being employed in branding context, including, love, passion, commitment, trust and engagement. The following sections explore these important consumer-brand relationships concepts including self-brand connection,[6] brand trust,[7] [8] brand commitment,[9] brand attachment[10] and brand love.[11] Consumer-brand relationships have thus become an umbrella term that encompasses a wide range of concepts as outlined above that have become central to brand management theory and are applied widely in branding practice.

Scholarly debate

Fournier, S (1998) Consumers and their brands: developing relationship theory in consumer research, *Journal of Consumer Research*, 24 (4), 343–73

Sheth, J N and Parvatiyar, A (1995) Relationship marketing in consumer markets: Antecedents and consequences, *Journal of the Academy of Marketing Science*, 23(4), 255–71

Self-brand connection

Self-brand connection is an important concept in branding that emerged in the mid-1990s. Self-brand connection builds on brand personality[12] and extended self-concept[13] wherein brands become an integral part of the consumer identity. This perspective posits that brands possess five distinct human-like qualities – sincerity, excitement, competence, sophistication and ruggedness – essentially forming a brand's identity. Extending this concept, Jennifer Escalas and James Bettman coined the termed self-brand connection, defined as an aggregate construct that captures the set of brand associations that are more meaningful and closely linked to the self-identity of a consumer.[14] Consumers choose a brand based on how well it may align with their self-image. In today's consumption-driven world, the notion that 'we are what we have' signifies how consumers extend their self-identity through objects, knowledge and habits. This concept is exemplified through actions like purchasing a prestige car to symbolize status or acquiring luxury clothing for societal recognition. Scholars have highlighted the importance of reference groups, which share similar beliefs and characteristics as the consumer, in shaping brand meanings.[15] Brands consistent with the ingroup positively impact self-brand connections, whereas those consistent with the outgroup have a negative effect.[16] Thus, self-brand connection operates not only individually but also collectively, encompassing family, group and national identities. Shared consumer passions for products or brands lead to identities expressed through concepts like brand communities,[17] brand tribes[18] and brand cults.[19] For consumers with high self-brand connection, their self-identity is tied to the brand. High self-brand connection can act as a barrier to negative events relating to the brand, including negative news or word-of-mouth, and brand rejection by others.[20] For instance, when Elon Musk decided to change the company name from Twitter to X, consumers reacted adversely by creating memes and demanding rollback to the original Twitter brand name.

When consumer identity is threatened by others rejecting the brand or outgroups using the brand, these consumers tend to trade up (i.e. buy a more premium version of the brand). For example, when young athletic consumers who have a strong self-brand connection with the brand Under Armour were informed that the brand was now preferred by non-athletic consumers, the athletic consumers demonstrated a greater willingness to upgrade and buy premium versions. Similarly, when young fashion-focused women with high self-brand connection to the brand Burberry were informed that working mums were avid consumers of the Burberry tote bag, they demonstrated a significant interest in purchasing a higher-priced version of the brand's handbags.[21] These examples demonstrate the dynamic relationship between consumers and the brands they use. Successful brands build strong connections with the consumers. The strength of self-brand connection acts as a buffer against adverse market events including negative word-of-mouth, service failures and reputation crisis.

Brand trust and brand commitment

Trust and commitment are basic aspects of any relationship. With the development of knowledge on consumer-brand relationship, why and how consumers trust their brands, and remain committed to these brands, have become important tenets of brand management discipline. Trust and commitment are by nature mutual and thus effort is required by both the brand and the consumer to maintain the relationship. The concept of brand commitment first emerged in the B2B relationships literature wherein the persistent desire to uphold a valued relationship between supplier and the manufacturer was explored.[22] In the consumer-brand relationships domain, commitment is characterized as a form of 'stickiness' fostering consumer loyalty even when satisfaction might be diminished.[23] Similarly, trust involves confidence in the integrity and reliability of the other party in the relationship.[24] Brand trust is defined as the willingness of the average consumer to rely on the ability of the brand to perform its stated function.[25] Thus, brand trust and brand commitment are interwoven as the former pertains to the brand delivering on its promise and the latter reflects the relationship strength that is formed based on the brand promise. In academic research, brand trust has been seen as a precursor to brand commitment which posits that relationships grounded in trust are esteemed to the extent that parties seek to commit to their continuation.[26] A brand makes a promise to gain and maintain consumer trust which, in turn, can lead to consumer commitment towards the brand.

BRANDING IN PRACTICE
Brand promise statements

Brands use catchy slogans and other tools to communicate their promise (as shown in Table 8.1). These promises can be functional, such as the price promise offered by many retailers such as Lidl, Target, Tesco, Wal-Mart and Wegmans. Many brands, on the other hand, highlight the pleasure of consuming the product, such as BMW, Marriott and Coca-Cola.

Not all brand promises are believed by consumers either. For instance, H&M, a fast fashion brand, and its claim on being good for the planet has been controversial among many consumer groups around the world. The brand has been given a low rating on its sustainability claims.[27] While H&M launched Conscious Collection, a line of clothing within the brand made of sustainably sourced materials, and in-store recycle bins, according to environmentalist Elizabeth Cline, less than 1 per cent of the clothes are collected back for recycling.[28] Of the clothes sent back to H&M, only 35 per cent of what's collected is recycled at all.[29]

Thus, catchy slogans of brand promise may not lead to consumer trust and commitment. However, a brand will have to act on the promises made to ensure that it is continued to be trusted.

Table 8.1   Example statements

Brand	Brand promise statement
Apple	Think different.
BMW	The ultimate driving machine.
Coca-Cola	To inspire moments of optimism and uplift.
Coors Light	The world's most refreshing beer.
De Beers	A diamond is forever.
Geico	15 minutes or less can save you 15% or more on car insurance.
H&M	More fashion choices that are good for people, the planet and your wallet.
Lidl	Big on quality, Lidl on price.
Marriott	Quiet luxury. Crafted experiences. Intuitive service.
Nike	To bring inspiration and innovation to every athlete in the world.
Target	Expect more, pay less.
Tesco	Every little helps.
Wal-Mart	Save money. Live better.
Wegmans	Consistent low prices.

SOURCE Power reviews[30]

Brand trust and brand commitment are multidimensional concepts. For example, brand trust is derived from several aspects, including shared values, competence, communication, opportunistic behaviour, reliability, integrity and benevolence.[31][32] Brand commitment is measured through three distinct dimensions, namely affective, continuance and normative.[33] Affective commitment entails a psychological attachment to the brand based on shared values and brand identification, linked to retention, repurchase, positive word-of-mouth and willingness to pay a premium. For instance, Apple consumers or Harry Potter fans (called Potterheads) queue up for hours in front of the stores in advance of a new product being launched (see Figure 8.2).

Continuance commitment reflects a rational dependence on the brand driven by limited alternatives or high switching costs, while normative commitment represents attachment due to personal obligation to the brand, influenced by social pressure and normative beliefs. While trust and commitment entail cognitive assessments of relationship-building benefits and risks, brand attachment and love address the emotional underpinnings of such relationships.

Figure 8.2 Consumers of Louis Vuitton waiting in a queue, showing the power of affective and normative commitment

SOURCE Photo by Melanie Pongratz on Unsplash

Brand attachment

Brand attachment reflects the strength of the bond connecting the brand with the self.[34] This bond is exemplified by the mental representation of the rich and accessible memory network which encompasses a consumer's positive thoughts and emotions pertaining to the brand and their own identity. Brand attachment consists of two sub-dimensions: self-brand connection (as discussed) and brand prominence. The brand prominence sub-dimension captures the salience of the cognitive and affective bond between the consumer and the brand. This salience is reflected in the immediate recall of the brand with perceived ease as well as the frequency with which brand-related thoughts and feelings are brought to mind.[35]

To create attachment among target consumers, brands have to focus on not only strengthening self-brand connection, but also, at the same time, they must enhance brand recall. To further improve brand recall, a strategically structured communications approach is recommended. For instance, L'Oréal Paris, a well-known global cosmetics brands, wanted to increase brand attachment among Canadian women in the 25–49 year age group. To achieve this, the brand posted sponsored advertisements showcasing models in a snowy outdoor shoot in Whistler, Canada. The eye-catching adverts used vibrant colours in the foreground with soft colours in background, and encouraged women to 'Dare to stand out from the crowd this winter' and 'Take winter beauty to new heights'. As a result, the brand achieved a 7-point lift in recommendations in this age group and doubled the average brand recall.[36] Similarly, after successfully revamping its iconic 500 model, the Italian automobile manufacturer Fiat launched the 500X crossover. In France, it targeted the over-35 potential car buyers using a structured YouTube-based campaign. The campaign achieved a 23 per cent increase in brand awareness and a 230 per cent increase in Google search traffic for the Fiat 500X model in France. The campaign even had a spillover effect wherein there was a 200 per cent increase in search volume for the Fiat brand.[37] The above examples show that structured and targeted brand communications, with high creative content that is original and relevant to the consumers, will lead to increase in self-brand connection and brand prominence. The increase in self-brand connection and prominence reflected in brand recall, in turn, increase brand attachment.

Brand love

A relatively recent conceptualization in consumer-brand relationships is brand love.[38] It encompasses the emotional needs that form the foundation of relationship-building. Similar to interpersonal love, brand love is the pinnacle of emotional attachment a consumer has with a brand. Scholars have examined brand love through a variety of methodologies and define brand love as the degree of passionate emotional attachment a satisfied consumer has for a particular brand.[39] Brand love differs from other brand-related emotions such as liking, because loved brands are deeply integrated with consumer identity and precludes negative feelings towards the brand. Based on the relational love prototype, scholars also argue that brand love is a fuzzy and complex concept. Thus, brand love encompasses a collection of 'thoughts, feelings, and actions that consumers arrange within a mental prototype'.[40]

Brand love can lead to several organizational advantages, including brand loyalty, positive word-of-mouth (WOM) and brand advocacy. Moreover, it can result in favourable brand associations, which subsequently forecast affective commitment and willingness to pay a premium price.[41] Managers can employ a variety of tactics to facilitate brand love among consumers including enabling passion-driven behaviours, self-brand integration, positive emotional connections and creating a sense of long-term relationship. For example, brands such as Patagonia and Body Shop created a sense of love among their customers by taking a consistent stance on specific global issues such as climate change and no animal testing for cosmetics.[42] Harley-Davidson is loved by its customers due to its creation and active management of a tightly-knit brand community. The brand regularly engages with its customers by creating emotional meaningful events such as music festivals or NASCAR races and through other digital engagements. Many consumers of Harley-Davidson even adorn the tattoo of the brand on their body, a show of love.

Thus, due to its emotional nature, brand love is often viewed as overlapping with brand passion, and emotional attachment, particularly in hedonic product categories, as opposed to utilitarian ones. This blurring of concepts raises questions about their distinctiveness, posing a research limitation concerning brand love.[43] The notion that brand love gives companies an advantage over 'unloved' competitors contradicts marketing empirical findings that show most brands, even the most beloved ones, have numerous sporadic buyers. Consumers often fail to perceive anything exceptional about the brands they use, even those they claim to love.[44] These critiques serve as a timely reminder to approach popular branding constructs with caution. Further empirical evidence from a behavioural perspective could assist in determining whether consumer love for brands is genuine and leads to better market performance or merely an academic concept with limited managerial relevance.

Scholarly debate

Batra, R, Ahuvia, A and Bagozzi, R P (2012) Brand love, *Journal of Marketing*, 76 (2), 1–16

Romaniuk, J (2013) What's (brand) love got to do with it?, *International Journal of Market Research*, 55 (2), 185–86

Brand engagement and customer experience

Brand engagement and customer experience are two essential pillars for successful branding, influencing how companies interact with their target audience and establish long-lasting connections. Brand engagement encompasses the emotional and cognitive relationship that customers form with a brand.[45] It goes beyond mere transactions, aiming to create meaningful interactions that foster loyalty and advocacy.[46] Successful brand engagement involves consistent messaging, immersive storytelling and a genuine alignment of values between the brand and its customers. By creating memorable experiences and eliciting positive emotions, companies can cultivate a strong sense of community and affinity among their customers.[47]

Customer experience, on the other hand, refers to the entirety of a customer's journey with a brand, encompassing every touchpoint from initial awareness to post-purchase interactions.[48] Customer experience is thus created by factors that brands control as well as outside its control, including influence of other people, consumer goals and purpose of shopping.[49] [50] In his book on customer experience management, Bernd Schmitt highlights five steps: (1) analysing the experiential world of the customers, (2) building the experiential platform, (3) designing the brand experience, (4) structuring the customer experience and (5) engaging in continuous innovation.[51] A seamless and delightful customer experience can significantly impact brand perception and loyalty.[52]

The intersection of brand engagement and customer experience is where brands can truly differentiate themselves from competitors. Engaging customers with consistent brand communications and authentic brand experiences at every touchpoint contributes to a positive customer journey.[53] When brand engagement strategies align seamlessly with a consistent customer experience, it results in a symbiotic relationship where customers not only buy products or services but also become emotionally attached to the brand's story and values. This interconnected approach fosters self-brand connection, encourages word-of-mouth marketing and positions the brand as more than just a transactional entity as well as a trusted companion.

BRANDING IN PRACTICE

Macmillan engagement campaign leads to additional
help for cancer sufferers

Macmillan, one of the largest UK-based charities in the fight against cancer, realized that cancer sufferers needed much more support in everyday tasks such as shopping, cleaning and ironing. Moreover, it was also observed from its research that one in four cancer patients did not have adequate support from family and friends.

To alleviate this issue, Macmillan's Team Up service came up with an idea of creating a region-specific, online marketplace that connected local community with cancer sufferers, so the patients could get vital everyday support. Additionally, the charity wanted to engage young volunteers from the local communities and make the experience safe and easy to use for everyone involved.

Macmillan employed a multichannel brand communications approach, wherein it used mobile technologies, traditional media and its in-person volunteering team to ensure the campaign's success. It used software to verify users' identity at a point of registration, created a unique brand identity that differentiated in colour and form factor from other Macmillan campaigns, and the dedicated community manager spent time working with local groups. The charity also ran bi-weekly user testing sessions to ensure buy-in from local communities.

This consistent and multipronged approach resulted in registrations exceeding 40 per cent of the target. While the campaign team assumed that support tasks by volunteers would be completed within three days of the cancer sufferer registering a task, the average task completion time was less than two days.[54] This case demonstrates the importance of consistent and creative brand communications supported by efficient processes, which can lead to successful brand engagement and fulfilling customer experience.

Brand engagement via digital and social media

In today's digital era, consumers not only expect high-quality products and services but also demand a personalized, convenient and intuitive journey. This includes factors like user-friendly interfaces, efficient problem-solving and personalized recommendations. Moreover, today's consumers rely on brand-related information from other consumers, rather than relying exclusively on marketing materials.[55] With increasing personalization, as seen on websites like Amazon or eBay, consumers now expect brands to treat them as a unique entity. Brands that prioritize and invest in enhancing their customer experience stand to gain a competitive edge, as satisfied customers are more likely to become repeat buyers and enthusiastic brand advocates.[56]

With emerging technological advancements such as social media, mobile commerce, web 2.0, virtual reality (VR), augmented reality (AR), multiplayer online games (MMORPG), eSports and artificial intelligence (AI), brand engagement via digital and social media has become extremely varied. Digital brand engagement, thus, has become critical for success in today's market. However, while offering opportunities for engaging with customers through a variety of platforms and technologies, it poses substantial challenges as brands have less control of their communications as explained in the following Branding in practice case.

BRANDING IN PRACTICE

Global recall of Samsung Galaxy Note 7: the power of consumer content and contempt in social media

On 2 August 2017, Samsung unveiled its flagship smartphone, the Galaxy Note 7, with great fanfare in New York, which boasted novel technologies including an iris scanner. By 19 August 2017, the phone was being sold in 10 markets including South Korea and United States with a scheduled launch in the European Union in October. However, within a week of the launch, customers started posting photos and videos of the phone overheating, exploding or catching fire. The news spread globally within hours and most major news outlets around the world were reporting it. While Samsung announced a voluntary global recall on 2 September 2017, more than 2.5 million Galaxy Note 7 phones were already sold in the market. On 8 September 2017, the Federal Aviation Administration of USA and airlines worldwide asked passengers with the Galaxy Note 7 to keep the phone turned off and not charge it throughout their journey. As consumer complaints about the phones surged, the US Consumer Product Safety Commission urged people to stop using the phone, leading Samsung to issue a formal recall on 15 September 2017.[57]

By 1 October 2017, Samsung started selling the phone again, stating the faults relating to the battery that caused the mishap was resolved. However, consumers who bought the new version started posting photos and videos again within a week, with viral videos of it on board a Southwest Airline flight in the USA emitting smoke and the plane having to be evacuated. With major US carriers like AT&T and T-Mobile stopping sales within a week, on 11 October 2017, Samsung announced it would stop selling the Galaxy Note 7 globally.

This example shows the power of content sharing on social media and how brands have to remain aware and agile in the face of consumer backlash. While product recalls have been a regular phenomenon in the market for decades, the advent of digital technologies has shifted the power base into the hands of the consumers. Three months after the recall and the stopping of production, Samsung announced that two separate problems with the lithium-ion batteries were to blame for the fires.[58]

The interactive nature of digital technologies coupled with global connectivity add further complexity to brand engagement challenges as outlined in the Samsung case. Consumers nowadays are not passive recipients of brand information, but act as co-creators.[59] Consumers create vast amount of audio-visual content and exchange amongst themselves through a variety of technologies.[60] For instance, text- and video-based product reviews, online forums, livestreaming and many other technological avenues are used by consumers to engage with and share their views about brands. For instance, livestream shopping is estimated to be worth $68 billion by 2026 in the USA alone.[61] However, the largest livestream shopping market in the world happens to be China wherein top streamers like Li Jiaqi (Austin Li) sell thousands of products in a few minutes through their live broadcasts.[62]

Digital brand engagement offers a unique opportunity for brands to gain knowledge about their customers. Through social media and other research and data mining platforms, brands are able to access vast amounts of consumer data. Such data includes consumer socio-demographics such as age, gender, location, income, education, family size, social network size and socio-psychographics including lifestyle, consumption preferences and preferred brands across categories. The abundance of data has led to new industries involving marketing technology (Martech), digital data analytics, data warehousing and data mining. Companies such as Palantir that specialize in Big Data analytics are utilizing machine learning and artificial intelligence which allows its clients, including brands, organizations and governments, to harness the power of data.[63] Brands that utilize this data in an efficient manner are able to build sustainable and successful engagement strategies. For instance, when launching a new CLA version of its car, Mercedes Benz hired five Instagram photographers through a competition where whoever got the most impressions would get to keep the car. This campaign received 87 million organic Instagram impressions with 2 million new likes. Similarly, Airbnb uses the campaign 'Don't just go there, live there' through which it posts photos generated by the hosts and guests on the Airbnb platforms about lived experiences. Each post received substantial engagement among consumers.

While all brands aim to build strong consumer-brand relationships, it is not always possible to create a strong attachment, connection, love and engagement. There are many brands to whom consumers demonstrate high levels of connection, love and engagement such as Apple, Samsung, Nike, Louis Vuitton and Harry Potter. At the same time, there are many other brands that are highly successful without having a strong self-brand connection, attachment or love. These brands are trusted by consumers, and often are bought solely out of habit, for example, Kellogg's corn flakes, Colgate toothpaste, Asos.com, Sony and Toyota. The key to building consumer-brand relationships is to deliver on the brand promise consistently and keep reminding the consumers through engaging brand communications.

Chapter summary

In this chapter, we have explored the origins and popular concepts of consumer-brand relationships that have roots in the relationship marketing theory. We explained a number of important branding concepts such as self-brand connection, brand trust, brand commitment, brand attachment, brand love and brand engagement. We demonstrated how each of these concepts can help brand managers to effectively manage their brands through developing stronger relationships with their target consumers. The importance of fulfilling the brand promise and how it can lead to satisfying and enhancing customer experience have also been highlighted. We have shown that using creative brand communications, brands, irrespective of their industry sector, can build substantial engagement in physical as well as digital domains.

Key concepts

- Consumer-brand relationship
- Self-brand connection
- Brand trust
- Brand commitment
- Brand promise
- Brand attachment
- Brand love
- Brand engagement

Exercise questions

1 Discuss the origins of consumer-brand relationships in branding.
2 Explain the importance of building strong self-brand connections for a brand.
3 Why are brand trust and commitment critical for any brand's success?
4 Using any three of the consumer-brand relationships concepts, critically examine a brand of your choice against its major competitor.
5 Using examples, identify successful and failed branding campaigns on social media.
6 Consumer-brand relationships are even more critical in the digital domain. Critically reflect on this statement.

CASE STUDY How social media sold Wall's ice cream

Wall's ice cream is a well-established name and used social media platforms to refresh their brand's personality and relevance. The authors used econometrics to isolate the sales impact of social channels on sales.

SOURCE www.mrs.org.uk/resources/social-media

Case questions

1 Examine the competitive market of ice cream and explain why Wall's decided to launch a social media campaign.

2 Explain the key highlights and the rationale for brand engagement strategy behind the 'Goodbye Serious' campaign.

3 Discuss the need for context-dependent social media engagement in the case study. In your view, what other social contexts over the summer months could be utilized by the brand to create further engagement?

4 Critically examine if the campaign was successful against its objectives.

5 Discuss the importance of brand engagement on social media for seasonal products and how they can strengthen consumer-brand relationships.

Endnotes

1 Sheth, J N and Parvatiyar, A (1995) Relationship marketing in consumer markets: Antecedents and consequences, *Journal of the Academy of Marketing Science*, 23 (4), 255–71

2 Fournier, S (1998) Consumers and their brands: Developing relationship theory in consumer research, *Journal of Consumer Research*, 24 (4), 343–73

3 Sheth, J N and Parvatiyar, A (1995) Relationship marketing in consumer markets: Antecedents and consequences, *Journal of the Academy of Marketing Science*, 23 (4), 255–71

4 Bagozzi, R P (1995) Reflections on relationship marketing in consumer markets, *Journal of the Academy of Marketing Science*, 23 (4), 272–77

5 Fournier, S (1998) Consumers and their brands: Developing relationship theory in consumer research, *Journal of Consumer Research*, 24 (4), 343–73

6 Escalas, J E and Bettman, J R (2003) You are what they eat: The influence of reference groups on consumers' connections to brands, *Journal of Consumer Psychology*, 13 (3), 339–48

7 Morgan, R M and Hunt, S D (1994) The commitment-trust theory of relationship marketing, *Journal of Marketing*, 58 (3), 20–38

8 Chaudhuri, A and Holbrook, M B (2001) The chain of effects from brand trust and brand affect to brand performance: The role of brand loyalty, *Journal of Marketing*, 65 (2), 81–93

9 Beatty, S E and Kahle, L R (1988) Alternative hierarchies of the attitude-behavior relationship: The impact of brand commitment and habit, *Journal of the Academy of Marketing Science*, 16, 1–10

10 Park, C W, MacInnis, D J and Priester, J (2008) Brand attachment: Constructs, consequences, and causes, *Foundations and Trends in Marketing*, 1 (3), 191–230

11 Batra, R, Ahuvia, A and Bagozzi, R P (2012) Brand love, *Journal of Marketing*, 76 (2), 1–16

12 Aaker, J L (1997) Dimensions of brand personality, *Journal of Marketing Research*, 34 (3), 347–56

13 Belk, R W (1988) Possessions and the extended self, *Journal of Consumer Research*, 15 (2), 139–68

14 Escalas, J E and Bettman, J R (2003) You are what they eat: The influence of reference groups on consumers' connections to brands, *Journal of Consumer Psychology*, 13 (3), 339–48

15 Berger, J and Heath, C (2007) Where consumers diverge from others: Identity signaling and product domains, *Journal of Consumer Research*, 34 (2), 121–34

16 Escalas, J E and Bettman, J R (2005) Self-construal, reference groups, and brand meaning, *Journal of Consumer Research*, 32 (3), 378–89

17 McAlexander, J H, Schouten, J W and Koenig, H F (2002) Building brand community, *Journal of Marketing*, 66 (1), 38–54

18 Cova, B and Cova, V (2001) Tribal aspects of postmodern consumption research: The case of French in-line roller skaters, *Journal of Consumer Behaviour*, 1 (1), 67–76

19 Belk, R and Tumbat, G (2005) The cult of Macintosh, *Consumption Markets & Culture*, 8 (3), 205–17

20 Khalifa, D and Shukla, P (2021) When luxury brand rejection causes brand dilution, *Journal of Business Research*, 129, 110–21

21 Wang, Y and John, D R (2019) Up, up, and away: Upgrading as a response to dissimilar brand users, *Journal of Marketing Research*, 56 (1), 142–57

22 Moorman, C, Zaltman, G and Deshpande, R (1992) Relationships between providers and users of market research: The dynamics of trust within and between organizations, *Journal of Marketing Research*, 29 (3), 314–28

23 Gustafsson, A, Johnson, M D and Roos, I (2005) The effects of customer satisfaction, relationship commitment dimensions, and triggers on customer retention, *Journal of Marketing*, 69 (4), 210–18

24 Morgan, R M and Hunt, S D (1994) The commitment-trust theory of relationship marketing, *Journal of Marketing*, 58 (3), 20–38

25 Chaudhuri, A and Holbrook, M B (2001) The chain of effects from brand trust and brand affect to brand performance: The role of brand loyalty, *Journal of Marketing*, 65 (2), 81–93

26 Shukla, P, Banerjee, M and Singh, J (2016) Customer commitment to luxury brands: Antecedents and consequences, *Journal of Business Research*, 69 (1), 323–31

27 https://directory.goodonyou.eco/brand/h-and-m (archived at https://perma.cc/W2NB-MLJH)

28 www.brandingmag.com/2019/12/12/hms-greenwashing-short-sighted-and-unethical/ (archived at https://perma.cc/X7TG-3D2X)

29 www.cbc.ca/news/business/clothes-recycling-marketplace-1.4493490 (archived at https://perma.cc/L2NF-Z9E9)

30 www.powerreviews.com/blog/brand-promise-examples/ (archived at https://perma.cc/988R-2H28)

31 Morgan, R M and Hunt, S D (1994) The commitment-trust theory of relationship marketing, *Journal of Marketing*, 58 (3), 20–38

32 McEvily, B and Tortoriello, M (2011) Measuring trust in organisational research: Review and recommendations, *Journal of Trust Research*, 1 (1), 23–63

33 Singh, J, Shukla, P and Schlegelmilch, B B (2022) Desire, need, and obligation: Examining commitment to luxury brands in emerging markets, *International Business Review*, 31 (3), 101947

34 Park, C W, MacInnis, D J, Priester, J, Eisingerich, A B and Iacobucci, D (2010) Brand attachment and brand attitude strength: Conceptual and empirical differentiation of two critical brand equity drivers, *Journal of Marketing*, 74 (6), 1–17

35 Ibid.

36 www.digitaltrainingacademy.com/casestudies/2015/08/taking_winter_beauty_to_new_heights.php (archived at https://perma.cc/R8CB-6V47)

37 www.thinkwithgoogle.com/marketing-strategies/video/fiats-500x-crossover-ad-drives-audience-engagement-on-youtube/ (archived at https://perma.cc/8A5L-VNHX)

38 Carroll, B A and Ahuvia, A C (2006) Some antecedents and outcomes of brand love, *Marketing Letters*, 17, 79–89

39 Ibid.

40 Batra, R, Ahuvia, A and Bagozzi, R P (2012) Brand love, *Journal of Marketing*, 76 (2), 1–16

41 Ibid.

42 www.thebodyshop.com/en-gb/about-us/activism/faat/a/a00018 (archived at https://perma.cc/NK8F-77ER)

43 Singh, J and Crisafulli, B (2022) *Brands and Consumers: A research overview*, Routledge, London

44 Romaniuk, J (2013) What's (brand) love got to do with it?, *International Journal of Market Research*, 55 (2), 185–86

45 Hollebeek, L (2011) Exploring customer brand engagement: Definition and themes, *Journal of Strategic Marketing*, 19 (7), 555–73

46 Obilo, O O, Chefor, E and Saleh, A (2021) Revisiting the consumer brand engagement concept, *Journal of Business Research*, 126, 634–43

47 Brodie, R J, Ilic, A, Juric, B and Hollebeek, L (2013) Consumer engagement in a virtual brand community: An exploratory analysis, *Journal of Business Research*, 66 (1), 105–14

48 Lemon, K N and Verhoef, P C (2016) Understanding customer experience throughout the customer journey, *Journal of Marketing*, 80 (6), 69–96

49 Verhoef, P C, Lemon, K N, Parasuraman, A, Roggeveen, A, Tsiros, M and Schlesinger, L A (2009) Customer experience creation: Determinants, dynamics and management strategies, *Journal of Retailing*, 85 (1), 31–41

50 Puccinelli, N M, Goodstein, R C, Grewal, D, Price, R, Raghubir, P and Stewart, D (2009) Customer experience management in retailing: Understanding the buying process, *Journal of Retailing*, 85 (1), 15–30

51 Schmitt, B H (2010) *Customer Experience Management: A revolutionary approach to connecting with your customers*, John Wiley and Sons

52 Grewal, D, Levy, M and Kumar, V (2009) Customer experience management in retailing: An organizing framework, *Journal of Retailing*, 85 (1), 1–14

53 Lemon, K N and Verhoef, P C (2016) Understanding customer experience throughout the customer journey, *Journal of Marketing*, 80 (6), 69–96

54 www.marketingweek.com/six-brand-case-studies-that-proved-the-value-of-customer-experience/ (archived at https://perma.cc/H7HS-S9F5)

55 Baumöl, U, Hollebeek, L and Jung, R (2016) Dynamics of customer interaction on social media platforms, *Electronic Markets*, 26, 199–202

56 Shawky, S, Kubacki, K, Dietrich, T and Weaven, S (2020) A dynamic framework for managing customer engagement on social media, *Journal of Business Research*, 121, 567–77

57 www.bbc.co.uk/news/technology-37615496 (archived at https://perma.cc/A63S-XP82)

58 www.nbcnews.com/tech/tech-news/samsung-finally-explains-galaxy-note-7-exploding-battery-mess-n710581 (archived at https://perma.cc/K2Q6-6LPJ)

59 Tajvidi, M, Richard, M O, Wang, Y and Hajli, N (2020) Brand co-creation through social commerce information sharing: The role of social media, *Journal of Business Research*, 121, 476–86

60 Hollebeek, L D and Brodie, R J (2016) Non-monetary social and network value: Understanding the effects of non-paying customers in new media, *Journal of Strategic Marketing*, 24 (3–4), 169–74

61 https://fitsmallbusiness.com/livestream-shopping-statistics/ (archived at https://perma.cc/MG5R-CPV5)

62 www.theguardian.com/world/2022/jun/09/li-jiaqi-chinese-influencer-career-tiananmen-square-tank-cake-stream (archived at https://perma.cc/8KEL-ASWU)

63 www.palantir.com/about/ (archived at https://perma.cc/BFS4-KSTR)

Brand extension 09

Overview

In this chapter, we discuss the fundamental concept of brand extension, and its pivotal role in brand management. As brands grow, they extend into different categories and lines, which pose new challenges for brand management. We provide details of research into drivers of brand, category and line extension. The extensions are not free from risks, and we highlight the advantages and disadvantages therein. In the following section, we include research insights into how consumers evaluate the extensions, based on different types of congruence or fit, as well as how the 'spillover' effects influence consumer perceptions. Lastly, we present how culture influences perceptions and attitudes towards brand extension.

Key learning outcomes

Upon reading this chapter, you should be able to

- Understand the fundamental concepts of brand, category and line extension
- Gain knowledge on the success factors of extensions, along with advantages and disadvantages of brand extension
- Comprehend how consumers evaluate brand extensions through the lenses of brand fit, product fit and spillover effects
- Know about the cultural influences of perceptions toward brand extensions

What is brand extension and its role in brand management?

Brand extension, a strategic marketing practice, involves extending a well-established brand into new product or service categories, leveraging the parent brand's equity to enhance the acceptance and success of the new offerings.[1] Brand extension as a strategic practice relies on the positive self-brand connection, brand trust and brand attachment, which consumers have developed towards the existing brand, leading to reduced perceived risk and increased willingness to try the new products offered by the brand.[2] Brand extensions are considered a preferred strategic tool because they are seen as a less risky approach to introducing new product lines. For instance, Apple's success from a comparatively small personal computer brand to a global behemoth can be attributed to successful brand extension in phones, music and streaming services. Similarly, Caterpillar, a heavy-machine product brand, has successfully extended its business into boots, apparels and other merchandise. Brand extension allows companies to tap into the parent brand's equity, and reduce the resources required for building a new brand.[3] Successful brand extension aligns with the concept of brand portfolio management, wherein firms strategically manage a set of related brands to optimize overall brand equity.[4]

Brand extensions also enable brands to diversify their product portfolios while maintaining a cohesive brand identity.[5] Thus, extensions allow brands to address changing customer needs, tastes, preferences, while remaining relevant. Scholarly literature highlights the significance of congruence between the parent brand's image and the extended product category for successful brand extension.[6] [7] In this context, brand extension's effectiveness hinges on the brand's ability to extend its core attributes and associations into the new domain.[8] For instance, initially focused on young consumers, Lego has successfully extended the brand through extensions that target adults (Lego Technic), architecture students (Lego Architecture), women (Lego Friends) and very young kids (Lego Duplo).[9] The brand has also used several thematic extensions by collaborating with very successful Hollywood franchises such as Star Wars, Disney, Marvel and DC Comics. This has even led to successful movie and television franchises as well.[10] In addition, Lego has extended the brand in cultural domains by collaborating with popular Korean pop band BTS and the Museum of the Modern Art (MoMA), as well as popular brands including Ikea, Adidas and Levi's.[11]

As discussed, brand extension serves as a crucial strategy within brand management. It harnesses the power of established brand equity to facilitate growth, reduce risk and enable diversification. By strategically extending into new categories, companies can cater to evolving consumer preferences while leveraging the positive perceptions associated with their parent brands. However, effective execution requires alignment between the parent brand and the extended offering, emphasizing the need for congruence in brand attributes and associations. Overall, brand extension underscores the dynamic interplay between brand equity, consumer perceptions and strategic innovation in the realm of brand management. In the next sections, we discuss different types, drivers, advantages and disadvantages of brand extensions.

Types of brand extensions – category and line extensions

As discussed in the previous section, brand extensions offer a less risky and less resource-intensive way for firms to enter into new or existing markets with new products. When a firm introduces a new brand, it has two choices: create a direct brand (e.g. BMW 3 series) or a sub-brand (e.g. Volkswagen Polo). In the above cases, BMW and Volkswagen are called parent brands. Over time, these sub-brands can also have their own extensions. For instance, Volkswagen Polo has 23 different extensions depending on the engine type, engine size, transmission type, colour and other features.[12] Thus, brand extensions can lead to substantial complexities for firms as new and innovative specifications are added. There are two major categories of brand extensions: category extension and line extension.

Category extension

Category extension involves introducing new products or services within a related or unrelated product category. For category extensions, the brand generally aims to maintain its core attributes. An example is Toyota's extension from manufacturing only petrol or diesel automobiles to producing hybrid technology, such as the Toyota Prius. This expansion allowed Toyota to leverage its reputation for fuel-efficient vehicles to create a new product line that addresses environmental concerns. Such related brand extensions can help a brand increase its market presence and market share. However, at times, it can also cannibalize the other extensions that exist within a parent brand's line up.[13] For example, Prius could cannibalize the market of Toyota Corolla and vice versa. Many brands also extend themselves in unrelated categories and can be very successful. For example, Amazon, the online retailer which started in 1994, decided to move into the cloud computing space almost a decade later. However, over time, Amazon Web Services (AWS) has become a global leader in this space and AWS generates more than 70 per cent of operating profits for Amazon (the parent brand).[14] Amazon has similarly ventured into a variety of category extensions with Kindle (e-reader), audio books (audible), mobile phone, tablets and other electronic devices (Fire and Alexa), electronic equipment (Amazon Basics), entertainment and gaming (Amazon Prime and Twitch), home security (Ring), domestic products including baby wipes, diapers and vitamin supplements (Amazon Elements), dog food (Wag) and groceries (AmazonFresh), among many others.

Line extension

Line extension occurs when a brand introduces variations or different versions of an existing product within the same product category. As consumer preferences evolve, a brand may add new features and remove existing features. To highlight this novelty a brand may create a line extension to benefit from the established brand recognition. For example, with consumers becoming aware of the sugar content in Coca-Cola products coupled with the spread of health consciousness among wider population, the brand introduced a variety of line extensions including Diet Coke, Coca-Cola Zero Sugar and Coca-Cola Zero Sugar Zero Caffeine. Further, the brand has introduced a number of different sizes from 250ml to 2ltr bottles and different types of packaging (i.e. glass, plastic bottles and cans). These variants extend the product line while keeping the brand consistent and recognizable.

Line extensions are carried out through a lens of product feature changes as observed in the example of Coca-Cola above. However, some brands use other mechanisms such as price to extend the brand. For instance, Tesla Motors has created entry-level options such as Model 3 and Model Y, mid-priced Model S and higher-tier Model X. Tesla has also announced a sports car version, Tesla Roadster, which is expected to be priced above $200,000.[15] This is called vertical brand extension, which is aimed at catering to different socio-economic segments of the market. When a brand introduces an extension that appeals to the higher-income segment of the market, it is called upward extension. On the other hand, if the brand extension caters to the lower socio-economic segments, it is identified as downward extension. For example, to fight the deep discounters such as Lidl and Aldi, in the UK groceries market, Tesco introduced downward brand extensions through Tesco Everyday Value and Tesco Discount. Moreover, to appeal to the less price-conscious consumers, Tesco developed an upward extension with its Tesco Finest range, which is priced at similar price point as some other national brands.

Brand extensions are quite common globally. According to the latest research, almost 70 per cent of new products in the consumer-packaged goods market in the US are brand extensions.[16] A study by market research firm Nielsen of top brands in 46 FMCG categories and 82 brand extensions in food and non-food categories, shows that in addition to promoting brand equity, brand extensions can grow incremental sales up to 38 per cent and contribute as much as 30 per cent to parent brand sales.[17] Moreover, the study also found that FMCG brand extensions were five times more successful than new product launches. In the next section, we discuss the drivers of brand extension.

Drivers of brand extension

While a large number of new product introductions are brand extensions, only 30 per cent of them survive the first two years.[18] Given that brand extension failure rate is nearly 70 per cent, it is vitally important for brand managers to obtain insights on the drivers for brand extension success. A plethora of academic studies over the past 30 years have attempted to understand the factors that drive brand extension success.[19] Figure 9.1 shows a conceptual framework that captures these drivers.

One of the foremost drivers of brand extension success is parent brand equity. This is reflected in consumer attitude, familiarity, quality perceptions and loyalty towards the parent brand.[20] As consumers may not be familiar with the new brand extension, they cannot make informed judgements regarding the new offering.[21] In such circumstances, they would use existing heuristics (knowledge structure or schema) attached with the parent brand to make buying decision. Another critical factor that drives brand extension success is extension fit, which reflects the perceived similarity between an extension and its parent brand. The extension fit is a multifaceted construct which comprises of usage fit (shared product usage contexts), goal fit (shared associations organized around common goals), feature or product fit (shared tangible product characteristics) and concept or brand fit (shared abstract brand images).[22] If the extension fit is high, consumers are more likely to retrieve and transfer parent brands related associations to the brand extension.

BRANDING IN PRACTICE
Examples of extension fit

Usage fit

Usage fit refers to a brand extension where the new product is used in a similar way as the existing product. An example of usage fit is BMW's extension from luxury cars to motorcycles (see Figure 9.1). Both products cater to a premium and performance-oriented audience, and the usage context of driving aligns well with the brand's identity.

Goal fit

Goal fit involves extending the brand to products that share a common purpose or goal with the existing brand. An instance of goal fit is Patagonia's expansion into the food industry. Known for its commitment to environmental sustainability, Patagonia launched Patagonia Provisions, a line of food products that align with the brand's values of responsible sourcing and ethical consumption.

Figure 9.1   BMW's extension from luxury car to motorcycle based on usage fit

SOURCE BMW

Figure 9.2   Apple uses simple design across devices based on feature and product fit

SOURCE Photo by Julian O'hayon on Unsplash

Feature/product fit

Feature fit occurs when the new product shares certain features or characteristics with the existing brand. An example of feature fit is Apple's extension from computers to smartphones (see Figure 9.2). Apple's reputation for innovation, design excellence and user-friendly interfaces translated seamlessly into the smartphone category with the introduction of the iPhone.

Concept/brand fit

Concept fit involves extending the brand to products that share a common underlying concept or essence. Disney, a well-established brand in the entertainment industry, extended its brand into the streaming service market with the launch of Disney+. The concept fit here lies in Disney's core identity of providing family-friendly, high-quality content. Disney+ offers a platform for streaming a wide range of Disney movies, TV shows and original content that aligns with the brand's concept of wholesome entertainment for all ages.

As already discussed, a large number of brand extensions fail, and the concept of fit remains a critical factor. For example, Colgate, a leading brand in oral care, attempted to extend its brand into the frozen food market in the 1960s with 'Colgate Kitchen Entrees' (for example, see Figure 9.3). However, the brand fit between toothpaste and frozen food was unclear and confusing to the consumers, resulting in scepticism and lack of credibility. Consumers found it difficult to associate a toothpaste brand with food products, leading to the failure of this brand extension attempt. Similar famous examples exist with the brand Virgin introducing cola in the UK market, and Zippo, the famous lighter brand, launching its clothing range.

Beyond brand fit, there are many other product fit failure examples. For instance, in the 1990s Harley-Davidson attempted to extend into the perfume market with a fragrance line. This product fit failure occurred because the essence of a motorcycle brand did not seamlessly translate into a completely different product category like perfume. The disconnect between the rugged image of Harley-Davidson motorcycles and the elegance and subtlety associated with perfumes resulted in consumer confusion and an inability to resonate with the new product. Similarly, when Cheetos, a popular snack brand, tried to extend its product line into the cosmetics market with 'Cheetos Lip Balm', the extension failed. *Cosmopolitan* magazine, a well-known woman's lifestyle magazine, extended its brand into the yogurt market, which also encountered failure. The above examples highlight the importance of carefully evaluating whether the extension fits with the parent brand. In a meta-analysis involving more than 150 research papers over the past 30 years, scholars show that strength of

Figure 9.3   Example of unsuccessful brand extensions

extension fit could increase the success of brand extension with a probability of 61.4 per cent. Thus, brands should ensure that their new offering aligns with their core attributes, values and consumer perceptions to create a meaningful and successful extension.

Other factors affecting brand extension

Brand extension success depends on several other factors beyond the parent brand's equity and extension fit. From a parent brand perspective, the industry in which the parent brand operates, the prestige of the parent brand and the variability of products already associated with the brand. For example, an automobile brand will find it difficult to move into the cola and drinks sector. However, many luxury brands are able to create brand extensions across categories. For example, Armani, while predominantly known for its ready-to-wear (Emporio Armani, Armani Jeans) and haute couture (Armani Collezioni) range, is also in the business of hotels and luxury villas (Armani Hotels), eyewear, leather goods, among others.

For the success of their brand extensions, brands use different cues to make the parent brand more accessible in consumers' minds. For example, Disney uses its name in its theme parks (e.g. Walt Disney World Resort, Disneyland Paris, Hong Kong Disneyland), streaming service (e.g. Disney+, Disney Channel, Disney Junior) and other assets.[23] Such cues allow the benefit of the parent brand equity transfer to extended products. However, if the brand extension is highly innovative and has its own cues that can distinguish it, the signalling role of parent brand equity becomes less relevant.[24] For example, the Star network, which runs more than 70 different TV channels in India, has 790 million viewers a month across India and in more than 100 countries, has been a subsidiary of Disney since 2017. However, most of its channels are still widely known by their original names and Disney's name is not incorporated everywhere. Similarly, ESPN is 80 per cent owned by Disney. However, the Disney brand is loosely associated with it.

Consumers' characteristics, such as their level of involvement, age and gender, can also be a critical factor in brand extension success. For example, some older consumers may find learning and processing new information more difficult. Hence, they rely on existing parent brand associations which strengthen the signalling associated with the brand extension and facilitate categorization processes.[25] Scholars argue that women and men process information differently and employ different levels of elaboration when analysing new stimuli.[26] Thus, by understanding their target segment socio-demographics, brand managers can employ appropriate positioning strategies to successfully extend their brand.

BRANDING IN PRACTICE
Brands that defy extension logic

When a brand becomes too identifiable as an exemplar for a particular category of product, extensions become difficult to achieve. For instance, there are brands that have become synonyms for a particular category of product or service such as Xerox (for photocopying), Google (for online search), Bubblewrap (wrapping), Uber (for taxi) and Hoover (for vacuum cleaning). These brands have adopted different strategies to extend their brands by creating a different parent or sub-brand. For example, Google is now part of a parent brand, Alphabet. Moreover, it has created several sub-brands that have grown to become global brands in their own categories such as Android (smartphone software), Pixel (smartphone hardware), YouTube (video streaming) and Nest (smart products).

There are also brands like Virgin that have defied the extension logic by expanding into many related and unrelated categories. Started as Virgin Records, a music company in the UK in 1970, Virgin has a vast portfolio of brand extensions that encompass health and lifestyle (Virgin Active), airline (Virgin Atlantic, Virgin Atlantic Holidays), hospitality (Virgin Experience Days, Virgin Hotels, Virgin Limited Edition, Virgin Voyages), mobile communications (Virgin Mobile), music (Virgin Music, Virgin Radio, Virgin Records), retail (Virgin Megastores, Virgin Gift Card, Virgin Wines), banking (Virgin Money) and space travel (Virgin Galactic) among many others.[27]

The parent brand 'Virgin' is associated with approximately 60 businesses with 49 sub-brands using the Virgin name. However, these extensions have not always been successful either. For instance, there have been a large number of failed ventures such as Virgin Nigeria (Airline), Virgin Cola (soft drinks), Virgin Vodka (spirits), Virgin Brides (retail), Virgin Cinemas (entertainment) and Virgin Rail (transport), etc.

One of the reasons Virgin is able to expand into so many product is because of its maverick founder, Richard Branson. The brand is loosely associated with the values of youthfulness, adventure, fun and rebelliousness. These values are constantly projected through a variety of brand communications including the image of Richard Branson.

Advantages and disadvantages of brand extension

Brand extension remains one of the most preferred market expansion strategies despite the high failure rate of new extensions. There are several advantages and disadvantages associated with brand extension strategy, as outlined in Tables 9.1 and 9.2. Successful brand extensions can not only be advantageous for the brand extension

Table 9.1   Advantages of brand extension with examples

Advantages of brand extension	Examples
1. Leverages existing brand equity and recognition.	Apple's extension from computers to smartphones with the iPhone.
2. Reduces costs by utilizing brand awareness.	Coca-Cola introducing Diet Coke and Coca-Cola Zero Sugar as line extensions.
3. Mitigates risk through consumer trust.	Amazon's extension into cloud computing with Amazon Web Services (AWS).
4. Enhances customer loyalty and retention.	Starbucks' extension into the Starbucks Rewards loyalty programme.
5. Achieves economies of scale by sharing resources.	Procter & Gamble's brand extension strategy for Tide detergent and Tide To Go stain remover.
6. Allows diversification without losing core identity.	Nestlé's extension into the pet food market with the Purina brand.
7. Encourages cross-promotion between different product lines.	Calvin Klein's brand extension from a premium fashion brand to perfumes, home furnishings and other categories.
8. Facilitates quick market entry with a recognized brand.	Tesla's extension into the electric truck market with the Cybertruck.
9. Builds consumer trust and acceptance faster.	Lego's extension into video games with Lego-themed games.
10. Enhances brand perception as innovative.	Google's extension into various technology areas like self-driving cars and AI.

Table 9.2 Disadvantages of brand extension with examples

Disadvantages of brand extension	Examples
1. Risk of brand dilution.	Kodak's extension into printers and ink products.
2. Misfit between parent brand and new category.	Colgate's extension into frozen food (Colgate Kitchen Entrees).
3. Potential cannibalization of sales.	Kellogg's extension of Nutri-Grain into cereal bars.
4. Negative perceptions transferred.	BP's extension with 'Beyond Petroleum' criticized for greenwashing.
5. Difficulty in creating distinct positioning.	Harley-Davidson's extension into the perfume market.
6. Dilution of brand image.	Virgin's extension into various industries including Virgin Cola.
7. Potential for channel conflicts.	P&G's extension of Tide into the dry cleaning business.
8. Complexity in managing multiple lines.	Disney's extension into Disney+ streaming services.
9. Diversion of resources from core business.	Heinz's extension into coloured ketchup.
10. Legal issues related to trademark conflicts.	Microsoft's extension of the Windows brand into Windows Phone.

but the parent brand as well. For instance, Apple's extension into the smartphone and later a variety of other electronic products market has made it one of the largest companies in the world over the past 15 years in terms of its valuation.[28] Similarly, Adidas Originals allowed Adidas to extend from footwear to clothing. However, on the other side it can hurt the parent brand sales also. For example, Cadbury's, which is known for its chocolates and candy products globally, launched instant mashed potato brand, Smash, which was successful initially. However, over time due to perceived quality issues associated with it, the extension had an effect on the parent brand quality association as well. So, after 20 years of introducing the instant mashed potato brand, Cadbury's eventually sold the Smash brand.

Brand extension – spillover effects

An important reason why brands employ extension strategy is to take advantage of the parent brand equity. The parent brands want the substantial equity that has garnered in the market to reflect in their brand extension. Consumers, when exposed to the brand extension, evaluate the new extension based on their pre-existing attitudes regarding the parent brand.[29] Based on this evaluation, they form their opinions regarding the brand extension and also regarding the parent brand. When these evaluations of brand extension reflect back in consumer attitudes towards the parent brand, it is termed *attitude spillover*. Attitudes are relatively stable psychological constructs.[30] Because of this stability, pre-existing attitudes toward the parent brand will be related highly to post-exposure attitudes toward that brand.[31] This cognitive transfer may lead to positive or negative change in the attitude towards the parent brand due to the associative network in consumers' minds.[32]

The spillover effect, thus, can be positive as well as negative. This phenomenon is particularly pronounced when consumers perceive strong connections or a clear thematic fit between the entities (i.e. the parent brand and the brand extension), resulting in a cognitive shortcut that further boosts the existing mental associations with the parent brand. For example, BMW extended the brand into the electric vehicle (EV) market with the BMW i series. BMW already had a reputation for luxury, performance and engineering excellence. With the introduction of i series EVs and its success, the parent brand BMW has gained credibility as an automobile brand in sustainable mobility through positive attitude spillover. An example of when attitude spillover can be negative is Johnson & Johnson (J&J), one of the world's largest healthcare companies with a large portfolio of baby-care products that are trusted by parents worldwide. In 2018, J&J initiated a voluntary recall of its popular Johnson's baby powder due to asbestos contamination in the USA.[33] This resulted in substantial negative spillover for the parent brand J&J in terms of its stock market valuation, legal compensation and reduction in market share.[34]

Chapter summary

In this chapter we explored the important concept of brand extension. We learnt that brand extension is a comparatively less risky approach for introducing new brands; however, its success rate is not substantially different to other new product launches. The chapter also explored the various types of brand extensions including category and line extensions and their sub-types such as vertical and horizontal extensions. Brand extension success relies on a number of factors including parent brand equity, extension fit, brand communications and consumer factors. There is no successful recipe for brand extension success as it depends on the interaction of a large number of market forces. There are a number of advantages and disadvantages of brand extension. Moreover, brand extensions can increase or decrease parent brand equity through positive or negative spillover effects respectively. Overall, brand extension remains one of the most popular strategies to introduce new products in the market.

Key concepts

- Brand extension
  - Category extension
  - Line extension
    - Vertical and horizontal brand extension
- Parent brand equity
- Brand extension fit
- Brand extension drivers
- Spillover effects

Exercise questions

1 Explain brand extension and its importance for brand managers.

2 Describe different types of brand extensions with examples.

3 What are the major drivers of successful brand extension? Explain with examples.

4 There is no universal recipe for successful brand extension. Critically reflect on this statement.

5 Choose any three multinational brands and identify their brand extensions. What new extensions would you recommend for these parent brands?

6 What are the advantages and disadvantages of brand extension?

7 Brand extension can create positive or negative spillover for the parent brand. Explain your viewpoint in detail with examples.

8 Review and discuss the key managerial takeaways from the following paper: Singh, J, Scriven, J, Clemente, M, Lomax, W and Wright, M (2012) New brand extensions: Patterns of success and failure, *Journal of Advertising Research*, 52 (2), 234–42.

CASE STUDY The risks and rewards of brand extensions through innovations in consumer products

Innovation-based brand extension is crucial for consumer products companies to drive growth, take market share from competitors and boost profit margins. However, most new product innovations fail to deliver sustained sales and profits.

The opening of the Museum of Failure in Sweden sheds light on a crucial paradox in the consumer products industry – the relentless pursuit of innovation amidst a high rate of product flops. While companies spend billions on research and development, hoping for 'new and improved' products to boost market share and profits, the museum serves as a stark reminder that success is far from guaranteed.

This case study analyses examples of successful and failed brand extensions based on innovations in the consumer products industry. It examines the product development process, pricing strategies and market reception over time to draw insights about innovation best practices.

The pressure to innovate stems from several factors including stagnant core markets, which compel companies to seek new avenues for growth. Additionally, established players like L'Oréal rely on innovation to maintain their share in competitive markets.

The spectrum of innovation showcased in the museum ranges from seemingly bizarre brand extensions like Lay's cappuccino-flavoured crisps, to packaging changes like Marmite's upside-down squeezy bottle. Similarly, cautionary tales like Unilever's Persil Power detergent, which destroyed clothes while removing stains, or Coca-Cola's Blak and Life beverages, which failed to capture consumer imagination are reminders that even global brands can get it wrong. However, truly impactful brand extensions, like Nescafé's Nespresso capsule pods, are rare and such product innovations take years to develop.

Some brand extensions can initially succeed, and then fail as well, when the company fails to take into account the brand's key message and usage.

Reckitt Benckiser (RB) is a global consumer health, hygiene and nutrition company. Its Scholl brand focuses on foot care products, holding a significant global market share. In 2014, Scholl launched a breakthrough electronic foot exfoliation device called the Velvet Smooth Express Pedi which uses spinning rollers to remove dead skin. Priced at $39, it was cheaper and more effective than existing manual scraping tools for removing hard skin on feet. The pedi device was a huge success and Scholl revenues from 2013 to 2015 quadrupled to €810 million. It captured a significant market share by changing consumer behaviour and habits around foot care rather than just attracting brand switchers. The success accounted for nearly half of RB's health division growth during 2014 and 2015.

In 2016, Scholl introduced a new Wet & Dry Pedi model with enhanced waterproof features at a 50 per cent price premium. The market rejected it, with revenues dropping 11 per cent in 2016. RB CEO Rakesh Kapoor stated they had 'over-innovated' too quickly after the original product and priced too high, failing to understand consumer willingness to pay. The failure represented the majority of RB's slowing sales growth in 2016.

While innovation is critical for growth in consumer products, companies must carefully balance risks and rewards. They should focus innovation on shifting consumer habits, avoid too-frequent incremental product revamps and ensure they price new offerings appropriately based on the value proposition. When done right, innovation can deliver step-function revenue growth and profits. But mistakes can lead to dramatic market failure and brand damage.

Case questions

1 What are the major factors behind the unsuccessful brand extensions identified in this case?

2 If you were to recommend a company planning a brand extension, what considerations would you keep in mind for the success of the extension?

3 Based on the various brand extensions failures highlighted in the case, critically reflect on the following statement: Brand extension failures are not industry dependent.

4 While innovating, a company should keep sight of customer needs and trends. Reflect on the above statement, suggesting how a brand can manage its new extensions.

Endnotes

1 Broniarczyk, S M and Alba, J W (1994) The importance of the brand in brand extension, *Journal of Marketing Research*, 31 (2), 214–28

2 Loken, B, Joiner, C and Houston, M J (2023) Leveraging a brand through brand extension: A review of two decades of research, *Brands and Brand Management*, Psychology Press, New York, pp 11–42

3 Pitta, D A and Katsanis, L P (1995) Understanding brand equity for successful brand extension, *Journal of Consumer Marketing*, 12 (4), 51–64

4 Peng, C, Bijmolt, T H, Völckner, F and Zhao, H (2023) A meta-analysis of brand extension success: The effects of parent brand equity and extension fit, *Journal of Marketing*, 87 (6), 906–27

5 Keller, K L and Lehmann, D R (2006) Brands and branding: Research findings and future priorities, *Marketing Science*, 25 (6), 740–59

6 Aaker, M D (1990) Brand extensions: The good, the bad, and the ugly, *MIT Sloan Management Review*, 31 (Summer), 47–56

7 Völckner, F, Sattler, H, Hennig-Thurau, T and Ringle, C M (2010) The role of parent brand quality for service brand extension success, *Journal of Service Research*, 13 (4), 379–96

8 Batra, R, Lenk, P and Wedel, M (2010) Brand extension strategy planning: Empirical estimation of brand–category personality fit and atypicality, *Journal of Marketing Research*, 47 (2), 335–47

9 https://sundaybricks.com/2018/07/04/lego-brand-extension/ (archived at https://perma.cc/4EY5-VKBN)

10 https://en.wikipedia.org/wiki/List_of_Lego_films_and_TV_series (archived at https://perma.cc/S5AB-9JA8)

11 www.prestigeonline.com/sg/lifestyle/culture-plus-entertainment/most-iconic-lego-collaborations/ (archived at https://perma.cc/EMV6-UHG3)

12 www.cartrade.com/volkswagen-cars/polo/faqs/how-many-versions-are-available-for-volkswagen-polo/ (archived at https://perma.cc/G5NV-ADAL)

13 Lomax, W, Hammond, K, East, R and Clemente, M (1997) The measurement of cannibalization, *Journal of Product and Brand Management*, 6 (1), 27–39

14 www.fool.com/investing/2022/07/07/aws-chief-says-amazons-most-profitable-segment-is/ (archived at https://perma.cc/BN5U-J4EF)

15 https://carbuzz.com/cars/tesla/roadster (archived at https://perma.cc/4QYX-S4QL)

16 Peng, C, Bijmolt, T H, Völckner, F and Zhao, H (2023) A meta-analysis of brand extension success: The effects of parent brand equity and extension fit, *Journal of Marketing*, 87 (6), 906–27

17 https://timesofindia.indiatimes.com/business/india-business/fmcg-brand-extensions-five-times-more-successful-than-new-product-launches-study/articleshow/17402963.cms?frmapp=yes&from=mdr (archived at https://perma.cc/6PP5-28NK)

18 https://nielseniq.com/global/en/insights/analysis/2019/bursting-with-new-products-theres-never-been-a-better-time-for-breakthrough-innovation/ (archived at https://perma.cc/AP7K-YY6S)

19 Singh, J, Scriven, J, Clemente, M, Lomax, W and Wright, M (2012) New brand extensions: Patterns of success and failure, *Journal of Advertising Research*, 52 (2), 234–42

20 Yoo, B, Donthu, N and Lee, S (2000) An examination of selected marketing mix elements and brand equity, *Journal of the Academy of Marketing Science*, 28, 195–211

21 Erdem, T and Swait, J (2001) Brand equity as a signaling phenomenon, *Journal of Consumer Psychology*, 7 (2), 131–57

22 Martin, I M, Stewart, D W and Matta, S (2005) Branding strategies, marketing communication, and perceived brand meaning: The transfer of purposive, goal-oriented brand meaning to brand extensions, *Journal of the Academy of Marketing Science*, 33 (3), 275–94

23 https://en.wikipedia.org/wiki/List_of_assets_owned_by_the_Walt_Disney_Company (archived at https://perma.cc/F6TZ-ZARA)

24 Peng, C, Bijmolt, T H, Völckner, F and Zhao, H (2023) A meta-analysis of brand extension success: The effects of parent brand equity and extension fit, *Journal of Marketing*, 87 (6), 906–27

25 Ibid.

26 Wang, P, Xiong, G and Yang, J (2019) Serial position effects on native advertising effectiveness: Differential results across publisher and advertiser metrics, *Journal of Marketing*, 83 (2), 82–97

27 www.virgin.com/about-virgin/virgin-group/overview (archived at https://perma.cc/QN5V-STZX)

28 www.ft.com/content/c3ad748f-c910-4a3c-8026-32890a6f3061 (archived at https://perma.cc/S7MH-7SD6)

29 Aaker, D A and Keller, K L (1990) Consumer evaluations of brand extensions, *Journal of Marketing*, 54 (1), 27–41

30 Ajzen, I and Fishbein, M (1977) Attitude-behavior relations: A theoretical analysis and review of empirical research, *Psychological Bulletin*, 84 (5), 888

31 Raufeisen, X, Wulf, L, Köcher, S, Faupel, U and Holzmüller, H H (2019) Spillover effects in marketing: Integrating core research domains, *AMS Review*, 9, 249–67

32 Simonin, B L and Ruth, J A (1998) Is a company known by the company it keeps? Assessing the spillover effects of brand alliances on consumer brand attitudes, *Journal of Marketing Research*, 35 (1), 30–42

33 https://edition.cnn.com/2019/10/18/health/johnson-and-johnson-baby-powder-recall-bn-trnd/index.html (archived at https://perma.cc/68KF-WDAQ)

34 www.theguardian.com/business/2023/jul/19/johnson-johnson-cancer-patient-lawsuit (archived at https://perma.cc/9H4W-T6KW)

Brand alliance or co-branding

10

Overview

In this chapter, we first explain the strategic concept of co-branding and its recent popularity alongside its benefits and risks. We then explain the conditions of success for co-branding, based on research insights. In the following section, we include the theories underpinning co-branding from a consumer perspective. We also present the notion of positive and negative perceptual spillovers due to co-branding. The final section deals with the recent application of co-branding in the form of cause-brand alliance.

Key learning outcomes

Upon reading this chapter, you should be able to

- Understand the concept of brand alliance or co-branding
- Comprehend the advantages and disadvantages of co-branding, including spillover effects
- Identify the drivers for successful co-branding
- Know about the psychology of co-branding
- Gain insights into cause-brand alliances

Defining co-branding

Co-branding or brand alliance is a strategic branding approach that involves the collaboration of two or more distinct brands in the creation and promotion of a new product or service.[1] This approach leverages the established equity, awareness and associations of each partner brand to create a synergistic effect that enhances customer perceptions, credibility and market reach. Co-branding manifests in various forms, such as ingredient co-branding ('Intel Inside', among various personal computers), promotional co-branding (McDonald's 'Happy Meals' with Disney toys), complementary co-branding (Nestlé and Starbucks coffee products), advertising alliances (Kellogg and Tropicana jointly advertising each other's products), bundling (Microsoft including McAfee anti-virus in its software), dual branding (Avis and Budget promoting each other together) and product combinations (Betty Crocker and Hershey's launching a milk chocolate together). The above forms of co-branding may overlap in their scope and function. For instance, dual branding may involve an advertising alliance and promotional co-branding as well. Overall, the aim of the involved brands is to leverage each other's brand equity.

Co-branding capitalizes on the combined equity of the two brands to yield a more potent and memorable impact on consumers.[2] In other words, in the context of co-branding the sum of the combined brand assets is greater than the parts of the individual brands.[3] In co-branding, partners selectively integrate their associations to create a congruent narrative, influencing consumers' perceptions of product quality, value and authenticity. For example, Dell computers use Intel processors to signal the high quality of its PCs, with the Intel logo prominently displayed on the computer.

Benefits and risks of co-branding

Academic researchers find that co-branding allows collaborating brands to leverage their brand associations in a more cost effective and less risky manner, as compared to traditional brand extension strategies.[4] Thus, there are a number of benefits of co-branding. Research suggests that co-branding results in increased brand awareness and access to new markets, and it can lead to a unique market positioning, resonating with a broader audience.[5] Moreover, complementary expertise and resources can result in improved product quality and innovation, ultimately enhancing customer satisfaction and loyalty.[6] As discussed in the previous chapter, brand extensions are not always successful, and more importantly, many brands cannot extend in different product categories due to their equity being too strongly attached to a particular product category. For example, McDonald's attempt to enter into the hospitality business by launching four-star hotels in Europe failed.[7] Thus, brand extensions, while remaining a preferred method of expanding into new products and new markets, is a highly saturated market phenomenon and does not lead to success in all cases. Co-branding, on the other hand, allows brands to avoid such risks by benefitting from the established images and associations of the partners. Due to these unique advantages, co-branding is observed in a variety of industries such as food and drink, retailing, air travel and financial services. In the last three decades, there has been a substantial increase in the number of products launched as an alliance of two brands. Notable examples include Nike and Apple's Sports Kit, Fiat and Mattel's limited-edition Barbie car, and Coca-Cola and OPI's line of nail lacquers.

There are arguably two most commonly cited benefits of co-branding. The first pertains to obtaining assets, both tangible and intangible, and the utilization of collective resources and skills, which help brands enter novel markets and consumer bases. The second benefit involves maximization of brand value, through augmenting revenue streams and strengthening customer-centric brand equity.[8] These benefits can be observed in any alliance context. For example, when a high-ranked university enters into an alliance with a low-ranked university (e.g. a dual degree), the added value of the dual degree aids the lower ranked university.[9] Thus, when an unknown or lesser-ranked brand partners with a highly reputable brand, consumers perceive the alliance based product to be of high quality and demonstrate greater choice confidence.

Since brand alliances involve utilization of collective resources and skills, from a financial perspective they are cheaper to execute compared to new product launches and in some cases brand extensions. Co-branding partners can combine resources; thus, the overall cost of promotion and other overheads are reduced for each partner.[10] For example, British Petroleum (BP) and Marks and Spencer's (M&S) have been alliance partners in the UK since 2005.[11] The brands share their equity and resources instilling confidence in consumers regarding quality of the products. By coming together, both brands are able to offer customers greater convenience and value. Similarly, in B2B markets co-branding leads to greater benefits for the lower equity brand.[12] Moreover, the experience of primary partner plays an important role and could lead to substantial effect on the quality evaluations,[13] enhanced outcomes for customers[14] and stock returns[15] of the co-branded products.

BRANDING IN PRACTICE
Volvo and Daimler AG join hands to develop fuel cell technology

A notable example of B2B brand alliance from Europe in recent years is the collaboration between Volvo Group and Daimler AG to develop fuel cell technology for heavy-duty commercial vehicles. In March 2021, these two prominent European automotive companies announced their intention to form a joint venture, named 'cellcentric GmbH and Co. KG', with the aim of advancing hydrogen-based fuel cell systems.[16]

This collaboration aligns with the companies' shared commitment to sustainable transportation solutions. By pooling their resources, knowledge and expertise, Volvo Group and Daimler intend to accelerate the development and deployment of hydrogen fuel cell technology in the commercial vehicle sector. This technology holds the potential to significantly reduce carbon emissions and contribute to a more environmentally friendly transport industry.

The partnership leverages the strengths of both companies, with Volvo Group's experience in vehicle development and Daimler's expertise in fuel cell technology, to create a synergistic effect. The alliance allows them to share research and development costs, mitigate risks and work towards a common goal that benefits not only their individual brands but also the broader transportation industry and the environment.

This example underscores how B2B brand alliances in Europe are increasingly focusing on innovation and sustainability, combining the strengths of different companies to drive technological advancements and address global challenges.

Academic research shows that co-branding has clear revenue generation and cost benefits. For example, when a manufacturer enters into an alliance with a supplier, it can lead to significant lower manufacturing costs, increased innovation and lower prices for the manufacturer. Similarly, it also increases the supplier profits. The alliance, in turn, can increase economies of scale and reduce the chances of competitors' entry.[17] Research evidence also suggests that co-branding can enhance brand sales and overall market share without the risk of cannibalizing the original brands.[18]

With the advantages of co-branding highlighted earlier, both academic researchers and businesses are keen to grasp its benefits; however, there is a lack of knowledge on the risks associated with this branding strategy.[19] Some of the risks inherent to co-branding pertain to the differences in strategic visions, legal and financial disagreements, or incompatible brand synergies.[20] A failure involving a partner brand can have undesirable consequences for the co-brand, as the alliance can be viewed negatively by consumers. This can result in customer dissatisfaction, negative word-of-mouth and reduction in brand loyalty.[21] Academic research also shows that negative events affecting any partner brand can affect the co-brand when the alliance is viewed as equally culpable for the offence. When the alliance is linked directly to the competence failure of an organization, consumers are likely to transfer this negative association to the other brand in the alliance.[22] For example, Southwest Airlines suffered negative publicity following a scandal and media hype surrounding the alleged treatment of captive whales by SeaWorld.[23] Given the longstanding partnership between Southwest Airlines and SeaWorld, the scandal led to a 35 per cent decline in SeaWorld's share price, public protests and criticism against Southwest Airlines and resultantly Southwest Airlines terminated the long-term alliance. Similarly, Ford received unfavourable media attention in the wake of the tyre scandal affecting its partner brand, Firestone.[24] The Firestone crisis led to the recall of over 20 million tires, the loss of market value for the partner brands and the termination of a nearly a 100-year relationship between Ford Motor Company and Firestone.

Beyond the partner brand spillover effects, negative spillover of alliance can also create memory traces among consumers. Such memory traces and associations can create unfavourable brand responses for future product launches.[25] Such an effect varies across the three crisis types. Based on controllability and intentionality, Timothy Coombs classifies crises into three types:

1 preventable (i.e. the brand knowingly breaches the law causing damage to consumers)

2 accidental (i.e. the brand lacks control over the crisis yet causes damage to consumers)

3 victim (i.e. the brand unknowingly causes damage to consumers due to the actions of a third party)[26]

This crisis typology has also spurred research on crisis response strategies that can reduce reputational damage for the brands. This is discussed in detail in Chapter 12. When a co-brand is involved in preventable crises it creates more negative responses from consumers when compared with accidental crises.[27] For example, research shows that, following a preventable crisis, the non-culpable brand in the alliance suffers from negative consumer perceptions even when enjoying high equity.[28] The above risks highlight the need for brands to be highly cautious when selecting a partner brand for a potential alliance. For example, Lego had to end its partnership with Shell following negative publicity about Shell's plans to drill in the Arctic, and Visa was drawn into the corruption scandal involving FIFA.

Currently, little is known in co-branding research regarding partner brands' failure to meet objectives, incompatible brand values, partner repositioning and other financial and legal issues, and to what extent it could attribute to unsuccessful co-branding partnerships.[29] Overall, while co-branding is highly popular in the marketplace due to its inherent benefits in brand equity, cost savings and consumer acceptance, it is not devoid of risks. In the next section, we discuss the conditions that lead to successful co-branding.

Scholarly debate

Lafferty, B A (2007) The relevance of fit in a cause–brand alliance when consumers evaluate corporate credibility, *Journal of Business Research,* 60 (5), 447–53

Simonin, B and Ruth, J (1998) Is a company known by the company it keeps? Assessing the spill over effects of brand alliances on consumer brand attitudes, *Journal of Marketing Research,* 35 (1), 30–42

Conditions for the success of co-branding

Academic researchers have highlighted four fundamental conditions that can lead to successful co-branding. These factors are:

1 attitudes toward the partner brands
2 familiarity of the partners
3 the complementarity between the product categories
4 the brand fit between the partners[30]

While positive attitudes and familiarity of partnering brands among target consumers are vital, product fit (i.e. the extent to which two product categories are compatible) and brand fit (i.e. the consistency of the partners brand image and personality) are equally important for co-branding success.

When there is a good fit between the brand alliance partners, consumers feel assured about the product.[31] Co-branding from brands that are seen as complementary to each other are viewed more positively than when the brands are not complementary. For example, in the below Branding in practice when IBM and SAP, two technology companies, enter into alliance, they represent category level fit or congruence. Similarly, the McDonald's and Coca-Cola alliance is seen favourably by consumers due to the complementarity between their product offering, i.e. fast-food and soft drink. Fit between brand images can also have a positive influence on co-branding evaluations.[32] For example, Nike and Apple are both seen as highly innovative brands in their respected product categories. Thus, both possess strong brand images that complement each other, resulting in successful co-branding. The above examples also captures the importance of consumer familiarity in co-branding success as both partners involved in co-branding are well-known.

Managers must be mindful of these four critical factors when deciding on their co-branding partner. When both partner brands possess positive attitudes in the market and have highly familiarity among consumers, but the product and brand fit is not strong, it can lead to an unsuccessful co-branding. For instance, Forever 21, a well-known fashion brand, entered into a promotional alliance with Atkins, the low-carb diet brand. Forever 21 shipped Atkins bars, which are used as a low-carb snacks for weight loss, with its customer orders. While both brands are well-known within their categories, there was a poor product and brand fit. Customers were unable to comprehend the complementarity between these brands and thus many were outraged when their plus size outfit orders arrived with a weight loss bar.[33] Both brands apologized to customers and ended their promotional alliance due to the poor product and brand fit.

Table 10.1   Successful brand alliances

Co-branding companies	Sector	Process
IBM and SAP	B2B	IBM and SAP have collaborated to integrate their technologies and offer businesses improved enterprise solutions. This partnership has combined SAP's enterprise software with IBM's cloud and services, enabling companies to leverage both brands' strengths for comprehensive business solutions.[34]
Nestlé and L'Oréal	B2C	These two global giants joined forces to create a line of nutritional cosmetics in 2002. Nestlé's expertise in nutrition and L'Oréal's knowledge of beauty products culminated in the 'Innéov' brand, offering beauty supplements designed to enhance skin and hair health. The partnership ended in 2015.[35]
Nike and Apple	B2C	Nike and Apple partnered in 2006 to create the Nike+iPod Sports Kit, a co-branded product that allowed users to track their athletic performance through their iPods and Nike footwear. This integration of fitness and technology showcased the synergy between the two brands.
Coca-Cola and McDonald's	B2C	This enduring co-branding collaboration that started in 1955 involves exclusive beverage offerings at McDonald's outlets. The 'McFloat' and 'McFizz' products, made with Coca-Cola beverages, are tailored for McDonald's menus, showcasing the synergy between fast food and soft drink brands.[36]
Airbus and Rolls-Royce	B2B	In the aerospace industry, Airbus and Rolls-Royce collaborated on the A350 XWB aircraft. Rolls-Royce provides the advanced Trent XWB engines for the Airbus A350, demonstrating the partnership's commitment to innovation and efficiency in aviation technology.[37]
Siemens and Bentley	B2B	Siemens, a global technology company, collaborated with Bentley Motors, a luxury car manufacturer, to integrate Siemens' technology into Bentley's production process. This partnership enhances Bentley's manufacturing efficiency, demonstrating the application of B2B co-branding in improving industrial processes.[38]
H&M and Versace	B2C	The collaboration between Swedish fashion retailer H&M and Italian luxury fashion brand Versace resulted in a limited-edition collection that combined Versace's iconic designs with H&M's accessibility. This co-branding effort made luxury fashion more affordable and accessible to a broader consumer base.[39]

(*continued*)

Table 10.1   (Continued)

Co-branding companies	Sector	Process
Samsung and Intel	B2B	Samsung, a South Korean electronics conglomerate, and Intel, an American technology company, collaborated to develop advance processors for various devices, including smartphones and smartwatches. This B2B partnership illustrates how global technology leaders can join forces to create competitive solutions.[40]
Tata Motors and Cummins	B2B	Tata Motors, an Indian automobile manufacturer, collaborated with Cummins, an American engine manufacturer, to produce engines for Tata's commercial vehicles. This B2B collaboration showcases how a partnership between a vehicle manufacturer and an engine specialist can lead to improved performance and efficiency.[41]
McDonald's and Pokémon	B2C	McDonald's and the popular franchise Pokémon collaborated on multiple occasions to offer Pokémon-themed toys with Happy Meals. This co-branding effort leveraged the appeal of Pokémon characters to attract young customers and boost sales.[42]
Uniqlo and Disney	B2C	Japanese apparel retailer Uniqlo teamed up with Disney to create limited-edition clothing collections featuring beloved Disney characters. This B2C collaboration capitalized on the nostalgia and popularity of Disney characters to drive customer engagement and sales.[43]

Psychological mechanisms of co-branding

With the increasing interest among managers in co-branding, academic researchers have also engaged in explaining the psychological mechanisms that can lead to successful co-branding. Four major theories – namely signalling theory, information integration theory, associative network theory and attitude accessible theory – have been regularly employed to explain co-branding success.

As discussed in Chapter 7, signalling plays a fundamental role in brand communication. People rely on communication signals from partner brands as perceivable indicators of co-branding that they cannot observe directly. Through partner brands' communication, consumers can derive quality cues and in turn also prescribe a reference price for the co-brand. For instance, when Nike and Apple, which are both premium brands within their categories, enter into an alliance, consumers assume that the product will be highly innovative, good quality and premium priced. Thus, partner brand signals can play an important role in co-branding.

Further to signalling, consumers also have pre-conceived attitudes and beliefs about partner brands. When a co-brand is launched, information integration theory[44] suggests that new attitudes are formed through the integration of new information regarding the co-brand with the existing attitudes, beliefs and perceptions of the two partner brands. Academic researchers have shown that judgements about the brand alliances are likely to be affected by prior attitudes towards each brand and that can lead to future judgements about the partner brands and the co-brand as well.[45] A key consideration for information integration theory is congruency between the partner brands. As explained earlier, if the product and brand fit is weak between the partnering brands, there are greater chances of co-branding failure.

As discussed in Chapter 6, associative network theory is critical for brand positioning. Similarly, in the case of co-branding, both partner brands have to spend substantial resources to create a condition wherein consumers can fuse the brand togethers as a single stimulus. Without creating such linked nodes in consumer memory structures,[46] co-brands would not be successful. For instance, a consumer will only be able to associate the stimuli relating to the co-brand if the alliance is continuously reinforced through advertisements, public endorsements, a variety of endorsements and promotions among other brand communications tools. A highly successful example of such an associative network is Heineken's sponsorship of UEFA Champions League. The sonic association created by Heineken with the words 'the champions' throughout its advertisements when Champions League games are played has allowed football viewing consumers to create a strong associated memory network between the two brands.

While associative network theory focuses on the memory connection, attitude accessibility theory is related to the strength of attitude. This theory proposes that the stronger the attitude towards a stimulus, the more easily it is accessed from memory. Thus, the stronger the attitude towards a brand, the easier it becomes for consumers to recall the brand.[47] According to this theory, the co-brand is evaluated based on how easily consumers can recall their attitudes towards the partner brands. Moreover, if one of the partner brands is easily accessible to consumers due to their strong attitudes, its related attitudes will take precedence in evaluating the co-brand. Thus, having equity between partner brands is vitally important.[48]

Social cause-brand alliance

The discussion in this chapter has predominantly focused on B2B and B2C co-branding which brings together two for-profit brands. There is an increasing trend of co-branding involving a for-profit and a not-for-profit brand, creating a cause-brand alliance. Cause-brand alliances focus on mutual benefits for both brands. The for-profit partner gains a positive attitude and is perceived as warm and trustworthy by consumers.[49] Similarly, the not-for-profit partner benefits from financial donations and can increase its reach among a larger group of potential donors.[50] Moreover, the partnership can lead to improved brand awareness, enhanced consumer trust, greater purchase intentions, higher profits and increased customer loyalty.[51]

Again, for cause-brand alliance to be successful, the four principles that we highlighted earlier in the section 'Conditions for the success of co-branding' are pertinent. More importantly, the fit between the brand and the cause is extremely important for consumers to accept the alliance. Consumers' attitudes and behaviours towards cause-related alliances are favourable when their perceptions of the cause are similar to their perceptions of the brand.[52] For example, the Pampers and UNICEF brand alliance is a longstanding and impactful partnership between Procter & Gamble's (P&G) Pampers brand, a global leader in baby care products, and the United Nations Children's Fund (UNICEF), a renowned international organization dedicated to children's welfare.[53] This collaboration is primarily focused on a critical global issue: maternal and newborn tetanus (MNT) elimination. Pampers committed to donating a portion of the proceeds from the sale of specially marked packs of its nappies to UNICEF. Each pack sold carries a '1 Pack = 1 Vaccine' message, indicating that the purchase of one pack of nappies would provide funding for one tetanus vaccine for a mother in need. UNICEF, with the financial support from Pampers, procures and distributes tetanus vaccines to healthcare facilities in countries where MNT is prevalent. UNICEF works with local health workers and communities to ensure that pregnant women receive these life-saving vaccines. The partnership extends beyond financial contributions. Pampers and UNICEF collaborate on educational programmes to raise awareness about the importance of vaccination and safe delivery practices, helping to reduce maternal and newborn tetanus cases. The Pampers and UNICEF partnership demonstrates how a successful cause-brand alliance can leverage the reach and resources of a global brand like Pampers to make a tangible impact on a critical global health issue, aligning with the not-for-profit brand's mission.

However, academic research also suggests that a cause-brand alliances can be successful even when there is an unclear fit.[54] The incongruity between the cause and the brand can be overcome if the alliance can lead to transference of positive emotions related to the cause on the brand. For example, Masterfoods (the parent company of Mars, Inc., the producer of M&M's brand candies) donated 50 cents for every bag of Pink and White M&M's sold to the Susan G. Komen Breast Cancer Foundation, a charitable organization that funds cancer research, education and screening.[55] In this case, M&M, which is a brand of chocolate, has no clear connection as a product or a brand with cancer research.

A weak fit between the cause and the brand could lead to controversy as well and can result in negative brand evaluation, wherein consumers question the for-profit brand's inferred or ulterior motive. Inferred motive is defined as the extent to which a customer believes a firm intended to maximize its own interests while engaging in a socially appropriate action that may sway consumer opinions.[56] While the brand supports a social cause altruistically, the action might be perceived as hypocritical. This hypocrisy perception occurs when the brand's observed behaviour is inconsistent with what it claims to be supporting. Such hypocritical behaviour can negatively affect consumer attitude and behaviour towards the brand.[57] For example, Kentucky Fried Chicken (KFC), one of the world's largest fast-food chains, launched its 'Buckets for the Cure' charitable campaign, to support breast cancer awareness and research. This initiative involved a pledge from KFC to donate 50 cents from each specially branded pink bucket of its grilled or Original Recipe chicken sold in KFC outlets in the month of October to Susan G. Komen foundation. However, this campaign was severely criticized by activists and other organization as 'pinkwashing'.[58] The term pinkwashing refers to a situation where a company or organization uses breast cancer awareness and the colour pink as a marketing tactic without making substantial contributions to the cause. Critics claimed that there was a contradiction between promoting breast cancer awareness and offering menu items that could be associated with unhealthy diets, which can contribute to various health issues, including obesity.[59] Thus, when brands engage in cause-brand alliances, they need to exercise caution in the selection of the social cause. A cause that could raise questions regarding the brand's core activity should be avoided. In the KFC case, the incongruity principle suggests that supporting a cause that is not directly connected with the food sector may have been more fruitful for KFC.

As noted earlier, cause-brand alliances are often met with scepticism from a wider body of stakeholders, specifically about fulfilling ulterior business motives in supporting a social cause. Such scepticism can cause significant resource waste as well as reputational damage for the brand. To overcome such a challenge, we suggest a five-step framework for achieving cause-brand partnership success. Table 10.2 describes the STEAM framework.

Table 10.2   STEAM framework for cause-brand alliance success

STEAM Framework	Explanation	Questions to ask
Specificity	• A brand should specify what exactly it wishes to achieve from a cause-brand alliance. Their objective should be aligned to the resource investment from the organization. • The brand should also examine the cause-related connection from a congruity perspective. • The brand should also focus on the partnering not-for-profit organization and the perceptions associated with them.	• Is the brand interested in donating money to a cause or is it genuinely interested in tackling social ills through action? • Is the cause in congruence with the brand's core business and value proposition? • Are the not-for-profit partner's values aligned with the cause and the brand's objectives?

(continued)

Table 10.2 (Continued)

STEAM Framework	Explanation	Questions to ask
Transparency	• The brand should transparently communicate what it aims to achieve through this cause-brand alliance to the not-for-profit partner. • The types of support that the brand provides to the cause should be set out clearly.	• Have we clearly identified the timeframe for our alliance? • Are we transparently communicating the resource expenditure? • Are we transparently communicating our objectives and desired outcomes to our partner and wider audiences?
Engagement	• Once the brand identifies the social cause, it needs to conceptualize the execution plan and engage with the multiple stakeholders that are involved with the cause. • Throughout the execution, the brand should identify the touchpoints that will aid the success of the cause-brand alliance.	• How are we engaged with stakeholders with varying views about the cause? • Have we engaged with both supporters and critics? • What are our physical and digital engagement strategies? • How are we optimizing our and the not-for-profit partner's communication expertise to signal our motives?
Accountability	• The brand should make sure that its actions beyond the cause-brand alliance are in line with the vision of the cause. • The cause-brand alliance should be supported by all ranks of the organization, including senior management. • The brand should accept that it has an obligation to take responsibility for unplanned outcomes.	• Are our actions in the wider market appropriately aligned with the cause we are supporting? • Is there a sufficient buy-in and support among senior management towards the cause-brand alliance? • Are we willing to accept responsibility for undesirable outcomes?
Measurability	• In this stage, the brand should demonstrate how is it achieving the specified objectives of the cause-brand alliance outlined in the first step. • The brand should hire an external neutral organization to evaluate the success of its cause-brand alliance.	• How is our cause-brand alliance performing? • What objectives are being fulfilled and where are we observing any deviation? • Have we engaged with a neutral organization to examine the effectiveness of our alliance activities?

Chapter summary

In this chapter, we explored an important concept in brand management, co-branding, which is also termed brand alliance. We first defined what is meant by co-branding and then examined its benefits and risks. Co-branding is highly popular in branding practice because it is seen as a less resource-intensive and less risky strategic approach, in comparison to new product launches and even brand extensions. However, there are a number of risks associated with co-branding as well. To develop a successful brand alliance, we identified four important principles, namely consumer attitudes, familiarity, fit between the products and the brand fit. We also observed several successful brand alliance examples that have stood the test of time in both B2B and B2C sectors. Focusing on academic research in co-branding, we also identified important theories in the field that can explain the underpinning psychological mechanisms driving the success of brand alliances. Finally, we explored the burgeoning field of cause-brand alliances wherein a for-profit and a not-for-profit organization engage in co-branding.

Key concepts

- Brand alliance or co-branding
- Spillover effects
- Product fit
- Brand fit
- Co-branding theories
  - signalling theory
  - information integration theory
  - associative network theory
  - attitude accessible theory
- Cause-brand alliance

Exercise questions

1 Define co-branding and explain why it remains a popular strategic approach in branding compared to new product launches.

2 What are the major benefits associated with co-branding?

3 Identify and explain the major risks associated with brand alliances and how it can hurt a partner brand.

4 Using examples explain the important principles that drive successful brand alliances.

5 Explain any two theories that underpin co-branding-related academic research. How can an understanding of these theories help design impactful brand alliances in practice?

6 Describe the notion of cause-brand alliance. Provide one example, reflecting on the reasons of cause-brand alliance success and failure.

CASE STUDY   Handwashing for life – Lifebuoy's global cause-brand alliances

Read the following case study from Unilever about Lifebuoy's Social Mission programmes and communications, which has encouraged more than 1 billion people to develop good handwashing habits.

Lifebuoy soap was first created in 1894 by William and James Lever, during a period where public health and personal hygiene was becoming of greater social interest. In the 21st century, Lifebuoy is one of Unilever's biggest brands, aiming to prevent illness and save lives through handwashing with soap, creating accessible hygiene products and promoting healthy habits. This includes a handwashing behaviour change programme, including across Asia, Africa and Latin America, and TV adverts.

Other initiatives have included:

- **Lifebuoy's response to Covid-19:** public service announcements in 17 countries to follow public health guidelines about handwashing with soap as a key measure to stay protected; 2021's **It's in Your Hands** campaign continued to emphasize the need for handwashing alongside social distancing, mask-wearing and vaccination; it strengthened its supply chains to keep factories running and products available; it donated over 20 million products, including soap, hand sanitizers and antibacterial wipes to various organizations and initiatives, including schools, hospitals, the elderly and taxi drivers across Asia Pacific, the Middle East and Africa.

- **H for Handwashing:** H for Handwashing was built on the premise that effective behaviour change must start at an early age. Aligning with teaching children the alphabet through simple word associations, this campaign aimed to transform the letter 'H' into a symbol for hygiene. This included providing educational materials and launching a downloadable book

- **Harnessing the power of digital:** Lifebuoy's mobile programme **Mobile Doctarni** is a voice-based service that delivers critical health and hygiene information to mothers living in rural parts of the world, where access to doctors, information and TV is limited. The programme was able to significantly increase handwashing with soap/liquids by about one occasion per day among mothers. Specifically among pregnant or new mothers, the frequency of handwashing vastly improved among participants exposed to the campaign – an average of 1.5 times increase in handwashing frequency.

- **Lifebuoy's new telehealth partnerships:** Lifebuoy is progressing its social mission by supporting more people to improve their health and hygiene through its **telehealth** partnerships (consultation through mobile devices). Lifebuoy has teamed up with leading telemedicine providers in India, Indonesia, Vietnam, Bangladesh and Pakistan to expand the reach of these vital platforms.

- **Partnerships tackling cross-cutting issues linked to hygiene:** expanding partnerships' portfolios beyond hygiene to improve adjacent health-related behaviours, e.g. malnutrition and immunization. That means forging impactful partnerships that focus on holistic health where hygiene has a cross-cutting impact, enabling us to tackle hygiene-related health issues such as malnutrition and immunisation.

SOURCES www.unilever.com/planet-and-society/health-and-wellbeing/handwashing-for-life/; Rabie, T and Curtis, V (2006) Handwashing and risk of respiratory infections: A quantitative systematic review, *Tropical Medicine and International Health*, 11 (3), 258–67; Luby S et al (2011) The effect of handwashing at recommended times with water alone and with soap on child diarrhea in rural Bangladesh: An observational study, *PLoS Med*, 8 (6); Unilever calculation based in part on information reported by NielsenIQ through its ScanTrack, MarketTrack and Retail Index Services for the Skin Cleansing Category (markets defined by Nielsen or Unilever) for the 52-week period ending: Ghana – Jun 2020; Egypt – Sep 2020; Denmark, Norway, Saudi Arabia, Sweden and UAE – Nov 2020; Argentina, Australia, Bangladesh, Brazil, Canada, China, France, Germany, Great Britain, Greece, Hungary, India, Indonesia, Italy, Malaysia, Mexico, Netherlands, New Zealand, Nigeria, Pakistan, Peru, Philippines, Russia, South Africa, Spain, Switzerland, Taiwan, Thailand, Turkey and Uruguay – Dec 2020; Hong Kong, Kenya, Poland and Vietnam – Jan 2021; Austria, Belgium, Chile, Portugal, Singapore and South Korea – Feb 2021; US – Mar 2021 (Copyright © 2021, NielsenIQ); www.lifebuoy.com/No1.html

Case questions

1 Go to Unilever's website and read its mission and vision. How does this cause-brand alliance fit with Unilever's strategic branding?

2 Examine the H for Handwashing cause-brand alliance using the STEAM framework.

3 Apply any two of the four theories underpinning brand alliances identified in this chapter to the success of the H for Handwashing cause-brand alliance.

4 Critically evaluate using the four fundamental principles of successful brand alliance discussed in the chapter how Unilever collaborated with various social causes and relevant not-for-profit organizations to create effective cause-brand alliances.

5 Reflect critically on how these cause-brand alliances benefitted Unilever.

6 Examine the case from a critic's perspective and recommend how other brands can learn from Unilever's approach to improve their chances of successful cause-brand alliances.

Endnotes

1 Singh, J, Quamina, L and Kalafatis, S P (2016) Strategic brand alliances: Research advances and practical applications, *The Routledge Companion to Contemporary Brand Management*, 120–35

2 Washburn, J H, Till, B D and Priluck, R (2000) Co-branding: Brand equity and trial effects, *Journal of Consumer Marketing*, 17 (7), 591–604

3 Rao, A and Ruekert, R W (1994) Brand alliances as signals of product quality, *Sloan Management Review*, 36 (1), 87–97

4 Besharat, A and Langan, R (2014) Towards the formation of consensus in the domain of co-branding: Current findings and future priorities, *Journal of Brand Management*, 21, 112–132

5 Washburn, J H and Plank, R E (2002) Measuring brand equity: An evaluation of a consumer-based brand equity scale, *Journal of Marketing Theory and Practice*, 10 (1), 46–62

6 Park, C W, Jun, S Y and Shocker, A D (1996) Composite branding alliances: An investigation of extension and feedback effects, *Journal of Marketing Research*, 33 (4), 453–66

7 https://hbr.org/2007/04/the-upside-of-falling-flat (archived at https://perma.cc/R6B8-3BW6)

8 Besharat, A (2010) How co-branding versus brand extensions drive consumers' evaluations of new products: A brand equity approach, *Industrial Marketing Management*, 39 (8), 1240–49

9 Kalafatis, S P, Ledden, L, Riley, D and Singh, J (2016) The added value of brand alliances in higher education, *Journal of Business Research*, 69 (8), 3122–32

10 Lambe, C J, Spekman, R E and Hunt, S D (2002) Alliance competence, resources, and alliance success: Conceptualization, measurement, and initial test, *Journal of the Academy of Marketing Science*, 30 (2), 141–58

11 www.bp.com/en/global/corporate/news-and-insights/press-releases/m-and-s-food-and-bp-extend-successful-forecourt-convenience-relationship.html (archived at https://perma.cc/L9KY-VY2T)

12 Kalafatis, S P, Remizova, N, Riley, D and Singh, J (2012) The differential impact of brand equity on B2B co-branding, *Journal of Business & Industrial Marketing*, 27 (8), 623–34

13 Helm, S V and Özergin, B (2015) Service inside: The impact of ingredient service branding on quality perceptions and behavioral intentions, *Industrial Marketing Management*, 50, 142–49

14 Dahlstrom, R and Nygaard, A (2016) The psychology of co-branding alliances: The business-to-business relationship outcomes of role stress, *Psychology & Marketing*, 33 (4), 267–82

15 Cao, Z and Yan, R (2017) Does brand partnership create a happy marriage? The role of brand value on brand alliance outcomes of partners, *Industrial Marketing Management*, 67, 148–57

16 www.volvogroup.com/en/news-and-media/news/2021/mar/news-3905968.html (archived at https://perma.cc/835J-7LFC)

17 Erevelles, S, Stevenson, T H, Srinivasan, S and Fukawa, N (2008) An analysis of B2B ingredient co-branding relationships, *Industrial Marketing Management*, 37 (8), 940–52

18 Swaminathan, V, Reddy, S K and Dommer, S L (2012) Spillover effects of ingredient branded strategies on brand choice: A field study, *Marketing Letters*, 23, 237–51

19 Singh, J, Quamina, L and Kalafatis, S P (2016) Strategic brand alliances: Research advances and practical applications, *The Routledge Companion to Contemporary Brand Management*, 120–35

20 Ibid.

21 Weber, K and Sparks, B (2004) Consumer attributions and behavioral responses to service failures in strategic airline alliance settings, *Journal of Air Transport Management*, 10 (5), 361–67

22 Votolato, N and Unnava, H (2006), Spill over of negative information on brand alliances, *Journal of Consumer Psychology*, 16 (2), 196–202

23 www.theguardian.com/world/2014/jul/31/southwest-seaworld-end-partnership (archived at https://perma.cc/NW2Q-XPZN)

24 https://en.wikipedia.org/wiki/Firestone_and_Ford_tire_controversy (archived at https://perma.cc/PQ87-7SYQ)

25 Suh, J and Park, S (2009), Successful brand alliance and its negative spill over effect on a host brand: Test of cognitive response hypothesis, *Advances in Consumer Research*, 36, 243–47

26 Coombs, W T (2007) Protecting organization reputations during a crisis: The development and application of situational crisis communication theory, *Corporate Reputation Review*, 10, 163–76

27 Singh, J and Crisafulli, B (2020) 'Corporate image at stake': The impact of crises and response strategies on consumer perceptions of corporate brand alliances, *Journal of Business Research*, 117, 839–49

28 Singh, J, Crisafulli, B, Quamina, L T and Kottasz, R (2020) The role of brand equity and crisis type on corporate brand alliances in crises, *European Management Review*, 17 (4), 821–34

29 Crisafulli, B, Dimitriu, R and Singh, J (2020) Joining hands for the greater good: Examining social innovation launch strategies in B2B settings, *Industrial Marketing Management*, 89, 487–98

30 Singh, J, Quamina, L and Kalafatis, S P (2016) Strategic brand alliances: Research advances and practical applications, *The Routledge Companion to Contemporary Brand Management*, 120–35

31 Park, C, Jun, S and Shocker, A (1996), Composite branding alliances: An investigation of extension and feedback effects, *Journal of Marketing Research*, 33 (4), 453–66

32 Simonin, B and Ruth, J (1998) Is a company known by the company it keeps? Assessing the spill over effects of brand alliances on consumer brand attitudes, *Journal of Marketing Research*, 35 (1), 30–42

33 https://edition.cnn.com/2019/07/24/business/forever-21-atkins-bars/index.html (archived at https://perma.cc/6WBY-N2ZU)

34 www.ibm.com/cloud/sap/alliance (archived at https://perma.cc/LQB3-34H2)

35 www.nestle.com/media/pressreleases/allpressreleases/loreal-nestle-end-joint-venture-inneov (archived at https://perma.cc/GYC2-U2ZV)

36 www.nytimes.com/2014/05/16/business/coke-and-mcdonalds-working-hand-in-hand-since-1955.html (archived at https://perma.cc/3RQP-AYV5)

37 www.rolls-royce.com/media/press-releases-archive/yr-2011/110619-power-enhanced-a350.aspx (archived at https://perma.cc/8F59-M38E)

38 https://press.siemens.com/global/en/pressrelease/siemens-and-bentley-systems-strengthen-their-strategic-alliance-and-joint-investment (archived at https://perma.cc/4R5S-HCYR)

39 www.vogue.co.uk/gallery/versace-for-hm-party (archived at https://perma.cc/6K9H-YLXK)

40 https://news.samsung.com/global/samsung-expands-collaboration-with-intel-to-advance-vran-innovation (archived at https://perma.cc/4CK5-XLNX)

41 www.cummins.com/news/releases/2023/04/26/cummins-inc-and-tata-motors-strengthen-their-30-year-alliance-power (archived at https://perma.cc/FB6L-22G7)

42 www.mcdonalds.com/gb/en-gb/family-hub/happy-meal.html (archived at https://perma.cc/W9FT-CWSR)

43 www.uniqlo.com/uk/en/content/IDdisney-stories21603.html (archived at https://perma.cc/G87C-ZLH6)

44 Anderson, N (1981), *Foundations of Information Integration Theory*, Academic Press, New York

45 Simonin, B and Ruth, J (1998) Is a company known by the company it keeps? Assessing the spill over effects of brand alliances on consumer brand attitudes, *Journal of Marketing Research,* 35 (1), 30–42

46 Anderson, J (1983) A spreading activation theory of memory, *Journal of Verbal Learning and Verbal Behaviour,* 22 (3), 261–95

47 Fazio, R, Powell, M and Williams, C (1989) The role of attitude accessibility in the attitude-behaviour process, *Journal of Consumer Research,* 16 (3), 280–88

48 Singh, J, Quamina, L and Kalafatis, S P (2016) Strategic brand alliances: Research advances and practical applications, *The Routledge Companion to Contemporary Brand Management,* 120–35

49 Galan-Ladero, M, Galera Casquet, C and Singh, J (2015) Understanding factors influencing consumer attitudes toward cause-related marketing, *International Journal of Non-profit and Voluntary Sector Marketing,* 20 (1), 52–70

50 Till, B D and Nowak, L I (2000) Toward effective use of cause-related marketing alliances, *Journal of Product & Brand Management,* 9 (7), 472–84

51 Krishna, A and Rajan, U (2009) Cause marketing: Spill over effects of cause-related products in a product portfolio, *Management Science,* 55 (9), 1469–85

52 Lichtenstein, D R, Drumwright, M E and Braig, B M (2004) The effect of corporate social responsibility on customer donations to corporate-supported non-profits, *Journal of Marketing,* 68 (4), 16–32

53 www.unicef.org/partnerships/pg-pampers (archived at https://perma.cc/X42Z-DVS3)

54 Lafferty, B A (2007) The relevance of fit in a cause–brand alliance when consumers evaluate corporate credibility, *Journal of Business Research,* 60 (5), 447–53

55 https://csnews.com/mms-dove-chocolate-support-breast-cancer-awareness (archived at https://perma.cc/A5F6-Y739)

56 Joireman, J, Grégoire, Y, Devezer, B and Tripp, T M (2013) When do customers offer firms a 'second chance' following a double deviation? The impact of inferred firm motives on customer revenge and reconciliation, *Journal of Retailing*, 89 (3), 315–37

57 Wagner, T, Lutz, R J and Weitz, B A (2009) Corporate hypocrisy: Overcoming the threat of inconsistent corporate social responsibility perceptions, *Journal of Marketing*, 73 (6), 77–91

58 www.bcaction.org/breast-cancer-action-calls-shame-on-kfcs-pink-buckets-campaign/ (archived at https://perma.cc/P45A-WLD8)

59 http://edition.cnn.com/2010/LIVING/homestyle/04/28/kfc.pink.bucket.campaign/index. html (archived at https://perma.cc/ALV9-YJCV)

Brand portfolio management   11

Overview

In this chapter, we first explain the concept of brand portfolio management, and discuss how different types of approaches to brand portfolio management lead to benefits and sometimes disadvantages. We then discuss how equity is locked and managed at different levels of a brand's portfolio. In the following section, we include the tactical elements of brand portfolio. The final section deals with the concept of corporate branding, the important levers and how organizations can manage corporate brands.

Key learning outcomes

Upon reading this chapter, you should be able to

- Understand the concept of brand portfolio management
- Comprehend the advantages and disadvantages of different brand portfolio management strategies
- Identify how brand equity is managed across levels
- Gain insights on tactical elements of brand portfolio management
- Understand the concept of corporate branding
- Grasp the important levers that help corporate brands distinguish themselves
- Develop an unerstanding of how to manage corporate brands

What is brand portfolio?

It is well-established that brands are created to communicate their value to customers. Brands are also a promise made by the manufacturer to their customers which signals price, quality, status and other relevant symbolic aspects. As a brand grows, many different customer segments get involved in buying and consuming the brand.

Many times, consumers use the same brand for varying reasons. For instance, some consumers may use a soft drink for quenching their thirst, while others may use it as party refreshment. Similarly, a health supplement may be used a consumer to reduce weight, while others may use it to remain fit. Thus, as the usage associated with the product differs, brand managers may want to align their brand's narrative to fit with their customer needs and wants. Moreover, with regular product innovations and additional features that are added, brands also aim to convey the differentiation between the older and new version of their products. For example, Apple launches a new iPhone variant every year. Further to that, many brands expand into multiple categories of products that are related or unrelated to their initial offering. Continuing with Apple, the company currently operates in personal computing, smartphone, wearable devices, sound equipment, television and home entertainment and is even planning to develop autonomous cars.

The growth of product categories and the proliferation of brands across the categories to serve multiple segments of customers creates immense complexities for brand managers. A brand's basic premise is to differentiate the product from competition. However, growing competition and a plethora of brands within the marketplace make it difficult for a brand to differentiate itself. Furthermore, as discussed earlier, with the growth of a single brand in multiple product categories, brand managers have to simplify and clearly distinguish their offering so consumers can easily identify the brand and remain connected.

BRANDING IN PRACTICE
Nokia's entry and exit from consumer electronics

Nokia, established in 1865 as a paper mill operation in Finland, expanded into rubber products, telecommunications, consumer electronics, personal computers, network equipment, mobile phones, operating systems, among other things. Moreover, within each of these categories, the brand Nokia had multiple product levels depending on customer segment requirements. For instance, to just serve the consumer electronics markets in the early 2000s, Nokia created a number of mobile phones such as the Nokia 3310, Nokia 6600, N73, N95 and E71. It also acquired a number of prominent brands across several categories: the hardware division of Sega to develop N-gage gaming devices, the online music distributor Loudeye Corporation, the media-sharing service Twango, the mobile advertising technology firm Enpocket, the digital mapping brand Navtaq, among many others. However, with the arrival of the Apple iPhone, the Nokia consumer electronics division struggled substantially. For instance, in 2007 when the Apple iPhone was launched, Nokia's Symbian operating system had a market share of 62.5 per cent within the mobile phone sector. However, by the end of

2008, this had fallen to 40.8 per cent, reducing to less than 15 per cent by the end of 2011.[1] In 2014, Nokia sold its mobile phone division with its brands.[2] However, at the same time, the Nokia brand has continued its acquisitions as well. For instance, in 2016, Nokia purchased French telecommunications equipment company Alcatel-Lucent, which also owns the iconic telecommunications firm Bell Labs.

This Nokia example shows how sometimes brands grow in different sectors, flourish and at times fail. Without a clear portfolio management strategy, brands can enter into categories of products without having clear expertise. Nokia was predominantly a B2B company that ventured into B2C market and flourished for a number of years. However, with continuous expansion into a variety of B2C categories, and without a clear brand portfolio management strategy, it had to withdraw from consumer electronics. The brand continues to operate successfully through its B2B portfolio.

Figure 11.1   Nokia had many globally successful phones such as the Nokia 5110

SOURCE Photo by Girl with red hat on Unsplash

Managing brand portfolio

To manage the challenge of brand proliferation and growth, brand managers need to plan branding from the perspective of portfolio management. Portfolio management refers to the systematic process of managing a collection of assets, investments, projects or products to achieve specific strategic objectives. It involves making decisions about the allocation of resources, risk management and the optimization of the portfolio to maximize returns or achieve other desired outcomes.[3] Brand portfolio management, thus, is the systematic process of identifying, structuring, managing, curating and communicating the brands under a company's control. Developing a portfolio management approach allows managers to create a clear and coherent structure to streamline their brands fitting with their strategic objectives, allocate appropriate marketing and communication resources based on each brand's growth potential, take appropriate acquisition or deletion decisions and manage the brand on a day-to-day basis. Brand portfolio management also helps consumers in understanding the differing traits and features of a brand within the portfolio and helps foster customer-brand relationships.

Brand portfolio management is not a rigid structure and can differ for each firm depending on their strategic brand vision and growth. In that regard, brand portfolios differ between competing brands. An important point to remember is that most brands do not start with a predetermined portfolio strategy. As a brand expands into new product categories and markets, complex hierarchies and levels emerge. As discussed in Chapter 9, brands have varieties of line and category extension strategies as they grow. Moreover, brands can move into new businesses that can further increase complexities. The business in practice regarding Nokia explains the complexities involved in brand management and the need for brand portfolio management.

Types of brand portfolio management strategies

Brands use a variety of strategies to successfully manage their portfolio. Three major brand portfolio management strategies that brands employ include: corporate branding, family branding and individual branding. Corporate branding is the highest-level brand in the hierarchy of brand portfolio management. It represents the parent company and all its products and services. For example, the corporate brand for Samsung is simply 'Samsung'. All of Samsung's products, such as smartphones, TVs and appliances, are branded under the Samsung corporate brand. On the other hand, there are corporate brands like Unilever and Diageo which function on the corporate level with a large portfolio of brands across various categories. These corporate brands serve as a relationship enhancer for the stakeholders. In the section on corporate branding in this chapter, we explain in further detail the importance of corporate branding and how it is a critical avenue for reputation management and brand identity.

Family branding involves the use of one overarching name for multiple products or product lines. For example, 'Microsoft Office' encompasses a suite of software applications like Word, Excel and PowerPoint. Many large firms use a unique family brand setting at product category level: Procter & Gamble use product category classification such as baby care, fabric care, family care, feminine care, grooming, hair care and oral care to set out the family of brands that operate within the same category. Within fabric care, Procter & Gamble owns brands such as Ariel, Bounce, Cheer, Downy, Dreft, Era, Gain, Rindex and Tide. These brands compete against each as well as other competitors in the market.

Within the family brands, there are individual brands. These brands have their own unique identity and are managed independently within the corporate structure. For instance, detergent brands such as Ariel, Gain and Tide also act as individual brands wherein they have their own variants for different pack sizes and formulations. Similarly, the Apple family brand includes individual brands such as the iPhone, iPad and MacBook, all with numerous variants based on their specifications and colours. Individual brands are all marketed under their own names, which helps to differentiate them from each other and from other brands in the market.

Brands also manage their portfolio cognisant of regional and cultural differences. For instance, Colgate toothpaste is sold globally, however, Sorriso is mostly available in Latin America and Elmex in Europe. An outline of the structure of Colgate-Palmolive is shown in Figure 11.2.

Figure 11.2   Brand portfolio management structure of Colgate-Palmolive

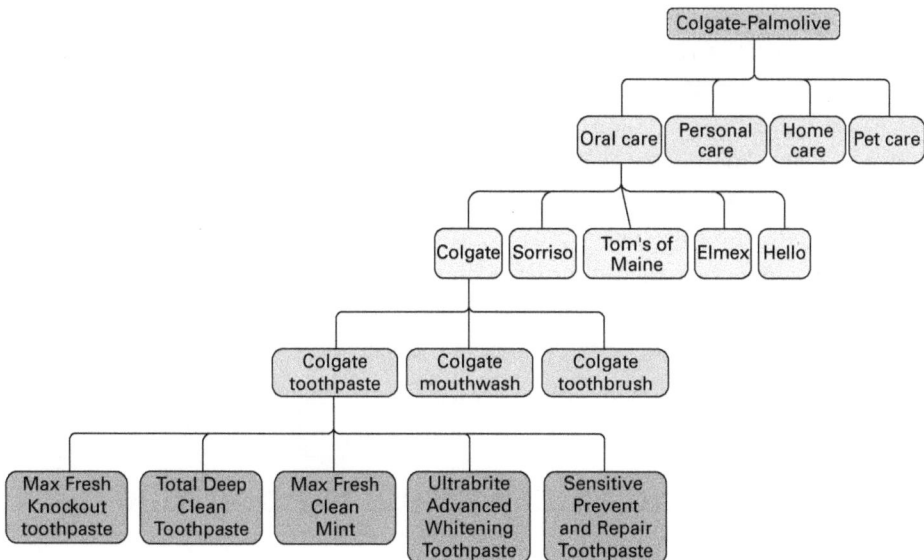

SOURCE Authors' compilation
NOTE The above only shows a few of the brand variants within the Colgate brand. Please visit www.colgate.com/en-us/products for the full brand portfolio.

Similarly, depending on the region and cultural associations, brands also include variants within their individual portfolio. For example, Coca-Cola in the UK is available in eight different pack sizes from a 150ml can to a 2.25ltr plastic bottle. In the USA, there are six pack sizes from 220ml to 2ltr.

Advantages and disadvantages

The portfolio management approach creates the structure and relationships between a company's brands and sub-brands. This approach has several advantages and disadvantages that impact a company's branding strategy. The biggest advantage of adopting brand portfolio management strategy is the clarity and consistency it provides for the parent brand and the sub-brands about their role with the hierarchy. It also makes it easier for consumers to understand how various products and services are related and thus increase brand recognition and trust. Further, brand portfolio management can also allow a corporate brand to leverage its brand equity across categories which makes it easier to enter into new product categories and international markets. The portfolio approach allows for efficient resource allocation as marketing and R&D efforts can be shared across related brands. This can reduce the cost of innovation and improve market penetration. Moreover, the brand portfolio management approach can help mitigate risks when one of the brands within a portfolio suffers from reputational damage due to a transgression.

The brand portfolio management approach provides clarity but at the same time due to market pressures, many brand managers tend to overextend the brand. This overextension can lead to brand dilution and cannibalization within the same product category. Moreover, each extension is associated with its own costs related to production, logistics, retail and communications. Thus, it can lead to resource allocation challenges. In addition, overextending brand portfolio and variants in particular can cause consumer confusion. For instance, there are more than 40 different variants of Colgate toothpaste available in the market including various flavours and ingredients (e.g. mint, charcoal, fluoride-free, etc.) and types of oral care (e.g. cavity protection, whitening, freshness, sensitive teeth care, etc.). Such levels of variety may lead to consumer confusion, decision postponement and reduced decision satisfaction at times.[4] When such overextension occurs, the portfolio management approach can allow the brand manager to evaluate the market performance of the extensions and make decisions regarding streamlining the portfolio size.

Managing brand equity across the portfolio

The brand portfolio management approach allows brand managers to unlock brand equity at every level of the portfolio. To leverage equity at each level, the following principles can be followed. First, a company has to decide on its *brand strategy* by defining its core values and distinction in terms of what the brand stands for. Second, based on the brand strategy, the company can decide its *brand positioning* strategy which will allow consistency and coherence of brand communication. Third, the strategy and the positioning will the guide the company in *developing and managing its brand portfolio*. Such a brand portfolio will, in turn, allow a brand to create a *roadmap for product development and brand extension*. Finally, by *monitoring and evaluating* the performance of each brand and its variants, the company can adjust the overall brand portfolio.

The brand portfolio management approach can guide a firm in its actions to leverage brand equity at each level of the portfolio. At the corporate brand level, the major brand equity considerations are reputation management, social responsibility and product/market development. For example, Kering group, which owns luxury brands including Gucci, Yves Saint Laurent, Bottega Veneta, Balenciaga, Alexander McQueen and Briony, among others, has a unique corporate level sustainability initiative that has resulted in the Kering brand publishing its first environmental profit and loss statement (EP&L) in 2016 and initiatives such as group wide sustainability targets for suppliers and its own brands, the banning of fur across product range and refusal to use models under 18 years old.[5]

Brand equity is locked in the positioning of various brands within the brand family. Thus, the overall brand family and the individual brands within the family can leverage brand equity through their strategic actions. For instance, within the fabric care brand family, Unilever has various detergent brands such as Surf, Omo (Persil in the UK; Skip in France, Portugal and Spain; Ala in Argentina; Via in Sweden; Breeze in Thailand and Philippines; and Rinso in Indonesia), and Neutral among others. Each brand is positioned slightly differently in the market. However, they all adhere to Unilever's principles of sustainability.[6] Surf is associated with value for money and concentrating on fun and playfulness, while targeting the price conscious consumer. The brand is also focused on families with young children, encouraging playing outside and getting dirty, while Bio Luvil targets adults and adult households predominantly focusing on clothes and fashion. Neutral diverts from these brands and focuses on skin sensitivities to detergent chemicals and fragrances. With each brand having its own position, they can choose varying communication strategies, tools and approaches to build and maintain their brand equity. Moreover, this allows the brands to explore varieties of co-branding strategies. For instance, Neutral collaborated with Allergy and Asthma Association within Finland, while Omo with its family focus partnered with the Olympic movement that encourages kids to be active in not-for-profit sports clubs.

Tactical management of brand portfolio

Brand portfolio is dynamic. As the company grows, it builds new brands, and acquires and discards brands to serve its current and potential customers according to its brand vision. This requires regular changes within the brand portfolio. There are a number of tactics that brands use to maintain their overall brand equity. These tactics include brand introduction, rejuvenation, transfer, extension and divestment.

Brand introduction is the process of launching a new brand into the market. This typically involves creating brand awareness, establishing a brand identity and building initial brand equity. Apple's introduction of the iPhone in 2007 is a notable example. Apple successfully introduced a new brand that revolutionized the smartphone industry by combining design, functionality and user experience. Brand rejuvenation, also known as brand revitalization, involves making changes to an existing brand that may include repositioning, redesigning or rebranding to appeal to a new or refreshed target audience. McDonald's uses this tactic often when it revamps its menu, offering different toys in Happy Meals, and redesigning the restaurant ambience to attract its customer base. Brand transfer refers to the practice of leveraging an established brand's equity to enter a new product category or market. It involves extending a brand's identity and reputation beyond its original scope. Nike successfully transferred its brand equity from athletic footwear to apparel, accessories and even technology, creating a broader brand presence that extends beyond shoes.

BRANDING IN PRACTICE

Twitter aims to rejuvenate itself by becoming the super app X

Since its inception, Twitter has been a news-led social media platform that focused on global socio-political trends. With the takeover by Elon Musk, Twitter was re-branded as X. Mr Musk highlighted the financial struggles of the brand and promoted his vision for the brand to become a super app such as WeChat in China that offers everything from messaging, video calls, micro-blogging, buyer-seller platform, forums and payments.

To rejuvenate the brand, X will need to use a variety of brand portfolio strategies to operate in different categories. It will also need to collaborate with a variety of organizations to provide the range of services it aims to deliver. For instance, the brand may collaborate with large travel organizations to build a hospitality and travel search option, connect with online auction companies to create a buyer-seller ecommerce platform and offer a payment gateway using Musk's earlier ventures, such as Paypal.

Alternatively, creating its own sub-divisions and sub-brands will require considerable resources and brand portfolio management effort in this saturated market. Communicating the value of the sub-brands will pose yet another challenge for X. A well-crafted brand portfolio can lead X to success.

Brand divestment involves the strategic decision to sell or discontinue a brand or brand portfolio. This can be done to focus resources on core brands, eliminate underperforming brands or address regulatory or competitive issues. Covergirl, the American cosmetics brand, was acquired by Procter & Gamble in 1989 and later on sold to Coty, Inc. in 2016. Brand divestment involves the tactical decision to sell, discontinue or spin off a brand from the brand portfolio. Companies may choose to divest brands that no longer align with their core business objectives, underperform or face regulatory or competitive challenges. In 2017, the Kraft Heinz Company divested several brands, including the sale of its cheese business to Lactalis, to focus on core brands and reduce debt. This divestment allowed Kraft Heinz to reallocate resources and streamline its portfolio.

Corporate branding

Corporate branding refers to the entire organization as a brand, as opposed to individual product or services.[7] Many companies now prominently display the organization as a brand. This practice is observed across a wide array of organizations, including for-profit, not-for-profit, non-governmental organizations, universities, sports teams and destinations.[8] In specific regions of the world, corporate branding has a well-established presence. For instance, in Japan, Korea and India, companies such as Mitsubishi, Samsung and Tata are long recognized as corporate brands engaged in a wide array of sectors, including shipbuilding, medical equipment, construction, financial services, software development and consultancy. This extends beyond these corporations' more recent reputations in the Western world, primarily for automobiles and consumer electronics.

Corporate branding offers a further distinctive identity beyond the product/service brand that can promote differentiation from competitors. Moreover, corporate branding can help the firm in developing and percolating a particular set of values, culture, people, programmes, assets and skills.[9] A strong corporate brand thus allows companies to straddle across sectors based on their values and ethos. For instance, DuPont is a corporate brand that has endured numerous shifts in its strategic direction over time. Initially, it ventured into gunpowder manufacturing, briefly explored the rapidly growing automotive industry in the early 20th century and later focused its efforts on polymers and innovative materials. Subsequently, it expanded into the energy sector and currently the brand identifies itself as a worldwide science company.[10] Similarly, IBM, the global technology behemoth, which started as a time clocks company, moved into punch card-based data processing, to computing, mainframe servers, personal computers, software, super computers, consulting and now into machine learning and artificial intelligence. However, the values and ethos associated with technological innovations have remained consistent throughout the company's evolution. Most industry sectors have large corporate brands that consumers identify with. For instance, within retail, there are global corporate brands such as Wal-Mart, Tesco and Carrefour. Similarly, in the aviation industry there are both manufacturing and service corporate brands, such as Airbus, Boeing, United Airlines, Turkish Airlines, Emirates and Menzies. Corporate brands not only offer the trust signals to consumers but also allow employees to develop a sense of identity and help build employee-company relationships.

Corporate brands have some overlaps in their characteristics with product brands; however, these are also distinct. The scope and scale of a corporate brand comprises the whole enterprise, the entire corporation and all its stakeholders, and not just one product or a group of products.[11] Moreover, corporate brands reflect the company's heritage, values and beliefs that define corporate brand identity. In comparison, product brands are often developed predominantly through the imagination of the brand management team and the advertising agencies. Further, product brands' main focus is consumers, while a corporate brand targets a much wider stakeholder group including employees, investors, suppliers, policy makers and society at large. Corporate brands are managed at a comparatively senior level of the organization, while many product brands are controlled and managed by middle managers.[12] In order to develop a successful corporate brand, it is vital that the values associated with the corporate brand are transmitted to the entire organization. This happens when there is a strong commitment from senior management at the highest levels.[13]

Corporate brand levers

Corporate brands allow companies to leverage their position through a variety of dimensions including heritage, value, reputation, personality and ethics/sustainability credentials.[14] While products and services tend to become similar over time, organizations are inevitably very different.[15] Corporate brand activities are organization wide, thus, initiatives supported by the corporate brand offer better resource utilization, management and wider acceptance compared to product brands. Due to closer stakeholder engagement compared to product brands, initiatives supported by corporate brands are seen as more credible and trustworthy.

Corporate brands can leverage a company's historical legacy, traditions and heritage to build a strong brand identity and foster connections with customers and stakeholders.[16] Such an approach can emphasize the company's longstanding market presence, values and contributions to the industry and society. For example, Coca-Cola often emphasizes its 135+ years of history and traditions, associating its brand with nostalgia and timeless refreshment. Coca-Cola's vintage advertisements and use of its classic logo help reinforce this heritage perspective.[17] The corporate brand can also utilize its historical legacy to showcase its authenticity. Adidas, for instance, effectively highlights its pivotal role not only in the realm of sports (by pioneering innovations like the first hand-forged spiked running shoes for various distance races, famously crafting Jesse Owens' footwear for the 1936 Berlin Olympics and introducing the first lightweight football boots with screw-in studs, as well as manufacturing footballs for numerous World Cups), but also in the realm of popular culture (as evidenced by its enduring association with dance music culture, for instance, the hip-hop pioneers Run DMC's track 'My Adidas'). Some corporate brands even add their establishment year within the logo itself to highlight their heritage and origin. For example, the beer brand Budweiser often includes the year 1876 in its logo, signifying the year the brand was founded. Similarly, the luxury brand Hermès uses the word Paris to signify its association with the leading fashion and luxury destination.[18] Moreover, Hermès also highlights its association as a high-end harness and saddle maker, by depicting the 'Duc-carriage' with a horse and rider.

In addition to heritage association, the corporate brand is a valuable tool for reputation management. Corporate brands reflect the values and culture of the organization that product brands may not convey. The values, culture and personality of the corporate brand allow both internal and external stakeholders of a brand to derive meaning associated with the brand and the organization.[19] Corporate brands are, thus, strongly connected with organizational reputation. A positive reputation can significantly impact a company's success and competitiveness.[20] Reputation is often regarded as one of a company's most valuable assets and can lead to increased customer trust, loyalty and competitive advantage.[21] Consumers are more likely to do business with companies they trust, and investors are more inclined to support financially stable and reputable organizations.[22] For instance, Apple is known for its strong corporate reputation, built on a combination of innovative products, sleek design and a commitment to customer privacy. The company's reputation for quality and reliability has contributed to its loyal customer base.

BRANDING IN PRACTICE
Nestlé corporate brand: heritage, values and reputation

Nestlé, founded in 1866 by Henri Nestlé, is a Swiss multinational food and beverage conglomerate known for its strong corporate brand heritage, values and reputation. It is the world's largest food company, with over 200 brands and products sold in over 190 countries.

Nestlé's corporate brand heritage is deeply rooted in the company's commitment to improving the nutrition and wellbeing of infants through the development of Farine Lactée, the world's first milk-based infant food. Nestlé continues to honour this heritage by positioning itself as a nutrition-focused company. This heritage aligns with Nestlé's mission to 'unlock the power of food to enhance quality of life for everyone, today and for generations to come'.[23]

Nestlé's corporate values, encapsulated in its 'Nestlé in Society' report, reflect its commitment to responsible business conduct, sustainability and ethical practices.[24] The company prioritizes areas like nutrition, water stewardship, environmental sustainability and social impact. Nestlé's 'Creating Shared Value' (CSV) approach integrates social and environmental concerns into its core business strategy, demonstrating a commitment to value creation for both shareholders and society.[25]

Nestlé maintains a strong global reputation through consistent product quality, transparency and ethical practices. Its reputation for safe and nutritious products extends to diverse markets worldwide. Nestlé's efforts to provide clean and safe drinking water in developing countries through its 'Water for Life' initiative showcases its commitment to global social responsibility.

Nestlé successfully utilizes its corporate brand heritage, values and reputation to maintain a global presence while fostering trust, sustainability and innovation. The vision put forward by the corporate brand helps unite the entire organization and foster trust with stakeholders. By aligning its actions with its heritage and values, Nestlé continues to be a leading force in the global food and beverage industry, illustrating the strategic importance of brand heritage and reputation for corporate brands.

Approaches to corporate branding

Depending on the organizational structure, managers decide about the visibility and identity the corporate brand should create, in comparison to its product brands. Companies generally employ three different approaches in this regard.[26] Some organizations use their corporate brand name across all the firm's activities and communications. This 'monolithic' corporate brand approach may also be used in conjunction with product brands. For instance, Amazon, the multinational technology and e-commerce company known for its vast online marketplace, cloud computing services and innovative ventures, employs a monolithic brand strategy across its diverse range of products and services, from e-commerce (i.e. Amazon.com) and Amazon Prime to Amazon Web Services (AWS).

The second approach to corporate branding focuses on 'endorsed and sub-brands' wherein the corporate brand offers an endorsement or support to the product brand.

The endorsement is aimed at adding credibility to the endorsed product brand or sub-brand in consumer minds, utilizing the strength of values of the corporate brand.[27] For example, Cadbury's Dairy Milk, Sony PlayStation or Polo by Ralph Lauren utilize the corporate brand's heritage, values and reputation. This approach is particularly useful when launching new brands or entering new product/service categories. The third approach involves giving little or no prominence to the corporate brand, with a clear focus on a product brand. When a corporate brand employs such an approach, some of its stakeholders, such as the shareholders, suppliers and partners, may know the corporate brand and its product brands. However, the end-users or the consumers may not be able to make a direct connection between the product and the corporate brand.[28] For instance, PepsiCo is known for its individual product brands such as Pepsi, Lay's, Gatorade, Tropicana and Quaker Oats. These brands are marketed separately and cater to different categories. Procter & Gamble (P&G) has a portfolio of several successful individual product brands, for example, Tide, Pampers, Gillette and Crest. Each of these brands has its own distinct identity and marketing strategy, although they are all owned by the corporate brand P&G.

Similar to product brands, corporate brands have a personality as well. The values and actions of a corporate brand reflected in individual or collective employee actions and behaviours set out its personality.[29] Three specific personality traits that are vital for corporate brands are highlighted by academic researchers, including being *passionate* and *compassionate* in addressing the market and stakeholders; *creative* and *disciplined* in its approach to markets; and *agile* and *collaborative* in addressing market dynamics and changes.[30] In the digital era, company websites have become an important vehicle for demonstrating these traits. In analysing corporate brand websites, researchers have identified personality traits such as sophistication, excitement, affection, popularity, competence and ruggedness, amongst others.[31][32] For example, the website of Kikkoman, a Japanese food and seasoning company with a global reach known for its soy sauce and a wide range of authentic Japanese condiments, highlights its corporate social responsibility (CSR) credentials and warm personality through its digital presence.

CSR, sustainability, activism and such other socio-politically relevant activities are mostly carried out by the corporate brand. Termed corporate brand citizenship, these initiatives reflect the values and wider societal concerns of the people within the organization. For example, the Swedish retailer Ikea sets out a sustainability strategy with an ambitious goal to become carbon positive, without relying on offsetting. In making this commitment, Ikea aims to reduce more greenhouse gas emissions than its value chain emits.[33] Similarly, Danone, one of the world's largest dairy companies, committed to substantially cut absolute methane emissions from its fresh milk supply chain by working with farmers, other companies and governments on regenerative practices.[34] Such commitment from corporate brands means that each product brand within the Ikea and Danone groups and its suppliers must engage in sustainable and carbon positive solutions.

However, at the same time, it is important to remember that many corporate brands still face allegations of greenwashing or corporate irresponsibility.[35] For example, while highlighting sustainability as a major strategic driver, as highlighted in the branding in practice above, Nestlé has been accused of using palm oil in its products, even though palm oil production is a major driver of deforestation.[36] Similarly, while H&M has devoted substantial resources towards sustainability, it has been criticized for its use of fast fashion, which is a major contributor to textile waste. H&M has also been accused of using misleading labels on its products, such as 'organic cotton' and 'sustainable'.[37] In 2015, Volkswagen was caught cheating on emissions tests for its diesel vehicles. The company had installed software in its vehicles that could detect when they were being tested and reduce emissions accordingly. This allowed Volkswagen to sell its vehicles as being more environmentally friendly than they actually were.[38] These cases highlight that, if not managed appropriately, corporate brands can also cause substantial harm to the organization's reputation and revenues. The next section, thus, discusses how to manage corporate brands.

Managing corporate brands

As corporate brands evolve, developing and managing a consistent and clear narrative becomes significantly complex. Managing corporate brands involves strategically shaping and overseeing the identity, reputation and perception of a company in the eyes of its stakeholders.[39] It encompasses defining the brand's values, mission and positioning, ensuring consistency in messaging and visual elements, and aligning all activities with the brand's core identity. Effective corporate brand management requires continuous monitoring of market trends and stakeholder feedback, as well as adapting to evolving consumer expectations and societal values.[40] Companies that excel in managing their corporate brands can foster trust, loyalty and positive associations, ultimately contributing to long-term success and competitive advantage in their respective industries.

A prominent scholar in corporate brand management, John Balmer, offered the **6Cs framework** for developing and managing a corporate brand. The 6Cs include culture, character, communication, constituencies, covenant and conceptualization.[41] *Culture* relates to the organization's shared values and beliefs. It is the foundation of the organization's character, and it is what binds the organization together. *Character* is the corporate brand's core values and beliefs which makes its distinct from competitors. The *communication* dimension allows the brand to communicate its character and culture to its stakeholders. *Constituencies* are the brand's stakeholders, such as the customers, employees, investors, suppliers and other community members. The corporate brand needs to understand the needs and expectations of its constituencies to effectively communicate its character to them. This, in turn, reflects in the relationship between the brand and its constituencies, referred to as the *covenant*. *Conceptualization* captures how the organization is perceived by its stakeholders. The corporate brand needs to continuously manage its stakeholders' perceptions in order to create a positive corporate image. By understanding and addressing these six dimensions of corporate branding, organizations can create strong corporate brands that are aligned with their strategic goals and that resonate with their stakeholders.

The framework is particularly useful for today's digital marketplace wherein organizations can demonstrate each of these 6Cs through their websites, social media communication and other digital channels including digital expos and trade shows. In the physical world, corporate brands engage with different stakeholders through different platforms. For example, at a trade show, a corporate brand engages with mainly suppliers and B2B customers. However, in a retail environment, the corporate brand is engaged with end customers. In digital environments, such as websites or social media, all stakeholders converge in the same space. Hence, a corporate brand has to be nurtured on digital platforms. Based on the 6Cs framework, the corporate brand needs to demonstrate its culture and character consistently with all constituencies. This, in turn, will lead to better covenant (relationship) and conceptualization. For example, the website of UPM, a leading Finnish forest industry company, providing information on their sustainable and innovative solutions in forestry, paper, pulp and biofuels. The website demonstrates UPM's commitment to sustainability, focusing on reducing emissions, promoting circular economy principles and responsible forest management. Its Biofore strategy drives innovations in renewable materials and contributes to a more sustainable future.

Chapter summary

In this chapter, we explored the concept of brand portfolio and understood why it is important for brands to employ a portfolio approach as they grow. There are multiple ways in which brand portfolio can be managed and each approach can have varying brand equity implications. We also identified various tactics of brand portfolio management. Corporate branding is a unique approach towards brand portfolio management wherein the whole organization is reflected a single brand. We learnt how and why corporate brands have become vitally important for today's businesses. We also explored the brand levers such as heritage, value, culture, personality and reputation which can be better communicated through corporate branding approach. Finally, we comprehended the issues involved in the effective management of corporate brands.

Key concepts

- Brand portfolio
- Brand portfolio management
- Portfolio management tactics
- Corporate branding
- Levers of corporate brands
- Management of corporate brands

Exercise questions

1 Define brand portfolio and why it is needed in today's marketplace.

2 Each brand can have its own unique way of portfolio management. Critically evaluate this statement using examples.

3 How can brand portfolio management affect brand equity across levels? Reflect on how brands can manage equity at each level.

4 Describe, using examples, the variety of tactics used by brands in managing their brand portfolio.

5 What is corporate branding? Why has it become important?

6 What benefits do corporate brands offer an organization?

7 Explain the 6Cs of corporate brand management.

CASE STUDY   Balancing convention and expansion

Tata's Global Branding Strategy, Tata Group, India's oldest and one of the largest private conglomerates, faced a crucial challenge in the late 20th century – reconciling its strong Indian identity with aspirations for global expansion. This case study examines the branding strategies employed by Tata Group regarding its major international acquisitions between 2000 and 2010. Specifically, it analyses the decisions to maintain standalone branding or integrate acquisitions under the Tata parent brand. The analysis reveals how Tata balances global growth ambitions with preserving brand equity in both local and global contexts during the integration process.

Founded in 1868, Tata Group grew into one of India's largest private sector entities by 2010, with over 100 companies in industries from steel to IT to hotels, and $70 billion in revenue. The company holds a strong association with Indian national identity and values like community service. However, since the 1990s, Ratan Tata, the group's leader, envisioned a global future, which raised concerns about the potential dilution of its core values and brand identity. This created a strategic challenge regarding brand architecture for major international acquisitions.

Conventional branding wisdom suggested unifying diverse acquisitions under the 'Tata' name, as exemplified by companies like GE. For example, GE applies its parent brand across the board to all new ventures and all new acquisitions, so its brands become GE Healthcare, GE Power and GE Capital, for example. However, Tata faced unique challenges, such as wanting to preserve its own Indian identity while at the same time wanting to respect acquired brands. In achieving this brand architecture approach, Tata Group adopted a flexible approach, defying conventional wisdom.

For instance, in 2000, Tata Tea acquired UK beverage firm Tetley Tea for $450 million. Tetley retained its distinct branding with modest visual association with Tata as the parent brand. Tata's logic was that Tetley held strong brand equity in the UK that would be diluted by rebranding it as Tata Tea. Similarly, in 2008, Tata Motors acquired the Jaguar and Land Rover auto brands for $2.3 billion. As iconic British car brands, Tata wanted to maintain their distinct brand identities to preserve their value. Rebranding risked weaker associations with Indian-made cars.

However, in 2007, when Tata Steel acquired Anglo-Dutch steelmaker Corus for $13 billion it used a different approach. After initial hesitation, Tata Steel rebranded Corus, which was a comparatively weak brand, as Tata Steel Europe in 2010 to better integrate operations.

Tata's case offers valuable insights into balancing tradition and expansion. Its success demonstrates that branding strategies must be tailored to specific contexts and challenges. Its different brand acquisition approaches reveals that Tata weighs rebranding decisions carefully based on perceptions of brand equity gains versus risks, in both local subsidiary and Tata corporate brand contexts. This nuanced, context-specific approach aims to balance Tata's global integration needs with retaining the value of strong legacy brands.

This case suggests that firms expanding globally through acquisition face heightened needs to manage brand architecture across portfolios and geographies. Brand integration decisions require weighing synergies against diluting or damaging established brand identities shaped by national cultures and business contexts. As Tata shows, pragmatic and context-specific rebranding choices can prove more successful than uniform integration policies. The case offers a compelling example of how a traditional company can successfully navigate the complexities of globalization while staying true to its core values.

Case questions

1 Visit www.tata.com/investors/companies and examine its brand portfolio in detail. Develop a brand portfolio structure as explained in Figure 11.1.

2 Critically reflect on the advantages and disadvantages of the brand portfolio management approaches employed by Tata and GE.

3 Discuss the preferred brand portfolio management tactics used by the Tata Group. Explain in detail why the company employs such tactics.

4 Visit the Tata Group website and critically examine how it uses the corporate brand levers of heritage, value and transparency.

5 Apply the 6Cs framework to analyse the corporate brand management strategy of the Tata Group.

Endnotes

1 www.statista.com/statistics/263438/market-share-held-by-nokia-smartphones-since-2007/ (archived at https://perma.cc/3S8G-F5S3)

2 www.wsj.com/articles/SB10001424052702304788404579521182171069704 (archived at https://perma.cc/BGV7-AC3Z)

3 Drake, P P and Fabozzi, F J (2010) *The Basics of Finance: An introduction to financial markets, business finance, and portfolio management*, vol. 192, John Wiley and Sons

4 Wang, Q and Shukla, P (2013) Linking sources of consumer confusion to decision satisfaction: The role of choice goals, *Psychology & Marketing*, 30 (4), 295–304

5 www.kering.com/en/sustainability/crafting-tomorrow-s-luxury/historic-commitment/ (archived at https://perma.cc/N5WV-8QUX)

6 www.unilever.co.uk/planet-and-society/ (archived at https://perma.cc/LZ6C-VWKP)

7 Keller, K L (2003) Brand synthesis: The multidimensionality of brand knowledge, *Journal of Consumer Research*, 29 (4), 595–600

8 Roper, S (2016) Branding the entire entity: Corporate branding, in *The Routledge Companion to Contemporary Brand Management*, Routledge, pp 354–65

9 Aaker, D A (1996), *Building Strong Brands*, The Free Press, New York

10 Roper, S (2016) Branding the entire entity: Corporate branding, in *The Routledge Companion to Contemporary Brand Management*, Routledge, pp 354–65

11 Hatch, M J and Schultz, M (2008), *Taking brand initiative: How companies can align strategy, culture and identity through corporate branding*, Jossey-Bass, San Francisco

12 Harris, F and De Chernatony, L (2001) Corporate branding and corporate brand performance, *European Journal of Marketing*, 35 (3/4), 441–56

13 Fetscherin, M and Usunier, J C (2012) Corporate branding: An interdisciplinary literature review, *European Journal of Marketing*, 46 (5), 733–53

14 Simoes, C, Singh, J and Perin, M G (2015) Corporate brand expressions in business-to-business companies' websites: Evidence from Brazil and India, *Industrial Marketing Management*, 51, 59–68

15 Aaker, D A (2004) Leveraging the corporate brand, *California Management Review*, 46 (3), 6–18

16 Burghausen, M and Balmer, J M (2014) Corporate heritage identity management and the multi-modal implementation of a corporate heritage identity, *Journal of Business Research*, 67 (11), 2311–23

17 Balmer, J M and Greyser, S A (eds.) (2003) *Revealing the Corporation: Perspectives on identity, image, reputation, corporate branding, and corporate-level marketing: An anthology*, Psychology Press

18 Shukla, P (2011) Impact of interpersonal influences, brand origin and brand image on luxury purchase intentions: Measuring interfunctional interactions and a cross-national comparison, *Journal of World Business*, 46 (2), 242–52

19 1 Roper, S (2016) Branding the entire entity: Corporate branding, in *The Routledge Companion to Contemporary Brand Management*, Routledge, pp 354–65

20 Van Riel, C B and Fombrun, C J (2007) *Essentials of Corporate Communication: Implementing practices for effective reputation management*, Routledge

21 Roberts, P W and Dowling, G R (2002) Corporate reputation and sustained superior financial performance, *Strategic Management Journal*, 23 (12), 1077–93

22 Syed Alwi, S F, Nguyen, B, Melewar, T C, Loh, Y H and Liu, M (2016) Explicating industrial brand equity: Integrating brand trust, brand performance and industrial brand image, *Industrial Management & Data Systems*, 116 (5), 858–82

23 www.nestle-esar.com/aboutus/missionvision (archived at https://perma.cc/4JFS-7U7Q)

24 www.nestle.com/sustainability (archived at https://perma.cc/784R-HWF4)

25 Porter, M E and Kramer, M R (2011) Creating shared value, *Harvard Business Review*, 89 (1–2), 62–77

26 Olins, W (1990) *The Wolff Olins Guide to Corporate Identity*, The Design Council, London

27 Balmer, J M (2012) Strategic corporate brand alignment: Perspectives from identity based views of corporate brands, *European Journal of Marketing*, 46 (7/8), 1064–92

28 Balmer, J M and Gray, E R (2003) Corporate brands: What are they? What of them?, *European Journal of Marketing*, 37 (7/8), 972–97

29 Simoes, C, Singh, J and Perin, M G (2015) Corporate brand expressions in business-to-business companies' websites: Evidence from Brazil and India, *Industrial Marketing Management*, 51, 59–68

30 Keller, K L and Richey, K (2006) The importance of corporate brand personality traits to a successful 21st century business, *Journal of Brand Management*, 14, 74–81

31 Okazaki, S (2006) Excitement or sophistication? A preliminary exploration of online brand personality, *International Marketing Review*, 23 (3), 279–303

32 Ankomah Opoku, R, Abratt, R, Bendixen, M and Pitt, L (2007) Communicating brand personality: Are the web sites doing the talking for food SMEs?, *Qualitative Market Research: An International Journal*, 10 (4), 362–74

33 www.ikea.com/gb/en/this-is-ikea/climate-environment/the-ikea-sustainability-strategy-pubfea4c210 (archived at https://perma.cc/4QLB-BTNJ)

34 www.reuters.com/business/sustainable-business/dairy-giant-danone-aims-cut-methane-emissions-by-30-by-2030-2023-01-17/ (archived at https://perma.cc/2BDY-TUKF)

35 Perks, K J, Farache, F, Shukla, P and Berry, A (2013) Communicating responsibility–practicing irresponsibility in CSR advertisements, *Journal of Business Research*, 66 (10), 1881–88

36 www.greenpeace.org/philippines/press/9990/greenpeace-calls-out-nestle-for-false-claims-on-plastic-neutrality/ (archived at https://perma.cc/P4C8-6TYX)

37 www.bigissue.com/news/environment/hm-greenwashing-is-disguising-the-reality-of-fast-fashion/ (archived at https://perma.cc/SMS6-9V6E)

38 https://environmentaldefence.ca/volkswagen-dieselgate-timeline/ (archived at https://perma.cc/ER8Y-D35L)

39 Balmer, J M (2012) Corporate brand management imperatives: Custodianship, credibility, and calibration, *California Management Review*, 54 (3), 6–33

40 Urde, M (2013) The corporate brand identity matrix, *Journal of Brand Management*, 20, 742–61

41 Balmer, J M and Greyser, S A (2006) Corporate marketing: Integrating corporate identity, corporate branding, corporate communications, corporate image and corporate reputation, *European Journal of Marketing*, 40 (7/8), 730–41

PART THREE
Managing contemporary brands

Managing negative events for brands

12

Overview

In this chapter, we first explain the overarching concept of brand crises and its impact on reputation management. We then discuss the three well-known types of crises – product harm, brand transgression, and service failure and recovery. Each subsection includes well-cited scholarly work and recent as well as classic examples of negative events for brands.

Key learning outcomes

Upon reading this chapter, you should be able to

- Understand the concept of brand crises and reputation management
- Comprehend the three types of negative events – product harm, brand transgression and service brand failure
- Gain insights into strategies of recovery and reputation management

Brand crises and reputation management

It is generally believed that negative information weighs heavily on people's minds.[1] For instance, consumers remember negative experiences more vividly. Prospect theory, a well-known theory in behavioural economics, identifies that people give greater emphasis to their losses compared to gains of the same size.[2] For example, the pain from losing \$1,000 could only be compensated by the pleasure of earning \$2,000. This is also known as 'negativity bias' in social psychology.[3] Negative events are a common occurrence in the marketplace. People do not always get treated in an optimal manner in their societal and organizational interactions. In organizational interactions, consumers do not always think about the individual treating them badly, rather the actions are scrutinized at a more macro level, wherein the entire organization is blamed. Brands, as the key communication tool for most organizations, find themselves at the forefront of these interactions. When any kind of crisis relating to the organization has an impact on its stakeholders, there is a potential for substantial reputational damage.

A brand crisis typically emerges from negative events that severely impact an organization's reputation, financial stability or operations, often leading to significant public scrutiny and loss of stakeholder trust.[4] Crises are often characterized by their unexpected nature, the threat they pose to core organizational values, the need for urgent decision making and the level of uncertainty they introduce. These events can vary in nature, such as financial scandals, product recalls, environmental disasters, ethical misconduct or cybersecurity breaches.[5] Volkswagen, a prominent German automobile maker, faced a brand crisis when it was revealed that the company had installed software in its diesel cars to manipulate emissions tests. This revelation led to a significant decline in Volkswagen's reputation, legal battles and imposition of large financial penalties.[6] The scandal had a lasting impact on the company's brand reputation and emphasized the importance of ethical conduct and transparency in the automotive industry. Volkswagen's handling of the brand crisis and response management strategy coupled with the financial penalties could have minimized the reputational damage, and helped maintain its sales growth worldwide.[7]

Negative events can trigger a domino effect, causing a chain reaction of problems that escalate into a full-fledged crisis, demanding strategic and well-coordinated responses from the organization.[8] For example, Enron, once a leading American energy company, collapsed due to an extensive accounting fraud. The scandal not only led to the bankruptcy of Enron but also damaged the reputation of Arthur Andersen, its auditing firm.[9] As Enron collapsed, to avoid further negative associations and to maintain its core reputation of competence, Arthur Anderson undertook an extensive re-branding exercise, renaming itself as Accenture. While Arthur Anderson's reputation was damaged due to the Enron scandal, Accenture continued to grow.[10] It is now a successful consulting organization, providing services for 89 of the Fortune Global 100 biggest companies in the world and for more than three-quarters of the Fortune Global 500 companies.[11] The Enron scandal is a classic example of how financial mismanagement and unethical practices can severely tarnish a brand and erode trust.

Crises can have far-reaching consequences, extending beyond the immediate event, and adversely affecting an organization's as well as it associated partners' brand image, market position, financial stability and overall sustainability. For instance, Cambridge Analytica, a British consulting firm, faced a major brand crisis when it was exposed for harvesting personal data from Facebook without consent. The scandal raised concerns about data privacy and manipulation of public opinion for political purposes. Facebook, which was closely associated with the scandal, also faced significant reputational damage and regulatory scrutiny. Therefore, an appropriate strategic response to brand crisis is required. Successful brand crisis management involves not only reactive responses but also proactive planning to anticipate potential crises and mitigate their impact.[12] Effective crisis management strategies encompass timely and transparent communication with stakeholders, crisis team coordination and learning from the crisis to implement improvements and prevent similar incidents in the future.[13]

In the aftermath of a brand crisis, organizations often find themselves at a crossroad, requiring careful navigation to rebuild trust and reputation. In this regard, effective brand communications play a crucial role in shaping perceptions and responses during and after a crisis. Clear, consistent, transparent and empathetic communication is essential in conveying the organization's commitment to resolution and recovery, fostering a sense of trust and credibility among stakeholders.[14]

Thus, reputation management is a crucial aspect of brand crisis management strategy that focuses on influencing, shaping and maintaining a positive perception of an organization among its stakeholders.[15] It involves a systematic approach to monitoring and managing the reputation of a brand following a negative event, which encompasses how it is perceived by customers, investors, employees and the broader public.[16] Academic researchers have long viewed reputation as a valuable intangible asset that directly affects a brand, and, in turn, an organization's financial performance and competitive advantage.[17] Many brands, therefore, actively engage in reputation management through effective communications, ethical business practices, social responsibility initiatives and building strong relationships with stakeholders to enhance their standing and credibility in the market.

Effective reputation management is crucial to mitigate the impact of brand crises and rebuild trust. Swift and transparent communication, corrective actions and a demonstrated commitment to addressing the issues at hand are essential components of successful crisis management and reputation recovery. The ability to bounce back from a brand crisis and rebuild a positive reputation is a testament to the resilience and adaptability of a good brand crisis strategy. In 2018, Starbucks faced a brand crisis after an incident where two African American men were arrested at a Philadelphia store for waiting without making a purchase. In response, Starbucks closed 8,000 company-owned stores in the United States for a day to conduct racial bias training for employees. This proactive action demonstrated the company's commitment to addressing the issue and fostering a more inclusive environment, contributing to brand recovery and a strengthened reputation for social responsibility.[18]

BRANDING IN PRACTICE

The horsemeat scandal and Tesco's reputation management:
what happened, the impact and what we learned

The horsemeat scandal in the UK was a major food safety threat that occurred in
2013. It involved the discovery of horsemeat in products that were labelled as beef.
The scandal had a big impact on the food industry and consumers alike. It also
raised concerns about the safety and traceability of food supply chains.[19]

Tesco was one of the major retailers involved in the horsemeat scandal. In 2013, it
was revealed that Tesco's own-brand burgers contained 29 per cent horsemeat.[20]
This was a major blow to Tesco's reputation, as it led to concerns about the safety
and quality of its products.

Tesco were able to quickly identify and address the root cause of the problem,
and took a number of steps to improve its food safety and supply chain management.
It tightened its supplier approval process, implemented DNA testing of meat
products and increased the amount of British meat it sourced. Tesco also became
more transparent about the supply of its products, and launched a new website
where customers could track the journey of their food from farm to fork.

In addition to these measures, Tesco also invested in reputation management
strategies to rebuild trust with consumers. It launched a number of advertising
campaigns that emphasized its commitment to food safety and quality. It also
engaged with customers on social media and through its customer service channels
to address their concerns.

Beyond the Tesco brand, the horsemeat scandal had several negative
consequences for the whole industry. It eroded consumer trust in the food industry
and led to a decline in sales of beef products. The scandal also had a significant
economic impact on the food industry, as businesses were forced to recall products
and implement new food safety measures.

In response to the scandal, the government introduced new food safety
regulations. These regulations included stricter requirements for food labelling and
traceability. The food industry also took steps to improve food traceability, such as
implementing DNA testing of meat products.[21]

The horsemeat scandal was a major wake-up call for the food industry. It showed
how vulnerable the food supply chain is to fraud and how important it is to have
robust food safety measures in place. While the industry has made progress since
the scandal, there is still more work to be done to prevent food fraud.[22]

Tesco's response to the horsemeat scandal was widely praised by industry
experts and the brand was able to recover from it and maintain its position as one of
the UK's leading retailers due to the brand-crisis-related reputation management
strategies it employed. However, the scandal served as a reminder of the importance
of food safety and supply chain management for all retailers.

Theoretical framework for brand crisis type identification and response

An important theoretical framework that helps understand brand crisis type and appropriate response is the situational crisis communication theory (SCCT).[23] The theory explains how organizations should communicate with their stakeholders during a crisis. The theory assumes that the main goal of crisis communication is to protect the organization's reputation, which is affected by how stakeholders attribute responsibility for the crisis and how they perceive the organization's response strategies.[24] SCCT also provides guidelines for selecting the most appropriate response strategies based on the type, history and relationship of the crisis. The theory posits that the most effective crisis response strategy depends on two key factors: the level of crisis responsibility (i.e. controllability) and the reputational threat posed by the crisis (i.e. impact). The level of crisis responsibility refers to the extent to which an organization could have controlled the crisis before it occurred. This can be influenced by a variety of factors, such as the nature of the crisis, the organization's past actions and the public's perception of the organization. Reputational threat refers to the potential damage to an organization's reputation because of the crisis. This can be affected by the severity of the crisis, the organization's response to the crisis and the public's reaction to the crisis.

Table 12.1 Crisis types

Crisis type	Explanation	Causes
Victim crisis	The organization is also a victim of the crisis. Weak attributions of crisis responsibility = Mild reputational threat	• Natural disaster: Acts of nature damage an organization such as an earthquake. • Rumour: False and damaging information about an organization is being circulated. • Workplace violence: Current or former employee attacks current employees onsite. • Product tampering/malevolence: External agent causes damage to an organization.
Accidental cluster	The organizational actions leading to the crisis were unintentional. Minimal attributions of crisis responsibility = Moderate reputational threat	• Technical-error accidents: A technology or equipment failure causes an industrial accident. • Technical-error product harm: A technology or equipment failure causes a product to be recalled.

(continued)

Table 12.1   (Continued)

Crisis type	Explanation	Causes
Preventable cluster	The organization knowingly placed people at risk, took inappropriate actions or violated a law/ regulation. Strong attributions of crisis responsibility = Severe reputational threat	• Human-error accidents: Human error causes an industrial accident. • Human-error product harm: Human error causes a product to be recalled. • Organizational misdeed with no injuries: Stakeholders are deceived without injury. • Organizational misdeed management misconduct: Laws or regulations are violated by management. • Organizational misdeed with injuries: Stakeholders are placed at risk by management and injuries occur.

According to SCCT, there are three types of crises: victim, accidental and preventable. Table 12.1 below summarizes the crisis types based on the criteria of controllability and impact.

Victim crises are those that are caused by external factors and are not the fault of the organization. Examples of victim crises include natural disasters, terrorism, product tampering or workplace violence. These types of crises have the lowest level of attributions of responsibility and reputational threat for the organization, as stakeholders tend to sympathize with the organization and view it as a victim of the situation. Therefore, the recommended response strategies for victim crises are to express concern, compassion and regret for the affected stakeholders, and to provide information and assistance as needed. A recent example of a brand involved in a victim crisis is the case of Nike and the Kobe Bryant crash. In January 2020, Kobe Bryant, his daughter Gianna and seven other people were killed in a helicopter crash. Nike was one of the first brands to respond to the tragedy, releasing a statement expressing its condolences to the Bryant family and the other victims. However, Nike was later criticized for its handling of the crisis, specifically for the way it marketed Kobe Bryant merchandise in the aftermath of the crash. Some people felt that Nike was exploiting Kobe Bryant's death for profit, and that its marketing campaigns were insensitive to the Bryant family and the other victims. Nike defended its actions, stating that it was simply trying to honour Kobe Bryant's legacy and to provide his fans with a way to mourn his loss. However, the criticism continued, and Nike eventually decided to pull its Kobe Bryant merchandise from the market.[25] This example shows how important it is for brands to be sensitive to the needs of victims and their families in the aftermath of a crisis. Brands should also be careful not to exploit victims for profit.

Accidental crises are those that are unintentional and result from technical or human errors. Examples of accidental crises include equipment failures, product recalls or data breaches. These types of crises have a moderate level of attribution of responsibility and reputational threat for the organization, as stakeholders may question the organization's competence or reliability, but not its intentions or ethics. Therefore, the recommended response strategies for accidental crises are to acknowledge the crisis, accept some responsibility, apologize or express sympathy, and explain how the organization will endeavour to prevent similar crises in the future. For example, in 2018 two Boeing 737 MAX aircraft crashed within five months of each other, killing 346 people. The crashes were caused by a software flaw in the aircraft's Manoeuvring Characteristics Augmentation System (MCAS), which was designed to prevent stalls. However, the MCAS system could be activated in error, causing the aircraft to nosedive. The Boeing crisis had a significant impact on the company. The 737 MAX was grounded worldwide for nearly two years, and Boeing lost billions of dollars in revenue. The company's reputation was also harmed, and it faced numerous lawsuits from the families of the crash victims. Boeing took a number of steps to address the crisis. It fixed the MCAS software flaw and made other changes to the 737 MAX to make it safer. The company also apologized to the families of the crash victims and offered compensation to them. The 737 MAX was recertified by aviation regulators in late 2020 and began flying again in early 2021.[26] However, the Boeing crisis is not over. The company is still facing lawsuits and investigations, and it continues to rebuild its reputation. This crisis demonstrates the need for product safety, transparency in communications and the importance of accountability.

Preventable crises are those that are intentional or result from negligence or misconduct. Examples of preventable crises include fraud, corruption, deception or illegal actions. These types of crises have the highest level of attributions of responsibility and reputational threat for the organization, as stakeholders may view the organization as dishonest, unethical or immoral. Therefore, the recommended response strategies for preventable crises are to admit full responsibility, apologize sincerely, express remorse and regret, and offer compensation or restitution to the affected stakeholders. Tesla and the death of drivers in self-driving car accidents demonstrates a preventable crisis.[27] In one of the cases, the driver was using Tesla's Autopilot feature, which allows the car to steer, accelerate and brake on its own. However, the car failed to see a trailer-truck crossing the road and crashed into it, killing the driver.[28] Tesla has been criticized for its handling of the crisis surrounding the autopilot feature. The company has regularly denied that Autopilot was to blame for many of the crashes, but later admitted that the feature was not perfect.[29] Tesla has also been accused of overselling the capabilities of Autopilot and of not doing enough to prevent drivers from using the feature in unsafe conditions.[30]

These crises do not always involve products and for-profit organization but can also occur for not-for-profit organizations. For example, in 2018, a Swedish television investigation revealed that United Nations Children's Fund (Unicef), a UN agency responsible for providing humanitarian and developmental aid to children worldwide, did not fulfil its promise to assist some of the children who claimed that they were sexually abused by French peacekeepers in 2014.[31] The investigation also showed that some of the children were homeless, out of school and living on the streets, despite Unicef's assurance that they were in its assistance programme. The case exposed the seriousness of the issue and the need for accountability and transparency from Unicef and other aid agencies. The case also highlighted the wider problem of sexual misconduct and abuse in the humanitarian sector, which has been under scrutiny after the Oxfam scandal that occurred in Haiti. In 2018, Oxfam, a globally leading charity from the UK that focuses on the alleviation of global poverty, was tackling 26 claims of recent and historical sexual misconduct investigations involving Oxfam staff.[32] This led Haitian authorities to suspend Oxfam operations in their country, an inquiry by the International Development Committee in the UK and dismissal of several staff members at Oxfam.[33] The charity implemented a number of whistleblowing and safeguarding procedures and established an independent global commission to review its approach to safeguarding culture in response to the scandal.

The SCCT suggests that the most effective crisis response strategy is the one that best matches the level of crisis responsibility and the reputational threat posed by the crisis. In that regard, the theory identifies three primary and one secondary crisis response strategies, as outlined in Table 12.2.

Table 12.2   Crisis response strategies

Crisis response	Approach	Examples
Primary	Deny	• Attack the accuser: Crisis manager confronts the person or group claiming something is wrong with the organization. • Denial: Crisis manager asserts that there is no crisis. • Scapegoat: Crisis manager blames some person or group outside of the organization for the crisis.

(continued)

Table 12.2 (Continued)

Crisis response	Approach	Examples
	Diminish	• Excuse: Crisis manager minimizes organizational responsibility by denying intent to do harm and/or claiming inability to control the events that triggered the crisis.
		• Justification: Crisis manager minimizes the perceived damage caused by the crisis.
	Rebuild	• Compensation: Crisis manager offers money or other gifts to victims.
		• Apology: Crisis manager indicates the organization takes full responsibility for the crisis and asks
Secondary	Bolster	• Reminder: Tell stakeholders about the past good works of the organization.
		• Ingratiation: Crisis manager praises stakeholders and/or reminds them of past good works by the organization.
		• Victimage: Crisis managers remind stakeholders that the organization is a victim of the crisis too.

In sum, SCCT is a valuable tool for organizations to identify the crisis type and develop an effective response plan. It can help organizations to create the most appropriate crisis response strategy based on the type of the crisis, as outlined in Tables 12.1 and 12.2.

SCCT provides an important theoretical lens in the field of corporate communications. It has applications in public relations, crisis communications and reputation management at corporate level. At the same time, in the field of marketing and branding, negative events are examined using analogous terms, namely, product harm, brand transgression and service failure, which are the focus of our next sections.

Product-harm crises

A product-harm crisis is a situation in which a product is found to be defective, dangerous or harmful to consumers, and thus damages the reputation and profitability of the brand or company that produces it.[34] It typically involves a well-publicized situation affecting a large group of customers.[35] Product-harm crises can have negative consequences for various stakeholders, such as consumers, investors, competitors, regulators and the media.[36] Product-harm crises can also affect consumer behaviour, such as purchase intentions, brand loyalty, word-of-mouth and online search.[37] Product-harm crises are strongly linked to product recall, wherein a firm asks its customers to return its defective product in order to replace, fix or reimburse it.

Product-harm crises can occur in any industry and market, and can be caused by various factors, such as manufacturing errors, design flaws, quality control failures, human negligence, sabotage or natural disasters. For example, in 2008, China experienced a major product-harm crisis when melamine, a toxic chemical used to make plastics, was found in infant formula and other dairy products. The crisis affected more than 300,000 babies and children who suffered from kidney stones and renal failure. Six children died and many others were hospitalized. The scandal damaged the reputation of Chinese dairy products and led to bans and recalls in many countries.[38] Similarly, in 2021, Peloton, a fitness equipment company, recalled its Tread and Tread+ treadmills after reports of injuries and one death involving a child, and pets who got trapped under the machines. The company faced a backlash from consumers and regulators for initially resisting the recall and downplaying the safety risks.[39] The recall affected about 125,000 units and cost the company $165 million in lost revenue.[40]

BRANDING IN PRACTICE
GM's ignition switch crisis and response

General Motors (GM), one of the global automobile giants, was involved in a case of product-harm crisis when more than 30 million vehicles were recalled.[41] The case involved a defect in the ignition switches of some of GM's small cars, such as the Chevrolet Cobalt and the Saturn Ion, which could cause the engine to shut off unexpectedly, disabling the power steering, power brakes and airbags. The defect was first detected by GM engineers in 2001, but the company failed to recall the affected vehicles until 2014, after more than a decade of inaction and denial. By then, the defect had been linked to at least 13 deaths and 31 crashes, although some reports suggest that the actual numbers could be much higher.[42]

The GM case sparked a public outcry and a series of investigations by the US government, regulators, media and consumers. GM faced lawsuits, fines, criminal charges and congressional hearings for its negligence and cover-up of the problem. The company also suffered a loss of reputation, trust and market share among its customers and stakeholders.[43] GM's CEO Mary Barra admitted that the company's culture was characterized by 'incompetence' and 'silos' that prevented effective communication and decision making on safety issues. She also apologized to the victims and their families and promised to make changes to prevent such a crisis from happening again.[44]

In response to this crisis, GM implemented a number of changes. For example, it created a new position of vice president of global vehicle safety to oversee all aspects of vehicle safety and report directly to the top management. The company also established a 'Speak Up for Safety' programme to encourage employees, dealers and suppliers to report any potential safety issues or defects without fear of retaliation. It hired an independent monitor to oversee GM's compliance with the terms of a deferred prosecution agreement with the US Department of Justice, which required GM to pay a $900 million fine and cooperate with ongoing investigations.[45] The company also had to set up a compensation fund for the victims of the ignition switch defect, administered by attorney Kenneth Feinberg, who had previously handled similar funds for the 9/11 attacks and the BP oil spill.

The GM case illustrates the importance of product safety and quality for any company that wants to maintain its competitive advantage and customer loyalty. It also shows how a product-harm crisis can have devastating effects on a company's performance, reputation and social responsibility. Therefore, companies should adopt proactive strategies to prevent, detect and respond to product-harm crises in a timely and effective manner.

Beyond product recall, product-harm crises can also lead to a reduction in trust towards competing brands due to negative spillover effect, as explained in the horsemeat scandal. Following a product-harm crisis, consumers may become more cautious about using products from the industry as a whole as they may perceive all brands in the industry to be involved in such practices. Academic research suggests that in a situation where a competing brand is engaged in a product-harm crisis, the brand should use varying tactics to avoid the negative spillover effects depending on their market position. For instance, leading brands should use bolstering, while follower brands should employ differentiation strategy to avoid negative spillover from a product-harm crisis affecting a competing brand.[46]

Brand transgression

Brand transgression is a term that refers to a brand's act that violates the norms or expectations of consumers, and thus damages the reputation and relationship of the brand with its customers.[47] While there is some overlap between product-harm crises and brand transgression, when the transgression involves harm caused by product defect, many transgressions involve ethical misconduct, social responsibility, social media crisis, celebrity endorsement scandals or simply a failure to live to the brand's promises. The latter aspects do not involve any physical harm to the consumer, but they can sever emotional ties and make the consumer question the financial and relational investment they have made in the brand. Thus, academic research on brand transgression is rooted in consumer-brand relationship literature, and has been studied from a variety of standpoints including anthropomorphism,[48] cross-cultural effects[49] and neuroscience,[50] among many others.

There are two distinct types of brand transgressions identified in academic literature: performance-related and performance-unrelated (or value-based). Performance-related transgressions occur when a brand fails to deliver functional benefits or meet customer expectations, such as product defects, service failures or quality issues. Performance-unrelated or value-based transgressions occur when a brand violates social or ethical norms or customer values, such as ethical misconduct, social media crisis or a celebrity endorsement scandal.[51] Both types of transgression can damage the reputation and relationship of the brand with its customers and stakeholders. For example, Turing Pharmaceuticals, after acquiring Daraprim, a drug that treats HIV/AIDS patients, raised the price from $18 to $750 a pill. This price hike was ascribed to be motivated by profiteering, and it caused a significant backlash from society, which forced Turing to offer substantial discounts to hospitals.[52] However, the prices were not brought back to the original price of the pill for individual patients. Moral transgressions such as this one do not affect the performance of a product, but they do betray the fundamental promise of the brand to its consumers. Such transgressions may or may not have substantial revenue or profit implications. However, the ethical challenges posed by these transgressions can cause reputational damage for the company, as well as the industry as a whole. For instance, Turing's profiteering tactic brought into focus the overall pricing strategies used by the pharmaceutical industry.[53]

Brand transgression can also involve wrongdoing by the organization towards their employees. For example, it was revealed that one of Apple's largest assembly plants in Longhua (China), run by Foxconn, which employs nearly 1.3 million Chinese workers, became infamous for the high suicide rate of its workers in 2010. The workers were subject to long hours, low wages and strict rules, which led to the high rate of suicides.[54] Such revelations led to substantial media scrutiny. However, the companies involved, that is, Apple and Foxconn, initially denied such challenges. Moreover, Foxconn even asked new hires to sign an anti-suicide pledge, undertaking that if they killed themselves, the company would not be blamed or pursued for compensation.[55] Rather than improving working conditions, the company used safety nets so workers would not be able to jump from the top of the buildings. To reduce further reputation damage, the company announced putting in place appropriate policies to improve worker welfare.

While brand transgressions remain rife in the marketplace, companies can use their consumer-brand relationships to reduce the potentially negative consequences. Academic research suggests that strong consumer-brand relationships can act as a buffer against brand transgressions. However, even when the relationship is weak, organizations' investment in resolving the consequences of the transgression can lead to a stronger relationship with a brand post-transgression.[56]

Service brand failure and recovery

Service failure and recovery is a rich area of academic research that has grown in prominence over the past four decades. Service failure occurs when the service performance of an organization falls below the expectations of its customers.[57] Service recovery, which is regularly examined in tandem with service failure, is defined as all the actions the organization could take to remedy the complaints or loss caused by a service failure.[58]

Service has become the cornerstone for most developed economies and is playing a large part in many emerging economies as well. Companies nowadays are increasingly focused on customer orientation, and at the same time, customers are demanding better service. Digital technologies are adding further transparency in customer-organization service dynamics. For example, customers can see reviews of the services offered by an organization prior to engaging with it and thus set their expectations accordingly. Moreover, customers are becoming increasingly vocal when companies do not meet their expectations, or they believe that they have been treated unfairly. Websites such as Tripadvisor, Trustpilot, Feefo and Yelp have become primary service failure reporting portals. In addition, social media such as X (formerly Twitter), YouTube and Facebook also play a prominent role in customers highlighting service failures which can lead to substantial reputational damage for an organization. For example, in March 2020, Robinhood, a popular stock trading app, experienced a major outage that prevented millions of users from accessing their accounts and trading stocks during a historic market rally.[59] The outage lasted for more than 16 hours and caused many users to lose money and miss out on trading opportunities. Robinhood apologized for the incident and offered compensation to some users but faced a lot of backlash and criticism from customers, regulators and lawmakers. The incident also damaged Robinhood's reputation and trustworthiness as a reliable platform for investors. A Twitter account 'Robinhood Class Action' gained more than 7,000 followers and some users even filed lawsuits against the company for negligence and breach of contract.[60] This is an example of how a service failure in a digital environment can have serious consequences for both customers and businesses.

BRANDING IN PRACTICE

United Airlines 'bumpgate' case

In 2017, to accommodate four crew members who needed to reach another destination for their flight next day, United Airlines (UA) offered passengers remuneration to take a later flight. However, when no passenger came forward, UA staff randomly picked names of four passengers and told them to deplane.[61]

While three passengers did so reluctantly, one passenger, Dr David Dao, did not. UA crew called officers of the Chicago Department of Aviation to forcibly remove Dr Dao from the plane. A video recording of bloodied and injured Dr Dao being removed from the plane was posted by one of the fellow passengers on social media, which immediately went viral and was seen by millions of people.

The next morning, United CEO Oscar Munoz issued a statement justifying what happened, describing it as 're-accommodating the customers'. Munoz also sent an email to United staff commending the actions of the crew. Facing backlash from other travellers, Munoz later apologized to Dr Dao. Moreover, UA also settled a lawsuit for a confidential amount with Dr Dao.

Since this incident, within the USA, involuntary denied boarding incidents have declined substantially from 4.29 per cent in 2017 to 0.61 per cent in 2021. When a flight is overbooked, airlines tend to be more proactive and generous in their incentive to avoid such service failures.[62]

Service failures occur in various contexts of consumer-service brand interactions. For example, it can be due to process failure, employee interactions, expectations and experience mismatch. Examples range from room or flight overbooking, flight cancellations or delay, impolite employees treating customers in an unfair or unequal manner, dirty hotel rooms, service delivery delay or failure and monetary overcharge, among many others. Thus, any service experience that fails to meet customer expectations is associated with service failure.[63] Consumers complain for various reasons including seeking redress through compensation or other means, the simple opportunity to voice anger and frustration or even as an altruistic act to help improve the service amongst others.[64] However, service failure may not always result in complaining behaviour. Many consumers do not complain because they are unable to find the time and effort required to complain. Consumers, especially in collectivistic contexts, associate complaining with loss of face for themselves as well as the employee, and thus may not complain.[65] Moreover, when customers have low expectations from an organization and a service failure occurs, they tend not to complain.[66]

Recent academic research shows that service failure involves three distinct stakeholders, namely the complainer, the organization and the bystander. Service failure

Table 12.3   Customer evaluations of service recovery experiences

	FAIR	UNFAIR
Distributive justice	'The waitress agreed that there was a problem. She took the sandwiches back to the kitchen and had them *replaced*. We were also *given a free drink*.'	'Their *refusal to refund* our money for the cold food was inexcusable.' 'The *situation was never remedied*. Once they had my money, they disappeared when I had problems.'
Procedural justice	'The representative was pleasant and *quick to resolve the problem*.' 'The *sales manager called me back* one week after my complaint to check if the problem was taken care of to my satisfaction.'	'*They should have assisted me with the problem* instead of giving me a phone number to call. No one returned my calls, and I never had a chance to speak to a real person.'
Interpersonal justice	'The loan officer was very courteous, knowledgeable and considerate – he kept me informed about the progress of the complaint.'	'The person who handled my complaint about... wasn't going to do anything about it and didn't seem to care.'
Informational justice	'The employee explained that the restaurant was full that evening.'	'The employee did not provide an explanation for the reason we had to wait for three hours in the waiting area.'

can result in affective as well as behavioural responses. For example, due to service failure, consumers may feel dissatisfaction, anger, frustration, helplessness, betrayal, desire for revenge or desire for avoidance.[67] It may also result in varying behavioural responses such as re-complaining, exiting the interaction and switching to another service provider.[68] Complaining is dependent on a number of other contingency factors including the customer-brand relationship strength, firm reputation and brand equity.[69]

Service failure theories

Three important theories – cognitive appraisal, attribution and justice theory – have been used regularly in service failure and recovery related academic studies. Cognitive appraisal theory relates to consumers' evaluation of the failure (primary appraisal) and the coping strategies employed by the consumers (secondary appraisal).[70] Attribution theory examines with whom and where the responsibility in the service failure process lies.[71] This attribution of failure can either be external or internal.[72] Grounded in the fairness principle,[73] justice and equity theories[74] have been regularly

Table 12.4   Justice (fairness) of service recovery

Distributive justice	Procedural Justice	Interpersonal justice	Informational justice
Monetary	• Voice	• Politeness	• Explanation
• Refund	• Speed	• Empathy	• Information
• Discount	• Accessibility	• Concern	• Follow-up
• Replacement	• Flexibility	• Effort	• Keeping up-to-date
• Upgrade		• Respect	
Non-monetary		• Honesty	• Admission of responsibility
• Apology			

employed by academic researchers to explain the service failure and recovery process. There are four types of justice perceptions: distributive, procedural, interactional and informational. Each type of justice perception can result in a variety of service recovery responses that can affect consumer fairness perceptions, as demonstrated in the examples in Table 12.3.

Distributive justice refers to the perceived fairness of the allocation of resources such as compensation, promotions and rewards. It captures the cost-benefit analysis that the customer undertakes when service failure occurs and the service brand attempts a failure recovery.[75] As detailed in Table 12.4, recovery grounded in distributive justice can reflect in refund, discount, replacement, upgrade and/or apology offered to the consumers by the service brand. **Procedural justice** is associated with the perceived fairness of the process of recovery claim which can be achieved through the speed of recovery, as well as a clear, transparent, accessible and flexible approach to the recovery process.[76] **Interactional justice** is the perceived equity of the treatment that consumers receive during the process of service failure in comparison to others. The politeness, honesty, concern, effort, respect and empathy shown by the service organization towards the consumers equitably can substantially augment consumers' interactional justice perceptions.[77] Finally, **informational justice** is concerned with the accuracy, clarity and timeliness of information that is provided in response to the service failure.[78] To achieve recovery in consumers' minds from an informational justice perspective, service brands can take actions such as admitting responsibility, explaining the circumstances, providing clear information, offering up-to-date information and following up with the consumers to avoid re-complaining.

With service becoming a central contributor for more and more economies, service failure and recovery is critically important for any brand that operates in a competitive marketplace. As outlined above, brand managers can proactively identify and prepare their service failure touchpoints and develop appropriate service recovery strategies using the justice theory framework.

Chapter summary

In this chapter, we comprehensively put together academic research and managerial examples pertaining to negative events that affect brands. We understood how and why brand crises occur and the importance of reputation management strategies. We provide a framework to clearly identify crisis types and effectively manage response strategies using the SCCT. We explain the notion of product-harm crisis as well as the incidence of brand transgression. Finally, grounded in the justice theory framework, we offer insights for brand managers to manage the service failure and recovery process successfully. In sum, brand managers should proactively endeavour to mitigate the impact of negative events.

Key concepts

- Brand crisis
  - Crisis types
  - Crisis response management
- Reputation management
- Product-harm crisis
- Brand transgression
- Service failure
- Service recovery

Exercise questions

1 Explain, using examples, why managers should proactively identify negative events that may affect their brands and develop appropriate reputation management strategies.

2 Find two real-life brand crisis cases, identify the crisis types and suggest appropriate crisis responses that can be employed using the SCCT framework.

3 Compare and contrast the concepts of product-harm crisis and brand transgression with examples.

4 Critically analyse the importance of service failure and recovery strategies for today's digital organizations.

5 Using an example of service failure that you were involved in, discuss how the organization would have employed the justice theory framework for an appropriate recovery effort.

CASE STUDIES   Brand crisis and response management

Case 1: Equifax and the data breach

What happened

On 29 July 2017 Equifax discovered a massive data breach which affected the personal information of up to 143 million Americans, including social security numbers and driver licences. The company believed that the hack had taken place several weeks earlier, even as early as mid-May.[79]

Equifax waited until September to make a public announcement of the problem.

The data thieves knew where to target. Equifax is one of three nationwide credit-reporting companies that track and rates the financial history of US consumers. The companies are supplied with data about loans, loan payments and credit cards, as well as information on everything from child support payments, credit limits, missed rent and utilities payments, addresses and employer history, which all factor into credit scores.

Subsequent events only made the situation worse: the website and consumer telephone lines set up by Equifax so that people could get information and sign up for credit protection were overwhelmed and it took weeks to get them working effectively. It was reported that three executives sold nearly $2 million in shares after the breach was discovered but before being publicly revealed. Equifax subsequently twice upped its estimate of the numbers of consumers impacted – by 2.5 million in October 2017 and by 2.4 million in February 2018.

What we learned

This is why we build crisis preparedness plans.

A data breach must have been very high on the potential risks that Equifax faced. Given its business, any data loss is serious.

A plan would have had laid out the crisis team, how they should work together, the steps to take, the initial messaging and statements, and the process for escalating the response as it got worse.

Nothing in Equifax's slow motion and bungled response suggested it had anticipated and planned for such an event.

Case 2: KFC and the shortage of chicken

What happened

In February 2018, KFC had to close more than half of its 900 stores in the United Kingdom because of a shortage of... chicken.[80]

The social and mainstream media enjoyed the irony of a chicken shop without any chicken and went to town on the story. The cause was a delivery problem after the chain switched its contract to DHL which said that due to 'administrative problems' a number of deliveries were cancelled or delayed. Loyal customers vented on Twitter and took their families to McDonald's. Some even complained to their local politicians.

Then KFC, even while struggling to get the restaurants re-opened, managed to switch the narrative entirely. It ran an apology advertisement that was extremely funny (especially to the brand's core younger consumers) while taking ownership of the problem, this involved a rearrangement of the letters KFC. The company was widely applauded by customers and the media for its deft handling of the situation and became the poster child for how to handle a crisis well.

What we learned

Among the key elements in a best-in-class crisis response plan are:

- An understanding of the brand's key stakeholder, particularly the core consumers. Who are they? Where are they? What are their key considerations? What's likely to be on their minds when the brand is facing challenges.

- An understanding of the brand's promise and 'voice'. How is it positioned? What's likely to support or break the trust in the brand in how it responds to a crisis.

KFC's clever, authentic and borderline obscene response showed it deeply understood both these factors. It knew its audience (young, hip and irreverent) and it followed through in exactly the kind of tone and language that was consistent with how the brand was positioned in other, more positive marketing.

The result was a swift abatement of the criticism for the closed stores – and the sound of widespread applause for a model crisis response.

Case questions

1 Using the SCCT framework, identify the crisis types for the two cases with your own justifications.

2 Critically evaluate the appropriateness of the response from each brand using the SCCT framework.

3 Suggest your own alternative response strategies that these brands could have employed using the SCCT framework.

4 Develop a 140/280 character social media response that the brand could use to reduce the reputational damage.

Endnotes

1 Rozin, P and Royzman, E B (2001) Negativity bias, negativity dominance, and contagion, *Personality and Social Psychology Review*, 5 (4), 296–320

2 Kahneman, D and Tversky, A (2013) Prospect theory: An analysis of decision under risk, *Econometrica*, 47 (2), 263–91

3 Ito, T A, Larsen, J T, Smith, N K and Cacioppo, J T (1998) Negative information weighs more heavily on the brain: The negativity bias in evaluative categorizations, *Journal of Personality and Social Psychology*, 75 (4), 887–900

4 Coombs, W T, Holladay, S J and White, R (2020) Corporate crises: Sticky crises and corporations, in *Advancing Crisis Communication Effectiveness*, Routledge, pp 35–51

5 Dutta, S and Pullig, C (2011) Effectiveness of corporate responses to brand crises: The role of crisis type and response strategies, *Journal of Business Research*, 64 (12), 1281–87

6 www.bbc.com/news/business-34324772 (archived at https://perma.cc/8T47-A5RQ)

7 www.statista.com/statistics/264349/sales-revenue-of-volkswagen-ag-since-2006/ (archived at https://perma.cc/AHZ4-G53F)

8 Coombs, W T and Holladay, S J (2014) How publics react to crisis communication efforts: Comparing crisis response reactions across sub-arenas, *Journal of Communication Management*, 18 (1), 40–57

9 www.britannica.com/event/Enron-scandal (archived at https://perma.cc/G6MJ-PW28)

10 https://brandstruck.co/blog-post/instructive-rebranding-case-studies-time-part-1/ (archived at https://perma.cc/G3S7-CYFC)

11 https://newsroom.accenture.com/fact-sheet/ (archived at https://perma.cc/BXQ2-BHNR)

12 Pearson, C M and Clair, J A (1998) Reframing crisis management, *Academy of Management Review*, 23 (1), 59–76

13 Fink, S and American Management Association (1986) *Crisis Management: Planning for the inevitable*, Amacom

14 Ulmer, R R, Sellnow, T L and Seeger, M W (2022) *Effective Crisis Communication: Moving from crisis to opportunity*, Sage Publications

15 Aula, P and Mantere, S (2020) *Strategic Reputation Management: Towards a company of good*, Routledge

16 Hutton, J G, Goodman, M B, Alexander, J B and Genest, C M (2001) Reputation management: The new face of corporate public relations?, *Public Relations Review*, 27 (3), 247–61

17 Fombrun, C J (1996) *Reputation: Realizing value from the corporate image*, Harvard Business Press

18 https://stories.starbucks.com/stories/2018/beyond-may-29-lessons-from-starbucks-anti-bias-training-and-whats-next/ (archived at https://perma.cc/2EXL-CLZZ)

19 www.bbc.com/news/uk-21418342 (archived at https://perma.cc/GGQ4-JYRG)

20 www.theguardian.com/uk-news/2013/oct/22/horsemeat-scandal-guardian-investigation-public-secrecy (archived at https://perma.cc/B9BQ-LRBL)

21 www.bbc.com/news/business-25715666 (archived at https://perma.cc/QS4U-8TMX)

22 https://en.wikipedia.org/wiki/2013_horse_meat_scandal (archived at https://perma.cc/A7WQ-ZRBZ)

23 Coombs, W T and Wicks, R B (2014) On responding to crisis: Testing the situational crisis communication theory, *Public Relations Review*, 40 (4), 588–600

24 Coombs, W T (2007) Protecting organization reputations during a crisis: The development and application of situational crisis communication theory, *Corporate Reputation Review*, 10, 163–76

25 www.inverse.com/input/style/nike-kobe-6-protro-mambacita-mamba-forever-sneakers-shoes-reselling-stockx-ebay-removed-listings (archived at https://perma.cc/2LR8-DC8S)

26 https://simpleflying.com/boeing-737-max-ultimate-guide/#faqs-about-the-boeing-737-max (archived at https://perma.cc/BAZ7-EABK)

27 www.nytimes.com/2023/01/17/magazine/tesla-autopilot-self-driving-elon-musk.html (archived at https://perma.cc/MLX3-8PPU)

28 www.shorenewsnetwork.com/2023/08/10/deadly-tesla-crash-in-virginia-sparks-new-federal-investigation/ (archived at https://perma.cc/7ZMC-MQQP)

29 www.theverge.com/2021/5/7/22424592/tesla-elon-musk-autopilot-dmv-fsd-exaggeration (archived at https://perma.cc/7SEF-88RD)

30 www.forbes.com/sites/nicholasreimann/2022/10/27/sec-investigating-tesla-over-autopilot-safety-claims-report-says/?sh=521820262329 (archived at https://perma.cc/AE8Q-7R8B)

31 www.theguardian.com/global-development/2018/feb/13/unicef-admits-failings-with-child-victims-of-alleged-sex-abuse-by-peacekeepers (archived at https://perma.cc/3KWP-8SNJ)

32 www.bbc.com/news/uk-43163620 (archived at https://perma.cc/W5BG-D65D)

33 www.bbc.com/news/uk-43112200 (archived at https://perma.cc/45MA-DC29)

34 Cleeren, K, Dekimpe, M G and van Heerde, H J (2017) Marketing research on product-harm crises: A review, managerial implications, and an agenda for future research, *Journal of the Academy of Marketing Science*, 45, 593–615

35 Dawar, N and Pillutla, M M (2000) Impact of product-harm crises on brand equity: The moderating role of consumer expectations, *Journal of Marketing Research*, 37 (2), 215–26

36 Khamitov, M, Grégoire, Y and Suri, A (2020) A systematic review of brand transgression, service failure recovery and product-harm crisis: Integration and guiding insights, *Journal of the Academy of Marketing Science*, 48, 519–42

37 Jang, S, Kim, J, Song, R and Kim, H (2018) Advertising strategy and its effectiveness on consumer online search in a defaming product-harm crisis, *Asia Pacific Journal of Marketing and Logistics* 30, 705–24

38 Cleeren, K, Dekimpe, M G and van Heerde, H J (2017) Marketing research on product-harm crises: A review, managerial implications, and an agenda for future research, *Journal of the Academy of Marketing Science*, 45, 593–615

39 www.consumerreports.org/home-garden/home-product-recalls/peloton-tread-tread-plus-treadmills-recalled-serious-safety-hazards-a6638931886/ (archived at https://perma.cc/V3FW-7C5D)

40 https://edition.cnn.com/2021/05/06/business/peloton-recall-losses/index.html (archived at https://perma.cc/A7Z8-Q27D)

41 www.vox.com/2014/10/3/18073458/ gm -car-recall (archived at https://perma.cc/MGL7-2Q8S)

42 www.npr.org/2014/03/31/297158876/timeline-a-history-of-gms-ignition-switch-defect (archived at https://perma.cc/3F9R-249P)

43 www.reuters.com/article/us-gm-recall-timeline-idUSKBN0F62WY20140701 (archived at https://perma.cc/8VKE-SLUK)

44 www.forbes.com/sites/danbigman/2014/06/05/general-motors-report-on-ignition-switch-crisis-finds-no-cover-up/?sh=34fcaf521e98 (archived at https://perma.cc/49C5-RCW8)

45 www.nytimes.com/2015/09/18/business/gm-to-pay-us-900-million-over-ignition-switch-flaw.html (archived at https://perma.cc/Z68C-KD7W)

46 Zhang, J and Lim, J S (2021) Mitigating negative spillover effects in a product-harm crisis: Strategies for market leaders versus market challengers, *Journal of Brand Management*, 28, 77–98

47 Aaker, J, Fournier, S and Brasel, S A (2004) When good brands do bad, *Journal of Consumer Research*, 31 (1), 1–16

48 Puzakova, M, Kwak, H, Ramanathan, S and Rocereto, J F (2016) Painting your point: The role of color in firms' strategic responses to product failures via advertising and marketing communications, *Journal of Advertising*, 45 (4), 365–76

49 Magnusson, P, Krishnan, V, Westjohn, S A and Zdravkovic, S (2014) The spillover effects of prototype brand transgressions on country image and related brands, *Journal of International Marketing*, 22 (1), 21–38

50 Reimann, M, MacInnis, D J, Folkes, V S, Uhalde, A and Pol, G (2018) Insights into the experience of brand betrayal: From what people say and what the brain reveals, *Journal of the Association for Consumer Research*, 3 (2), 240–54

51 Dutta, S and Pullig, C (2011) Effectiveness of corporate responses to brand crises: The role of crisis type and response strategies, *Journal of Business Research*, 64 (12), 1281–87

52 https://money.cnn.com/2015/11/25/news/companies/turing-pharmaceuticals-daraprim-price-drop/ (archived at https://perma.cc/82XE-4TP7)

53 www.science.org/content/blog-post/what-do-about-turing-and-others (archived at https://perma.cc/R5NM-SBGU)

54 Merchant, B (2017) *The One Device: The secret history of the iPhone*, Little, Brown

55 www.cbsnews.com/news/what-happened-after-the- foxconn -suicides/ (archived at https://perma.cc/6CBW-FTZG)

56 Park, J K and John, D R (2018) Developing brand relationships after a brand transgression: The role of implicit theories of relationships, *Journal of the Association for Consumer Research*, 3 (2), 175–87

57 Smith, A K, Bolton, R N and Wagner, J (1999) A model of customer satisfaction with service encounters involving failure and recovery, *Journal of Marketing Research*, 36 (3), 356–72

58 Khamitov, M, Grégoire, Y and Suri, A (2020) A systematic review of brand transgression, service failure recovery and product-harm crisis: Integration and guiding insights, *Journal of the Academy of Marketing Science*, 48, 519–42

59 www.cnbc.com/2020/03/09/robinhood-app-down-again-during-another-historic-trading-day.html (archived at https://perma.cc/9XAG-26M9)

60 https://fortune.com/2020/03/09/robinhood-crash-third-time-stock-market/ (archived at https://perma.cc/237U-HUYH)

61 https://eu.usatoday.com/story/travel/news/2019/04/09/david-dao-doctor-dragged-off-united-flight-speaks-out/3408956002/ (archived at https://perma.cc/YMN6-ZDSV)

62 https://thepointsguy.com/news/whats-changed-since-dr-dao-was-dragged-off-a-united-airlines-flight-five-years-ago/ (archived at https://perma.cc/7S6P-LQJV)

63 Khamitov, M, Grégoire, Y and Suri, A (2020) A systematic review of brand transgression, service failure recovery and product-harm crisis: Integration and guiding insights, *Journal of the Academy of Marketing Science*, 48, 519–42

64 Singh, J and Wilkes, R E (1996) When consumers complain: A path analysis of the key antecedents of consumer complaint response estimates, *Journal of the Academy of Marketing Science*, 24, 350–65

65 Wan, L C (2013) Culture's impact on consumer complaining responses to embarrassing service failure, *Journal of Business Research*, 66 (3), 298–305

66 Choi, S and Mattila, A S (2008) Perceived controllability and service expectations: Influences on customer reactions following service failure, *Journal of Business Research*, 61 (1), 24–30

67 Singh, J and Crisafulli, B (2015) Customer experiences in service failure and recovery, in S Sahdev, K Purani and N Malhotra (eds.), *Boundary Spanning Elements and the Marketing Function in Organizations – Concepts and empirical studies*, Springer International Publishing AG, Switzerland, pp 117–36

68 Singh, J (1988) Consumer complaint intentions and behavior: Definitional and taxonomical issues, *Journal of Marketing*, 52 (1), 93–107

69 Choi, S and Mattila, A S (2008) Perceived controllability and service expectations: Influences on customer reactions following service failure, *Journal of Business Research*, 61 (1), 24–30

70 Joireman, J, Grégoire, Y and Tripp, T M (2016) Customer forgiveness following service failures, *Current Opinion in Psychology*, 10, 76–82

71 Grégoire, Y, Laufer, D and Tripp, T M (2010) A comprehensive model of customer direct and indirect revenge: Understanding the effects of perceived greed and customer power, *Journal of the Academy of Marketing Science*, 38, 738–58

72 Dunn, L and Dahl, D W (2012) Self-threat and product failure: How internal attributions of blame affect consumer complaining behavior, *Journal of Marketing Research*, 49 (5), 670–81

73 Homans, G C (1974) *Social Behavior: Its elementary forms*, Harcourt Brace Jovanovich

74 Rawls, J (2001) *Justice as Fairness: A restatement*, Harvard University Press

75 Voorhees, C M and Brady, M K (2005) A service perspective on the drivers of complaint intentions, *Journal of Service Research*, 8 (2), 192–204

76 del Río-Lanza, A B, Vázquez-Casielles, R and Díaz-Martín, A M (2009) Satisfaction with service recovery: Perceived justice and emotional responses, *Journal of Business Research*, 62 (8), 775–81

77 Bacile, T J, Wolter, J S, Allen, A M and Xu, P (2018) The effects of online incivility and consumer-to-consumer interactional justice on complainants, observers, and service providers during social media service recovery, *Journal of Interactive Marketing*, 44 (1), 60–81

78 Shin, H, Casidy, R and Mattila, A S (2018) Service recovery, justice perception, and forgiveness: The 'other customers' perspectives, *Services Marketing Quarterly*, 39 (1), 1–21

79 https://en.wikipedia.org/wiki/2017_Equifax_data_breach (archived at https://perma.cc/Y8P5-WCXJ)

80 www.wired.co.uk/article/kfc-chicken-crisis-shortage-supply-chain-logistics-experts (archived at https://perma.cc/H56Q-66WQ)

Luxury branding   13

Overview

In this chapter, we first explain the context of luxury branding, definitions and growth. We then talk about the principles underpinning luxury products and branding, including brand signalling, value perceptions and symbolism. In the following section, we discuss the contemporary growth challenges faced by the luxury brands, including counterfeiting, masstige brands, sustainable luxury and luxury democratization. Finally, we bring in the developments of luxury marketing in the digital sphere.

Key learning outcomes

Upon reading this chapter, you should be able to

- Understand the concept of luxury, definitions and the growth of the sector
- Comprehend the principles and theories underpinning luxury branding
- Gain insights into the current growth challenges in the sector
- Understand how digital revolution is impacting the luxury sector

The unique context of luxury branding

The fascination with luxury has captivated the human mind throughout history, spanning past, present and future (see Figure 13.1). This enduring allure has transcended time, from ancient civilizations to today's rich and the nouveau riche, where yearnings for opulence remain constant. Whether we look at the ornate gold-clad sarcophagi and vibrant wall paintings of the Egyptian civilization, intricately crafted wooden architecture and exquisite silk work of the Chinese culture or the ornate gold jewellery and stonework of the Indus Valley civilization, luxury has always played a pivotal role in establishing power, status and social hierarchy.

This penchant for luxury persists in the art, craftsmanship and lifestyle of both pre-and post-Renaissance European societies. Even in today's modern marketplace, the concept of luxury continues to captivate consumers worldwide. However, a

Figure 13.1   Human beings have always been fascinated with exquisite objects

SOURCE Author's

critical issue arises when attempting to define luxury, given its contextual and transient nature. The *Oxford English Dictionary* defines luxury as a state of great comfort or elegance, often involving significant expense, or as an inessential, desirable item that is expensive or hard to obtain.[1]

This definition illustrates the multifaceted nature of luxury, encompassing both a state of being and coveted objects. For example, a Rolls-Royce may be seen as inessential, desirable, expensive and associated with great comfort and elegance. However, with the 'democratization' of luxury, where there is greater access to once-exclusive goods, defining luxury becomes more complex.[2] In the Western developed markets, where handbags are considered essential, and luxury brands such as Louis Vuitton are more accessible, questions about luxury's essence arise.

To address this broad definition, scholars in management and psychology have adopted a trait-specific approach to define luxury. For instance, traits associated with luxury include old-fashioned, pleasant, good taste, flashy and expensive.[3] Later research highlights six specific traits attached with all types of luxury, such as premium price, excellent quality, scarcity, ancestral heritage, aesthetics and superfluousness.[4] However, researchers focusing on the fashion industry only suggest luxury fashion brands have overlapping traits like heritage, exclusivity, premium price, design signature, environment and service, along with culture, brand identity and marketing communication.[5] Other researchers have proposed traits such as rarity, cost, change, transformation, expenditure, distinction, excess and pleasure.[6] Exclusivity

Figure 13.2   Red roses have lost their luxury status in recent times due to easy availability

SOURCE Unsplash/Becca Tapert

and uniqueness are also vital traits in luxury.[7] Luxury brands create and maintain a rarity principle, generating high awareness while remaining comparatively rare and difficult to obtain.[8] For instance, Ferrari limits its annual car production to create a scarcity premium.[9]

A third approach to defining luxury emphasizes experiential aspects, recognizing the contextual nature of luxury. Luxury, in this context, becomes a reflection of beauty and art applied to functional items, and a conveyance of culture and life-style.[10] The meaning of luxury depends on contextual factors, as what is considered luxurious can change over time. For example, presenting out-of-season flowers as a gift, such as a rose on the Valentine's Day, was once a luxury. However, red roses are now available throughout the year and have become accessible across the social strata due to global production and logistics advancements (Figure 13.2).

In summary, luxury is a multifaceted concept that can be defined through various lenses, including a generic definition, a trait-based approach or an experiential per-spective. An amalgamation of these approaches provides a more comprehensive un-derstanding of luxury. A new definition of luxury encapsulating the above approaches is proposed: *Luxury is a significantly comfortable state of being, achieved through the possession of aspirational goods, services and/or meanings that are desired by oneself and/or significant others, based on the collective past and present experiences.*[11] Luxury brands serve as a means to attain this state and encompass goods, services or constructs, which offer symbolic aspirational meaning embedded in societal consciousness, reflecting the contextual and transient nature of luxury.

What makes a product a luxury brand?

Luxury by definition involves aspiration, desires and societal meanings. Thus, in almost every sector there are luxury brands. For example, Bentley in automobiles, Louis Vuitton in fashion and leather goods, Christian Louboutin in shoes, Chopard in jewellery, Hermès in silk scarves and Patek Philippe in watches. In the previous section, we identified a number of traits – high quality, exclusivity, rarity and scarcity, heritage, price, unique design and innovation, and perceived symbolism – that separate a luxury brand from a non-luxury brand.

Exclusivity derived through the scarcity principle is a fundamental concept in the luxury goods industry which emphasizes the importance of limited availability in enhancing the desirability and prestige of luxury products.[12] This principle suggests that when luxury brands restrict the quantity of a particular product or limit its availability in the market, it creates a perception of exclusivity, which in turn increases consumer demand.[13] Consumers are more inclined to desire and value items that are perceived as scarce or hard to obtain due to the innate human tendency to seek uniqueness and social distinction through ownership of exclusive items.[14] As a result, luxury brands strategically employ scarcity as a means to maintain their brand's aura of exclusivity and elevate the perceived value of their products.[15] The rarity principle, though it is used interchangeably with the scarcity principle by many, differs as it emphasizes the innate uniqueness or exceptional qualities of a luxury product.[16] Rarity does not require limiting the availability through production processes, as managed by Ferrari and De Beers. However, rarity could be inherent to the product itself due to the use of rare materials, intricate craftsmanship or unique design elements.[17] For instance, the Fabergé Lady Compliquée is a remarkable luxury watch known for its intricate craftsmanship and artistic design. This timepiece features a mesmerizing dial that pays homage to the famous 'Peacock Egg' of 1908 from Fabergé. It features a hand-engraved peacock in 18 karat gold, a diamond-set bezel and a retrograde hand-winding movement. The Lady Compliquée exemplifies Fabergé's heritage of creating exquisite, one-of-a-kind pieces that blend horological precision with artistic elegance, making it a coveted collector's item for those who appreciate the fusion of haute horologerie and fine artistry. While these principles share similarities, it is important to note that luxury brands may employ both strategies simultaneously and prioritize one over the other. The choice between the scarcity principle and rarity principle depends on the brand's identity, marketing strategy and the specific product in question.

As discussed previously, luxury is highly contextual. In this regard, the brand's origin plays an important role. People regularly incorporate brand origin in their decision making.[18] For instance, Swiss watches, Italian leather goods, French perfume, Belgian chocolate, Scotch whisky and Chinese silk are used as important cues in buying decisions. French and Italian luxury brands are able to charge substantial premiums due to their brand origin which other brands cannot. Hence, to benefit from this typical consumer preference, many luxury brands from emerging markets often employ French or Italian-sounding names to evoke a sense of European sophistication and heritage, which can enhance their perceived prestige and appeal to a global luxury consumer base.[19] For instance, Indian luxury brand Hidesign uses sub-brand names such as Dione, Keira, Cindy, Kelly and Heidi. Similarly, the Japanese lingerie brand Ravijour combines French words to evoke a touch of European luxury.[20]

Scholarly debate

Kapferer, J N and Valette-Florence, P (2016) Beyond rarity: The paths of luxury desire. How luxury brands grow yet remain desirable, *Journal of Product and Brand Management*, 25 (2), 120–33

Shukla, P (2011) Impact of interpersonal influences, brand origin and brand image on luxury purchase intentions: Measuring interfunctional interactions and a cross-national comparison, *Journal of World Business*, 46 (2), 242–52

Luxury brand signalling, symbolism and value perceptions

Luxury brand signalling is a critical aspect of how high-end brands communicate their exclusivity, quality and prestige to consumers.[21] It involves using various cues and signals to convey the unique attributes and desirability of luxury products. One key signalling strategy is through price positioning.[22] Luxury brands often set their prices significantly higher than their competitors, signalling their commitment to premium quality and exclusivity. For example, brands like Rolex and Hermès are known for their high price tags, which signal their luxury status and attract consumers seeking products associated with superior craftsmanship and status.

Another essential element of luxury brand signalling is through branding and logo design. Luxury brands often invest heavily in creating distinctive logos and brand imagery that are instantly recognizable and associated with prestige.[23] For instance, the interlocking 'C' logo of Chanel and the iconic monogram of Louis Vuitton serve as powerful signals of luxury and craftsmanship, allowing consumers to showcase their affiliation with these brands. Additionally, limited edition and exclusive collaborations with renowned designers or artists, such as the partnership between Louis Vuitton and Jeff Koons, can further enhance the brand's signalling of uniqueness and desirability.[24] In summary, luxury brand signalling encompasses various strategies, including pricing, branding and collaborations, to convey exclusivity and prestige to consumers. These signals help consumers identify and connect with luxury brands, fostering a sense of aspiration and desire for their products while maintaining their elevated status in the market.

Symbolic motivations arise from the aspiration for social prestige and status.[25] These motivations manifest in a consumption pattern that communicates significance and information regarding one's social standing, identity, personality and personal preferences.[26] When a product or service serves as a symbol, its value is determined by the social status and influence it conveys within the network, rather than its intrinsic cost.[27] The theory of network effects, also known as network externalities, provides an explanation that the symbolic value individuals assign to a product or service is influenced by the growing number of users.[28] Thus, the more people who own a luxury brand, the more desirable it becomes to others. This is because luxury brands are often seen as status symbols, and people want to be associated with brands that are popular and exclusive. For example, Balenciaga, the Spanish luxury fashion house, founded in 1917, has grown in popularity among young consumers for its avant-garde design and its high-end luxury clothing. Interestingly, the more shocking designs the brand has introduced, the more popular it has become. This symbolic motivation and the resulting practice of symbolic consumption of luxury brands are observed across historical periods.[29]

Thorstein Veblen, in his seminal 1899 work on the theory of the leisure class, argued that a substantial portion of goods consumption was driven by the desire to attain and affirm one's social status.[30] He contended that affluent members of society engaged in consumption to create 'invidious comparisons', whereas those with fewer resources pursued 'pecuniary emulation'. This concept was further expanded by economists introducing network externalities. These externalities, often called 'network effects', occur when the value of a product or service increases as more people use it. For example, the more the number of people own smartphones, the more useful they become because people can easily communicate with others and access various apps and services. Based on the above logic, economists assert that three primary motivational factors underpin the inclination to engage with luxury brands: the snob effect, the bandwagon effect and the Veblen effect.[31]

Buyer motivations

Snob motivation refers to people's desire for unique goods. This motivation dampens consumer demand for a luxury brand because more people are buying the brand. The underlying reason is due to the negative effects of the expanding network, also known as the *negative network effect*. In other words, the consumer of the luxury brand is unable to differentiate from others through the uniqueness of their consumption.[32] Hence, popularity of a luxury brand can destroy its utility for the snobbish consumers.[33] For example, Burberry, a British luxury brand, faced a period of struggle in the early 2000s when its iconic check pattern became associated with lower socio-economic youth segments and rampant counterfeiting. This led to substantial reputational damage and decline in sales as the traditional Burberry buyers shunned the brand.[34] Burberry subsequently underwent a major rebranding effort which also involved jettisoning the infamous check print. This helped the brand to regain its previous status as a true luxury fashion house. Having reclaimed its luxury status, Burberry reintroduced the pattern 13 years later.[35] Luxury brands, therefore, should carefully monitor and maintain the exclusivity and uniqueness signals associated with their offerings.

In contradiction to snob motivation, bandwagon motivation arises when consumers purchase luxury brands because of their popularity. The bandwagon effect is observed when demand for a luxury brand is increased because socially relevant individuals and groups are also consuming it at a given price. For example, consumers may buy a luxury brand that is being endorsed by a popular social media influencer, a celebrity or a relevant group of people. Thus, the bandwagon effect is similar to positive network effects, where a product becomes more desirable as its popularity increases.[36] This associated consumption of luxury brands grounded in the bandwagon effect is driven by social approval and a sense of belonging to the relevant status groups. Consumers use these luxury brands as signals about their status and belonging to the social community. Luxury brands, thus, have to strike a balance between their popularity and exclusivity. For example, the brand Von Dutch, launched in the mid-1990s became highly popular for its trucker hats, jackets and t-shirts in the early 2000s with celebrities such as Beyoncé, Paris Hilton, Whitney Houston, Madonna, Britney Spears and Justin Timberlake adorning the brand.[37] However, in the late 2000s the brand experienced a rapid decline due to saturation driven by its increasing popularity and counterfeiting.[38] As the above example illustrates, if too many people own a particular luxury brand, the exclusivity, rarity and uniqueness may get diluted, which, in turn, will trigger the snob effect, resulting in consumers abandoning the brand. However, if the brand remains too exclusive, many consumers would not be able to purchase it, and thus could result in sales revenue and profits losses.

Veblen motivation, on the other hand, refers to the traditional definition of conspicuous consumption regarding the willingness of people to buy high-end luxury goods in order to display their wealth and financial prowess.[39] Herein, the perceived prestige and desirability of a luxury brand increase as its price rises, contrary to the law of demand. In other words, consumers are drawn to higher-priced luxury items as a symbol of status and exclusivity. This suggests that due to Veblen motivation, a luxury brand's price increase might not lead to loss of sales.

Classifying luxury

Considering the complex characteristics of both the construct of luxury and value, luxury has been classified from various perspectives, encompassing functional, experiential, hedonic and symbolic dimensions. As previously mentioned, the historical significance of luxury in shaping individual and social identities is widely acknowledged. This has led to substantial research on value perceptions associated with luxury brands that reflect *functional*, *social* and *personal* aspects. *Functional* value represents what the luxury goods or services 'do' in the real world, rather than what they 'represent'.[40] Consumers anticipate that a luxury product should be practical, exhibit excellent craftsmanship and possess a distinctiveness that fulfils their desire for differentiation.[41] For instance, since inception, Louis Vuitton trunks were designed with exceptional functionality, capable of enduring the extensive world travels of their clientele. Likewise, Patek Philippe underscores its heritage and enduring quality in watchmaking through its advertising tagline, 'You don't truly possess a Patek Philippe; you simply care for it for the succeeding generation.' Academic research suggests that highlighting price, quality and uniqueness can allow luxury brands to demonstrate their functional value.[42] The assessment of the overall value of any luxury brand continues to heavily involve social value perceptions. These perceptions stem from its image and symbolism in connection with or separation from demographic, socio-economic and cultural-ethnic reference groups.[43]

Social value perceptions relate to the instrumental aspect of impression management and are driven by outer-directed consumption preferences and reflect in social salience and social identification.[44] Scholars have highlighted how luxury brands strategically position themselves to create associations with exclusive social circles or cultural references, amplifying their allure and social value in the eyes of consumers.[45] Consequently, these social value perceptions serve as a vital dimension in understanding the intricate dynamics of luxury brand consumption through both acquisition and display of luxury brands. Luxury brands regularly utilize this dimension. For example, Louis Vuitton's 'Neverful' handbag campaign was accompanied by the tagline 'Neverful. Never out of style', highlighting the social approval and classic nature of the product.

While social referencing and status signalling have received significant attention throughout the history of luxury branding debate, an important thought that is becoming more prominent in recent times is the idea of luxury consumption directed towards pleasing the self.[46] *Personal* value perceptions associated with luxury brands are grounded in self-enhancement which relates to the expressive dimension of impression management.[47] Luxury brands exploit personal value perceptions through three sub-dimensions that reflect the internal and external facets of the self through materialism and hedonism associated with luxury brand consumption. For example, Gucci, the famous Italian fashion house, is known for its bold and flamboyant designs. Its advertising often features young and attractive people who are having fun and enjoying themselves. This creates a sense of excitement and hedonism, which can be appealing to consumers.

BRANDING IN PRACTICE
Supreme exploits luxury brand symbolism and value perceptions

Supreme, the iconic streetwear brand founded in New York City in 1994, has remarkably transformed streetwear culture by successfully utilizing luxury brand signalling, symbolism and value perceptions to engage customers. What began as a small skateboarding shop in downtown Manhattan has evolved into a global cultural phenomenon, with consumers across the world eagerly buying into in the brand's unique blend of streetwear and luxury. The brand is known for its limited-edition products, high prices and association with hip-hop culture.

Supreme cleverly employs luxury brand signalling by adopting a minimalist yet instantly recognizable logo – the bold red box with 'Supreme' in white Futura Heavy Oblique font. This iconic branding serves as a symbol of exclusivity and authenticity. Supreme's limited product releases, typically in small quantities, create a sense of scarcity, driving up demand and reinforcing the brand's luxury appeal. The collaboration with luxury fashion houses like Louis Vuitton further elevated Supreme's status, showcasing its ability to align with traditional luxury while maintaining its streetwear roots.

Supreme understands the power of symbolism. The brand's ability to incorporate cultural references, often subversive or nostalgic, into its designs, resonates with its core audience. Supreme has effectively tapped into the symbolism of counterculture, skateboarding and hip-hop, establishing itself as a symbol of rebellion and authenticity. Items like the Supreme Box Logo Hoodie have become status symbols within streetwear culture, signifying not just clothing but a lifestyle and identity.

Supreme's limited editions and collaborations generate anticipation and excitement, contributing to the perception that owning a Supreme product is an achievement. The resale market for Supreme items, where certain pieces can fetch prices many times their original retail value, reinforces the idea that Supreme offers both financial and social value. Customers view Supreme as an investment, where the value of ownership extends beyond the utility of the product itself.

As a result of these strategies, Supreme has been able to successfully exploit luxury brand signalling, symbolism and value perceptions and has become one of the most successful fashion brands in the world.

Contemporary growth challenges for luxury brands

As the marketplace evolves, luxury brands, which were once the preserve of the elite, are now desired by other socio-economic classes as well. The business growth aim often conflicts with the scarcity and rarity principles of luxury branding and the knowledge on why and how consumer commit to luxury brand is nascent.[48] Luxury brands are also faced with the choice of following the successful branding practices of non-luxury brands, for instance corporate social responsibility, sustainability, digitization, corporate identity and value management, the dilemma of the luxury brand extending into 'masstige' and brand dilution due to counterfeiting. This section examines several such contemporary challenges that are faced by the luxury brands.

Given their visibility and high symbolic and cultural capital, consumers increasingly expect luxury brands to engage in and be vocal about various social issues such as sustainability, climate change and racial equality.[49] While known for their exclusivity, many luxury brands are embracing ethical practices in response to consumer demand and their own strategic vision.[50] Yet, the impact of these efforts on their profitability remains uncertain, with mixed research findings.[51] It should be noted, however, that such society-oriented practices are aimed towards strengthening the luxury brand's image and attitudes, rather than for increasing profitability or market performance. While some luxury brands at the corporate level such as the Kering group (owner of Gucci, Balenciaga, Brioni, etc.) have achieved high sustainability rankings, consumer attitudes towards the individual luxury brands and their sustainability initiatives appear ambivalent.[52] In contrast, others show that depending on the appeal used by the luxury brands, consumers prefer sustainable luxury brands. For example, when a brand uses self-pride appeal-based communication, it heightens the luxury dimension, however, a gratitude appeal in communication increases the sustainability association.[53] Gucci's Chime for Change campaign, launched in 2013, is a global initiative advocating for gender equality and women's empowerment. The brand raises awareness and funds for various projects aimed at improving the lives of women and girls worldwide, focusing on education, healthcare and justice.

Most luxury brands concentrate their corporate social responsibility efforts on the supply side, focusing on sustainable raw materials, procurement processes and labour management. For example, Prada has developed a new code of conduct for the group's suppliers to improve its sustainability and social responsibility credentials and converted all the production of virgin nylon into regenerated nylon.[54] Similarly, Tiffany & Co. is committed to responsible sourcing of diamonds and has implemented initiatives to track the provenance of their stones, ensuring they come from ethical and environmentally responsible sources. Some also engage in demand-side initiatives, such as charity events and partnerships with non-profit organizations. For example, Burberry has a comprehensive CSR programme that includes sustainability efforts like reducing its carbon footprint and water usage. They also invest in communities through educational and philanthropic initiatives.[55] Similarly, for its re-nylon project, Prada will fund 1 per cent of its proceeds to the Sea Beyond charity.[56]

The rapid growth of luxury brands in recent decades is largely attributed to the increasing demand from emerging markets such as China, India, Russia and Brazil.[57] The consumers in emerging markets may not have same per capita income as their developed market counterparts, however, there is a substantial growth in the so-called nouveau riche segment who aspire for global luxury brands.[58] To satisfy the demand of the growing customer base globally, luxury brands have engaged in a variety of brand extensions. These have been termed at times as 'accessible luxury',[59] 'masstige'[60] or 'democratization'.[61] One prominent example is the expansion of Italian fashion house Gucci into the world of fragrance and beauty. By applying its distinctive design aesthetic and luxury appeal to perfumes, makeup and skincare products, Gucci successfully extended its brand into the beauty sector, attracting a wider audience while maintaining its premium image. Another example is Louis Vuitton's foray into the realm of luxury travel and hospitality with their Louis Vuitton Maison concept. Through this extension, Louis Vuitton offers customers a holistic brand experience, including hotels, restaurants and cultural spaces, reinforcing the brand's commitment to luxury and craftsmanship in a new and immersive way.[62] Similarly, Armani has extended its brand in haute couture, ready-to-wear, eyewear, home furnishings, fragrances, hospitality including clubs, hotels and resorts, restaurants, and museums, as well as beauty and food products.[63] While such brand extensions allow these luxury brands to reach wider audiences, it has also meant loss of focus. For instance, academic research shows that when luxury brands extend themselves to engage middle-class consumers, traditional luxury consumers tend to abandon democratizing luxury brands.[64]

Counterfeiting

Counterfeiting poses significant challenges for luxury brands, affecting their reputation, revenues and intellectual property rights.[65] Such challenges are also substantiated by growing research evidence.[66] The counterfeit luxury goods market is estimated to be a $1.2 trillion economy.[67] The counterfeiting of luxury goods has become increasingly sophisticated, making it difficult for consumers and even experts to distinguish fake products from genuine ones. This not only erodes consumer trust but also damages the brand's image as counterfeits often lack the quality and craftsmanship associated with luxury items. The global luxury industry loses billions of dollars annually due to counterfeit sales (Figure 13.3).

Figure 13.3   Counterfeiting remains a big business across the world

SOURCE Author's

This loss not only affects the revenue stream of luxury brands but also hinders their ability to invest in innovation and maintain their competitive edge.[68] Moreover, the proliferation of counterfeits can lead to legal battles, as luxury brands seek to protect their intellectual property rights, incurring significant legal expenses. For example, it is estimated that French luxury group LVMH spends as much as $17 million every year on anti-counterfeiting legal expenses.[69] Additionally, the availability of counterfeit products in online marketplaces has exacerbated the problem, making it harder for luxury brands to control the distribution and sale of fake goods. For example, Amazon removed more than six million counterfeit luxury and non-luxury goods in 2022 alone.[70] These challenges highlight the pressing need for luxury brands to invest in anti-counterfeiting measures to protect their brand equity and maintain their exclusivity. To fight counterfeiting, luxury brands are also investing in the latest technological solutions including blockchain. For instance, several leading luxury brands including LVMH, Prada and Cartier have partnered in establishing the Aura Blockchain Consortium, which offers shoppers tamper-proof access to information about the product's supply chain and proof of ownership.[71] Luxury brands are also using other initiatives such as microprinting and holograms, serial numbers and RFID tags, and unique design patterns to fight the counterfeiters.

Digitalizing luxury

One of the foremost challenges faced by luxury brands is digitization. For hundreds of years, luxury brands were largely available in large cosmopolitan cities of the world such as London, Venice, Monte Carlo, New York and Paris. However, the rapid pace of digital evolution adds increasing challenges for luxury brands as they are now globally desired and are spurred to engage with customers residing in remote corners of the world. Consequently, this expansion has notably broadened luxury brands' reach and the esteem attributed to them by the consumers.[72] Furthermore, it has provided luxury brands with the means to establish meaningful interactions with both current and prospective customers, extending beyond the confines of physical retail spaces. Internet technologies provide a dynamic platform for luxury brands to engage with the consumers, contrasting with the one-way communication channels of the past, such as print and TV ads. Yet, they bring forth significant challenges. Initially, many luxury brands were hesitant to embrace these technologies, leading to delayed online presence and the emergence of luxury portals, for instance, Net-a-Porter and Farfetch.[73] The second challenge is the depth and quality of engagement. While the internet allows global connections, it diminishes the traditional luxury shopping experience, impacting service quality and personal interactions. Maintaining a consistent, high-quality digital experience is a major challenge for the luxury brands.[74] Furthermore, online commerce threatens the uniqueness and exclusivity, historically linked with luxury. In the past, customers had to invest substantial effort to gather information about luxury brands. However, social media now facilitates easy comparisons of attributes such as price, style and trends among peers.[75] Thus, alongside customer engagement, luxury brands face the task of managing multi-channel expectations while preserving a unique and exclusive brand narrative.[76]

Luxury brands have also embraced digitalization to communicate their social engagement initiatives. In particular, many luxury brands are engaging in brand *activism*, wherein a brand takes a stand on contemporary social political challenges.[77] Using social media, luxury brands have become increasingly vocal about their views on socio-political issues. For instance, following the George Floyd murder by the police and the rise of Black Lives Matter movement, many prominent luxury brands including Gucci, Fendi, Louis Vuitton and Dior have taken a stance and spoken out against racial injustice in their social media outlets. Burberry also announced its boycott of Xinjiang cotton sourcing from China due to concerns over alleged human rights abuses in the region, over social media.[78] It also allowed the brand to engage in a dialogue with today's digital savvy consumers. Such brand activism initiatives by luxury brands receives attention from global media outlets and the public at large, and helps to strengthen their image.

Luxury brands are also embracing the latest immersive digital technologies for communicating with customers. For instance, Ralph Lauren, Gucci, Burberry and several other brands have opened their collections on the video game Roblox, which is especially popular among the young players.[79] Similarly, Balenciaga has collaborated with globally popular game Fortnite and launched a range of hoodies, clothes and skins.[80] Gucci has partnered with The Sandbox to create a virtual world called Gucci Vault. Gucci Vault is a space where users can collect digital Gucci items, such as non-fungible tokens (NFT) and virtual clothing. In collaboration with Superplastic, a company that creates digital characters and toys, Gucci created a collection of 100 NFT. This collaboration features the digital artworks of Superplastic characters, Janky and Guggimon, in Gucci-inspired designs. The NFTs were sold on the OpenSea marketplace and raised over $2 million.[81] While faced with technical glitches and other setbacks, Dolce & Gabbana and Tommy Hilfiger were among the major names participating in the first ever Metaverse Fashion Week, which saw the brands create elaborate experiential boutiques in the Decentraland metaverse.[82] Such initiatives heighten the experiential dimension of luxury branding.

Digitalization has allowed substantial customization opportunities for luxury brands. Many luxury brands have embraced the practice of customization to enhance the online shopping experience for their discerning clientele. Luxury brand customization allows customers to personalize products, whether it's a bespoke suit, a monogrammed handbag or custom-fitted jewellery. This online trend not only caters to individual preferences but also amplifies the exclusivity associated with luxury consumption. Through user-friendly digital platforms, customers can select materials, colours and design elements, effectively co-creating their unique luxury items. Brands like Louis Vuitton, Burberry, Longchamp and Rolex have integrated these customization options seamlessly into their websites, enabling customers to engage with their products in a more intimate and personal way. Luxury customization practices online not only cater to the desire for unique, one-of-a-kind items but also strengthen brand loyalty and engagement in the digital realm, where the concept of bespoke luxury has found a new and thriving home.

While many luxury brands are embracing social media and other digital technologies, some exclusive brands are shunning social media and attempt to replicate their customers' unique experience digitally through other avenues. For example, Bottega Veneta shut down its social media accounts in 2021 and devised a special app to curate customer experience.[83] Other brands such as Rolls-Royce, Balenciaga and Celine also use social media sparsely, to maintain their exclusivity focus.

Luxury brands in the digital marketplace are adapting to the evolving landscape by leveraging online platforms to reach wider audiences and cater to the changing preferences of tech-savvy consumers. They prioritize e-commerce, offering exclusive online shopping experiences while maintaining their aura of exclusivity. Digital strategies, such as immersive content, social media engagement and limited-edition digital releases, are now integral to luxury brands' presence, ensuring they stay relevant and alluring in the digital age.

Chapter summary

In this chapter, we examined the unique context of luxury branding. While the conventional brand management concepts apply equally to luxury, it is a complex construct that has been defined through varied lenses, such as the generic, trait-based and experiential. The trait approach to luxury allows us to understand the distinction between luxury and non-luxury brands. Luxury brands thrive on their unique symbolism, signalling and value perceptions. Various counteracting forces such as snob, bandwagon and Veblen motivations drive luxury brand consumption. We also learnt the various types of values that are important for luxury brands including social, personal and functional value. With the growth of luxury brands globally, there are a number of challenges relating to socio-political engagement, brand extension and counterfeiting that these brands face. Finally, we understood how luxury brands are embracing digital technologies to strengthen their brand image and customer-brand relationships.

Key concepts

- Luxury branding
  - Luxury brand signalling
  - Luxury brand motivations
  - Luxury value perceptions
- Difference between luxury and non-luxury brands
- Luxury brand activism
- Counterfeiting
- Democratization/masstige
- Digital luxury

Exercise questions

1 Discuss the different approaches used in defining luxury.

2 Critically reflect on what makes a product a luxury brand.

3 Explain the snob, bandwagon and Veblen motivations that underpin luxury branding using examples.

4 Discuss the different value perceptions that drive luxury consumption.

5 Describe in detail the contemporary growth challenges faced by luxury brands.

6 How are luxury brands embracing digital technologies? Explain with examples.

7 Using examples, explain how luxury brands should engage in activism particularly using the social cause-brand image fit concept.

CASE STUDY   Can luxury fashion brands ever really be inclusive?

Read the following article by Paurav Shukla and Dina Khalifa, which examines the extent to which luxury fashion brands can be inclusive. Many invest in initiatives to address environmental concerns, e.g. the Kering group aiming to reduce greenhouse gas emissions by 50 per cent by 2025 or health issues (such as LVMH providing their manufacturing facilities to make free hand sanitizer in France). However, there is doubt that the exclusive nature of luxury brands (out of the price range for most consumers) can ever align with a public image of sustainability and environmental or social awareness.

SOURCE https://theconversation.com/can-luxury-fashion-brands-ever-really-be-inclusive-165187

Case questions

1 Critical reflect on whether 'luxury brands can really be inclusive', based on the traits associated with luxury.

2 This case study suggests that many luxury brands' approach to inclusivity is a reaction to a crisis. Explain using examples.

3 What kind of symbolic motivations can be triggered among consumers when luxury brands engage in activism?

4 Through your own web search, identify examples of luxury brands that have proactively embraced the idea of inclusivity.

5 Identify ways in which luxury brands can improve their equality, diversity and inclusion initiatives through online and offline initiatives.

Endnotes

1 www.oed.com/dictionary/luxury_n?tab=meaning_and_use (archived at https://perma.cc/R45C-RRXK)

2 Shukla, P, Rosendo-Rios, V and Khalifa, D (2022) Is luxury democratization impactful? Its moderating effect between value perceptions and consumer purchase intentions, *Journal of Business Research*, 139, 782–93

3 Dubois, B and Laurent, G (1994) Attitudes toward the concept of luxury: An exploratory analysis, *Asia-Pacific Advances in Consumer Research*, 1 (2), 273–78

4 Dubois, B, Czellar, S and Laurent, G (2005) Consumer segments based on attitudes toward luxury: Empirical evidence from twenty countries, *Marketing Letters*, 16 (2), 115–28

5 Fionda, A M and Moore, C M (2009) The anatomy of the luxury fashion brand, *Journal of Brand Management*, 16 (5–6), 347–63

6 Michaud, Y (2013) *Le nouveau luxe: Expériences, arrogance, authenticité*, Stock

7 Ko, E, Costello, J P and Taylor, C R (2019) What is a luxury brand? A new definition and review of the literature, *Journal of Business Research*, 99, 405–13

8 Phau, I and Prendergast, G (2000) Consuming luxury brands: The relevance of the 'rarity principle', *Journal of Brand Management*, 8, 122–38

9 www.autocar.co.uk/car-news/business/ferrari-preserve-uniqueness-limiting-production-numbers (archived at https://perma.cc/A8QH-ZG28)

10 Kapferer, J N (2015) *Kapferer on Luxury: How luxury brands can grow yet remain rare*, Kogan Page Publishers

11 Shukla, P (2020) *Luxury Value Perceptions: A cross-cultural perspective*, Aalto University Press

12 Shukla, P, Rosendo-Rios, V, Trott, S, Lyu, J and Khalifa, D (2022) Managing the challenge of luxury democratization: A multicountry analysis, *Journal of International Marketing*, 30 (4), 44–59

13 Rosendo-Rios, V and Shukla, P (2023) The effects of masstige on loss of scarcity and behavioral intentions for traditional luxury consumers, *Journal of Business Research*, 156, 113490

14 Amaldoss, W and Jain, S (2005) Conspicuous consumption and sophisticated thinking, *Management Science*, 51 (10), 1449–66

15 Kapferer, J N and Bastien, V (2012) *The Luxury Strategy: Break the rules of marketing to build luxury brands*, Kogan Page

16 Phau, I and Prendergast, G (2000) Consuming luxury brands: The relevance of the 'rarity principle', *Journal of Brand Management*, 8, 122–38

17 Kapferer, J N and Valette-Florence, P (2016) Beyond rarity: The paths of luxury desire. How luxury brands grow yet remain desirable, *Journal of Product & Brand Management*, 25 (2), 120–33

18 Shukla, P (2011) Impact of interpersonal influences, brand origin and brand image on luxury purchase intentions: Measuring interfunctional interactions and a cross-national comparison, *Journal of World Business*, 46 (2), 242–52

19 Cakici, N M and Shukla, P (2017) Country-of-origin misclassification awareness and consumers' behavioral intentions: Moderating roles of consumer affinity, animosity, and product knowledge, *International Marketing Review*, 34 (3), 354–76

20 www.ravijour.com/about/ (archived at https://perma.cc/VK7L-WBZJ)

21 Dubois, D, Jung, S and Ordabayeva, N (2021) The psychology of luxury consumption, *Current Opinion in Psychology*, 39, 82–87

22 Parguel, B, Delécolle, T and Valette-Florence, P (2016) How price display influences consumer luxury perceptions, *Journal of Business Research*, 69 (1), 341–48

23 Han, Y J, Nunes, J C and Drèze, X (2010) Signaling status with luxury goods: The role of brand prominence, *Journal of Marketing*, 74 (4), 15–30

24 Hagtvedt, H and Patrick, V M (2009) The broad embrace of luxury: Hedonic potential as a driver of brand extendibility, *Journal of Consumer Psychology*, 19 (4), 608–18

25 Shukla, P and Rosendo-Rios, V (2021) Intra and inter-country comparative effects of symbolic motivations on luxury purchase intentions in emerging markets, *International Business Review*, 30 (1), 101768

26 Kastanakis, M N and Balabanis, G (2014) Explaining variation in conspicuous luxury consumption: An individual differences' perspective, *Journal of Business Research*, 67 (10), 2147–54

27 Berger, J and Ward, M (2010) Subtle signals of inconspicuous consumption, *Journal of Consumer Research*, 37 (4), 555–69

28 Katz, M L and Shapiro, C (1985) Network externalities, competition, and compatibility, *The American Economic Review*, 75 (3), 424–40

29 McNeil, P and Riello, G (2016) *Luxury: A rich history*, Oxford University Press

30 Veblen, T (1899) *The Theory of the Leisure Class*, Viking-Penguin, New York

31 Leibenstein, H (1950) Bandwagon, snob, and Veblen effects in the theory of consumers' demand, *The Quarterly Journal of Economics*, 64 (2), 183–207

32 Tian, K T and McKenzie, K (2001) The long-term predictive validity of the consumers' need for uniqueness scale, *Journal of Consumer Psychology*, 10 (3), 171–93

33 Kastanakis, M N and Balabanis, G (2014) Explaining variation in conspicuous luxury consumption: An individual differences' perspective, *Journal of Business Research*, 67 (10), 2147–54

34 www.vogue.co.uk/article/burberry-banned (archived at https://perma.cc/D4TP-UNX8)

35 https://nandininachiar.medium.com/how-did-burberry-break-free-from-the-rigid-fist-with-which-it-was-held-by-the-chav-subculture-6ee258eefb08 (archived at https://perma.cc/58LL-ZXPU)

36 Shukla, P and Rosendo-Rios, V (2021) Intra and inter-country comparative effects of symbolic motivations on luxury purchase intentions in emerging markets, *International Business Review*, 30 (1), 101768

37 www.ranker.com/list/what-happened-to-von-dutch/matt-manser (archived at https://perma.cc/6MA8-LUUN)

38 www.adweek.com/brand-marketing/the-great-fail-von-dutch-from-price-tags-to-tie-tags (archived at https://perma.cc/3VTN-R9MA)

39 Shukla, P and Rosendo-Rios, V (2021) Intra and inter-country comparative effects of symbolic motivations on luxury purchase intentions in emerging markets, *International Business Review*, 30 (1), 101768

40 Shukla, P (2012) The influence of value perceptions on luxury purchase intentions in developed and emerging markets, *International Marketing Review*, 29 (6), 574–96

41 Wiedmann, K P, Hennigs, N and Siebels, A (2009) Value-based segmentation of luxury consumption behavior, *Psychology & Marketing*, 26 (7), 625–51

42 Shukla, P and Purani, K (2012) Comparing the importance of luxury value perceptions in cross-national contexts, *Journal of Business Research*, 65 (10), 1417–24

43 Vigneron, F and Johnson, L W (2004) Measuring perceptions of brand luxury, *Journal of Brand Management*, 11 (6), 484–506

44 Chattalas, M and Shukla, P (2015) Impact of value perceptions on luxury purchase intentions: A developed market comparison, *Luxury Research Journal*, 1 (1), 40–57

45 Shukla, P, Singh, J and Banerjee, M (2015) They are not all same: Variations in Asian consumers' value perceptions of luxury brands, *Marketing Letters*, 26, 265–78

46 Wiedmann, K P, Hennigs, N and Siebels, A (2009) Value-based segmentation of luxury consumption behavior, *Psychology & Marketing*, 26 (7), 625–51

47 Shukla, P (2012) The influence of value perceptions on luxury purchase intentions in developed and emerging markets, *International Marketing Review*, 29 (6), 574–96

48 Shukla, P, Banerjee, M and Singh, J (2016) Customer commitment to luxury brands: Antecedents and consequences, *Journal of Business Research*, 69 (1), 323–31

49 Sipilä, J, Alavi, S, Edinger-Schons, L M, Dörfer, S and Schmitz, C (2021) Corporate social responsibility in luxury contexts: Potential pitfalls and how to overcome them, *Journal of the Academy of Marketing Science*, 49, 280–303

50 https://theconversation.com/can-luxury-fashion-brands-ever-really-be-inclusive-165187 (archived at https://perma.cc/CQ5M-GZHN)

51 Achabou, M A and Dekhili, S (2013) Luxury and sustainable development: Is there a match?, *Journal of Business Research*, 66 (10), 1896–903

52 Kapferer, J N and Michaut-Denizeau, A (2014) Is luxury compatible with sustainability? Luxury consumers' viewpoint, *Journal of Brand Management*, 21 (1), 1–22

53 Septianto, F, Seo, Y and Errmann, A C (2021) Distinct effects of pride and gratitude appeals on sustainable luxury brands, *Journal of Business Ethics*, 169, 211–24

54 www.pradagroup.com/en/sustainability/prada-impact/impact.html (archived at https://perma.cc/YRU2-N98S)

55 https://burberrycareers.com/content/Responsibility/?locale=en_GB (archived at https://perma.cc/KYR4-B337)

56 www.pradagroup.com/en/sustainability/environment-csr/prada-re-nylon.html (archived at https://perma.cc/Z2JP-6LFH)

57 Singh, J, Shukla, P and Schlegelmilch, B B (2022) Desire, need, and obligation: Examining commitment to luxury brands in emerging markets, *International Business Review*, 31 (3), 101947

58 Shukla, P, Rosendo-Rios, V, Trott, S, Lyu, J and Khalifa, D (2022) Managing the challenge of luxury democratization: A multicountry analysis, *Journal of International Marketing*, 30 (4), 44–59

59 De Barnier, V, Falcy, S and Valette-Florence, P (2012) Do consumers perceive three levels of luxury? A comparison of accessible, intermediate and inaccessible luxury brands, *Journal of Brand Management*, 19 (7), 623–36

60 Kumar, A, Paul, J and Unnithan, A B (2020) 'Masstige' marketing: A review, synthesis and research agenda, *Journal of Business Research*, 113, 384–98

61 Shukla, P, Rosendo-Rios, V and Khalifa, D (2022) Is luxury democratization impactful? Its moderating effect between value perceptions and consumer purchase intentions, *Journal of Business Research*, 139, 782–93

62 www.architecturaldigest.com/story/first-louis-vuitton-hotel-paris (archived at https://perma.cc/3H79-6ZU4)

63 www.armani.com/en-gb (archived at https://perma.cc/7H2N-EDGT)

64 Rosendo-Rios, V and Shukla, P (2023) When luxury democratizes: Exploring the effects of luxury democratization, hedonic value and instrumental self-presentation on traditional luxury consumers' behavioral intentions, *Journal of Business Research*, 155, 113448

65 Wilcox, K, Kim, H M and Sen, S (2009) Why do consumers buy counterfeit luxury brands?, *Journal of Marketing Research*, 46 (2), 247–59

66 Khan, S, Fazili, A I and Bashir, I (2021) Counterfeit luxury consumption: A review and research agenda, *Journal of Consumer Behaviour*, 20 (2), 337–67

67 https://blog.gitnux.com/luxury-replica-statistics/ (archived at https://perma.cc/7H2N-zzzz)

68 Eisend, M, Hartmann, P and Apaolaza, V (2017) Who buys counterfeit luxury brands? A meta-analytic synthesis of consumers in developing and developed markets, *Journal of International Marketing*, 25 (4), 89–111

69 www.warc.com/newsandopinion/news/why-luxury-keeps-struggling-with-its-counterfeits-problem/42145 (archived at https://perma.cc/LFJ7-L3HC)

70 www.globallegalpost.com/news/amazon-removed-six-million-counterfeit-products-in-2022-in-fight-against-fakes-1721087115 (archived at https://perma.cc/3B2T-3TAJ)

71 https://auraluxuryblockchain.com/members (archived at https://perma.cc/83R9-62VJ)

72 Chevalier, M and Gutsatz, M (2020) *Luxury Retail and Digital Management: Developing customer experience in a digital world*, John Wiley and Sons

73 https://luxurysociety.com/en/articles/2010/09/should-luxury-brands-use-twitter (archived at https://perma.cc/A59W-7RLN)

74 Heine, K and Berghaus, B (2014) Luxury goes digital: How to tackle the digital luxury brand–consumer touchpoints, *Journal of Global Fashion Marketing*, 5 (3), 223–34

75 Godey, B, Manthiou, A, Pederzoli, D, Rokka, J, Aiello, G, Donvito, R and Singh, R (2016) Social media marketing efforts of luxury brands: Influence on brand equity and consumer behavior, *Journal of Business Research*, 69 (12), 5833–41

76 Pangarkar, A, Arora, V and Shukla, Y (2022) Exploring phygital omnichannel luxury retailing for immersive customer experience: The role of rapport and social engagement, *Journal of Retailing and Consumer Services*, 68, 103001

77 Moorman, C (2020) Commentary: Brand activism in a political world, *Journal of Public Policy & Marketing*, 39 (4), 388–92

78 www.reuters.com/world/china/burberry-becomes-first-luxury-brand-suffer-chinese-backlash-over-xinjiang-2021-03-26/ (archived at https://perma.cc/FA8V-QXUF)

79 https://edition.cnn.com/style/article/fashion-metaverse-millions-september-issues/index.html (archived at https://perma.cc/AAC9-RZPA)

80 www.vogue.com/article/balenciaga-fortnite-partnership (archived at https://perma.cc/PCS5-JQUF)

81 www.nft-stats.com/collection/superplastic-supergucci (archived at https://perma.cc/CG67-JYNX)

82 https://edition.cnn.com/style/article/fashion-metaverse-millions-september-issues/index.html (archived at https://perma.cc/GXM4-R6WX)

83 www.wmagazine.com/fashion/bottega-veneta-instagram-deleted-why (archived at https://perma.cc/3KH4-VNPU)

Sensory branding and neuromarketing

14

Overview

In this chapter, we first explain the role of sensory perceptions in creating and sustaining brand differentiation. We then discuss the types of human sensory perceptions, with examples of how brands use these perceptions. In the following section we discuss crossmodal sensory perceptions and the latest advancements in research. In the final section, we discuss neuromarketing and its impact on branding practice.

Key learning outcomes

Upon reading this chapter, you should be able to

- Understand sensory branding
- Gain insights into types of sensory perceptions
- Develop an understanding of 'crossmodal' sensory perceptions
- Comprehend applications of neuromarketing perspectives in branding

The role of human sensory perceptions

Human sensory perceptions are the processes by which people receive, select, organize and interpret information from the external world through their five senses: sight, hearing, smell, taste and touch. Sensory perceptions play a crucial role in consumer decision making, as they influence how consumers perceive, evaluate and choose products and services.[1] Sensory perceptions also affect consumers' emotions, memories, preferences and satisfaction.[2] In the physical retail environment, marketers have long understood the power of sensory perceptions in guiding consumer decision making and brand choices. For instance, academic research showed that when retail

Figure 14.1   Since 2018, all Apple stores use a signature scent developed in collaboration with renowned perfumer Christophe Laudamiel

SOURCE Unsplash.com/Mihály Köles

stores use smells that are perceived as warm (e.g. vanilla, cinnamon), compared to cool (e.g. peppermint, eucalyptus), consumers assumed the environment to be more socially dense, that is, they perceived the presence of others in the environment (Figure 14.1). In such warm-scented retail environments, social density perceptions also lead to a sense of loss of power, or perceived control of their surroundings. Interestingly, the perceived loss of power results in consumers preferring power-compensatory behaviour which encourages buying expensive brands.[3] Appropriate use of sensory elements within the retail environment has become a well-established tool that encourages browsing, time spent within store, employee interactions and purchase behaviour. Advancements in sensory marketing research has provided new avenues for retailers to interact and engage with their customers.

Brands use sensory perceptions to create differentiation and distinctiveness in the market by offering unique sensory experiences that appeal to consumers' senses and creating positive associations with the brand. Differentiation refers to the extent to which a brand is perceived as different from its competitors on attributes that are relevant and important to consumers. Distinctiveness refers to the extent to which a brand is easily recognizable and memorable among other brands in the same category.[4] Once established, the distinctive sensory features associated with the brand turn in valuable distinctive assets,[5] as discussed in Chapter 4.

Some examples of how brands build *distinctive sensory assets* successfully using sensory perceptions are:

- Sight: Brands can use visual elements such as colours, shapes, logos, characters, images, fonts, packaging, product design and service delivery to create distinctive visual identities that attract consumers' attention and convey the brand's personality and values.[6] For example, Coca-Cola uses its iconic red colour and script logo to create a strong visual identity that is easily recognizable and associated with happiness and refreshment.

- Hearing: Brands can use auditory elements such as sounds, music, jingles, slogans, voiceovers and sound effects to create distinctive auditory identities that capture consumers' attention and evoke emotions and memories.[7] For instance, Netflix uses its famous sonic branding approach to create a distinctive auditory identity.

- Smell: Brands can use olfactory elements such as scents, fragrances, aromas and odours to create distinctive olfactory identities that stimulate consumers' senses and influence their mood and behaviour.[8] Coffee shop brands use the smell of freshly brewed coffee to create a distinctive olfactory identity that attracts consumers and enhances their experience of the brand.

- Taste: Brands can use gustatory elements such as flavours, tastes, textures and sensations to create distinctive gustatory identities that satisfy consumers' senses and preferences.[9] Ice-cream brand Baskin & Robbins continuously creates unique and appealing flavours, such as Rocky Road, Buttercream Cupcake, Mango Coconapple, Sumatra Coffee Toffee and many others.

- Touch: Brands can use tactile elements such as materials, shapes, textures, temperatures, weights and vibrations to create distinctive tactile identities that appeal to consumers' senses and perceptions.[10] For example, 3D and 4D movies offered by cinemas focus on tactile feedback for a more immersive viewer experience.

Human sensory perceptions are important factors in consumer decision making, as they affect how consumers perceive and evaluate products and services. Brands can use sensory perceptions to create differentiation and distinctiveness in the market by offering unique sensory experiences that appeal to consumers' senses and create positive associations with the brand.

Scholarly debate

Biswas, D (2019) Sensory aspects of retailing: Theoretical and practical implications, *Journal of Retailing*, 95 (4), 111–15

Zha, D, Foroudi, P, Jin, Z and Melewar, T C (2022) Making sense of sensory brand experience: Constructing an integrative framework for future research, *International Journal of Management Reviews*, 24 (1), 130–67

Types of sensory influences in branding

The five types of sensory influences as outlined in the previous section have been widely researched. In this section, we discuss the importance of these cues in branding.

Visual elements in branding

Visual perceptions are often the first sensory cues that customers get exposed to in a physical or digital environment. For example, before even entering a physical store, a customer can see the brand name, colours, windows, lights, layout, employee appearance, in-store crowding and other ambient features. Similarly, in a digital environment, it is primarily the visual cues that customers first see. For instance, while browsing through a website or an app, customers experience colour, style, format and other visual features. Thus, due to the variety, visual cues are usually observed more often than any other sensory cues.[11] Brand managers focus substantial resources on visual composition of their brand including logo, fonts, format, colours and packaging. The visual sensory perceptions drive unique consumer behaviour. For example, research shows that creative packaging can make customers more curious and encourage them to process the information, leading to buying decisions.[12] In this section, we focus on several important visual cues that consumers consider in their decision making including colour, fonts, characters and images, across physical and digital domains.

Colour is one of the most salient and influential visual elements that captures consumers' attention and evokes emotional responses. Colour includes three dimensions: hue, saturation and value. Hue refers to the wavelength composition of a colour, saturation corresponds to the degree of intensity, richness, strength or purity of a colour, and value reflects the relative lightness or darkness of a colour.[13] Each of these dimensions can influence how brand meaning is conveyed. For example, red can signify passion, excitement, urgency or danger, depending on the situation and the culture.[14] Fast food restaurants, accordingly, often use red in their store space and branding. In addition, when choosing colours, brand managers need to be cognizant about the additive and subtractive nature of colour. Additive colours (red, green, blue; RGB) are used mostly in digital mediums (e.g. computers, tablets and mobile phones) as these devices create colours by adding one set of hues to another. Subtractive colour models (cyan, magenta, yellow and black; CMYK) are used in print mediums (e.g. newspapers, magazines), where colour creation occurs due to the absorption of certain wavelengths of colour while reflecting other wavelengths to the reader.

Colour can also convey meanings and associations that are biologically, culturally and contextually dependent.[15] According to the psychology of colour, colours can have different effects on consumers' moods, attitudes and behaviours. For instance, warm colours like red, orange and yellow can generate biological responses through stimulating arousal, appetite, increased attention and impulsiveness, while cool colours like blue and green can induce relaxation, trust and calmness.[16][17] In addition, colour has a strong cultural dependency.[18] Red, for instance, is considered auspicious in China and India, and preferred by brides at their wedding; while it also signifies love in Western cultures, and is ascribed to symbolize annual festivities such as Valentine's Day. Ascriptions of colours across cultures may have developed historically, drawing cultural meanings rooted in the cultural psyche over time.[19] Some examples of the cultural meanings of colours are presented in Table 14.1. Colour can also affect consumers' perception of product attributes, such as quality, taste, freshness or price.[20] For example, consumers perceived a chocolate bar as more expensive when it was wrapped in gold foil than in silver foil.[21] The above examples show the crucial role of colour in creating brand associations across cultures. Brands should, therefore, be cognizant of the impact on colour in their communications and branding.

Fonts are another visual element that can influence consumers' perception and evaluation of textual information. Fonts can communicate personality traits, emotions and values that are consistent, or inconsistent, with the message or the brand image.[22] For example, serif fonts are often associated with tradition, elegance and authority, while sans serif fonts are seen as modern, clean and simple.[23] Fonts can also affect consumers' subjective cognitive processing of information, such as readability and comprehension; its recommended that as large a type size as possible is used in brand communications.[24] For example, a study found that large fonts used in warning labels reduced college students' intentions to use e-cigarettes.[25] Another study found that dynamic right-slanted fonts in ads increase consumers' behavioural intentions.[26] The font shape and typeface congruence facilitates stimulus processing, thereby positively affecting perceptions of brand credibility, brand aesthetics and brand value; the latter reflected in higher price expectations.[27] For example, in the wine industry it is understood that font width can produce difference meanings re-

Table 14.1   Different meanings of colours across cultures

Colour	Cultural meanings
Black	Thailand: bad luck Hinduism: restoring chakra energies Europe: mourning, cool, funeral, death
Blue	Europe: soothing, bridalwear China: immortality Middle East: protection
Orange	Ireland: Protestants The Netherlands: favourite colour Hinduism: sacred
Red	Europe: danger, excitement, love China: luck and fame Celtic: death, afterlife
Green	Islam: hope, virtue China: exorcism USA: money
Yellow	Egypt: mourning Buddhism: wisdom Japan: courage

Figure 14.2 Wine companies use different fonts for the bottle labels to demonstrate varying levels of taste

SOURCE Unsplash.com/Louis Hansel

garding brand identity and product properties – for instance bold fonts are thought to be reflective of strong taste, while thin fonts a delicate taste (Figure 14.2).[28]

Fonts also affect the pressing of the payment button in digital commerce. For example, angular fonts, compared to round fonts, are perceived as harsh and thus remind consumers about the pain of payment, thus reducing consumer purchase intentions.[29] Thus, successful branding requires an appropriate level of understanding of the way fonts can influence consumer perceptions and decision making.

Anthropomorphism, the attribution of human characteristics to a brand, is another important visual sensory branding approach. Brands regularly use human or human-like characters in their logos, communications including advertisements, social media posts and other promotions. Such character-driven features can help brands convey emotional meaning. For instance, the logo of Amazon has an arrow going from A to Z which conveys the brand serving all types of products and the yellow arrow is set out to represent a smile, evoking a sense of reliability and happiness. Hermès, the iconic luxury brand, conveys its history and heritage of leather goods craftsmanship by highlighting a picture of a Duc-carriage with a horse. Other brands that use animals in their logos include Puma, Red Bull, Polo Ralph Lauren, Firefox, Lacoste, Crocs, Jaguar and Ferrari.

The use of anthropomorphic characteristics is used beyond the logo by many brands. Some brands use animals with human-like traits to convey their features. For instance, the insurance company Churchill uses a British bulldog, the price comparison portal comparethemarket.com uses a meerkat, the battery brand Duracell uses a rabbit and the cereal brand Kellogg's uses Tony the Tiger. Using animal characters, brands try to communicate culturally construed meanings associated with the animal as the brand's own features, such as the loyalty and sincerity of a dog, the curiosity of a meerkat, the energy of a rabbit and the power of a tiger.

Other brands use more human-like characters in their communications as mascots including the Michelin man, Ronald McDonald, M&M spokescandies, Mickey Mouse by Disney, Rich Uncle Pennybags in Monopoly by Hasbro, Mario by Nintendo and Jolly Green Giant by B&G foods. Similar to animal characters used by other brands, human-like characters allow brands to utilize the wide range of emotional attributes. Academic research on cuteness of characters suggests that the use of anthropomorphic characters drives either careful or hedonic behaviours among consumers depending on the kind of mental representation of *kindchen-schema* (baby schema) they trigger. For instance, when the anthropomorphism is identified as just cute (e.g. baby face on a product advertisement), it creates a mental representation of vulnerability and caretaking, and thus leads to careful behaviour.[30] On the other hand, products that are whimsically cute (e.g. a stapler that looks like a crocodile) can lead to hedonic behaviours.[31] Thus, the correct alignment of characters with the emotions integral to a brand can guide consumer decision making.

Digital domains, on the other hand, are unique because visual sensory perceptions take primacy as customers cannot touch or feel the product. Thus, brands primarily rely on visual aids, as outlined above, for building a better customer experience. In this regard, the use of images, browsing ease, interactivity and adaptability are paramount.[32] For instance, too many images on a web page may take a lot of time to load if the internet connection is weak and may reduce the customer's propensity to wait, stay and interact with the brand. Similarly, if a web page lacks interactivity and cannot adapt to the hardware device screen size, it may reduce the optimal experience.

Appropriate use of colours, fonts and anthropomorphism can increase the visual aesthetics in both the physical and digital domains and can lead to satisfactory customer experience.[33] Thus, the optimal use of visual elements in digital brand communications is crucial for effective digital branding.

Auditory elements in branding

In Chapter 4 we discussed the concept of sonic branding. Brands have long used auditory sensory perceptions above and beyond visual perceptions to create a distinctive image. The auditory aspects of branding, such as jingles, slogans, specific music tone, sound effects and voiceovers, can act as reminder and aid recall of a brand. For example, the lion's roar in MGM movies has been used for nearly 100 years, and more recently, the signature opening sounds of Amazon Prime and Netflix have become well recognized. Such auditory cues can trigger thoughts about the brand even when a brand name is not mentioned.[34] Beyond recognition and recall, auditory cues can help brands convey their product traits. For example, for food products such as crisps or potato chips, the sound produced through the biting action in an advert can convey the crispness and freshness of the chips.[35]

Further, how the brand name sounds is crucial. It is believed that almost 40 per cent of a product's success may be attributed to a well-chosen brand name.[36] Understanding the science of phonetics and sound symbolism is important for brand managers. Academic researchers examining the linguistic attributes of top brands have shown an apparent overrepresentation of the letters A, B, C, K, M, P and S, when compared to the occurrence of these letters in the English dictionary.[37] Moreover, greater fit between a brand name and its sound symbolism can convey the desired meanings for customers. For example, a hiking boot brand with a sound symbolism of ruggedness (e.g. Mammut, Timberland) and a moisturizing product with a sound symbolism of softness (e.g. Dove, Olay) are preferred by the customers.[38] Similarly, longer brand names (three-syllabic length or more) are perceived to convey greater social status and higher social position compared to shorter names (e.g. Lamborghini, Chanel).[39] In addition, rounded or back vowel sounds (e.g. /o/ as in frosh) is perceived as richer and creamier for an ice-cream brand.[40] Apart from vowels, consonants also play an important role in brand recognition. Research suggests that brand names that begin with hard consonants (e.g. Pepsi, Pantene) lead to greater brand recognition.[41]

Brands also embed auditory elements in their products to capture attention and create the optimal customer experience. For example, motorcycle and car brands devote substantial resources to how their engine sounds. Similarly, most smartphone manufacturers include a click sound when a photograph is taken, while in reality there is no manual switch involved. Perfume companies also invest in making sure that optimal spraying sound is created when the spray nozzle is pressed by the consumer.[42]

Beyond the embedded sonic elements in branding, external auditory elements can also influence consumer decision making. For example, in physical retail brand environments, music piped through the stereo system can influence customers' pace of browsing, shopping time and product choices. Auditory elements including tempo, style/genre, volume and familiarity of music can also influence consumer choices.[43] Counterintuitive to consumer perception, individuals actually spend longer in shops when exposed to unfamiliar music. It is suggested that familiar music can increase consumer arousal, which in turn, may lead to speedier shopping.[44] The genre of music played can also influence consumer brand choices. When supermarkets played French music in the background, consumers increasingly bought more French wine than German wine. However, when German music was played in the background, the preference was reversed.[45] Moreover, classical music increased consumers' willingness to pay for hedonic products such as expensive wines, while country music increased utilitarian purchases.[46] Music and sound in general, thus, play an important role in branding and creating lasting brand associations.

Haptic elements in branding

Touch and feel are key components in consumer decision making of almost all products. Thus, the haptic element is an important aspect of consumer brand choices. For example, when buying a sofa, consumers often try to visit home furnishing stores and sit on different types of sofas to get a feel for them.

Similarly, when buying clothes or a car, many consumers regularly attempt to experience the product first-hand (Figure 14.3). The haptic inputs offer consumers information about four properties of a product: texture, hardness, temperature and weight.[47] Such inputs can drive consumer decision making. For instance, when choosing bed mattresses, some consumers prefer soft, while other prefer hard mattresses. While consumers can perceive the texture of a mattress in a physical home furnishing shop, they cannot do so in the digital environment. Thus, leading direct-to-consumer brands such as Simba, Emma, Casper and Nectar, highlight the levels of firmness of their products in their advertising and communications. Further, to enhance user experience, smartphone brands such as Apple and Samsung spend considerable resources on designing optimal haptic inputs.

Figure 14.3   Understanding the power of haptics, many stores allow consumers to touch and feel the product freely

SOURCE Unsplash.com/Clark Street Mercantile

The need for touch is critical for consumers in evaluating products. It is a growing interest area of academic research, and new insights are continuously adding to our knowledge. Placing a product behind glass can inhibit touch, however, it can also increase the perceived luxuriousness of the brand.[48] Many luxury brands, thus, place their products inside a glass box or put up barriers so that shoppers cannot touch the product. However, this can also cause shopper frustration.[49] Academic research shows that allowing consumers to touch the brand can enhance perceived ownership effect, and this, in turn, can lead to greater purchase intentions.[50] At the same time, products that are previously touched by other shoppers are evaluated less favourably, which is called the product contamination effect.[51] Although these research findings may seem inconsistent, it is clear that touch has an important impact on consumer in-store behaviour, and is a potent topic of further research and applications in retail branding.

In many countries people mostly use cutlery, such as a spoon, fork or chopsticks, instead of their fingers to eat food. Thus, the manual haptic feedback through fingers is mostly absent. In these countries, consumers mostly rely on oral haptics, feeling things through their mouth, when making judgements about food products. Thus, many food and beverage brands are spending considerable resources on understanding oral haptics.[52] For example, foods with hard and rough (vs soft and smooth) haptic properties are perceived as healthier.[53] Such findings have important implications for consumer wellbeing.

Olfactory elements in branding

Olfactory branding is the use of scent to create a distinctive and memorable identity for a brand, product or service. It can enhance the emotional connection between consumers and brands, as well as influence their behaviour and preferences.[54] Olfactory branding can also differentiate a brand from its competitors and create a competitive advantage in the market by creating fragrance-related cues in customer minds (Figure 14.4). For example, walking outside a coffee shop in the morning, the smell of roasted beans may trigger the purchase of coffee and other related products, such as croissants or muffins.

Olfactory branding is based on the premise that smell is a powerful and primal sense that can evoke memories, emotions and associations.[55] Smell is also closely linked to taste, which can affect the perception of food and beverage products. It can influence mood, cognition and wellbeing, as well as social and cultural interactions. Research suggests that scented environments can enhance employee productivity, improve perceptions of product quality, increase duration of retail visit and purchase intentions among consumers, and boost consumers' willingness to pay.[56] For example, British Airways has developed a unique scent that is diffused in its terminals, lounges and planes. The scent is designed to create a pleasant, relaxing and adventurous mood

Figure 14.4   Smell is a powerful trigger for consumer action and brands use it regularly in their marketing efforts

SOURCE Unsplash.com/bundo

for travellers. The scent is also used in the airline's bathroom soaps and hand lotions.[57] Similarly, retail brand Abercrombie & Fitch uses its own line of scents in stores to instigate customer arousal and purchase intentions.[58] Olfactory or scent branding is also used by hospitality brands such as Hyatt, Taj, John Lewis, Starbucks and Disney among many others.[59]

However, olfactory branding is not a one-size-fits-all strategy. Smell sensitivities vary among individuals based on the environmental and cultural aspects. People living in less-polluted environments tend to have better sense of smell compared to those living in highly polluted environment.[60] Smells may have a cultural aspect, with preferences, associations and meanings differing across cultures. For example, in Hinduism, jasmine is considered sacred to goddess Shakti, who embodies fertility and divine energy. Similarly, in Sufi mysticism, the fragrance of jasmine is often used as a symbol of the soul's journey toward union with the divine. On the other hand, in Thai and Chinese cultures, jasmine is often associated with femininity and grace.[61]

In the Philippines, jasmine fragrance symbolizes purity, simplicity and humility, and it is often used in religious offerings and as a symbol of national pride. While in most Western cultures, jasmine fragrance is associated with purity and virtue, in some parts of South Asia, including Sri Lanka, jasmine garlands are placed on the bodies of the deceased as a gesture of respect and to mask the scent of decay.[62] Therefore, olfactory branding needs to consider the cross-cultural differences in olfaction and language, as well as the context and purpose of scent usage.

Gustatory elements in branding

Gustatory (i.e. taste) branding is a powerful and effective way of creating and managing a brand image, as it can influence the perception, preference and behaviour of consumers, and create a lasting and emotional connection with them. Gustatory branding is usually associated with food products. For example, with regularly used products such as toothpaste or mouthwash and indulgent products such as chocolates or ice cream, gustatory associations are crucial.[63] The Swiss chocolate brand Lindt is known for its high-quality and premium products, which are characterized by their smooth and rich taste, as well as their distinctive shapes and packaging. Lindt uses gustatory branding to convey its brand values of excellence, tradition and innovation, and to create a strong emotional bond with its customers, who associate Lindt with indulgence, pleasure and happiness.[64] Moreover, gustatory branding is not limited to food products only. It is used by a variety of other products wherein taste sense is employed.[65]

Gustatory branding can also help a brand to stand out from the crowd, to adapt to different markets and cultures, and to communicate its values and personality.[66] Gustatory branding is, therefore, an essential component of a successful brand management strategy for food and beverage brands. There are five different tastes that the human sensory system can evaluate: sweet, salty, bitter, sour and umami. The taste sensors across the tongue pick up the taste sensations and accordingly drive sensory perceptions.

Gustatory branding can be used to differentiate a brand from its competitors, to enhance customer loyalty and satisfaction, to create a sense of identity and belonging, and to evoke positive emotions and associations. Gustatory branding can also be used to communicate the brand values, personality and positioning, as well as to create a sensory synergy with other elements of the brand, such as the visual, auditory, olfactory and haptic aspects. Nespresso, the coffee brand, which is part of the Nestlé group, uses gustatory branding to create a distinctive and consistent taste experience for its customers, who can choose from a variety of flavours and intensities of coffee capsules. Nespresso also uses gustatory branding to position itself as a luxury and sophisticated brand, which offers convenience, quality and customization to its customers.[67]

Crossmodal sensory perceptions

While the above section highlights the various sensory influences in branding, these human senses do not operate in isolation. In other words, consumers use various senses together to arrive at their overall sensory perception. This insight has led to substantial research in the field, known as crossmodal sensory perceptions, wherein researchers examine the effects of a combination of sensory influences to understand human decision making.[68]

Crossmodal sensory experience research provides interesting insights for branding. It has been shown to influence the perceptions, preferences and behaviour of consumers, and can create a lasting and emotional connection with them. By appealing to multiple senses, brands can create a distinctive and memorable association with their products or services.[69] Moreover, as explained earlier, the combination of sensory perceptions can help brands communicate their values and personality, create a sense of identity and belonging, and evoke positive emotions and associations.[70] Crossmodal sensory experience is a powerful and effective way of creating and managing a brand image, as it can help a brand to stand out from the crowd, to adapt to different markets and cultures, and to create a multidimensional engagement with consumers.[71]

Figure 14.5   Images of food can arouse visual, gustatory and even olfactory reflections

SOURCE Unsplash.com/Louis Hansel

Table 14.2 Crossmodal sensory perception examples

Crossmodal pairing	Approach	Real-life examples
Visual-auditory	• Pairing uplifting music with energetic visuals in a sports apparel ad to convey a sense of excitement and motivation. • Using soothing music and calming visuals in a spa ad to create a sense of relaxation and tranquillity.	Nike's 'Just Do It' campaign combines powerful visuals of athletes in action with rousing music to create a sense of empowerment and motivation.
Auditory-haptic	• Incorporating crisp sounds when consumers interact with a product's packaging to enhance the perceived quality and premium-ness. • Using subtle vibrations in a smartphone notification to provide a more tactile and engaging experience.	BMW cars feature a variety of audible feedback sounds, such as the iconic door chime, to enhance the driving experience and reinforce brand identity.
Olfactory-visual	• Creating a signature scent for a retail store that complements the brand's visual identity and enhances overall shopping experience. • Using evocative food scents in restaurants to increase appetite and customer satisfaction.	Victoria's Secret employs a specific fragrance throughout their stores and products, creating a consistent brand identity.
Gustatory-visual	• Presenting food dishes with visually appealing arrangements and colour combinations to enhance taste perception. • Using descriptive language in food descriptions to stimulate the imagination and heighten the anticipation of taste.	M&M uses colourful packaging and playful visuals to enhance the perceived taste and enjoyment of their product.
Haptic-visual	• Employing soft, luxurious textures in product packaging to convey a sense of quality and value. • Using high-quality graphics and textures in digital interfaces to create a more immersive and engaging experience.	Chanel and Louis Vuitton use high-quality materials and craftsmanship in their packaging, creating a sense of luxury and exclusivity.

Let's expand on this. Gustatory perceptions generally operate in conjunction with visual and olfactory perceptions. The taste of a food or drink is not only determined by its flavour, but also by its multisensory inputs (Figure 14.5). For instance, a

75 per cent cacao dark chocolate has a sweet and bitter taste, yet the taste experience is much more complex and rich when we consider its dark and intense colour, its fruity aroma, its crisp sound when we bite it and its smooth texture when it melts in our mouth.[72] Similarly, changing the colour of a soft drink can change image perceptions attached to it, even though the taste remains the same.[73] The powerful link between the smells of food, the production of saliva and the desire for food has been well known to the food and beverages companies for a long time. Therefore, they use artificial scents of their products, such as cookies, pizza and cinnamon rolls, to lure shoppers in malls. The Hershey's store in Times Square uses artificial chocolate aromas to tempt customers to buy their chocolate.[74] Researchers find that even changing image placement, such as displaying the product image lower on the packaging, enhances flavour heaviness perceptions and could have implications for healthy eating decisions.[75] However, when these other sensory perceptions are not available, gustatory perceptions tend to get distorted.[76] For example, when smell and sight are constrained, potatoes can taste similar to apples, and red wine can taste similar to coffee.[77]

Crossmodal cues are used by brands in their advertising, packaging and other visual and sonic communications. For instance, the sound of a can of Coca-Cola being opened and poured into a glass is a crossmodal cue that enhances the perception of the taste and refreshment of the drink. Similarly, the shape and colour of the Toblerone chocolate bar are crossmodal cues that evoke the association with Swiss Alps and premium quality of the product. Researchers also show that the pitch of a sound and brightness of a colour can direct visual attention wherein objects that are light-coloured attract visual attention when a high-pitched sound is heard. Contrarily, dark-coloured objects attract visual attention when a low-pitched sound is heard.[78] Such crossmodal sensory perception can influence advertising on visual media, such as TV and digital media.

Crossmodal sensory experiences play a crucial role in branding, providing brands with a powerful tool to influence consumer perceptions and forge deeper connections with their audience. By understanding and harnessing the interplay between the senses, brands can create immersive and memorable experiences that resonate with consumers on an emotional level, ultimately driving brand loyalty and success.

Ethics of sensory marketing and branding

While it offers an important avenue for brands to engage with their customers, the ethical implications of sensory marketing raise critical questions about its impact on consumer autonomy and the potential for manipulative practices. On the one hand, sensory marketing can play a positive role in consumer decision making by providing consumers with additional information about products and enhancing their overall shopping experience through sensory exploration (see Table 14.3). For instance, in-store sampling of food products allows consumers to taste and evaluate the product before making a purchase, reducing the risk of post-purchase dissatisfaction. Similarly, the ambient scent of freshly baked bread in a bakery can create a welcoming atmosphere and signal the high quality of the products. Moreover, sensory marketing can be used to communicate brand identity and values effectively. For example, a luxury perfume brand might employ elegant packaging, soft textures and a sophisticated fragrance to convey a sense of luxury and exclusivity. This multisensory approach can create a stronger emotional connection with consumers, fostering brand loyalty and positive brand associations.

On the other hand, the power of sensory marketing also raises concerns about its potential to manipulate consumer behaviour and lead to undesired purchases (Figure 14.6). The use of intense or overpowering sensory stimuli can overwhelm consumers, making it difficult for them to make rational decisions. Additionally, sensory marketing techniques can be particularly effective in targeting vulnerable populations, such as children, who may be more susceptible to persuasive messaging. Research has shown that sensory marketing can influence consumers' perceptions of product quality, price and even taste.[79] Studies have demonstrated that products presented in high-quality packaging are perceived as being of higher quality and worth a premium price, even if the product itself is identical to a lower-priced product in less attractive packaging.[80]

Figure 14.6   Sensory marketing and branding raises important ethical questions

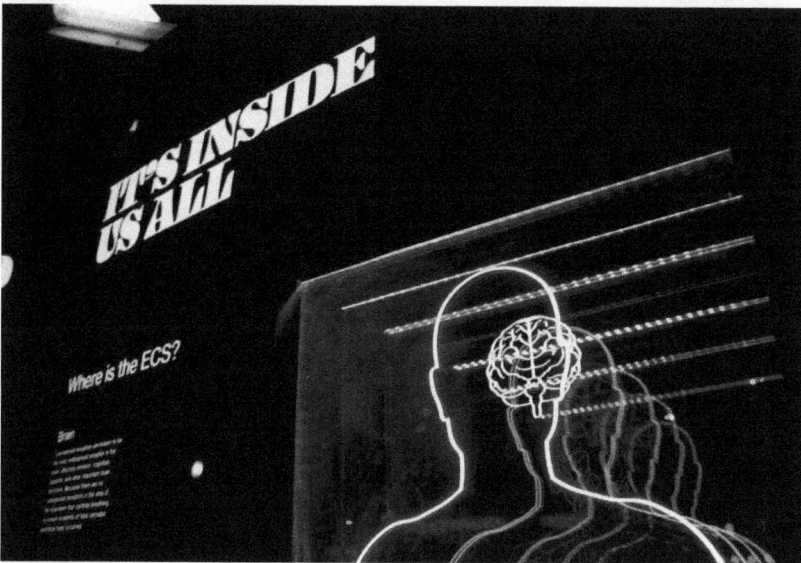

Table 14.3   The positives and negatives associated with sensory branding

Positive associations	Negative associations
Recognize and remember a brand or product by creating a distinctive and memorable sensory identity or signature.	Buy impulsively or compulsively by triggering their subconscious desires, cravings and urges through sensory stimuli.
Evaluate and compare a brand or product by highlighting its attributes, benefits and quality through sensory cues.	Spend more or waste more by influencing their perception of value, quantity and quality through sensory illusions.
Enjoy and appreciate a brand or product by creating a pleasant and satisfying sensory experience that enhances their mood, wellbeing and loyalty.	Consume unhealthily or unsustainably by appealing to their sensory hedonism, indulgence and gratification.

Furthermore, the use of sensory cues can influence in-store behaviour, leading to impulse purchases and increased spending. For example, the aroma of freshly baked cookies in a grocery store can evoke positive emotions and cravings, prompting consumers to add cookies to their carts, even if they had not originally planned to purchase them. The ethical implications of sensory marketing are further complicated by the growing use of neuromarketing techniques, which measure brain activity to understand consumer preferences and behaviour. While neuromarketing has the potential to provide valuable insights into consumer behaviour, it also raises concerns about privacy and the potential for manipulation.[81]

In conclusion, sensory marketing and branding raise ethical questions and challenges for both marketers and consumers. Marketers need to consider the moral implications and responsibilities of using sensory marketing and branding, and be aware that their actions do not lead to exploiting, deceiving or harming consumers. Consumers, too, need to be aware of the potential influence and impact of sensory marketing and branding, and exercise their critical thinking, self-control and informed choice. Sensory marketing and branding can be powerful and positive tools for creating and managing a brand image, but should be used with caution and understanding towards the consumers.

Neuromarketing

As our understanding of sensory aspects have developed over the past two decades, researchers have attempted to understand the neural activities that drive consumer decision making. This has led to the novel field of neuromarketing which applies neuroscience and cognitive science to marketing, aiming to understand and influence consumer behaviour and decision making.[82] Neuromarketing can help marketers optimize their strategies, products and other marketing communications by measuring the brain's responses to different stimuli.[83] Neuromarketing can also reveal customer needs, motivations and preferences more precisely than the traditional methods such as surveys, observations, interviews and focus groups.[84]

Neuromarketing assumes that most consumer decisions are not made consciously but are driven by non-conscious processes by neural networks in the brain.[85] At its core, it explores the fundamental concept that human behaviour is deeply rooted in neural activity. The human brain, an intricately wired neural network, processes and interprets sensory information, generating emotions, thoughts and, ultimately, actions. Neuromarketing aims to tap into these neural activities and connections, understanding how external stimuli, such as brand communication, trigger specific brain responses and influence consumer behaviour. In sum, neuromarketing seeks to access and unravel the intricate relationship between the human brain and behaviour and provide more accurate and reliable insights than self-reported data.

Neuromarketing researchers use a variety of methods and tools to collect and analyse data from consumers. Some of the methods involve neuroimaging tools like EEG (electroencephalography), fMRI (functional magnetic resonance imaging) and SST (steady-state topography), which register the brain's electrical activity and functions. Other methods use eye tracking and facial coding to infer consumers' feelings and preferences.[86] Each method has its advantages and disadvantages, depending on the research objectives, budget and feasibility. For instance, EEG is a relatively cheap, portable and fast method that can measure the brain's activity in real time, but it has low spatial resolution and can be affected by external noise.[87] fMRI is a more expensive, invasive and slow method that can measure the brain's functions with high spatial resolution, but it has low temporal resolution and can be uncomfortable for the participants.[88] Eye tracking is a simple, non-invasive and affordable method that measures consumers' attention and interest, but it cannot capture the emotional and cognitive aspects of consumer behaviour.[89] Facial coding is a method that can measure consumers' emotional expressions, but it can be influenced by cultural and individual differences.[90]

BRANDING IN PRACTICE

Neuromarketing in action: Philips leverages brain science
for packaging optimization

Philips, a global leader in electronics and healthcare, sought to optimize the packaging of their new steam iron, aiming to enhance consumer appeal and purchasing decisions. Recognizing the power of subconscious emotional responses in influencing consumer behaviour, it turned to Neurensics, a neuromarketing firm specializing in measuring brain activity to understand consumer preferences. The primary objective of this study was to determine whether the orientation of the hand holding the iron on the packaging would influence consumer perception and purchase intent.

Neurensics employed magnetic resonance imaging (MRI), a brain-imaging technique that measures activities from the entire brain, both conscious and unconscious, including rational and emotional thoughts. Participants were shown both images, one with a right hand holding the iron and the other with a left hand.

The MRI results revealed that packaging featuring a right hand holding the iron elicited significantly higher activation in brain regions associated with positive emotions, reward processing and purchase intent, compared to the packaging with a left hand. The left-hand-holding-iron image resulted in negative feelings including repulsion and disgust. This finding suggests that the right-handed packaging resonated more strongly with consumers as nearly 90 per cent of the population is right-handed and have a natural tendency to hold the iron in the right hand.

Based on the neuroimaging evidence, Philips concluded that packaging featuring a right hand holding the iron would be more effective in capturing consumer attention, evoking positive emotions and ultimately driving purchase decisions. This insight led Philips to adopt the right-handed packaging design for their new steam iron.

This case study highlights the value of neuromarketing in understanding consumer subconscious preferences and optimizing marketing strategies. By employing brain-imaging techniques, Philips gained valuable insights into the emotional impact of their packaging designs, enabling them to make data-driven decisions that could potentially boost sales and enhance brand success.

Neuromarketing has various applications in branding, such as advertising, digital marketing, product design, packaging, pricing and sales.[91] Brand managers can utilize neuromarketing techniques to assess the emotional impact of advertising campaigns, identifying the elements that resonate with consumers. This data can inform creative decisions including designing more effective and persuasive campaigns, testing different messages and media, and measuring the impact of advertising on consumer behaviour. Similarly, by understanding the pricing sensitivities of the consumers through neuromarketing, managers can develop optimal pricing strategies to maximize profitability while maintaining consumer satisfaction.[92] For example, PepsiCo used two methods, standard survey and EEG, to understand the impact of increasing price of its Lay's chips by 0.25 Turkish Lira on consumers in Turkey. A traditional survey predicted a sales drop of 33 per cent and the brand becoming non-profitable. On the other hand, EEG predicted a 9 per cent sales drop with the brand remaining profitable. PepsiCo decided to increase the prices and the sales dropped by only 7 per cent while the brand remained profitable.[93]

Within the digital domain, neuromarketing can help optimize websites, apps and social media platforms, by analysing how consumers navigate, interact and engage with digital content. Using neuromarketing, brand managers can measure consumer preferences for product features and packaging. This understanding can guide product development, ensuring that products align with consumer desires and maximize market appeal. For instance, Campbell Soup used eye tracking and biometrics to test different designs of their soup cans which resulted in different colour packaging for different soup lines with a smaller logo, more vibrant and steamy photos without spoons.[94] Similarly, BMW used neuromarketing for product design optimization, wherein it identified that consumers had stronger emotional reactions to cars with curved designs, and thus, the brand launched curved lines and contours in its BMW 3 series, and found greater success compared to previous models.[95]

Scholarly debate

Lee, N, Chamberlain, L and Brandes, L (2018) Welcome to the jungle! The neuromarketing literature through the eyes of a newcomer, *European Journal of Marketing*, 52 (1/2), 4–38

Lim, W M (2018) Demystifying neuromarketing, *Journal of Business Research*, 91, 205–20

Overall, neuromarketing is a fascinating and growing field that offers many opportunities and challenges for brands and consumers alike. It enables brands to gain deeper insights into their consumers' actions and choices and helps them design attractive and convincing campaigns and product offerings that meet their customers' needs. Notwithstanding, similar to sensory marketing, neuromarketing tools can be prone to unethical use, and brand managers need to be circumspect regarding its applications.

Chapter summary

This chapter discussed the latest developments in the field of sensory branding and neuromarketing. It offered insights on how human sensory perceptions play a key role in consumer decision making. We then explored five sensory influences – visual, auditory, haptic, olfactory and gustatory. We also learnt that these sensory influences do not operate in isolation and consumers use crossmodal sensory perceptions in their brand choices and other decision making. While the use of sensory perceptions in influencing consumer decision making is becoming increasingly common, there are ethical challenges that brand managers need to be aware of. Finally, we discussed how neuromarketing developments are helping brands make informed decisions regarding consumer choices leading to greater success.

Key concepts

- Sensory perceptions
  - Visual perceptions
  - Auditory perceptions
  - Haptic perceptions
  - Olfactory perceptions
  - Gustatory perceptions
- Crossmodal sensory perceptions
- Sensory marketing and branding
- Neuromarketing

Exercise questions

1 Using examples from three different sectors, explain how brands use different sensory aspects in influencing consumer decision making.

2 Give examples of how brands across products and services employ different visual sensory elements to influence consumer choice.

3 Critically examine the importance of studying crossmodal sensory perceptions for better branding applications.

4 Sensory marketing and neuromarketing can have both positive and negative effects on brands. Critically evaluate this statement.

5 Explain the various neuromarketing techniques researchers use to understand consumer decision making. Explain how neuromarketing may be a better approach to study consumer choices as compared to traditional research methods.

CASE STUDY   How the travel industry uses your sense of smell to enhance your holiday

Read the following article from 2016, which looks more closely into how tourism and travel operators may use sensory marketing – specifically the sense of smell – to provide a unique experience.

SOURCE https://theconversation.com/how-the-travel-industry-uses-your-sense-of-smell-to-enhance-your-holiday-180520

Case questions

1 Rank the sensory marketing elements according to their importance for the travel and tourism industry. Provide justification for your ranking.

2 Critically evaluate the ethical aspects of sensory marketing in travel and tourism industry.

3 Discuss what crossmodal sensory perceptions can be utilized by brands to connect with their customers in the travel industry.

4 Based on the case study, develop a sensory marketing campaign for an existing retail brand.

Endnotes

1 Krishna, A (2012) An integrative review of sensory marketing: Engaging the senses to affect perception, judgment and behavior, *Journal of Consumer Psychology*, 22 (3), 332–51

2 Hultén, B (2011) Sensory marketing: The multi-sensory brand-experience concept, *European Business Review*, 23 (3), 256–73

3 Madzharov, A V, Block, L G and Morrin, M (2015) The cool scent of power: Effects of ambient scent on consumer preferences and choice behavior, *Journal of Marketing*, 79 (1), 83–96

4 Sharp, B and Romaniuk, J (2016) *How Brands Grow*, Oxford University Press, Melbourne

5 Romaniuk, J (2018) *Building Distinctive Brand Assets*, Oxford University Press, Melbourne

6 Sample, K L, Hagtvedt, H and Brasel, S A (2020) Components of visual perception in marketing contexts: A conceptual framework and review, *Journal of the Academy of Marketing Science*, 48, 405–21

7 Melzner, J and Raghubir, P (2023) The sound of music: The effect of timbral sound quality in audio logos on brand personality perception, *Journal of Marketing Research*, 60 (5), 932–49

8 Keller, A (2017) *Philosophy of Olfactory Perception*, Springer

9 Biswas, D (2016) 15 sensory aspects of branding, in F Dall'Olmo Riley, J Singh and C Blankson (eds.), *The Routledge Companion to Contemporary Brand Management*, pp 218–28

10 Peck, J (2011) Does touch matter? Insights from haptic research in marketing, in A Krishna, *Sensory Marketing*, Routledge, pp 17–31

11 Biswas, D, Labrecque, L I, Lehmann, D R and Markos, E (2014) Making choices while smelling, tasting, and listening: The role of sensory (Dis)similarity when sequentially sampling products, *Journal of Marketing*, 78 (1), 112–26

12 Shukla, P, Singh, J and Wang, W (2022) The influence of creative packaging design on customer motivation to process and purchase decisions, *Journal of Business Research*, 147, 338–47

13 Labrecque, L I (2020) Color research in marketing: Theoretical and technical considerations for conducting rigorous and impactful color research, *Psychology & Marketing*, 37 (7), 855–63

14 www.forbes.com/sites/princeghuman/2023/03/28/how-the-neuroscience-of-color-impacts-consumer-behavior/

15 Singh, S (2006) Impact of color on marketing, *Management Decision*, 44 (6), 783–89

16 Lichtlé, M C (2007) The effect of an advertisement's colour on emotions evoked by attitude towards the ad: The moderating role of the optimal stimulation level, *International Journal of Advertising*, 26 (1), 37–62

17 www.designhill.com/design-blog/color-theory-how-do-colors-play-a-big-role-in-consumer-behavior/

18 www.shutterstock.com/blog/color-symbolism-and-meanings-around-the-world (archived at https://perma.cc/ZVU5-CVLB)

19 Hutchings, J B (1998) Color in anthropology and folklore, in *Azimuth*, vol. 1, North-Holland, pp 195–208

20 Spence, C (2018) Background colour and its impact on food perception and behaviour, *Food Quality and Preference*, 68, 156–66

21 Allen, L L (2010) Chocolate fortunes: The battle for the hearts, minds, and wallets of China's consumers, *Thunderbird International Business Review*, 52 (1), 13–20

22 Wu, R, Han, X and Kardes, F R (2021) Special fonts: The competing roles of difficulty and uniqueness in consumer inference, *Psychology & Marketing*, 38 (1), 86–100

23 www.fonts.com/content/learning/fontology/level-1/type-anatomy/serif-vs-sans-for-text-in-print (archived at https://perma.cc/3HVV-8F4N)

24 Pillai, K G, Katsikeas, C S and Presi, C (2012) Print advertising: Type size effects, *Journal of Business Research*, 65 (6), 865–68

25 Lee, H Y, Lin, H C, Seo, D C and Lohrmann, D K (2018) The effect of e-cigarette warning labels on college students' perception of e-cigarettes and intention to use e-cigarettes, *Addictive Behaviors*, 76, 106–12

26 Mead, J A, Richerson, R and Li, W (2020) Dynamic right-slanted fonts increase the effectiveness of promotional retail advertising, *Journal of Retailing*, 96 (2), 282–96

27 Van Rompay, T J and Pruyn, A T (2011) When visual product features speak the same language: Effects of shape-typeface congruence on brand perception and price expectations, *Journal of Product Innovation Management*, 28 (4), 599–610

28 Celhay, F and Remaud, H (2018) What does your wine label mean to consumers? A semiotic investigation of Bordeaux wine visual codes, *Food Quality and Preference*, 65, 129–45

29 Park, J, Velasco, C and Spence, C (2022) 'Looking sharp': Price typeface influences awareness of spending in mobile payment, *Psychology & Marketing*, 39 (6), 1170–89

30 Sherman, G D, Haidt, J and Coan, J A (2009) Viewing cute images increases behavioral carefulness, *Emotion*, 9 (2), 282

31 Nenkov, G Y and Scott, M L (2014) 'So cute I could eat it up': Priming effects of cute products on indulgent consumption, *Journal of Consumer Research*, 41 (2), 326–41

32 Dou, Q, Zheng, X S, Sun, T and Heng, P A (2019) Webthetics: Quantifying webpage aesthetics with deep learning, *International Journal of Human-Computer Studies*, 124, 56–66

33 Wan, H, Ji, W, Wu, G, Jia, X, Zhan, X, Yuan, M and Wang, R (2021) A novel webpage layout aesthetic evaluation model for quantifying webpage layout design, *Information Sciences*, 576, 589–608

34 Biswas, D, Labrecque, L I, Lehmann, D R and Markos, E (2014) Making choices while smelling, tasting, and listening: The role of sensory (Dis)similarity when sequentially sampling products, *Journal of Marketing*, 78 (1), 112–26

35 Zampini, M and Spence, C (2004) The role of auditory cues in modulating the perceived crispness and staleness of potato chips, *Journal of Sensory Studies*, 19 (5), 347–63

36 Alashban, A A, Hayes, L A, Zinkhan, G M and Balazs, A L (2002) International brand-name standardization/adaptation: Antecedents and consequences, *Journal of International Marketing* 10 (3), 22–48

37 Schloss, I (1981) Chickens and pickles, *Journal of Advertising Research*, 21 (6), 47–49

38 Pathak, A, Velasco, C and Spence, C (2020) The sound of branding: An analysis of the initial phonemes of popular brand names, *Journal of Brand Management*, 27, 339–54

39 Pathak, A, Velasco, C, Petit, O and Calvert, G A (2019) Going to great lengths in the pursuit of luxury: How longer brand names can enhance the luxury perception of a brand, *Psychology & Marketing*, 36 (10), 951–63

40 Yorkston, E and Menon, G (2004) A sound idea: Phonetic effects of brand names on consumer judgments, *Journal of Consumer Research*, 31 (1), 43–51

41 Biswas, D (2019) Sensory aspects of retailing: Theoretical and practical implications, *Journal of Retailing*, 95 (4), 111–15

42 Biswas, D, Labrecque, L I, Lehmann, D R and Markos, E (2014) Making choices while smelling, tasting, and listening: The role of sensory (Dis)similarity when sequentially sampling products, *Journal of Marketing*, 78 (1), 112–26

43 Garlin, F V and Owen, K (2006) Setting the tone with the tune: A meta-analytic review of the effects of background music in retail settings, *Journal of Business Research*, 59 (6), 755–64

44 Yalch, R F and Spangenberg, E R (2000) The effects of music in a retail setting on real and perceived shopping times, *Journal of Business Research*, 49 (2), 139–47

45 North, A C, Hargreaves, D J and McKendrick, J (1999) The influence of in-store music on wine selections, *Journal of Applied Psychology*, 84 (2), 271

46 North, A C, Sheridan, L P and Areni, C S (2016) Music congruity effects on product memory, perception, and choice, *Journal of Retailing*, 92 (1), 83–95

47 Klatzky, R L, Lederman, S J and Reed, C (1987) There's more to touch than meets the eye: The salience of object attributes for haptics with and without vision, *Journal of Experimental Psychology: General*, 116 (4), 356–69

48 Logkizidou, M, Bottomley, P, Angell, R and Evanschitzky, H (2019) Why museological merchandise displays enhance luxury product evaluations: An extended art infusion effect, *Journal of Retailing*, 95 (1), 67–82

49 Peck, J and Childers, T L (2003) Individual differences in haptic information processing: The 'need for touch' scale, *Journal of Consumer Research*, 30 (3), 430–42

50 Peck, J and Shu, S B (2009) The effect of mere touch on perceived ownership, *Journal of Consumer Research*, 36 (3), 434–47

51 Argo, J J, Dahl, D W and Morales, A C (2006) Consumer contamination: How consumers react to products touched by others, *Journal of Marketing*, 70 (2), 81–94

52 Biswas, D, Szocs, C, Krishna, A and Lehmann, D R (2014) Something to chew on: The effects of oral haptics on mastication, orosensory perception, and calorie estimation, *Journal of Consumer Research*, 41 (2), 261–73

53 Ibid.

54 Biswas, D (2019) Sensory aspects of retailing: Theoretical and practical implications, *Journal of Retailing*, 95 (4), 111–15

55 Errajaa, K, Daucé, B and Legoherel, P (2020) Consumer reactions to olfactory congruence with brand image, *Journal of Retailing and Consumer Services*, 52, 101898

56 Minsky, L, Fahey, C and Fabrigas, C (2018) Inside the invisible but influential world of scent branding, *Harvard Business Review*, https://hbr.org/2018/04/inside-the-invisible-but-influential-world-of-scent-branding (archived at https://perma.cc/9SQK-XTL8)

57 www.scentcompany.it/en/news/olfactory-marketing-the-best-examples-of-scent-branding/ (archived at https://perma.cc/4R96-AP2Z)

58 https://theconversation.com/how-the-travel-industry-uses-your-sense-of-smell-to-enhance-your-holiday-180520 (archived at https://perma.cc/ER8N-WZZQ)

59 www.scentcompany.it/en/news/great-examples-of-olfactory-marketing/ (archived at https://perma.cc/RP8B-SGMQ)

60 Sorokowska, A, Sorokowski, P and Frackowiak, T (2015) Determinants of human olfactory performance: A cross-cultural study, *Science of the Total Environment*, 506, 196–200

61 www.petalrepublic.com/jasmine-flower/ (archived at https://perma.cc/W8H9-CXWP)

62 https://medium.com/@howardmitchell1921/which-park-avenue-beer-shampoo-is-best-a-comprehensive-guide-10df92eebbbf (archived at https://perma.cc/5WED-5GN4)

63 Biswas, D (2019) Sensory aspects of retailing: theoretical and practical implications, *Journal of Retailing*, 95 (4), 111–15

64 www.chocolate.lindt.com/world-of-lindt/tasting-with-5-senses (archived at https://perma.cc/HN7G-ZN9B)

65 www.gq.com/story/valentines-day-edible-underwear-taste-test (archived at https://perma.cc/FY38-TWTG)

66 Krishna, A and Elder, R S (2021) A review of the cognitive and sensory cues impacting taste perceptions and consumption, *Consumer Psychology Review*, 4 (1), 121–34

67 www.theguardian.com/food/2020/jul/14/nespresso-coffee-capsule-pods-branding-clooney-nestle-recycling-environment (archived at https://perma.cc/54J7-KZLR)

68 www.psy.ox.ac.uk/research/crossmodal-research-laboratory (archived at https://perma.cc/9CUQ-DDAA)

69 Spence, C and Gallace, A (2011) Multisensory design: Reaching out to touch the consumer, *Psychology & Marketing*, 28 (3), 267–308

70 Spence, C, Puccinelli, N M, Grewal, D and Roggeveen, A L (2014) Store atmospherics: A multisensory perspective, *Psychology & Marketing*, 31 (7), 472–88

71 Hagtvedt, H and Brasel, S A (2016) Cross-modal communication: Sound frequency influences consumer responses to color lightness, *Journal of Marketing Research*, 53 (4), 551–62

72 Krishna, A and Elder, R S (2021) A review of the cognitive and sensory cues impacting taste perceptions and consumption, *Consumer Psychology Review*, 4 (1), 121–34

73 Hoegg, J and Alba, J W (2007) Taste perception: More than meets the tongue, *Journal of Consumer Research*, 33 (4), 490–98

74 www.cleveland.com/fighting-fat/2010/04/marketers_know_its_hard_to_resist_foods_when_youre_tempted_by_scents_fighting_fat.html (archived at https://perma.cc/PKG9-LQFH)

75 Togawa, T, Park, J, Ishii, H and Deng, X (2019) A packaging visual-gustatory correspondence effect: Using visual packaging design to influence flavor perception and healthy eating decisions, *Journal of Retailing*, 95 (4), 204–18

76 Kühn, S and Gallinat, J (2013) Does taste matter? How anticipation of cola brands influences gustatory processing in the brain, *PloS one*, 8 (4), e61569

77 Herz, R (2009) *The Scent of Desire: Discovering our enigmatic sense of smell*, Harper Collins

78 Hagtvedt, H and Brasel, S A (2016) Cross-modal communication: Sound frequency influences consumer responses to color lightness, *Journal of Marketing Research*, 53 (4), 551–62

79 Spence, C (2020) On the ethics of neuromarketing and sensory marketing, *Organizational Neuroethics: Reflections on the Contributions of Neuroscience to Management Theories and Business Practices*, 9–29

80 Shukla, P, Singh, J and Wang, W (2022) The influence of creative packaging design on customer motivation to process and purchase decisions, *Journal of Business Research*, 147, 338–47

81 Spence, C (2020) On the ethics of neuromarketing and sensory marketing, *Organizational Neuroethics: Reflections on the Contributions of Neuroscience to Management Theories and Business Practices*, 9–29

82 Lim, W M (2018) Demystifying neuromarketing, *Journal of Business Research*, 91, 205–20

83 Morin, C (2011) Neuromarketing: The new science of consumer behavior, *Society*, 48 (2), 131–35

84 Lee, N, Broderick, A J and Chamberlain, L (2007), What is 'neuromarketing'? A discussion and agenda for future research, *International Journal of Psychophysiology*, 63 (2), 199–204

85 Harrell, E (2019) Neuromarketing: What you need to know, *Harvard Business Review*, 97 (4), 64–70

86 Fortunato, V C R, Giraldi, J D M E and de Oliveira, J H C (2014) A review of studies on neuromarketing: Practical results, techniques, contributions and limitations, *Journal of Management Research*, 6 (2), 201

87 Khurana, V, Gahalawat, M, Kumar, P, Roy, P P, Dogra, D P, Scheme, E and Soleymani, M (2021) A survey on neuromarketing using EEG signals, *IEEE Transactions on Cognitive and Developmental Systems*, 13 (4), 732–49

88 Ariely, D and Berns, G S (2010) Neuromarketing: The hope and hype of neuroimaging in business, *Nature Reviews Neuroscience*, 11 (4), 284–92

89 dos Santos, R D O J, de Oliveira, J H C, Rocha, J B and Giraldi, J D M E (2015) Eye tracking in neuromarketing: A research agenda for marketing studies, *International Journal of Psychological Studies*, 7 (1), 32

90 Gill, R and Singh, J (2020, December) A review of neuromarketing techniques and emotion analysis classifiers for visual-emotion mining, in *2020 9th International Conference System Modeling and Advancement in Research Trends* (SMART), IEEE, pp 103–08

91 Zurawicki, L (2010) *Neuromarketing: Exploring the brain of the consumer*, Springer Science and Business Media

92 Lee, N, Chamberlain, L and Brandes, L (2018) Welcome to the jungle! The neuromarketing literature through the eyes of a newcomer, *European Journal of Marketing*, 52 (1/2), 4–38

93 www.neurensics.com/en/case-lays-how-neuropricing-increased-lays-profits (archived at https://perma.cc/VAT4-D2CK)

94 www.neurosciencemarketing.com/blog/articles/your-brain-on-soup.htm (archived at https://perma.cc/37RR-CQ8G)

95 www.iienstitu.com/en/blog/which-brands-are-using-neuromarketing (archived at https://perma.cc/E345-HB9U)

Branding on social media and digital brand analytics 15

Overview

In this chapter, we first explain the rise of social media branding. In the following section, we explain how brands use social media to create and build customer engagement. This is followed by a discussion on the rise and the prominence of social media influencers in digital brand communications. We then sum up the good practices and pitfalls to avoid in social media branding. In the final section, we explain the usefulness and applications of brand analytics data.

Key learning outcomes

Upon reading this chapter, you should be able to

- Understand the role of social media in brand communications
- Develop insights into ways of creating brand engagement through social media
- Develop understanding of the role of social media influencers in branding, including good practices
- Comprehend the basics of brand analytics

The advent of social media branding

Human beings have an innate need to belong and to connect with other humans.[1] Moreover, being social animals, we also possess curiosity about what others are doing and how we should behave in social settings to achieve our desired goals and favourable outcomes. These social aspects have driven people to engage in a variety of social endeavours, which in modern society has led to the rise of social media. The *Oxford English Dictionary* defines social media as 'websites and applications which enable users to create and share content or to participate in social networking'.[2]

While digital social media websites are a novel invention that emerged in the early 2000s, the notion of social media networking and interactions is grounded in the electronic information exchange that started with Morse Code.[3] The advent and commercialization of the internet created a new information exchange revolution that allowed a variety of communication options between brands, consumers and other stakeholders through email, bulletin boards and forums, real-time chatting, blogs and vlogs, and other digital communication avenues. Avenues that allowed consumers and brands to communicate and exchange information easily were social media networking websites. The first social media networking website experiments attempted to connect people through geographic proximity or similar lived experiences, such as geocities.com, classmates.com and sixdegrees.com. Based on the buzz created by these social media networking websites, a number of new platforms emerged, including Friendster and Myspace, followed by the now highly popular websites and apps such as Facebook and X (formerly known as Twitter). With increasing internet availability and access, coupled with broadband infrastructure improvement, these social media networking websites, which were predominantly text-based communication, allowed greater audio-visual content, with the rise of new age social media such as YouTube, Instagram, Snapchat, WeChat, Telegram and TikTok. While many of these social media networks succeeded in engaging users, many others failed, including Google initiatives such as Orkut, Google+, Buzz, Apple's Ping and other independent platforms such as YikYak.[4]

Currently, it is believed that there are more than 5 billion internet users of which almost 90 per cent use social media.[6] As Figure 15.1 shows, many social media networks have more than 2 billion regular users. The rise of the internet with increasing usage by consumers offered brands an opportunity to create meaningful and dynamic engagement. This led to brand's own websites, multi-retail platforms such as Amazon.com, auction platforms such as eBay.com and social media interactions through brand's own webpages, and other content. Social media networks allowed communication between consumers and brands, as well as consumers and consumers.

Consumers are now likely to use social media for almost every stage of their consumption process, including information search, alternative selection, decision making, word-of-mouth and the acquisition, use and disposal of products and services.[7] Moreover, social media network websites allow brands an opportunity to develop and communicate their identity, and gain commercial, non-commercial and social mileage via a variety of means that was not possible previously. For example, when searching about a product or service, consumers regularly scour social media pages created by the brand and read other consumers' views to make purchase decisions. For instance, Starbucks is known for its customer-centric social media presence. The brand frequently interacts with its customers on social media, answering questions, addressing concerns, and sharing fun and engaging content. Starbucks also hosts

Figure 15.1 Most popular social networks worldwide as of January 2023, ranked by number of monthly active users[5]

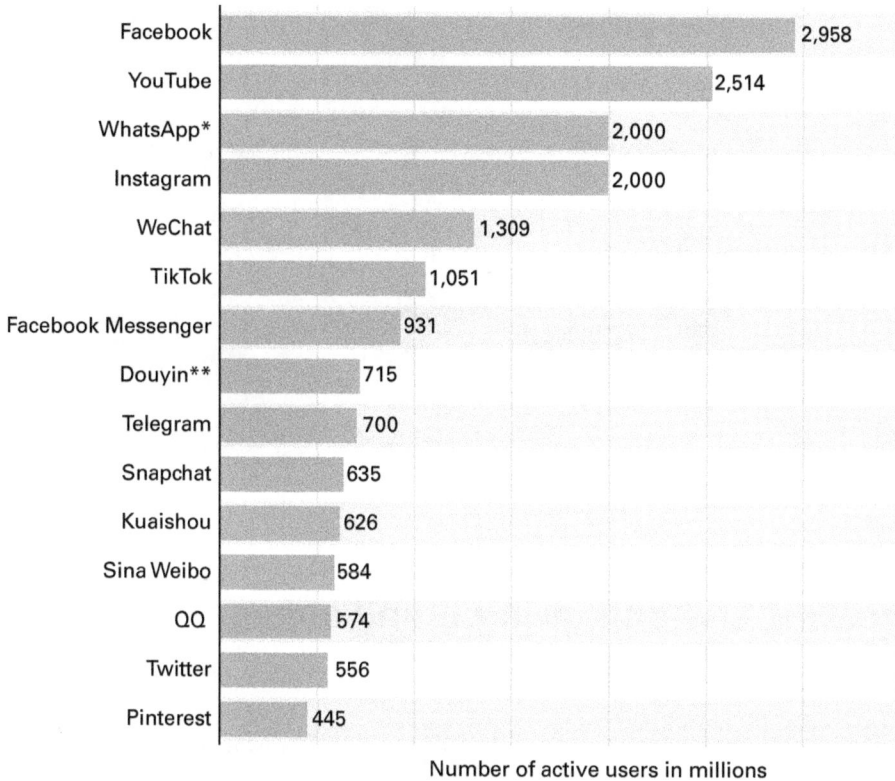

Social Network	Number of active users in millions
Facebook	2,958
YouTube	2,514
WhatsApp*	2,000
Instagram	2,000
WeChat	1,309
TikTok	1,051
Facebook Messenger	931
Douyin**	715
Telegram	700
Snapchat	635
Kuaishou	626
Sina Weibo	584
QQ	574
Twitter	556
Pinterest	445

Number of active users in millions

contests and giveaways throughout the year, giving customers the chance to win prizes such as free coffee, gift cards and merchandise. Such initiatives make the consumer feel that the brand is responsive to their needs and thus increase their trust in the brand.

Moreover, consumer-to-consumer electronic word-of-mouth on social media influences decision making.[8] This electronic word-of-mouth, also termed user-generated content (UGC), is used by brands to promote itself further. For example, GoPro, the camera brand, encourages its users to share their GoPro footage on social media using the hashtag #GoPro. GoPro then reposts and shares this content on its own social media channels, inspiring other users to get out and adventure with their GoPro cameras. In addition, initiatives such as Facebook Marketplace (see Figure 15.2) have given rise a new type of commerce called social commerce that can help consumers acquire and sell a variety of products and services on social media network websites.[9]

Figure 15.2   Consumers buy and sell a variety of products on social commerce marketplaces such as Facebook Marketplace

SOURCE Author's

Creating and enhancing brand engagement through social media

As the reach and usage of social media grows among consumers, it offers brands ample opportunities for creating and enhancing brand engagement. Brands can provide different types of information that can help consumer decision making. For example, brands can offer utility-focused information on social media, including product information, updates on product innovations, delivery aspects and comparison to competitors. Similarly, using more hedonic approach of communication, brands can motivate consumers to participate on their social media pages via contests, raffles and rewards. Moreover, brands can also use the dynamic nature of communication on social media to engage consumers in product feature innovations. By posting new product features on social media, brands can get real-time feedback about the product attributes preferred by the consumers. For example, many food and drink, fashion and clothing, and cosmetic brands have dedicated product testing programmes where they invite a select group of followers to test out new products and provide feedback. These programmes are often run through social media platforms such as Instagram and Facebook.

An industry report suggests that in several product categories 80 per cent of consumers make buying decisions based on a friend's social media post, and brands that offer content that is relatable tend to attract more consumers.[10] Companies that interact meaningfully with their audience beyond advertisements or product listings

Figure 15.3   The 6C framework of social media engagement

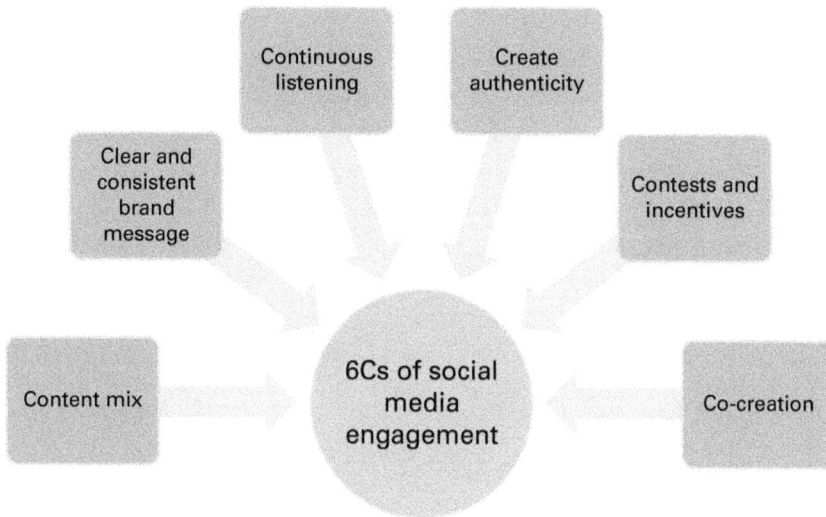

SOURCE Adapted from Parent et al. (2011, 219–29)

create a positive impact. Beyond the utilitarian and hedonic communications, the social nature of social media networks allows brands to tap into consumer conversations and understand the deeper associations, emotions and opinions of consumers.[11] For instance, despite the challenges faced by fashion retailers during the coronavirus pandemic, Boohoo Group (which includes PrettyLittleThing and Nasty Gal) managed to thrive. Boohoo's social media strategy has been integral to its success, with influencer endorsements enabling the brand to target and engage a young audience on Instagram (where it now has more than 12.6 million followers). Boohoo cleverly adapted its content to stay relevant, such as using #BoohooInTheHouse – a hashtag relating to 'stay at home style' during the Covid-19 lockdown. Similarly, other social selling platforms like Depop regularly offer mini-interviews with their content creators and sellers on social media to engage similar audience. The brand's page also offers content creators advice on topics such as 'how to make a listing that sells', 'how to take great photos', 'how to sell even faster', etc. Engaging social media users in co-creating content can help a brand in a variety of ways. For instance, it can increase brand identification and consumer enthusiasm to engage with the brand. At the same time, other consumers may find the co-creation approach more trustworthy and thus pay greater attention to such content. Academic research suggests that compared to company advertising, user-generated content on social media tends to generate a significantly positive brand attitude.[12]

As the above examples demonstrate, brands should actively engage in social media platforms for several practical reasons. Firstly, visibility and reach are significantly amplified through social media. With billions of active users across various platforms, brands can connect with a vast audience, including potential customers who might not have encountered their products or services otherwise. Such amplification can lead to higher penetration for the brand and contribute to overall sales and market share. Secondly, social media provides a direct line of communication between brands and consumers. By actively participating in conversations, responding to queries and addressing concerns, brands can build trust and satisfaction, fostering positive relationships. Thirdly, social media allows for real-time feedback. Brands can gather insights from comments, likes, shares and direct messages to improve their offerings and tailor marketing strategies.

Moreover, to enhance their customer engagement, brands should employ the following effective practices as identified in the 6C framework (see Figure 15.3).

Content mix: Academic research has shown that creative content tends to generate curiosity, and in turn, enhance motivation to process information.[13] Thus, a brand's social media posts should have creative, relevant, valuable and shareable content. This can include a mix of informative posts, entertaining videos and user-generated content. For example, Taco Bell uses social media to share behind-the-scenes glimpses, exclusive promotions and interactive stories. Their creative content keeps followers engaged and motivated to view and process upcoming menu items or events.

Clear and consistent brand message: Maintaining a clear and consistent communication tone and style across all social media channels helps reinforce brand associations and identity. Whether it is witty and playful or professional and informative, the voice should align with the brand's values. Several important psychological theories, including the stereotype content model (i.e. warmth vs competence)[14] or brand personality types (i.e. sincerity, excitement, competence, sophistication and ruggedness)[15] could help brands in developing a consistent brand message. For instance, a brand such as IBM, which is perceived by consumers to be competent, should use messages that reflect their competence. Alternatively, a brand that is perceived as warm should adopt a message accordingly. For example, Oreo wants to be seen as a playful and warm brand. To that end, Oreo celebrated its 100th anniversary with the 'Daily Twist' campaign. Each day for 100 days, Oreo posted a creative image related to a current event or holiday on Facebook and Twitter. The campaign encouraged followers to engage by guessing the twist or sharing their own ideas.

Continuous listening: Brands should continuously monitor social media conversations related to their industry and products. By gathering competitive market intelligence, a brand will be able to understand and predict market trends, new product launches or feature enhancements, which could then feed into their own product development and innovation. Moreover, listening to customer feedback and addressing concerns promptly, brands can build stronger consumer-brand relationships which, in turn, demonstrate responsiveness and care, and more importantly increase trust towards the brand among consumers.[16] Burt's Bees, an organic-product-focused cosmetics firm known for its beeswax and lip balm, actively interacts with followers on Twitter by answering questions and replying to comments. They take the time to engage with their audience, making followers feel heard and valued. By signing off comments with a real representative's name, they humanize their brand communications, and build stronger connections.

Create authenticity: Authenticity matters. Brands can demonstrate their authenticity through communicating integrity, sincerity, continuity and symbolism.[17] Brands should avoid overly promotional content and focus on building genuine connections with the consumers. When brands communicate their message authentically on social media, it reduces consumer scepticism and increases trust.[18] Responding to comments individually and showing appreciation for user-generated content signals authenticity. For example, the *Guardian*, a more than 200-year-old newspaper from the UK, is globally associated with serious journalism. Keeping up with its impression in public minds, the brand uses a formal and reserved tone in sharing its news posts on social media.

Contests and incentives: Running contests, giveaways and exclusive promotions encourages users to participate actively. Such activities are generally associated with a sense of pleasure. It motivates consumers to participate anticipating rewards based on the pleasure principle.[19] The reward mechanism further encourages consumers re-visit and re-engage with the brand's social media campaign. It also creates a sense of community around the brand. Goldfish Crackers ran a creative contest called the '#GoForTheHandful Duet Challenge' on TikTok. They challenged participants to duet with pro basketball player Boban Marjanović by attempting to hold more Goldfish crackers in one hand than Boban's record of 301. The entries were hash tagged with #GoForTheHandful, making it easy to search for and watch challengers pile Goldfish crackers in their hands. The winner received Goldfish for a year and earned the title of Official Goldfish Spokeshand. The contest garnered an impressive 11.5 billion views on TikTok.

Co-creation: Encouraging users to share their experiences with the brand (through photos, reviews or testimonials) boosts engagement and serves as powerful social proof. When other consumers create content involving the brand, consumers tend to trust it more as organic word-of-mouth. Moreover, such content is highly valued by consumers as they assume it to be a result of real interest and passion from the content creator.[20] For example, Airbnb leverages user-generated content on Instagram. They encourage travellers to share their Airbnb experiences using specific hashtags (#Airbnb or #LiveThere). By featuring these photos on their official account, Airbnb not only engages users but also showcases unique accommodations worldwide.

BRANDING IN PRACTICE

Gymshark: a fitness brand with a social media edge

Gymshark is a UK-based fitness brand that offers stylish, comfortable and functional clothing and accessories for men and women. Founded in 2012 by Ben Francis and Lewis Morgan, Gymshark has grown from a small online store to a global phenomenon with over 15 million followers across various social media platforms.

One of the key communications strategies that Gymshark employs on social media is to create engaging and authentic content that showcases its brand values and culture. For example, Gymshark regularly posts motivational quotes, fitness challenges, behind-the-scenes videos, customer testimonials and user-generated content on its main Instagram account @gymshark (which has more than 6.4 million followers). Gymshark's posts are highly relevant to its target audience, with the majority of imagery captured in a gym environment and with gym equipment or weights, thus adding clarity and consistency of brand message. Listening to its customers, Gymshark also consciously includes a balance of men and women in its posts and showcases the inclusive nature of the business by featuring varied athletes and diverse groups of people. Gymshark also has separate Instagram accounts for different segments of its audience, such as @gymsharkwomen (3.4 million followers).

Another strategy that Gymshark uses on social media is to collaborate with influential fitness personalities such as Whitney Simmons, Steve Cook and Nikki Blackketter. These influencers, also known as Gymshark Ambassadors, promote the brand's products, share their workout routines and tips, and interact with their fans on Instagram, YouTube, TikTok and other channels. Gymshark also co-creates products with some of these influencers, such as the Whitney Simmons Collection and the Nikki B x Gymshark Collection.

Through the lens of the 6C framework of social media engagement, Gymshark has created an effective social media presence that demonstrates its passion for fitness, innovation and community. This enhances its brand image and loyalty among its customers, as well as attracting new customers who are inspired by its products and values.

The role of social media influencers in brand building

Before the advent of social media networks, the main avenue for brands to communicate their message was either through print or electronic media available in any given market. This mainly included newspapers, magazines, radio and television. Depending on their budget, brands chose appropriate avenues to influence their consumers. A few brands, such as Tupperware, Avon and Amway, use consumer-to-consumer communications as their key marketing channel. Brands have long relied upon subject experts and opinion leaders for their specialized knowledge. These public personalities were employed to support brands' claims and market their offerings. The aim was to influence consumer product choice using the authenticity and trustworthiness of the expert.[21] For example, Oral-B used a long-term campaign suggesting that it is the preferred toothpaste of dental professionals.

With the commercialization of the internet in the mid-1990s onwards, consumer content creation increased manyfold. At this time, blogging emerged as a particular tool that allowed consumers to share their own opinions, in many cases free of charge. Many bloggers started writing about their own usage and product experiences which were read and commented by other consumers. The rise of social media networks in the mid-2000s allowed a substantial increase and dynamism in consumer-to-consumer communications. Consumers could communicate with the content creator in real-time, share their views and get instant feedback as well. This led to the advent of unique types of individuals who started sharing their own opinions about specific products or services based on their own usage and experience. These influential individuals over time garnered many followers, giving rise to the modern-day social media influencers. Influencer marketing has become the cornerstone of current branding practices. The global influencer marketing market has observed rapid growth from $1.7 billion in 2016 to $21.1 billion in 2023 and Instagram is considered the leading platform for influencer marketing.[22]

BRANDING IN PRACTICE
The rise of the social media influencer: Zoella

Social media influencers are individuals who have established credibility and popularity in a specific industry, or niche, by creating and sharing original content on various online platforms. They can influence the opinions, behaviours and purchasing decisions of their followers, who often regard them as authentic, relatable and trustworthy sources of information and entertainment. Social media influencers have emerged as a new type of celebrity and marketing agent in the digital era, challenging the traditional notions of fame, authority and communication.

A prominent and successful social media influencer whose fame rose with the rise of social media in the early 2010s is Zoe Sugg, better known as Zoella, who started her career as a YouTuber and blogger in 2009. Initially, Zoella wrote blog posts and created YouTube videos on her own life experiences. As her popularity grew, she started discussing her consumption of beauty and fashion brands. Zoella is widely regarded as one of the pioneers and leaders of the influencer industry, especially in the UK, where she was named the highest-earning female social media influencer under 30. In 2023, Zoella had nearly 11 million followers online with 1.1 billion views of the content she has created. She has created her own beauty and fashion line, written books and has actively promoted hers as well as other brands. She has also received numerous awards and recognition for her online presence and impact, such as being listed among 'Britain's most influential Tweeters' by *The Telegraph* and being appointed as a digital ambassador for Mind, a mental health charity.

Zoella's success is attributed to her variety, quality, frequency and personality of her content; her collaborations with other YouTubers and brands; her loyal and engaged audience; her recognizable, reputable and profitable personal brand; and her ability to overcome or cope with the controversies and criticisms that she faced.

An interesting question is why social media influencers have become so popular and influential. Academic researchers have examined this phenomenon by employing different theories and have provided several explanations, which are discussed below. A number of influential theories, including para-social relationships, reference group effect and congruity theory, have been used in academic research to explain the reasons behind the rapid growth of influencer economy on social media.

Unlike the influencers of the past, who were subject experts or celebrities, many social media influencers are seen as more relatable, credible and authentic. These influencers are relatable because most of them start from an ordinary background and have interests and a demographic similar to their followers. Many influencers post about their daily lives, respond to their followers regularly, often hold live discussions and build stronger connection with their followers. Thus, social media influencers are able to build congruence with their followers. As they use or promote a brand, their followers' approval of the endorsed brand increases due to the congruity.

With increasing number of followers, social media influencers and their followers build a kind of para-social relationship. Para-social relationships are one-sided relationships between followers and the social media influencer. In this type of relationship, the follower invests effort and resources in terms of emotions, time and money to continue the relationship with the influencer. However, the influencer is unlikely to be aware of such efforts by an individual follower as they have a large following. For example, James Stephen Donaldson, known as MrBeast, has over 312 million followers on his various YouTube channels. The followers are attracted by the creative content provided by these social media influencers and follow them and their endorsements in a one-sided manner. Para-social relationships offer a number of advantages for followers: feeling increased belonging, enhanced self-esteem, reduced loneliness and stronger social connections.[23] However, these can lead to negative consequences as well wherein these relationships can interfere with a follower's real-life relationships[24] and interactions leading to increased anxiety, loneliness and social isolation.[25]

By nature, most human beings like to be part of social groups. These social groups, termed as reference groups, are groups of individuals that have significant relevance for consumers and influence consumers' evaluations, aspirations and behaviour. To remain connected with the community of other followers, many followers buy products promoted by the influencers. With the increased congruency and the strength of relationship with the influencers, consumers find recommendations from influencers as more credible and authentic compared to company advertisements.[26] Moreover, with other followers liking, commenting, purchasing products or services recommended by influencers, consumers also find social proof to support their consumption.[27]

Consumers are increasingly consuming social media content. On most social media, the content is continuously updated, leading to 'bottomless scrolling'. Most people highlight positive aspects of their lives on social media, including their travel, food and other experiences. This is especially true of social media influencers who portray their public persona to be larger than life with fresh content added frequently. Influencer actions are aimed to engage their followers who constantly consume content due to 'fear of missing out' (FOMO).[28] FOMO occurs when consumers feel that their peers are receiving something enriching and gratifying, which they are not, and could lead to feelings of concern, apprehension and consternation.[29]

Scholarly debate

Hudders, L, De Jans, S and De Veirman, M (2021) The commercialization of social media stars: A literature review and conceptual framework on the strategic use of social media influencers, *International Journal of Advertising*, 40 (3), 327–75

Singh, J, Crisafulli, B, Quamina, L T and Xue, M T (2020) 'To trust or not to trust': The impact of social media influencers on the reputation of corporate brands in crisis, *Journal of Business Research*, 119, 464–80

Types of social influencers

Brand managers have different types of social media influencers to select from. Two important distinctions about the types have emerged: one is dependent on the existing popularity and professional standing of the social media influencer, while the other focuses on the number of followers. On the basis of number of followers, social media influencers are categorized into nano, micro, macro and mega influencers (see Figure 15.4). While there is no consensus about their exact number of followers, as a general guideline it is assumed that nano influencers are those with fewer than 10,000 followers. This is because they are new to social media or have a niche audience. They also tend to have a close relationship with their followers. Micro-influencers have between 10,000 and 100,000 followers. They are typically experts in their field and have a loyal following. Micro-influencers are a good choice for brands that want to target a specific niche audience. For example, Elyse Miller, a fitness coach, has approximately 25,000 followers and fits into the micro-influencer category. Macro-influencers have between 100,000 and 1 million followers. They are well-known in their industry and have a large reach. Macro-influencers can be effective for brands that want to increase brand awareness and reach a large audience. For example, Ashley Galvin (537,000 followers) is a fitness and yoga coach who promotes brands such as FRÉ hair repair serum. Mega-influencers have over 1 million followers. They are typically celebrities or social media stars. Mega-influencers can be effective for brands that want to quickly reach a global audience and generate buzz.

With regards to existing popularity and professional expertise, three types of social media influencers have emerged: (a) celebrity influencers; (b) expert influencers; and (c)

Figure 15.4   Social media influencer sphere of influence by number of followers

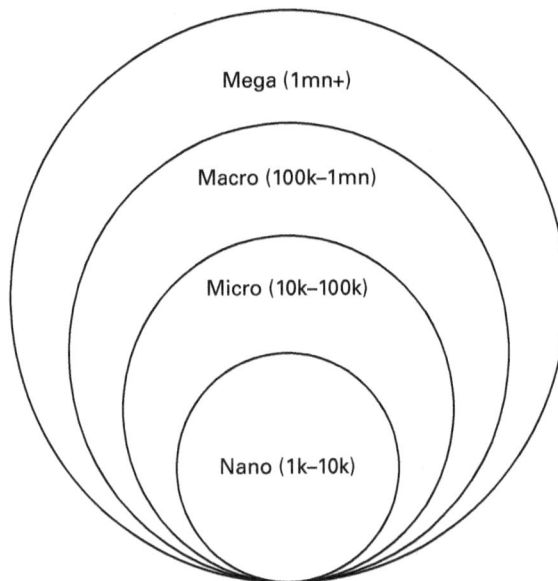

Mega (1mn+)

Macro (100k–1mn)

Micro (10k–100k)

Nano (1k–10k)

SOURCE Authors

celebrity-expert combined influencers. For example, Selena Gomez (499 million followers), one of the top pop singers who promotes brands such as Adidas, Pantene and Coach, is a celebrity social media influencer. Similar top celebrity influencers include Cristiano Ronaldo (787 million followers), Lionel Messi (530 million followers), Justin Bieber (477 million followers) and Kylie Jenner (450 million followers). Expert influencers are those who possess subject expertise in the area of their promotion. These experts generally belong to categories such as beauty, fashion, fitness, travel and lifestyle. For example, Huda Kattan, a beauty influencer, has more than 50 million followers on social media. Similarly, YouTuber Mark Rober, a former NASA engineer, promotes technology gadgets and has more than 26 million followers. Some of these social media influencers can become combined celebrity-expert influencers when they promote a product or service that is within their domain of expertise. For example, when Virat Kohli (231 million followers), one of the top cricket players, promotes cricket equipment, he takes on the role of an expert-celebrity combined influencer.

BRANDING IN PRACTICE
How to select an appropriate influencer for your brand

With the growing impact of social media influencers, brands need appropriate guidelines on how to choose a social media influencer. The following questions and reflections provide a guide for brand managers in selecting an appropriate social media influencer for their campaigns.

Are they an expert?

- Are they considered an expert in their respective field?
- How well will their image fit with the brand?
- Have they ever been invited to speak at an event?
- Have they received awards or been recommended by anyone in the industry?

Do they have an engaged community?

- How engaged is their community?
- What questions does the community ask and how well does the influencer answer them?
- How likeable are they among their community?

How many people are their posts reaching?

- Reach can help you understand how many views an influencer's post is likely to get.
- The more eyeballs on content, the higher the chance of boosting brand awareness.

Who are they reaching?

- Check the demographics of the community to ensure the brand is relevant to them – particularly if targeting a very specific demographic.
- Consider audience demographics such as interests, gender, age group and locations.
- Will you be targeting the right people if the message reaches them?

Have they worked with other brands?

- In general, this is fine, but if the influencer has worked with a competitor for a very long time, it can be difficult to shift the attention away from that competitor since their association with the influencer may stick.

Do they post regularly?

- Posting multiple times a week will have a direct impact on other metrics such as engagement rate, reach, loyalty, etc.

The above questions can help brands to select an appropriate social media influencer.

As discussed, social media influencers have become integral to modern day consumption and provide brand managers with a novel avenue to communicate and reinforce their brand associations and values. Social media influencers are found to be more relatable, credible and authentic by consumers and thus offer a complementary source of communication for brand managers beyond conventional advertising. Choosing an appropriate social media influencer is critical for brand managers. The following section captures the important aspects to consider when branding on social media.

The dos and don'ts of branding on social media

Social media has become pivotal for brand success in today's marketplace. However, the success is not equally shared, as some brands excel in engaging with their customers and other stakeholders on social media, while others find it a struggle. Thus, it is important for the brands to understand how to achieve success on social media.

As discussed previously, the 6C framework of brand engagement can help brands achieve success on social media. However, there are several pitfalls that brands can avoid in their activities on social media. Many unsuccessful brands

Figure 15.5 Share of Instagram influencers involved in fraud worldwide by number of followers[30]

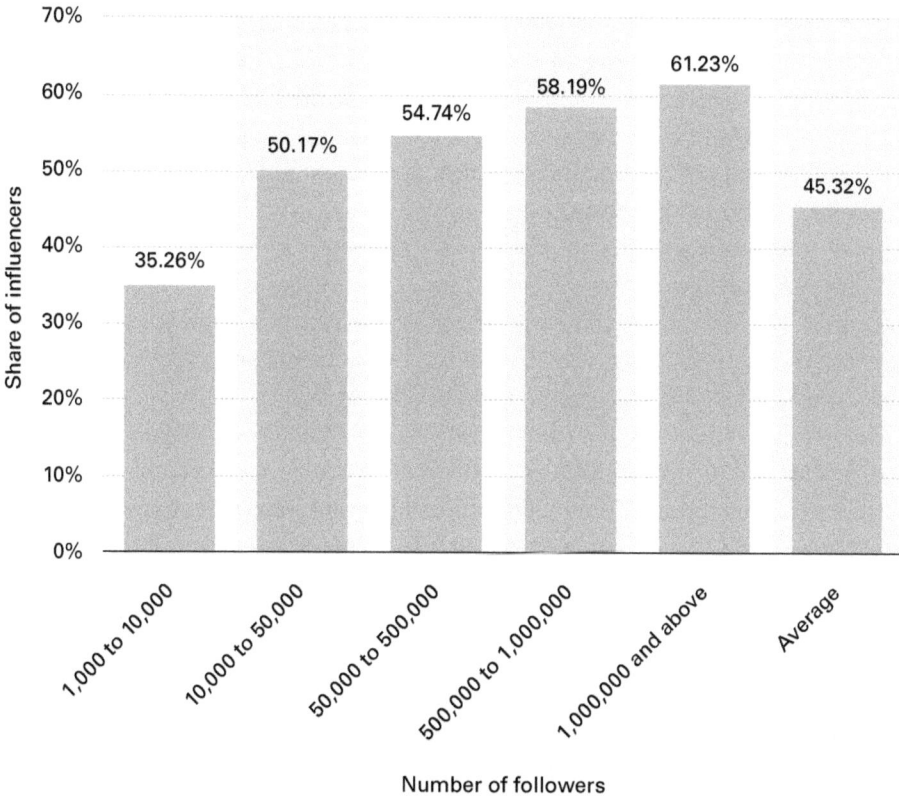

develop their campaigns without having a clear audience or plan in terms of how to engage with the target audience. While social media is used by different types of consumers, as discussed in earlier chapters, different consumer segments engage with the brand for varying reasons. Thus, the starting point for a successful social media campaign is developing a clear plan of engagement based on understanding the audience being targeted.

When developing their social media engagement plan, many brands tend to focus too much on creativity, ignoring the importance of consistency and clarity of their message. It is quite common for brands to seize on wrong trends on social media as well. Veering away from their central engagement theme can be detrimental and thus brands need to balance creativity with consistency. For example, Dove, the personal care brand from Unilever, wanted to engage in the dialogue around diversity. However, its Facebook advertisement showed a black woman turning into a white woman after using Dove lotion.[31] Dove faced significant social media backlash from its followers and the public. This dented the company's long-running diversity campaign and the brand had to apologize.

Another issue for brands is that they fail to engage with the relevant audience and do not have in place a clear post-campaign engagement plan. Social media is a dynamic engagement medium wherein the audience continuously engages with the brand. Some brands have a tendency to post social media campaigns similar to their advertisements on TV or newspapers with the assumption that it is the conventional one-sided communication. Moreover, some brands do not allocate sufficient resources towards post-campaign social media engagement and thus get overwhelmed in the face of a negative response. In addition, many brands focus only on negative comments and do not support the customers who share positive comments and experiences associated with the brands. This is particularly observed within hospitality and other service sectors. Brands should naturally engage with customers who express negative views to provide satisfactory service recovery. However, they should also engage with customers who share positive comments and experiences to reinforce brand associations and encourage repeat patronage.[32]

We have earlier discussed the selection process for social media influencers. However, many brands find themselves unclear about how to choose the right social media influencers for their campaigns. Many brands tend to engage influencers based on number of followers only. This may not be an optimal use of brand resources as there are several instances of unethical practices associated with influencer marketing. As Figure 15.5 shows, approximately half of influencers have an inflated number of followers.

The types of follower number fraud can take various forms including fake followers, fake comments made by bots and creation of pods. To inflate numbers of followers, many influencers buy fake followers. These **bought followers** are added gradually to help disguise the fact that they are not real. Similarly, many influencers buy **bot comment services,** that sell automated 'likes' and 'comments' to make audiences believe that an influencer is generating a positive reaction to posts, images and videos. Learning from the Massively Multiplayer Online Role-Playing Games (MMORPGs), many people on social media form alliances (also called Pods) to provide positive comments and 'likes' on each other's posts. Some influencers build their brand by making deals with these pods, which calls into question how genuine these alliances are since they aren't built on real, organic interest. The Branding in practice below offers guidance on how to identify signs of fraud and a practical checklist to avoid engaging with influencers that may have engaged in such fraud.

BRANDING IN PRACTICE
Signs of social media influencer fraud and a practical checklist

Social media follower fraud is not easy to detect. However, a brand can identify the signs of fraud by examining the following:

Sudden spike in followers

- A sudden spike not explained by another factor like a major event.

- Major events that could organically boost the number of followers include a live streaming session, a recent appearance at a fan get-together or a popular video that went viral.

Unequal ratio of likes/comments to number of followers

- Has a relatively low number of followers and a very high number of likes and comments, in this case likes/comments could be auto-generated.

Comments don't align with posts

- Comments on an influencer's social media platform don't have anything to do with what that influencer posted. For example, the influencer posted a video of a dog eating his lunch, but the comments talk about an entirely different subject.

In addition, the **8-point checklist** below can be used to spot an influencer marketing fraud.

Has the influencer got...

1 A verification badge?
2 A solid account history that shows consistent and original posts?
3 Proof of organic audience growth over time?
4 A history of quality posts?
5 High engagement on their posts?
6 An engaging and complete Instagram profile?
7 Examples of successful past campaigns, partnerships and sponsorships?
8 A history of promoting products and brands in a way that is consistent with brand values?

While providing a truly exciting avenue, social media engagement is fraught with a number of pitfalls. Brands should carefully traverse the social media space and engage with their audience. Importantly, as outlined above, it is highly recommended that brands avoid engaging with influencers who are involved in social media fraud of any kind, as it can be detrimental to the brand in the long run. Digital brand analytics can help brands in understanding and improving social media engagement, which is the focus of our next section.

Understanding brand social media analytics

As brands have increased their engagement on social media, a new field of research has emerged that focuses on data analytics that can help brands in achieving their social media related aims and objectives. Social media analytics is a relatively new field of research that can help understand brand exposure, lead generation, fan loyalty and online traffic on social media.[33] Brands can use a variety of data in their analytics process. Academic researchers identify seven types of data that can help brands in social media analytics.[34] Table 15.1 explains different data types and sub-types that can be utilized for social media analytics.

These data types and sub-types are examined through a variety of analytical techniques including text mining, sentiment analysis, web analytics, network analytics, descriptive *social media* analytics and image analytics. *Text mining* involves content-based analysis of mostly text-based data including reviews, posts, comments, etc. using techniques such as keyword retrieval, topic modelling and cluster analysis.[35] *Sentiment analysis* particularly focuses on the sentiment conveyed within the text.[36] Techniques such as opinion mining and aspect-oriented classification are used in sentimental analysis regularly.[37] *Web analytics* is a different branch of social media analytics that focuses on web-page-related characteristics, such as speed of loading, content and images used, with the use of website crawling/spidering, cloud computing and search log analysis.[38] [39] *Network analytics* taps into the structure of existing relationships between various entities on social media including between users and between users and brands, among others. Techniques such as *social network analysis*

Table 15.1   Data types and sub-types that can be used for social media analytics

Data	Sub-types
User-generated data	• CG-textual data (reviews, comments, posts, enquiries, tweets, Wikipedia pages) • CG-linguistic data
Platform-based data	• Structured data (ratings, stars, rankings) • Profile data (gender, age, followers) • Consumption data
Metadata	• Post-level (volume, length) • Webpage-level (web traffic)
Network data	• Links between users • Links between words
Firm-generated data	• Webpages, posts, comments, product descriptions
Temporal data	• Real-time data, posting time
Rich media data	• Geotag and image

SOURCE Wang et al (2021)

examine human networks, while *semantic network analysis* explores the linkage between products/objects.[40] *Descriptive social media analytics* captures the standard statistical analysis such as frequency and counts.[41] *Image analytics* is a novel analytical approach that aims to analyse visual content on social media through techniques such as image classification and feature descriptors.[42] Depending on their requirements, brands can use the above - mentioned data types and analytics techniques to better understand their social media presence and engagement.

To engage with different social media users, many brands engage in social testing. Social testing on social media is a method of evaluating the effectiveness of different content, strategies or tactics, on various social media platforms. It involves creating and comparing different versions of the same post or campaign and measuring its performance based on a predefined goal. The goal could be to increase engagement, traffic, conversions or any other metric that is relevant to the brand's objectives. Social testing can help brands gain data-driven insights into their audience preferences, behaviour and response to different types of content. It can also help them optimize their social media strategy and allocate their resources more efficiently.

Different types of social tests exist on social media, including A/B testing, spilt testing and multivariate testing. *A/B testing* is the simplest form of social testing, where two versions of the same post or campaign are shown to a random subset of the target audience and their performance is compared. For example, a marketer could test whether adding emojis to their Instagram captions increases engagement or not. HubSpot Academy observed that out of more than 55,000 page views, only 0.9 per cent of those users were watching the video on their homepage. By creating three different variants of the homepage, HubSpot were able to identify a particular homepage style that increased video viewing by 6 per cent and resultant sign-ups.[43] *Split testing*, a variant of A/B testing, involves splitting the entire audience into two or more groups and each group is shown a different version of the post or campaign. The performance of each group is then compared to determine which version is more effective. For example, a marketer could test how different posting times affect the reach and engagement of their Twitter posts. *Multivariate testing* is a more complex form of social testing, where multiple variables are changed simultaneously, and their combined effect is measured. For example, a marketer could test how different combinations of copy, image and headline affect the click-through rate of their Facebook advertisements. Netflix regularly uses multivariate testing to improve the usability of their user interface including content, buttons and styles, amongst many other variables.[44]

Social media analytics testing is highly valuable for improving social media marketing outcomes for brands. It can help brands to understand their audience better, create more engaging and relevant content, and optimize their social media strategy. By using social media analytics and testing tools, brand managers can save time and resources and make data-driven decisions that support their branding objectives.

Chapter summary

In this chapter, we first explored how social media evolved and how brands began engaging on social media. As social media has become an important part of many consumers' daily lives, brands engagement has become critical. In this regard, we offered the 6C framework of social media engagement that focuses on content, consistency, continuity, creating authenticity, contests and co-creation. We also discussed how some brands that are using the 6C framework are successful in today's digital marketplace. A significant aspect of the social media world are influencers, and we discussed the rise and importance of social media influencers for successful brand engagement. We also provided guidelines on how to select appropriate social media influencers. Furthermore, success on social media depends on several good practices that a brand should follow. Finally, we discussed the different digital analytics tools and techniques that brands can use to increase their chances of success on social media.

Key concepts

- Social media
- Brand management
- Social media influencers
  - Selection
  - Fraud
- Social media brand analytics

Exercise questions

1 Select any brand of your choice and examine how its social media engagement differs on any three different social media platforms.

2 Choose three brands and investigate their activities on social media platforms highlighting their branding goals.

3 Choose any brand of your liking that is active on social media and critically evaluate their engagement by applying the 6C framework.

4 Imagine you are a brand manager planning to engage a social media influencer based on their follower numbers.

   a. Identify two influencers each based on their sphere of influence (i.e. nano, micro, macro or mega).

b. Examine their recent social media posts and critically evaluate their appropriateness using the criteria provided in this chapter (see the Branding in practice box on pages 283–84).

5 Imagine you are invited as a consultant by a company that is planning to engage with their customers on social media. Explain the importance of brand social media analytics to the company marketing team.

CASE STUDY Wimbledon: match point for digital marketing

This case study, written by Clodagh O'Brien in 2023, is about Wimbledon's digital marketing strategy. It looks at how Wimbledon has used innovative technologies and techniques to continuously attract young audiences (and potential life-long fans) and promote the sport in an engaging way. Audience segmentation, online and offline content creation, and the use of various communications are covered here. Brand partnerships and advertising through those partnerships is also examined. Capitalizing on celebrity attendance is another aspect to the strategy but the priority is protecting the image and brand itself (e.g. trademarking its colours).

Finally, embracing AI and encouraging tennis players to endorse/take part in marketing are part of the strategy.

SOURCE https://digitalmarketinginstitute.com/blog/wimbledon-match-point-for-content-marketing

Case questions

1 Not all sports fans are alike. How does Wimbledon use audience segmentation to engage with different types of tennis fans on social media?

2 What are the various ways in which Wimbledon uses different social media for consumer engagement? Critically evaluate Wimbledon's marketing and social media strategy employing the 6C framework of social media engagement.

3 Wimbledon has partnered with many established brands. Examine any one of the integrated campaigns that involves Wimbledon and a partner brand and recommend suggestions for further refinement for the next Wimbledon tournament.

4 Explain how Wimbledon is using AI and data analytics to improve brand engagement.

5 Tennis stars are social media influencers themselves. If you were a social media manager at Wimbledon, what steps would you take to make sure that an appropriate social media influencer is chosen to represent the brand using the guidelines suggested within the Branding in practice box on pages 283–84?

Endnotes

1   Baumeister, R F and Leary, M R (1995) The need to belong: Desire for interpersonal attachments as a fundamental human motivation, *Psychological Bulletin*, 117 (3), 497–529

2   www.oed.com/dictionary/social-media_n?tab=meaning_and_use#99272386371 (archived at https://perma.cc/2R65-BASN)

3   https://online.maryville.edu/blog/evolution-social-media/ (archived at https://perma.cc/JPY7-L67Y)

4   www.searchenginejournal.com/failed-social-media-sites/303421/ (archived at https://perma.cc/5WH4-9AYT)

5   www.statista.com/statistics/272014/global-social-networks-ranked-by-number-of-users/ (archived at https://perma.cc/EGE2-L5S9)

6   www.statista.com/topics/1164/social-networks/#editorsPicks (archived at https://perma.cc/Q386-8MMK)

7   Chahal, H, Wirtz, J and Verma, A (2020) Social media brand engagement: Dimensions, drivers and consequences, *Journal of Consumer Marketing*, 37 (2), 191–204

8   Erkan, I and Evans, C (2016) The influence of eWOM in social media on consumers' purchase intentions: An extended approach to information adoption, *Computers in Human Behavior*, 61, 47–55

9   Zhang, K Z and Benyoucef, M (2016) Consumer behavior in social commerce: A literature review, *Decision Support Systems*, 86, 95–108

10 www.forbes.com/sites/forbesagencycouncil/2022/04/28/how-social-media-impacts-consumer-buying/?sh=36f8328a337d (archived at https://perma.cc/FA2C-42UV)

11 Hollebeek, L D, Glynn, M S and Brodie, R J (2014) Consumer brand engagement in social media: Conceptualization, scale development and validation, *Journal of Interactive Marketing*, 28 (2), 149–65

12 Müller, J and Christandl, F (2019) Content is king–But who is the king of kings? The effect of content marketing, sponsored content and user-generated content on brand responses, *Computers in Human Behavior*, 96, 46–55

13 Shukla, P, Singh, J and Wang, W (2022) The influence of creative packaging design on customer motivation to process and purchase decisions, *Journal of Business Research*, 147, 338–47

14 Kervyn, N, Fiske, S T and Malone, C (2012) Brands as intentional agents framework: How perceived intentions and ability can map brand perception, *Journal of Consumer Psychology*, 2 (2), 166–76

15 Aaker, J L (1997) Dimensions of brand personality, *Journal of Marketing Research*, 34 (3), 347–56

16 Chaudhuri, A and Holbrook, M B (2001) The chain of effects from brand trust and brand affect to brand performance: The role of brand loyalty, *Journal of Marketing*, 65 (2), 81–93

17 Morhart, F, Malär, L, Guèvremont, A, Girardin, F and Grohmann, B (2015) Brand authenticity: An integrative framework and measurement scale, *Journal of Consumer Psychology*, 25 (2), 200–18

18 Moulard, J G, Raggio, R D and Folse, J A G (2016) Brand authenticity: Testing the antecedents and outcomes of brand management's passion for its products, *Psychology & Marketing*, 33 (6), 421–36

19 Kivetz, R and Simonson, I (2002) Earning the right to indulge: Effort as a determinant of customer preferences toward frequency program rewards, *Journal of Marketing Research*, 39 (2), 155–70

20 Sorensen, A, Andrews, L and Drennan, J (2017) Using social media posts as resources for engaging in value co-creation: The case for social media-based cause brand communities, *Journal of Service Theory and Practice*, 27 (4), 898–922

21 McCracken, G (1989) Who is the celebrity endorser? Cultural foundations of the endorsement process, *Journal of Consumer Research*, 16 (3), 310–21

22 www.statista.com/topics/2496/influence-marketing/#topicOverview (archived at https://perma.cc/QAW9-VFXF)

23 Gleason, T R, Theran, S A and Newberg, E M (2017) Parasocial interactions and relationships in early adolescence, *Frontiers in Psychology*, 8, 246529

24 www.theguardian.com/media/2022/feb/13/too-close-for-comfort-the-pitfalls-of-parasocial-relationships (archived at https://perma.cc/X7HR-7FFT)

25 www.medicalnewstoday.com/articles/parasocial-relationships (archived at https://perma.cc/J96Y-MURH)

26 Ooi, K B, Lee, V H, Hew, J J, Leong, L Y, Tan, G W H and Lim, A F (2023) Social media influencers: An effective marketing approach?, *Journal of Business Research*, 160, 113773

27 Rohde, P and Mau, G (2021) 'It's selling like hotcakes': Deconstructing social media influencer marketing in long-form video content on YouTube via social influence heuristics, *European Journal of Marketing*, 55 (10), 2700–34

28 Tandon, A, Dhir, A, Almugren, I, AlNemer, G N and Mäntymäki, M (2021) Fear of missing out (FoMO) among social media users: A systematic literature review, synthesis and framework for future research, *Internet Research*, 31 (3), 782–821

29 Przybylski, A K, Murayama, K, DeHaan, C R and Gladwell, V (2013) Motivational, emotional, and behavioral correlates of fear of missing out, *Computers in Human Behavior*, 29 (4), 1841–48

30 www.statista.com/statistics/1250681/share-of-instagram-influencers-involved-in-fraud-worldwide/ (archived at https://perma.cc/9FN8-LRMT)

31 www.theguardian.com/world/2017/oct/08/dove-apologises-for-ad-showing-black-woman-turning-into-white-one (archived at https://perma.cc/7Q99-YN2Q)

32 Kim, W G, Lim, H and Brymer, R A (2015) The effectiveness of managing social media on hotel performance, *International Journal of Hospitality Management*, 44, 165–71

33 Moon, S and Iacobucci, D (2022) Social media analytics and its applications in marketing, *Foundations and Trends in Marketing*, 15 (4), 213–92

34 Wang, Y, Deng, Q, Rod, M and Ji, S (2021) A thematic exploration of social media analytics in marketing research and an agenda for future inquiry, *Journal of Strategic Marketing*, 29 (6), 471–91

35 Gandomi, A and Haider, M (2015) Beyond the hype: Big data concepts, methods, and analytics, *International Journal of Information Management*, 35 (2), 137–44

36 Fan, W and Gordon, M D (2014) The power of social media analytics, *Communications of the ACM*, 57 (6), 74–81

37 Lee, A J, Yang, F C, Chen, C H, Wang, C S and Sun, C Y (2016) Mining perceptual maps from consumer reviews, *Decision Support Systems*, 82, 12–25

38 Chen, H, Chiang, R H and Storey, V C (2012) Business intelligence and analytics: From big data to big impact, *MIS Quarterly*, 36 (4), 1165–88

39 Ordenes, F V, Ludwig, S, De Ruyter, K, Grewal, D and Wetzels, M (2017) Unveiling what is written in the stars: Analyzing explicit, implicit, and discourse patterns of sentiment in social media, *Journal of Consumer Research*, 43(6), 875–94

40 Gandomi, A and Haider, M (2015) Beyond the hype: Big data concepts, methods, and analytics, *International Journal of Information Management*, 35 (2), 137–44

41 Aswani, R, Kar, A K, Ilavarasan, P V and Dwivedi, Y K (2018) Search engine marketing is not all gold: Insights from Twitter and SEOClerks, *International Journal of Information Management*, 38 (1), 107–16

42 Miah, S J, Vu, H Q, Gammack, J and McGrath, M (2017) A big data analytics method for tourist behaviour analysis, *Information & Management*, 54 (6), 771–85

43 https://blog.hubspot.com/marketing/a-b-testing-experiments-examples (archived at https://perma.cc/C46D-4G8X)

44 https://netflixtechblog.com/what-is-an-a-b-test-b08cc1b57962 (archived at https://perma.cc/B4VX-AW5P)

Global and cross-cultural branding   16

Overview

In this chapter, we first highlight how brands operate in the global environment. In the first section, we discuss the role of culture in brand communications. The chapter includes the advent of the 'born global' brands and their unique features. In the final sections, we reflect upon contemporary issues in global branding, such as country of brand origin, global brand naming dilemmas and misclassification of brand names as a strategy. The chapter offers key insights into how to manage global brands successfully.

Key learning outcomes

Upon reading this chapter, you should be able to

- Understand the global branding environment
- Appreciate the impact of culture on international branding
- Develop an understanding of the digital era global brands
- Gain insights into the latest developments in global branding strategies

Branding in the global environment

As discussed in Chapter 2, historically most brands started off as local and remained that way for long periods. However, as globalization allowed trade between far flung markets, brands became international symbol of trust between manufacturers, traders and consumers. New transport means including railways, shipping and air transport allowed brands to expand globally in the 20th century. The 21st century brought a new wave of expansion through digital technologies and the rise of social media, as discussed in Chapter 15. Thus, the evolution of marketplaces, transportation and technologies now allows brands to operate globally without having to establish locally first, as was the case in the past.[1]

Academic researchers distinguish global brands from local brands based on their geographical reach and marketing activities. Today's global brands serve different geographical regions with the same brand name and similar marketing strategies and characterize an important aspect of global consumer culture. Local brands, in contrast, are marketed in a specific country or a geographical area.[2] For example, KitKat, the much-loved chocolate brand from Nestlé, has adapted to local tastes in Japan by introducing more than 300 limited-edition seasonal and regional flavours, such as Baked Potato, Sake and Wasabi, while continuing its standardized global brand communication.

Operating in global environments offers several benefits for brands.[3] Firstly, brands get access to large consumer and business markets. This allows brands to increase brand awareness, revenues, market share and achieve economies of scale in branding activities. Secondly, operating in a global environment offers financial stability to brands. For instance, if one market is facing economic downturn, brands can focus on other growth markets and maintain their revenue streams. Global branding also helps brand explore, examine and adapt to various global cultural trends.[4] This can help with product innovations, advertising effectiveness and engaging with global customer segments.

However, such opportunities are also coupled with substantial challenges such as environmental degradation, income inequalities, workers' rights, child labour and fuelling over-consumption, among many others.[5] For example, British Petroleum (BP), the global oil giant, was involved in a legal and environmental disaster in 2010, when the Deepwater Horizon oil rig exploded and sank in the Gulf of Mexico, killing 11 workers and releasing about 4 million barrels of oil into the sea.[6] BP was found guilty of gross negligence and misconduct, and faced billions of dollars in fines, penalties, claims and cleanup costs. The oil spill had devastating effects on marine life, wildlife, economy and people's health in the Gulf region. Similarly, Shell, another leading oil firm, was involved in an environmental crisis involving crude oil spillage in Nigeria.[7] Fashion brands such as H&M, Boohoo, Zara, Primark, Gap and many others have courted controversy regarding their environmental impact and labour rights.[8]

BRANDING IN PRACTICE
Uniqlo: a global brand with a local fit

Uniqlo is one of the most successful and innovative global apparel brands from Japan, with a presence in over 25 countries and territories. The company sells a wide range of products, including casual wear, innerwear, accessories and functional clothing. Uniqlo's global marketing strategy is based on the idea of 'LifeWear', meaning that it provides simple, high-quality and versatile clothing that enhances the lives of its customers.

One of the ways that Uniqlo does this is by offering products that fit the local needs and preferences of its customers. For example, in India, Uniqlo launched a brand called the Kurta Collection, which features traditional Indian garments with modern design and technology. In France, Uniqlo created a brand called Inès de la Fressange, which is a collaboration with a famous French model and designer inspired by Parisian chic and elegance. In Australia, Uniqlo developed a brand called Ultra Light Down, which is a lightweight and compact down jacket that can be worn in various seasons and occasions. The above are examples of product customization that appeals to local consumer preferences.

Further, Uniqlo localizes its global brand communications by creating socially responsible and impactful campaigns that connect with its target audiences. For example, it created a campaign called Peace for All in collaboration with celebrities and artists who have designed t-shirts. The profits from the sale of these t-shirts, more than $4.7 million to date, is donated to charity sector organizations such as the UNHCR, Save the Children and PLAN International.

By offering relevant and meaningful products and campaigns to the local markets, Uniqlo has been able to establish its global brand identity, while also satisfying the different needs and wants of its customers. The company's global marketing strategy has enabled it to achieve high levels of customer patronage, brand awareness and social impact across the world.

Branding in global environments presents several opportunities, while, at the same time, there are inherent risks involved that need to be managed. Hence, brand managers should be aware of global socio-political, economic, technological and legal issues (the PESTL factors) and appropriately adjust their strategies. In addition, culture plays a pivotal role in global brand management, as discussed in the following section.

The role of culture in branding

Culture is often described as a collection of ideas, customs and social behaviour of a particular people or society. Culture, while transmitted across generation to generation, is a dynamic concept and thus evolves over time. Culture and branding are interwoven. Brands offer a symbolic representation of culture as consumers use brands in their activities for meaning making. Cultural theorists help us understand how societies at a macro level get influenced by cultural forces. One of the most famous cultural frameworks is proposed by Geert Hofstede which identifies societies on six cultural dimensions, as detailed in Table 16.1.

Table 16.1   Macro cultural dimensions proposed by Geert Hofstede[9]

Dimension	Definition	Example	Countries
Power distance	The extent to which the less powerful members of a society accept and expect that power is distributed unequally.	High power distance cultures tend to have centralized authority, hierarchical structures and large gaps between the rich and the poor. Low power distance cultures tend to have decentralized authority, flat structures and small gaps between the rich and the poor.	High – Philippines (94), Mexico (81) Low – Austria (11), New Zealand (22)
Individualism vs collectivism	The degree to which individuals are integrated into groups or expected to look after themselves.	Individualistic cultures tend to value personal freedom, autonomy and achievement. Collectivistic cultures tend to value group harmony, loyalty and conformity.	Individualist – USA (91), Australia (90) Collectivist – Guatemala (6), Pakistan (14)
Masculinity vs femininity	The distribution of roles and values between the genders.	Masculine cultures tend to value competitiveness, assertiveness and ambition. Feminine cultures tend to value cooperation, nurturance and quality of life.	Masculine – Japan (95), Italy (70) Feminine – Sweden (5), Costa Rica (21)
Uncertainty avoidance	The tolerance levels of a society to uncertain or ambiguous situations.	High uncertainty avoidance cultures tend to have strict rules, regulations and rituals. Low uncertainty avoidance cultures tend to have flexible norms, tolerance and openness.	High – Greece (100), Uruguay (98) Low – Singapore (8), Denmark (23)
Long-term vs short-term orientation	The extent to which a society exhibits a pragmatic future-oriented perspective rather than a conventional historical or short-term point of view.	Long-term oriented cultures tend to value perseverance, thrift and adaptation. Short-term oriented cultures tend to value tradition, stability and reciprocation.	Long-term – South Korea (100), China (87) Short-term – Nigeria (13), Norway (35)

(continued)

Table 16.1   (Continued)

Dimension	Definition	Example	Countries
Indulgence vs restraint	The extent to which a society allows relatively free gratification of basic and natural human desires related to enjoying life and having fun.	Indulgent cultures tend to value happiness, leisure and personal expression. Restrained cultures tend to value duty, moderation and self-discipline.	Indulgence – United Kingdom (69), Brazil (59) Restraint – Saudi Arabia (14), Poland (29)

Figure 16.1   Comparing macro cultural dimensions across countries

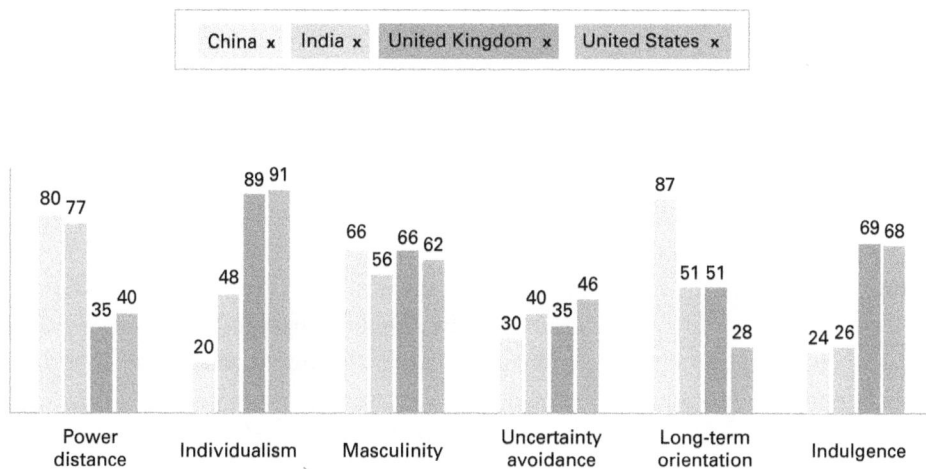

SOURCE www.hofstede-insights.com/country-comparison-tool

Figure 16.1 captures the country level macro cultural differences that can influence brand consumption as well. For example, China and India both have high power distance scores, which reflect a society that believes that inequalities amongst people are acceptable and there is appreciation for hierarchy and a top-down structure in society and organizations. From a branding perspective, this has substantial implications. For example, a brand consumed by the superiors or higher-status consumers will be preferred more by people in the lower echelons of the hierarchy.[10] The figure also shows stark differences between the USA and China for the individuals/collectivism dimension. In individualist societies, ties between individuals are loose and people are expected to look after themselves first. For example, the well-known 'American dream' of a prosperous lifestyle is a representation, wherein people hope for a better quality of life and a higher standard of living than their parents. The belief is that anyone, regardless of their status can 'pull up their socks' and raise themselves up from poverty. In collectivist cultures, cohesive in-group behaviour is the norm. Thus, people tend to follow their social group's behaviour closely. The rapid rise of livestreaming-based purchases in China is an example of this behaviour and the industry is estimated to have generated more than \$480 billion in 2022.[11]

Similar to the macro cultural framework proposed by Geert Hofstede, different frameworks also exist that identify country-level cultural differences. Other cultural theory researchers including Fons Trompenaars and Charles Hampden-Turner offered a different framework to understand diversity in global business. They identified dimensions such as universalism vs particularism, neutrality vs affectivity, individualism vs communitarianism, specific vs diffuse, internal vs external control and achievement vs ascription orientation.[12] A number of other frameworks exist that examine country cultures from the perspective of language, religion and geography.[13] The Hofstede framework remains one of the most popular globally.

While these macro frameworks explain country level differences, at individual or a micro-group level, people may or may not represent the country level cultural trait. For example, China is identified as a collectivist culture (see Figure 16.1), however, many individuals living in China could be highly individualistic. Similarly, there could be many American or British consumers who will be collectivist at an individual level, however, their country cultural trait is individualist. Thus, the macro cultural frameworks have been criticized in academic literature for over-simplification, over-generalization and at times rigidity as they do not take into consideration the dynamically evolving nature of cultural norms. For example, as mentioned, livestreaming-based sales are quite popular in China; however, it is not as popular in many other collectivist countries including India, Mexico and Pakistan. Thus, it could be challenging for a global brand to assume that they can standardize their products or services in a market based on macro cultural traits.

Frameworks based on micro level traits

Considering the challenges associated with macro cultural frameworks in global branding, academic researchers have proposed frameworks that are based on micro or individual level cultural traits. For instance, self-construal, that is how individuals define themselves vis-à-vis others, is useful to cultural differences at individual level. An individual can possess two different types of self-construal: independent or interdependent. Independent self-construal is characterized by the primary focus on oneself rather than the group. Contrarily, individuals with stronger interdependent self-construal demonstrate a strong sense of group affiliation and fundamental connectedness with others over their individual preferences and wishes.[14] Similarly, another important micro level cultural construct is associated with consumer thinking styles, involving holistic vs analytical thinking.[15] Holistic thinkers, mostly

Figure 16.2 The same object, a dining table with chairs, is construed differently depending on culturally motivated individual thinking styles

SOURCE Unsplash.com/shche_team

associated with East Asian countries, tend to reflect on the whole situation or context and focus on relationships between things. On the other hand, analytical thinkers, mostly associated with Western countries, are focused on rules and logic, cause and effect, and examine complex problems through individual parts. For example, while buying a dining table, a holistic thinker will consider the function of the table as a space for social or family gathering to enjoy a meal together. An analytical thinker, however, will see the dining table in terms of its quality, aesthetics, comfort and functionality (see Figure 16.2).

A substantial body of literature in branding, particularly pertaining to Consumer Culture Theory (CCT), examines the role of consumption culture.[16] CCT scholars are interested in consumption culture at individual or group level. CCT research examines consumption culture using varied lenses including how consumers derive their own identity markers using brands;[17] how they form and demonstrate belonging to a cultural notion through brand communities or tribes;[18] why and how consumers follow global or local trends; and socio-historic patterns associated with brands.[19]

These macro and micro cultural frameworks can help brand managers establish appropriate strategies to develop stronger customer-brand relationship across culturally homogenous or heterogeneous markets. However, brand managers need to remain conscious that they may have to use multiple macro and micro frameworks to achieve success in global markets.

Standardization vs customization

Riding the wave of globalization, many brands are entering other markets than their own country of origin. However, what strategy to use to enter foreign markets is a hotly debated topic. A seminal viewpoint was presented in this regard by Professor Theodore Levitt in his 1983 article published in the *Harvard Business Review* titled 'The globalization of markets'.[20] Levitt argued for a standardization approach suggesting that 'companies must learn to operate as if the world were one large market – ignoring superficial regional and national differences' (p 92). However, proponents of an alternative approach termed as customization argue that cultural differences, local customer characteristics and preferences should be taken into consideration.[21] This important debate has a further addition, suggesting the third approach of glocalization, which is a hybrid strategy that combines elements of both standardization and customization by adapting the global standardization strategy to local markets while maintaining some core elements that are consistent across all markets.[22] Each approach has its own advantages and disadvantages, as discussed in Table 16.2.

Another important aspect to consider is the difference in product and communication standardization vs customization. Product customization is driven by production process streamlining and could have significant costs associated with logistics. For example, a laptop nowadays may be assembled in one country,[23] however, its components may come from more than 30–40 different countries.[24] Moreover, brands should take into consideration consumers preferences. On the other hand, communication customization may differ based on mostly customer preferences. For example, automobile brands adopt their products between the UK and the US as cars are driven on different sides of the road. However, as both countries share substantial cultural norms and a common language, the communications can be standardized to a large extent. On the other hand, Coca-Cola sells the same product, with the same logo and packaging, in most countries. However, its communication is highly customized and involves local celebrities and events. For example, in China, Lu Han, a popular singer, actor and dancer, is Coca-Cola's brand endorser, while in India, it uses Bollywood film celebrities such as Aamir Khan, Aishwarya Rai and Ranbir

Table 16.2 Advantages and disadvantages of standardization, customization, and glocalization

Approach	Advantages	Disadvantages	Brands that use such an approach
Standardization	• A consistent brand image and reputation across the world • Economies of scale and lower costs due to mass production and distribution. • Transferable experience and knowledge among brand teams. • Easier control and coordination of branding activities.	• Misalignment with customer needs, wants and expectations in different markets • Reduced responsiveness and flexibility to changing market conditions and customer feedback. • Potential legal, ethical or cultural issues, due to ignoring local norms and regulations. • Loss of competitive advantage due to lack of differentiation from competitors.	• Apple is known for its standardized products, design, packaging, pricing and advertising across the world. Apple relies on its strong brand image and reputation to appeal to customers in different markets, without compromising on its quality and innovation. • Starbucks uses standardization to create a consistent customer experience and brand identity across the world. Starbucks offers the same core products, such as coffee, tea and pastries, with the same logo, store design and service standards in every market.
Customization	• Higher customer satisfaction and brand loyalty due to meeting their specific needs and wants. • Increased market share and profitability of the brand due to creating a unique value proposition for each market. • Enhanced brand communication creativity and innovation due to exploring new opportunities and challenges in each market. • Improved brand social responsibility and reputation due to respecting local cultures and values.	• Higher costs and complexity due to developing and managing different products and brand campaigns for each market. • Inconsistent brand image and identity across the world. • Difficulties in transferring brand experience and knowledge among marketing teams. • Challenges in controlling and coordinating branding and marketing activities.	• KFC uses customization to adapt its menu, ingredients, flavours and promotions to suit local tastes and cultures. For example, in China, KFC offers congee, egg tarts and soy milk; in India, it offers vegetarian options and spicy sauces; and in Japan, it offers fried chicken as a Christmas meal. • Netflix uses customization to offer different content, languages, subtitles and recommendations for each market. Netflix also produces original content that reflects the local culture, history and values of each market.

(continued)

Table 16.2 (Continued)

Approach	Advantages	Disadvantages	Brands that use such an approach
Glocalization	• Balancing the trade-offs between brand message and feature standardization and customization. • Leveraging the global brand equity while catering to local customer preferences. • Achieving synergies between global and local brand teams. • Enhancing the flexibility and responsiveness to market changes.	• Finding the optimal level of adaptation for each market for each brand. • Managing the potential conflicts or inconsistencies between global and local branding and marketing objectives. • Allocating the resources and responsibilities between global and local brand teams. • Measuring the performance and effectiveness of glocalization.	• IKEA uses glocalization to combine its global brand identity with local customer needs. IKEA offers the same products, design, quality and low prices across the world. However, it also adapts its product names, sizes, colours, styles and catalogues to suit local cultures and lifestyles. • Toyota uses glocalization to achieve both global efficiency and local responsiveness. Toyota offers some global models of cars with the same logo and quality standards across the world. However, it also adapts its car features and prices to suit local market conditions and customer preferences.

Kapoor. Similarly, in the Middle East region, Coca-Cola has engaged with local Arabic singers such as Nancy Ajram, and football players.

BRANDING IN PRACTICE

Types of customization offered by some brands

Burger King, a globally recognized fast-food brand originating from the United States, illustrates a robust strategy of customizing its offerings to meet distinct consumer preferences and cultural differences in various markets.

Burger King embraces localized product customization through culinary adaptations that respect regional taste profiles. In India, where vegetarianism is popular, Burger King innovatively offers a diverse range of vegetarian options, featuring plant-based patties and unique local flavours. This culinary customization aligns with the cultural and dietary preferences of the Indian market, showcasing Burger King's commitment to providing appealing choices for a diverse customer base.

Moreover, Burger King understands the importance of respecting religious beliefs and customs. In Middle Eastern markets, where Halal dietary guidelines are crucial, it ensures that its menu strictly adheres to Halal requirements. This consideration for religious customs underscores Burger King's dedication to providing inclusive and respectful product offerings.

Additionally, Burger King effectively customizes its promotional and marketing strategies to align with regional events, festivities and trends. In countries where specific cultural celebrations are significant, it tailors advertising campaigns and limited time offers to coincide with these events. This approach demonstrates Burger King's adeptness in leveraging local culture to enhance brand engagement and relevance.

In summary, Burger King's approach to product customization illustrates a commendable understanding of local tastes, cultural considerations and market dynamics. By adapting menus, marketing strategies and culinary choices, Burger King effectively navigates the global fast-food landscape, reinforcing its position as a popular and adaptable brand in the industry.

'Born-global' brands in the digital age

Most multinational brands, such as Microsoft, Coca-Cola, Phillips and Siemens, grew big in their home markets before they went overseas. Born-global brands, a concept emerging in the late 20th century, broke this tradition and swiftly internationalized from their inception, operating on a global scale from a very early stage. This phenomenon challenges traditional internationalization theories, such as the Uppsala Model,[25] which emphasized incremental and experiential international expansion. For example, of the 300 largest publicly listed UK companies in 2008, fewer than 30 per cent generate half of their total revenues from international sales.[26] However, many 'born-global' firms generate a very high percentage of their revenues from international markets. The rise of born-global brands has been attributed to factors such as advancements in technology, globalization and shifts in consumer behaviour.[27]

The roots of this rapid internationalization can be traced to the mid-1980s when technological advancements, especially in communication and transportation, facilitated global operations for startups and SMEs.[28] This was further fuelled by new market conditions such as increased globalization, market liberalization and regional integration, which created substantial opportunities globally for new entrants.[29] For example, Logitech, a Swiss-American brand that designs, manufactures and markets computer peripherals and software, was founded in 1981. Within a few years of its establishment, Logitech had expanded its operations to Europe, Asia and North America, establishing itself as a global leader in its industry. Similarly, Cochlear, a global leader in the ear implant market, was established in Australia in 1983 to develop and manufacture implantable hearing devices for people with severe to profound hearing loss. The brand's early internationalization strategy involved establishing partnerships with hospitals and research centres worldwide, enabling it to quickly expand its global reach.

The emergence of the internet in the 1990s exponentially accelerated the trend, enabling firms to reach a global audience almost instantly. For example, established in 1999, ASOS, an online fashion retailer that targets young adults, embraced the potential of e-commerce early on, establishing a global online presence and expanding its reach to over 200 countries. Similarly, Booking.com, an online travel agency that was founded in 1996 in the Netherlands, allows customers to book hotels, flights, car rentals and other travel services worldwide. It has become one of the largest travel e-commerce companies in the world over time.

Born-global brands leverage digital platforms, e-commerce and social media to establish a global presence, enabling them to engage with diverse consumer segments. Their strategies often involve utilizing online platforms to bypass traditional barriers to internationalization.[30] For example, launched in 2003 in Luxembourg, Skype, a communication brand that provides video chat and voice calls over the internet, had 50 million users globally by 2005 and more than 600 million in just five years. The brand's innovative technology which reduced communications costs and its user-friendly interface enabled it to gain rapid global adoption, becoming a household name within a few years of its launch. Similarly, Spotify, the Swedish audio streaming and media services brand, was founded in 2006. The brand used global licensing agreements that allowed it to quickly expand its reach to over 180 countries, establishing itself as a leading player in the music streaming industry. Most of the leading digital brands that we know and use today are born-global including Amazon (retail and ecommerce), Dell (computing hardware), eBay (auctions), Google (search engine), Instagram (social media), Netflix (video streaming), Paypal (finance) and Xiaomi (smartphones). Thus, born-global brands are not sector-dependent and have emerged across a variety of industries globally.

In conclusion, born-global brands represent a paradigm shift in international business and branding, challenging conventional models and highlighting the transformative influence of market changes, technology and transportation, on global market entry strategies.

BRANDING IN PRACTICE
Supercell: born-global gaming

Supercell is a mobile gaming company founded in Helsinki, Finland, in 2010. The company is best known for its hit games such as Clash of Clans, Clash Royale, Brawl Stars and Hay Day.[31] The company has achieved remarkable success in the global mobile gaming market, with over 100 million daily active players and billions of dollars in revenue.[32]

Supercell's success was based on external environmental factors such as the rapid penetration of the internet in most parts of the world and the rise of social media as well as smartphone technology. Moreover, the company's unique culture and strategy which focused on creating high-quality and engaging games for a global audience from inception helped its gaming brand's substantial success.

Supercell adopted a 'cell' structure, where small and independent teams of developers worked on their own projects with full autonomy and responsibility. Leveraging the power of data and analytics that was available due to digital advancements, the brand used real-time feedback and metrics to optimize the game design, monetization and marketing. This also allowed the company to quickly retire game brands that did not resonate with players.

Understanding global consumer preferences, the company was able to expand its game brand portfolio into different genres, such as strategy, card, action and casual games, to appeal to a diverse and loyal fan base. Its born-global nature allowed the company to engage with other born-global brands from different markets such as Tencent (China), SoftBank (Japan) and NetEase (China), to access new markets, especially in Asia.

In 2012, Supercell was recognized as the best Nordic startup company and chosen as the Finnish game developer of the year.[33] The following year, the brand won the Finnish Technology Educator 2013 competition, and the company was chosen as the software entrepreneur of the year.[34] The research and consultancy agency T-Media chose Supercell as Finland's most reputable company in their Luottamus and Maine (Trust and Reputation) report.[35]

In conclusion, Supercell is a remarkable example of how a born-global brand can create a successful impact worldwide. Supercell has demonstrated its ability to create high-quality and engaging games that have attracted millions of fans around the world. However, Supercell also needs to be aware of the challenges and risks that it faces in sustaining its innovation and popularity in the future.

The role of brands' country of origin

In a number of earlier chapters, we discussed the role of country of origin in branding. Country of origin is one of the most researched aspects of international marketing.[36]

Historically, categories of products associated with particular countries, such as French perfumes, Chinese silk, Indian spices and Italian food, allowed traders to charge a premium for the origin of their product. As markets and technology evolved, advance industrialized countries such as Germany and Switzerland became well known for their high quality, precision engineering and performance in specific sectors such as automobiles and watch-making respectively. Further developments in the domain of branding over the years led to the emergence of brands from these countries that imbued the characteristics of provenance for their benefit, leading to the concept of 'brand origin'.[37]

A brand's country of origin refers to the perceived or actual geographic location associated with a brand or product.[38] The concept has further evolved to encompass the country, region or city where the brand is headquartered, manufactures its products and sources its materials.[39] A brand's country of origin can affect consumer perceptions, preferences, attitudes and loyalty towards it, as well as its positioning, differentiation and communication in the market.[40] For example, BMW, Audi and Volkswagen regularly highlight their German origin. Similarly, most Swiss watch brands prominently mention 'Swiss-made' to utilize the positive origin perceptions that consumers have.

Not all countries have positive origin perceptions associated with them however. Thus, brands use foreign-sounding names to circumvent negative perceptions associated with their actual country of origin. This practice, known as foreign branding, aims to evoke positive associations with a different country or culture, thereby enhancing brand appeal and overcoming potential biases. Wanko, Hotwind, Scat and

Marisfrolg (the L is silent) are all Chinese brands attempting to tap into the appeal of Western sophistication. Some brands have even employed fonts and words that mimic the logos of megabrands, like Adidos, Hike, Cnoverse and Fuma.[41] Such branding endeavours could also lead to cultural appropriation. For instance, there is a Chinese eyewear brand called Helen Keller with the motto 'you see the world, the world sees you'; notwithstanding the fact that Helen Keller was both blind and deaf.

Such origin-avoidance effect is not only common in the Eastern emerging markets but also occurs around the world. For instance, Parfois, a women's accessories brand from Portugal, uses a French-sounding name to convey a sense of elegance and sophistication. The brand is now available in 70 countries with more than 1,000 stores. Caffè Nero is a British brand with an Italian sounding name. Dolmio, a leading brand of pasta sauce, which carries an Italian-sounding name was originally launched as Alora in Australia by Masterfoods. However, when test-launching its products in the UK, the brand name was changed to Dolmio to sound more Italian, which has now become global. Ginsu knives, which are much-loved by American consumers, were originally branded as Quikut. Through market research the company found that Quikut lacked panache, and thus the company created a new brand name that alluded to the exceptional sharpness and durability of a Japanese sword, Ginsu. Currys, a UK retailer previously known as Dixons, launched Matsui in the 1980s as a brand for its consumer electronics products to profit from the positive perceptions of Japanese electronics in consumer minds. The brand name and logo suggested a Japanese origin, with a sun symbol and the slogan 'Japanese Technology Made Perfect'. However, the Matsui products were actually made in the UK with imported parts, and had no connection to Japan or its technology. Similarly, Røde Microphones, a leading audio technology brand, is spelt with an 'ø' in the middle which gives the impression that the company is Scandinavian, when it is in fact Australian.

All the above examples of cloaking the country of origin with brand names exist because people demonstrate different levels of positive or negative associations with country of origin. In academic research, the positive effects of country of origin are studied under the label of consumer affinity, and the negative effects are studied as consumer animosity. Consumer affinity refers to the positive feelings and preferences that consumers have for products from certain countries, usually their own or those with similar cultures, values or history.[42] Consumer animosity refers to the negative feelings and aversions that consumers have for products from certain countries, usually those with political, military or economic conflicts or disagreements with their own.[43] For example, some American consumers may have a high affinity with products made in the USA or Canada, but high animosity for products made in China or Iran. Thus, many brands use foreign-sounding names to avoid negative associations with their original country of origin and take advantage of positive origin associations with foreign names. Academic research, however, shows that when consumers find out a brand has been acting in a deceptive manner, they tend to punish the brand

Figure 16.3 Apple uses language mentioned in the image to avoid stating 'made in China'

Designed by Apple in California
Assembled in China

SOURCE Author's

by avoiding purchase and spreading negative word-of-mouth.[44] Thus, brands trying to rapidly expand into new product categories or markets should exercise circumspection when planning to use foreign-sounding names, as this might not be beneficial in the long term if consumers associate such practice with deception.

Globally successful brands have acceptance from consumers worldwide. Thus, a different country of manufacturing or assembly is not perceived as negative for them. For example, in its global brand communications, including its product packaging, Apple uses the wording 'Designed by Apple in California. Assembled in China' rather than stating 'made in China' (see Figure 16.3). In doing so, Apple utilizes the positive associations people have with California-based technology companies. It also demonstrates that the product is produced in another country and thus captures the globalness of the brand Apple. Similarly, it is widely known that most global automobile brands such as Ford, Mercedes, Volkswagen and Toyota have their design origin and manufacturing plants in many different countries. This shows the power of global branding.

Chapter summary

This chapter captured the global environment in which today's brands have to operate to be successful. We also examined the important role that macro and micro culture plays in international markets. We looked at how brands are using a variety of approaches to succeed in a global environment. For example, some brands use standardization while others use customization, and some others use a hybrid approach. With the rise of globalization and digital technologies, born-global brands have emerged defying conventional wisdom that brands first need to be strong in their local market before venturing into foreign markets. Finally, we discussed the critical role of brand's country of origin and the different tactics and strategies used by the brands. The chapter provides several key applications and insights for successful global branding.

Key concepts

- International branding
- Global branding
- Culture
  - Macro culture
  - Micro culture
- Standardization
- Globalization
- Glocalization
- Born global
- Country of origin
  - Brand origin

Exercise questions

1 Describe the advantages and challenges of operating in a global environment for brands.

2 Using your own examples, explain how brands utilize macro and micro cultural influences for building successful consumer-brand relationships.

3 Critically evaluate the statement 'In order to succeed in global markets, brands should take into account cultural differences.'

4 Using the standardization vs customization debate, discuss, with examples, the pros and cons of each approach.

5 Critically evaluate the role of increasing globalization and technology in rise of 'born-global' brands.

6 Using the country of origin debate, explain why companies try to mask their brand origin and its short-term and long-term impact.

CASE STUDY   Zeekr: navigating the global expansion of a Chinese premium EV brand

This case examines the international growth strategy of Zeekr, the premium electric vehicle (EV) brand owned by the Chinese automaker Geely. It focuses on Zeekr's 2023 launch plans in the Middle East and Europe, as well as its ambitions to go public in the USA. The case analyses how Zeekr approaches overseas expansion amid trade tensions and competitive pressures in the EV space.

Founded in 2021 and backed by Geely, Zeekr operates in the premium EV segment competing with brands like Audi, BMW and Polestar. Zeekr delivered around 150,000 vehicles in its first two years exclusively in China. However, with slowing EV sales growth and intensifying competition in China, Zeekr announced plans to expand internationally. This includes a $1 billion IPO in the USA as well as market launches in Europe and the Middle East in 2023.

In September 2022, Zeekr signed agreements to launch in Saudi Arabia, UAE, Qatar and Bahrain in partnership with leading dealers. It aims to capture a share in underdeveloped premium EV segments in these markets. Zeekr is offering competitive pricing compared with gas-powered rivals and expects 10,000 units of sales across the four Middle Eastern markets by 2025. The move aligns with China's deepening economic ties in the region.

Concurrently, Zeekr decided to enter Europe, starting with the Netherlands and Sweden in the later part of 2022. However, Zeekr and other Chinese EVs have faced regulatory pushback in Europe regarding unfair subsidies. This could hamper growth plans in the medium term.

Zeekr confidentially filed for a $1 billion US IPO that would be the largest Chinese listing since DiDi, a vehicle-for-hire company similar to Uber, in 2021. The offering comes amid strained diplomatic ties, limiting Chinese IPOs in the USA, and seeks to raise capital for global expansion.

Zeekr's Middle Eastern expansion represents a bold move to capitalize on emerging EV markets. Zeekr exemplifies Chinese EV startups expanding overseas for growth and funding amid intensifying domestic competition. However, navigating international markets poses an array of challenges, such as protectionist policies, competitive dynamics and cultural differences across regions. As such, these firms must adapt their branding, pricing and strategic focus across different geographies.

The case suggests EV makers with global ambitions must balance seizing opportunities in new markets with mitigating regulatory risks and executing expansion plans sustainably. As a young brand, Zeekr provides an interesting test case for how emerging Chinese EV brands can internationalize competitively.

Case questions

1 Based on your reading of the case and the chapter, evaluate the cultural challenges Zeekr may face in becoming a global brand.

2 Imagine that Zeekr is planning to launch its high-end cars in your country. Using the macro and micro cultural aspects discussed in the chapter, what advice would you give to the brand about adapting to local consumer preferences?

3 In marketing their product successfully across the world, what type of product and communication customizations will Zeekr have to perform? Explain using examples.

4 Critically reflect on the decision by a Chinese firm to use Zeekr as a brand name in view of the country-of-origin debate.

Endnotes

1 Steenkamp, J B E (2020) Global brand building and management in the digital age, *Journal of International Marketing*, 28 (1), 13–27

2 Gürhan-Canli, Z, Sarial-Abi, G and Hayran, C (2018) Consumers and brands across the globe: Research synthesis and new directions, *Journal of International Marketing*, 26 (1), 96–117

3 Ibid.

4 Yu, L (2003) The global-brand advantage: Research indicates that buyers are more likely to perceive value in global brands, (Marketing) *MIT Sloan Management Review*, 44 (3), 13–14

5 Steenkamp, J B (2017) *Global Brand Strategy: World-wise marketing in the age of branding*, Springer

6 www.britannica.com/event/Deepwater-Horizon-oil-spill/Environmental-costs (archived at https://perma.cc/6V57-U3F9)

7 www.amnesty.org/en/latest/news/2023/02/nigeria-shell-oil-spill-trial/ (archived at https://perma.cc/KT89-8FB6)

8 www.business-humanrights.org/en/from-us/media-centre/fashion-brands-failing-to-protect-workers-from-labour-abuse-in-myanmar (archived at https://perma.cc/AX2P-YYSP)

9 www.hofstede-insights.com/ (archived at https://perma.cc/FC9H-VAZX)

10 Shukla, P and Rosendo-Rios, V (2021) Intra and inter-country comparative effects of symbolic motivations on luxury purchase intentions in emerging markets, *International Business Review*, 30 (1), 101768

11 www.reuters.com/world/asia-pacific/chinas-livestreaming-attracts-young-hopefuls-competition-grows-2023-08-15 (archived at https://perma.cc/X7FS-ZFR2)

12 Trompenaars, F and Hampden-Turner, C (2011) *Riding the Waves of Culture: Understanding diversity in global business*, Nicholas Brealey International

13 Ronen, S and Shenkar, O (2013) Mapping world cultures: Cluster formation, sources and implications, *Journal of International Business Studies*, 44, 867–97

14 Markus, H R and Kitayama, S (1991) Culture and the self: Implications for cognition, emotion, and motivation, *Psychological Review*, 98 (2), 224

15 Nisbett, R E, Peng, K, Choi, I and Norenzayan, A (2001) Culture and systems of thought: Holistic versus analytic cognition, *Psychological Review*, 108 (2), 291–310

16 Arnould, E J and Thompson, C J (2005) Consumer culture theory (CCT): Twenty years of research, *Journal of Consumer Research*, 31(4), 868–82

17 Schau, H and Gilly, M C (2003) We are what we post? Self-presentation in personal web space, *Journal of Consumer Research*, 30 (3), 385–404

18 Cova, B, Kozinets, R V and Shankar, A (eds.) (2007) *Consumer Tribes*, Routledge

19 McNeil, P and Riello, G (2016) *Luxury: A rich history*, Oxford University Press

20 Levitt, T (1983) The globalization of markets, *Harvard Business Review*, May–June, 92–102

21 Baalbaki, I B and Malhotra, N K (1995) Standardization versus customization in international marketing: An investigation using bridging conjoint analysis, *Journal of the Academy of Marketing Science*, 23 (3), 182–94

22 Robertson, R (1995) Glocalization: Time-space and homogeneity-heterogeneity, *Global Modernities*, 2 (1), 25–44

23 www.ft.com/content/1a68ef89-92f2-4e35-856a-122d4e461571 (archived at https://perma.cc/8L3D-9ZPB)

24 Freidman, T (2005) *The World Is Flat*, Farrar, Straus and Giroux, New York

25 Johanson, J and Vahlne, J E (1977) The internationalization process of the firm—a model of knowledge development and increasing foreign market commitments, *Journal of International Business Studies*, 8, 23–32

26 www.london.edu/think/born-global (archived at https://perma.cc/J74B-33EN)

27 Cavusgil, S T and Knight, G (2015) The born global firm: An entrepreneurial and capabilities perspective on early and rapid internationalization, *Journal of International Business Studies*, 46, 3–16

28 McDougall, P P, Shane, S and Oviatt, B M (1994) Explaining the formation of international new ventures: The limits of theories from international business research, *Journal of Business Venturing*, 9 (6), 469–87

29 www.london.edu/think/born-global (archived at https://perma.cc/REG9-AC3U)

30 Coviello, N and Munro, H (1997) Network relationships and the internationalisation process of small software firms, *International Business Review*, 6 (4), 361–86

31 https://supercell.com/en/about-us/ (archived at https://perma.cc/7TJ6-4W8T)

32 https://aws.amazon.com/solutions/case-studies/supercell-video (archived at https://perma.cc/4BSL-GX75)

33 https://yle.fi/aihe/artikkeli/2012/11/02/vuoden-suomalainen-pelikehittaja-valittiin-lahjoitti-koko-summan-movemberille (archived at https://perma.cc/A2NG-BS6S)

34 https://web.archive.org/web/20150402114837/http://talotekniikka-lehti.fi/2013/10/10/supercell-voitti-vexvelle-kunniaa/ (archived at https://perma.cc/J5ZM-BESM)

35 www.talouselama.fi/uutiset/suomen-hyvamaineisimmat-supercell-kone-ja-kolmatta-et-muuten-arvaa/667e0a04-7bb5-3c4d-b79c-aa0da8f01eaf (archived at https://perma.cc/24GS-Z4VF)

36 Samiee, S and Chabowski, B R (2021) Knowledge structure in product – and brand origin-related research, *Journal of the Academy of Marketing Science*, 49, 947–68

37 Thakor, M V (1996) Brand origin: Conceptualization and review, *Journal of Consumer Marketing*, 13 (3), 27–42

38 Shukla, P (2011) Impact of interpersonal influences, brand origin and brand image on luxury purchase intentions: Measuring interfunctional interactions and a cross-national comparison, *Journal of World Business*, 46 (2), 242–52

39 Chen, S, Wright, M J, Gao, H, Liu, H and Mather, D (2021) The effects of brand origin and country-of-manufacture on consumers' institutional perceptions and purchase decision-making, *International Marketing Review*, 38 (2), 343–66

40 Cakici, N M and Shukla, P (2017) Country-of-origin misclassification awareness and consumers' behavioral intentions: Moderating roles of consumer affinity, animosity, and product knowledge, *International Marketing Review*, 34 (3), 354–76

41 www.nytimes.com/2014/12/27/business/international/adidas-and-hotwind-in-china-brands-evoke-foreign-names-even-if-theyre-gibberish.html (archived at https://perma.cc/XHG4-BRCH)

42 Oberecker, E M, Riefler, P and Diamantopoulos, A (2008) The consumer affinity construct: Conceptualization, qualitative investigation, and research agenda, *Journal of International Marketing*, 16 (3), 23–56

43 Riefler, P and Diamantopoulos, A (2007) Consumer animosity: A literature review and a reconsideration of its measurement, *International Marketing Review*, 24 (1), 87–119

44 Cakici, N M and Shukla, P (2017) Country-of-origin misclassification awareness and consumers' behavioral intentions: Moderating roles of consumer affinity, animosity, and product knowledge, *International Marketing Review*, 34 (3), 354–76

INDEX

NB: page numbers in *italic* indicate figures or tables

Looking for another book?

Explore our award-winning
books from global business
experts in Marketing and Sales

Scan the code to browse

www.koganpage.com/marketing

More books on Branding from Kogan Page

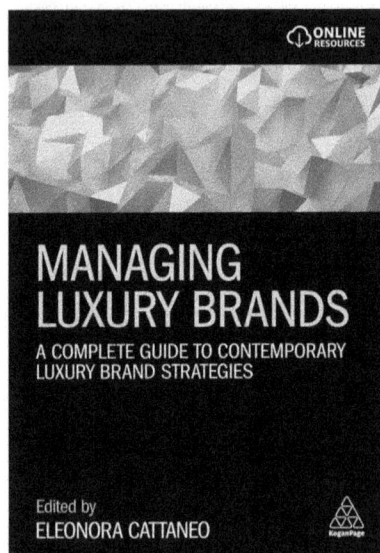

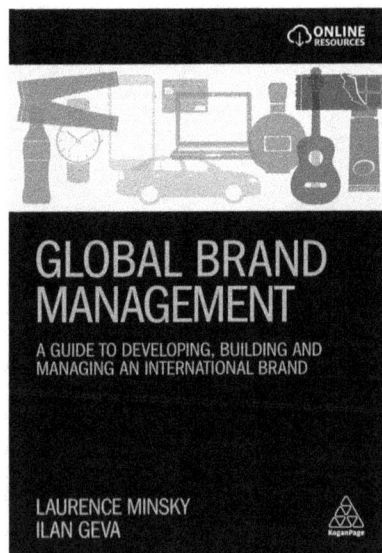